Spirituality and
Social Responsibility

Spirituality and Social Responsibility

Vocational Vision of Women in The United Methodist Tradition

EDITED BY

Rosemary Skinner Keller

Abingdon Press
Nashville

SPIRITUALITY AND SOCIAL RESPONSIBILITY: VOCATIONAL
VISION OF WOMEN IN THE UNITED METHODIST TRADITION

Copyright © 1993 by Abingdon Press

This book is printed on acid-free, recycled paper.

Library of Congress Cataloging-in-Publication Data

Spirituality and social responsibility : the vocational vision of women in the United Methodist
    tradition / edited by Rosemary Skinner Keller.
        p.   cm.
    Includes bibliographical references and index.
ISBN 0-687-39236-5 (alk. paper)
1. Women, Methodist—Biography. 2. Women in church work—Methodist Church. 3.
Church and social problems—Methodist Church. I. Keller, Rosemary Skinner.
BX8493.S77   1993
287'.6'0922—dc20
[B]   92-42140
                                                                                              CIP

Scripture quotations, unless otherwise noted, are from the Revised Standard Version of the
Bible, copyright © 1946, 1952, 1971 by the Division of Christian Education of the National
Council of Churches of Christ in the USA. Used by permission.

The quotation noted Phillips is from J. B. Phillips, *The New Testament in Modern English*
(Macmillan), copyright © J. B. Phillips, 1958, 1959, 1960, 1972.

Quotations noted KJV are from the King James or Authorized version of the Bible.

93   94   95   96   97   98   99   00   01   02 — 10   9   8   7   6   5   4   3   2   1

MANUFACTURED IN THE UNITED STATES OF AMERICA

CONTENTS

INTRODUCTION

ROSEMARY SKINNER KELLER

The vocational visions of two women, whose stories are shared in this book, graphically convey the unity of spirituality and social responsibility in the lives of women in the United Methodist tradition.

The first vision unfolds through the life journey of Thelma Stevens, who served The Methodist Church for its lifetime, from 1940–1968, as Executive Secretary for Christian Social Relations and Local Church Activities of the Women's Division of the Board of Missions. Born on a farm in Mississippi and the youngest of nine children, Thelma was only six years old when her mother died. Out of her grief, she decided to leave home. Reaching a nearby stream, Thelma became entangled in thorns, and some embedded themselves in her hand. Her brother found his little sister, crying, and took her home.

Alice Knotts writes: "The thorn in Stevens's hand became for her a parable of life. Years later when she was grown, a thorn, long ago forgotten, festered and came out of her hand. As an adult, Stevens saw that racial bigotry was a festering thorn in the hand of the church and society."

During her teenage years, Thelma was disillusioned with the church, whose upright members practiced segregation and defied the good life as she knew it. For she had played with black as well as white girls and boys for as long as she could remember.

At age sixteen, she experienced a conversion, which profoundly formed her life. The girls' basketball team, which she was coaching in a one-room rural schoolhouse, took her into the woods to view the lynching of a black teenager.

Thelma pledged to herself that "if the Lord would ever let me live long enough I would spend the rest of my life working for basic fairness and justice and safety for black people." And she did, though her commitment expanded to a more inclusive social responsibility to break down barriers of sex and class, as well as race, which separated all people. As her vocational vision matured, she chose to work through the church where she found mentors and colleagues who, in the biblical prophetic tradition, committed their lives to the task of Jesus' disciples: to build a new global order based upon his teachings.

The formative vision of a festering thorn of racial bigotry could be affirmed by each woman in this book, for all responded to God's call to prophetically witness against injustice.

A second vision unifying the subjects of these biographical studies is contained in the metaphor of a "sisterhood of shared fire," the experience of Jennie Fowler Willing. Joanne Brown tells the story of Willing as a grass-roots organizer committed to "women's work for women," in the expression of female missionary society members of Protestant denominations at the turn of the century. Willing believed it more important that 5,000 women give a few cents a year for mission work than that one woman give a hundred dollars. The fire of the Holy Spirit was a communal vision setting ablaze the lives of women in Methodist fashion as they sought to spread gospel holiness and reform the continent, indeed to transform the world. And Willing knew that the contagion of "shared fire" would bring meaning, dignity, and empowerment to the women who served, as they came to value their own lives as well as those whom they served.

Episodes from the lives of Thelma Stevens and Jennie Fowler Willing point toward the significance of a volume on the subject of spirituality and social responsibility, a vocational vision of women in the United Methodist tradition. Biographical studies are more than accounts of one woman or one man's life, from which we can separate our own experience. Stories of individuals, and the movements and institutions to which they related, appeal to us because we identify with, empathize with, and are radically challenged by another person's vocational journey. If the subject is well chosen, that subject's life story becomes a prism of a wider world of experiences, ideas, values, and historical moments, and expands our view of life. In contrast, studies of ideas, values, and even of events may not reach us with the same intensity and motivational power.

The fifteen writers of this volume recover stories of women who lived from the era of the American Revolution up to the present time, with the final three chapters devoted to women living in the 1990s. Through their subjects, the writers represent a feminist analysis of women and religion. They recognize that the church has fallen short of its calling to spirituality and social responsibility growing out of the witness of Jesus Christ. However, their faith and their scholarship continues to be based on commitment to that vision and to the task of working within the institution of the church and reforming it.

The vocational vision of women in the United Methodist tradition was not characterized from the earliest years by a mature "sisterhood of shared fire" addressing the festering thorns of racism, sexism, classism, and militarism in church and society. Rather, the pioneers whose stories are told here consistently tested the perimeters of women's role, and their vision matured as they challenged and stretched the acceptable boundaries.

That pattern is set in the first two articles about women in the early Republic, Catherine Livingston Garrettson, who lived during the era of the American Revolution, and Eliza Clark Garrett, who took part in the movement westward and the settlement of Chicago in the early nineteenth century. Both were white women of middle or upper-middle-class society whose ministries of philanthropy foretold those of laywomen in missionary societies and United Methodist women's organizations of the late nineteenth and twentieth centuries.

Diane Lobody writes "'A Wren Just Bursting Its Shell:' Catherine Livingston Garrettson's Ministry of Public Domesticity." Born into the aristocratic but passionately revolutionary Livingston family of upstate New York, Catherine (1752–1849) married the Methodist itinerant preacher Freeborn Garrettson, defying the cherished conventions of her Anglican and Dutch Reformed background. Foremost, wealthy people professed politely reasonable piety and did not have conversion experiences. But Catherine was irrevocably converted to the Social Holiness movement and turned to the Lord to "make me a profitable servant. Set me upon some work. I long to be doing something."

Her activist Methodist temperament found its outlet in her "ministry of public domesticity" within her home. The Garrettson household became "Traveler's Rest," a retreat center or Christian hostel for traveling and weary clergy. Providing a sanctuary to fulfill her own gifts as preacher, teacher, evangelist, and pastor, Catherine "created the space—interior and exterior—within which she could fulfill a ministry that honored her without disrupting her world view," Lobody writes. In keeping with John Wesley's pronouncement that the world was his parish, Catherine Garrettson devised "an equally generous vision of the boundaries of her household." Perhaps she also created a model for use of some of our overly private property two centuries later.

Eliza Clark Garrett (1805–1855) and her husband, Augustus, saw no future in remaining on a debt-ridden farm shared with siblings in New York state. They envisioned a more abundant life on the advancing frontier. In 1835, they settled in Chicago. Augustus rapidly gained wealth and was twice elected mayor. After their conversion, Augustus and Eliza conceived a dream for an alternative use of their financial resources: the building of a Methodist seminary to train illiterate men to be pastors in the West.

In "Eliza Garrett: To Follow a Vision," Ila Fisher concurs with nineteenth-century Methodist historian Abel Stevens that Augustus "knew his duty, but he did it not." After her husband's death, Eliza acted out of her spirituality and social responsibility to provide resources for founding the second institution for ministerial education of The Methodist Church in America, Garrett Biblical Institute. Eliza also envisioned an educational institution for female education, but after her untimely death the executors of her estate determined that so long as "the demands are so great for the Biblical Institute they can hardly be considered urgent for the establishment of a Female College." We will never know whether Eliza was aware of the tentative commitment of her executors to the education of women, Fisher states, but her legacy of "women's ability to shape and initiate institutions" is realized increasingly today.

Black and white women born prior to the Civil War were formed both by the revivalistic spirit of the Holiness tradition and the social reform fervor that permeated churches of the United Methodist heritage and the nation. Amanda Berry Smith (1837–1915), a black woman who was an ex-slave and washerwoman, represents extreme class as well as racial differences from the white women preceding and following her in this book. She was joined with them in her Methodist commitments to conversion and sanctification. However, testimonies to her powerful evangelical preaching on four continents make it clear that the spirituality of the Holiness tradition was more natural to her than to her white sisters.

In "Amanda Berry Smith: A 'Downright, Outright Christian,'" Nancy Hardesty and Adrienne Israel develop the double bind of racism and sexism, which followed Smith throughout her ministry. She met hostility from both white and black people and was considered a "speckled bird" by some African Americans because she ministered to both races. Smith's confidence that she belonged to "royal stock" of the black race created a strong sense of self undergirded by her spiritual conviction. Although Smith's autobiography focuses on her spirituality, Hardesty and Israel open the door to her social reform commitments to temperance and to civil rights and education of African American children during Reconstruction. Amanda's articulation of her faith in a "downright, outright" way is a gift to women and men today.

Previous studies of Frances Willard (1839–1898) have focused on her mature years and her contribution as president of the National Woman's Christian Temperance Union to temperance and other social reform movements in the late nineteenth century. Carolyn Gifford, who has studied Willard and the forty-nine volumes of her Diary in greater depth than any other scholar, tells the story of a lesser known period in Willard's life that is crucial to the content of this book. In "'My Own Methodist Hive': Frances Willard's Faith as Disclosed in Her Journal, 1855–1870," Gifford describes the spiritual foundations of Willard's childhood and early adult years that undergirded her later commitment to social responsibility.

Moral earnestness, emphasis on doing one's duty, and the struggle to build character were nurtured in the "Methodist Hive" of the Willard home. Further, these values were representative of American Victorian society and the middle-class culture that it fostered. To Willard, the moral life equaled the holy life, which was lived in conformity to God's will. Further, God required conversion, even of one reared in the lively and intense Methodist spiritual community of intellectual and moral striving. By the time Frances was twenty, her moral quest had become a vocational one. She sought to find useful work to enable her to "be good and do good." Beginning with Frances Willard, the "cause of women," the advocacy of women's self-development to fulfill whatever they believed God called them to be and do, becomes a foremost commitment of United Methodist women studied in this book. To live out of God's vision for their lives also meant to Willard that women were enabled to "enter every place" in society.

Jennie Fowler Willing (1834–1916) was a peer, heroine, and mentor of Frances Willard, who inspired and motivated her vocationally. Joanne Brown's essay, "Shared Fire: The Flame Ignited by Jennie Fowler Willing," traces Willing's vocational journey, a "life of resolute aim" which replaced a "life of aimless reverie," in Frances Willard's words. Their goal constituted the vision of mainstream Methodist women of the middle and late nineteenth century. Brown conveys through Willing the beliefs in conversion, sanctification, and perfection, and the activist commitment to build a better world, as they evolved in the Wesleyan tradition in America.

Willing was a laywoman who organized the early Woman's Foreign Missionary Society, had a preacher's license, taught in a university, became active in temperance, and opened a settlement house. We understand why Frances Willard saw her as the ideal model of useful nineteenth-century womanhood, the fulfillment of the WCTU "Do Everything Policy." Even more important for today was Willing's vision, as a precursor of liberation theology, that members of subject races must be helped to value their own dignity and then be trusted by middle-class reformers to make their paternalistic masters "comprehend that lesson." Further, Willing's model of shared leadership, her ability to lead without being a dominant personality in groups, commends her to women and men in positions of authority today.

Anna Oliver (1840–1892) is distinguished in United Methodist history as the first woman to graduate from a North American theological seminary, Boston University School of Theology, in 1876, and as the first woman, along with Anna Howard Shaw, to seek ordination in The Methodist Episcopal Church, in 1880. However, Oliver follows in the train of Willard and Willing. Her spirit of personal and social holiness, moral earnestness, and activist temper also led her into a broadly conceived ministry of social reform, including education of black and white children and protests against alcohol, women's dress code, and inadequate health care for women.

In his article, "Evangelism and Social Reform in the Pastoral Ministry of Anna Oliver: 1868–1886," Kenneth Rowe traces the inclusive ministry of preaching and social justice that preceded her unsuccessful campaign for ordination. Most sobering is her effective work in church growth and the spiritual deepening of her congregations in Passaic, New Jersey, and Brooklyn, New York, followed by the failure of church authorities to sanction her ordination. Maintaining the vision of her favorite biblical text (KJV), "Behold, I have set before thee an open door, and no *man* can shut it," Oliver was clear that she gained her genuine authority from God. After being rebuffed by the General Conference, she returned to her inclusive ministry as a preaching evangelist and social reformer until her death.

With her pen, Ida B. Wells-Barnett (1862–1931) exerted a radical protest for the human rights of her African American race. Recovery of Wells-Barnett's life has shed light on her struggle against lynching. Going farther, in "Because God Gave Her Vision: The Religious Impulse of Ida B. Wells-Barnett," Emilie Townes demonstrates the connection of her spirituality with her social justice stance.

While teaching in Memphis before her marriage, Wells also wrote for black newspapers. In her columns, she "forged a deep and abiding spirituality rooted in the black church in the South." Applying her faith to social questions, she protested against the condition of schools for black children and caste distinctions in worship services. Her primary cause throughout her adult life lay in her struggle against lynching and brutalization of blacks. Influenced by the formative "cult of true womanhood" among white women, Wells exalted black women's moral influence and responsibility for their race. She stood up against the powerful WCTU and Frances Willard for their insensitivity to blacks, particularly in regard to lynching. Wells-Barnett found difficulty in relating to group causes, making her most important contribution individually through her journalistic protests.

In reading each of these essays it becomes increasingly difficult to understand how the life stories, and even the names, of most of these women are virtually unknown today. No account of lost history is more startling than that of Katharine Bushnell (1855–1946), the subject of Dana Hardwick's essay "Man's Prattle, Woman's Word: The Biblical Mission of Katharine Bushnell." The socially prophetic ministry of Bushnell for more than seventy years, growing out of her conservative biblical grounding, follows in the train of Willing's ministry in its application to needs of the contemporary social and global scene.

Like Willing and most Holiness followers of the nineteenth century, Bushnell believed in the inerrancy of the biblical text. However, such infallibility and inspiration of God's word applied only to the original text.

At the heart of her closely interwoven spirituality and social responsibility, Bushnell was convinced that sex-biased translations of the Bible, "man's prattle," were the underlying cause of the subordination and oppression of women throughout the world. Born in rural, down-state Illinois, Bushnell became a licensed physician and committed herself to world mission work. She spent the majority of her adult years exposing forced prostitution in China, India, and the United States, as well as its connection to the opium traffic of China. Bushnell worked in close collegiality with other women in international missions fields and in the World WCTU. In the last twenty-five years of her life, after age sixty-five, she turned to her task of devising an interpretation of the Bible to free women to take their proper "place in the divine economy."

"Sisters in Christ: American Women Missionaries in Ewha Women's University," by Kyung-Lim Shin-Lee, traces the relationships formed by three American women sent to Korea by the Woman's Foreign Missionary Society of The Methodist Episcopal Church in the late nineteenth and twentieth centuries to found and lead the first educational institution for women in Korea. Education, first at Ewha Hak-dang, an elementary and secondary school, and then at Ewha University, was of high caliber from its founding in 1886. However, the social responsibility to advance education was not the primary purpose of the institutions. Fundamentally, the missionaries had a spiritual purpose to convert Koreans to Christianity, and education was needed to accomplish that goal. In fact, spiritual and social purposes have always been inseparably joined. Missionaries and Korean women committed themselves to faith and learning together to free Korean women from the binding traditions of men over women and to train them for leadership in church and society.

Kyung-Lim Lee sensitively establishes that, because of language barriers and limited contact with Korea, it was more difficult for Mary Scranton (1832–1909), the first missionary principal of Ewha Hak-dang, to make "true Korean women" than "true Christian women." Increasingly, the succeeding missionary presidents of Ewha University, Lulu Frey (1868–1921) and Alice Appenzeller (1885–1950), identified more closely with the Korean society and women, though the imposition of American culture was always an issue. Lee helps us see the ambiguities, for she asks a key question: What would the status of Korean women be today if missionaries had not dared to oppose firm traditions?

Georgia Harkness (1891–1974) was the preeminent female theologian of American Protestantism prior to the late-twentieth-century emergence of a distinguished and growing number of feminist theologians. Primarily, Harkness was a folk theologian, less a creator of new theological trends among scholars than an interpreter to laity and clergy. Further, she was an applied theologian, who insisted that theology issue in prophetic ethical action. As a seminary professor and author of thirty-seven books and countless articles in church journals, Harkness's influence on clergy, laity, and institutional church structures throughout the mid-twentieth century was inestimable.

In "Georgia Harkness—Theologian of the People: Evangelical Liberal and Social Prophet," Rosemary Keller interprets Harkness, first, as a Methodist in responsibly translating Wesleyan theology into its twentieth-century setting, and second, through her pen and political activism, as a leader within the denomination and ecumenical Protestantism to bring the socially active temperament of Wesleyanism to bear on institutional church structures. This essay focuses on Harkness's journey in relating evangelicalism and liberalism in her faith stance. It further lifts up her challenge to the church to witness against racism, sexism, and militarism by reforming its own structures and calling society to accountability. Harkness confronted both clergy and laity with their prophetic task, beginning with the local church and extending to all wings.

Many readers of this volume who remember Thelma Stevens (1902–1990) will personally agree that no white woman identified more closely and sensitively with black women than she did. In "Thelma Stevens: Crusader for Racial Justice," Alice Knotts persuasively demonstrates the religious foundations of Stevens's social activism. Her mandates for Christian social action were the teaching of Jesus and the Methodist Social Creed. Through her pivotal position and magnetic leadership in directing the Department of Christian Social Relations and Local Church Activities, Stevens was responsible for molding the Women's Division of the Board of Missions as the prophetic arm of Methodism.

Throughout her thirty years of service in the general structure of The Methodist Church, Stevens always affirmed that its heart and life were in the local congregation. "All action is local," she contended, as she consistently empowered congregations to hold the wider organization accountable to its Christian service. Although her professional years were focused more on the struggles against racism, in "retirement" she addressed sexism within the church. She was deservedly proud of her formative role in the birth of the Commission on the Status and Role of Women in The United Methodist Church. No woman better deserves the distinction as the "grand dame" of twentieth-century Methodism than does Thelma Stevens.

The final three essays in this volume grow out of experiences of lay and clergywomen who are living today and address issues confronting many of us as we journey vocationally. Alice Chai writes "The Struggle of Asian and Asian American Women Toward a Total Liberation: A Korean Methodist Woman's Vocational Journey." She sets the context of an Asian and Asian American Christian feminist theology, drawing on the historical and cultural consciousness of women in Eastern societies and the intersection of sexism, racism, and classism in their experience. In place of a section of documents like those in other chapters, Chai relates aspects of her own vocational journey and the importance of spirituality and social responsibility in her life.

Chai stresses the importance of the heritage of Asian foremothers' experience for the development of a feminist theology by Asian women in their respective communities today. As is true of women in other settings of Eastern and Western culture, Korean women such as Chai experience a double-edged relationship with Christianity. Although the Christian faith has provided them a spirituality to resist oppressive social structures, the church has been an instrument in sustaining patriarchal domination within church and society. Chai's primary commitment is to development of an Asian feminist theology. Through her own witness, she is helping to create that vision and to actively spearhead efforts to combat structures that promote sexual exploitation, injustice, and poverty of Asian women and men.

Mary Elizabeth Moore's essay, "One Spirit—Many Stories: Contemporary Laywomen Share Their Vocational Visions," is based on interviews with eight women of Chinese American, African American, and European American heritage, who live in Hawaii and throughout the continental United States and are active in professional and volunteer capacities in church and society today. These women are in the midst of their life's vocational journeys, and Moore organizes their responses around common threads, such as their early initiation in the faith, the gift of mentors in their lives, and their activism in making decisions and taking stands that moved them along in their spiritual and social responsibility.

Unlike many of the women presented earlier, these women do not stand out as radical pioneers for social justice. However, they all have an acute awareness of world problems and relate to a variety of pressing social causes in the world today. We cannot look back upon their lives or our own with the sense of completion that we saw in the lives of the foremothers already studied here. Their value to us is highly personal. They acknowledge that they are not certain where God is leading them but that they feel God is actively at work in their lives now. The most common thread that emerged, Moore writes, was that vocation is a response to God's call, and that a primary responsibility given with the call is to help make the world a better place for all. We who are also in the midst of vocational living, which is "evolving and being filled with surprises along the way," can identify with the experience of ambiguity in the lives of Moore's subjects.

The book concludes with an essay written by Barbara Troxell, "Honoring One Another with Our Stories: Authority and Mutual Ministry Among United Methodist Clergywomen in the Last Decade of the Twentieth Century." Her interviews with twelve clergy sisters who are bishops, district superintendents, and staff members of general agencies of the church again raise concerns close to the daily nurture of persons on vocational journeys today. Because women have been coming to seminary on the ordination track in large numbers only since 1970, the rise of women into local church pastorates and other positions of authority has been recent. Troxell raises issues in her interviews that particularly address this first generation of women who are coming into clergy and professional lay leadership in large numbers.

A vision of "the Gospel Way of Life" should be a safeguard against taking on authority in inappropriate, unjust ways. Part of the prophetic truth that must be spoken today, Troxell states, is that women must make a fresh exploration of the meaning of servant ministry and self-giving, as well as self-affirmation and empowerment. Clergywomen must address directly problems among themselves, including jealousy toward and resentment of other women in leadership and the inability to hear others' stories without feeling threatened in their own journeys. Lay and clergywomen alike must see that hard, clear, mutually selfless searching is not antithetical to personal spiritual empowerment, if they are to gain the vocational vision to be prophetic and pastoral agents of change in the church.

Almost 125 years ago, in 1875, Anna Oliver wrote "that it is impossible for us to believe in a moment that we shall receive equal consideration with men." Anna Oliver could not conceive such a vision, but she, and each foremother studied in this volume, continually strove for that goal. As we follow in their train, we need searchingly to discern the spirituality and social responsibility at the heart of our vocational visions.

The words of Sharon Brown Christopher, one of the six women now serving as bishops in The United Methodist Church, set a standard for all women and men:

> My call is to live a life that becomes the Gospel and has everything to do with integrity. . . . My way of being in the world flows from one Source, God, who calls me toward the living of a vision of life as God intends it to be.

I invite you to enter into the lives of women in the United Methodist tradition who have responded to that call and help us to form our vocational visions today.

Rosemary Skinner Keller
Evanston, Illinois
August 1992

Catherine Livingston Garrettson

CHAPTER 1

"A WREN JUST BURSTING ITS SHELL"

Catherine Livingston Garrettson's
Ministry of Public Domesticity

DIANE H. LOBODY

I dreamed of some severe trials of too painful a nature to be written or
remembered if they should ever come to pass. In the conclusion I found
myself in a large room, with many dear friends. I was dancing alone. But I
cannot by any description, convey an idea of the beauty and harmony of this
dance; and the attitudes, and graceful steps, I found myself to my great surprise mistress of.[1]

The luminous images and lambent narrative of Catherine Livingston
Garrettson's dream evocatively prophesied her own resolution to the
dilemma that confronted the first generations of women who devoted
their lives to The Methodist Episcopal Church. Invigorated by the liberating message of Wesleyan teachings, stimulated by the democratic rhetoric
of early republican politics, emancipated by their own experiences of conversion, and empowered by their transforming encounters with God,
women like Catherine Garrettson were energized for Christian service.
The constraints of the culture in which they lived, however, defined the
arenas in which women's vocations could be exercised. No matter how
compelling the conviction that God had called her, no respectable Protestant woman could formally engage in a public ministry at the turn of the
nineteenth century without scandalizing society, embarrassing her family,
and disconcerting the institutional church.

Catherine's dream in 1790 presaged the gracefully subversive manner
by which she would eventually choreograph a ministry that was contigu-
ous both with her own integrity and with the expectations of her culture.[2]
The balanced movements in this dream narrative are striking: Acute suffering sets the stage for and propels her into the dance; her suitably feminine public performance takes place in a socially acceptable location;
she dances within the circumstances of a harmonious community, but

19

is utterly autonomous and dances beautifully and competently alone.

The ministry upon which Catherine was to embark a few years later was symbolically akin to this dream dance. Years of personal anguish, both before and after her conversion to Methodism, shaped the message and the environment of her ministry. She performed some of the most public functions of ministry (teaching, evangelism, pastoral care) in entirely domestic settings, and carved out for herself a way to answer her call to Christian service without questioning the restrictions of church and society that barred women from formal church vocations. But the home in which she was principally to center her ministry could by no means be characterized as a private household, and Catherine, like so many women in those liminal decades, began inexorably to stretch the perimeters of the domestic, and tentatively cracked open the boundaries between the public and the private.

Catherine Garrettson was by her background singularly poised to straddle the border between public and private life. The sixth of ten surviving children, Catherine was born in 1752 into the astonishingly wealthy and politically powerful Livingston family of Rhinebeck, New York. Generations of crafty Livingstons and industrious Beekmans converged in the union of Catherine's parents, Judge Robert Livingston and Margaret Beekman; at their marriage the two conjoined their bodies, their souls, and more than three quarters of a million acres of prime Hudson River Valley real estate. Catherine and her siblings were nestled in an environment that afforded economic privilege, social prominence, emotional security, and familial affection. All of the children, girls as well as boys, were educated as rigorously as possible; Catherine and her five sisters were not banished to the traditionally feminine arts of needlework and the pianoforte, but like their brothers wrestled with the sciences, French, and Enlightenment philosophy.

The Livingston family lived in a comfortable, stimulating, and well-mannered world, moving smoothly and familiarly in rarefied social circles. Mercy Otis Warren was a regular correspondent of the Livingston sisters, and Catherine's intimate observations of such luminaries as Alexander Hamilton and George Washington are sprinkled in her own letters. The Livingston women were butterflies of the New York social scene, but they were not vacuous women; their intelligence was nurtured not only by their unusual education but also by the enriching ethos of the Livingston family's political involvement.

Enormous wealth unavoidably summons concomitant power. Judge Livingston, breaking tradition with the reprehensibly self-serving ambitions of his forebears, committed his energies to public service in the practice of law. Later appointed to the provincial Supreme Court, the judge was also regularly elected to the colonial legislature, and worked diligently to craft a moderate colonial response to the increasingly repressive actions of the British government. Although instinctively conservative, the Judge became pertinaciously radical as the colonies simmered under British rule, and by the early 1770s every member of the Livingston family was an impassioned revolutionary. When war broke out in 1775, Catherine's brothers and brothers-in-law were thrust into the political and military limelight. Her oldest brother, Robert, was a delegate to the Continental Congress and elected to the committee charged with drafting the Declaration of Independence; two other brothers served as officers (and heroes) in the army; three sisters married prominent military leaders; and sundry cousins were equally well-positioned.

The political connections formed in the caldron of the Revolutionary War were solidified and rewarded in the new republic. After the peace, Livingston men and the husbands of Livingston women were regularly elected or appointed to significant offices in state and national government. The Livingston women, not ever inclined toward reticence on any issue, were thoroughly accustomed to including themselves in the discussions, travels, and activities of their assorted male relatives. For these women, linked by blood and by love to men whose trade was politics and whose discourse was power, public and private life readily commingled. The women, of course, wielded no direct political power; they could not vote, much less participate in the structure of the new government. But in the first decades of the infant nation, their homes—the homes of the legislators and cabinet officers and diplomats who were their brothers and husbands—were public households, where dignitaries stopped for tea, policy was debated over lunch, and statecraft found a permanent place at the dinner table.

Even as these Livingston public households modeled the setting for Catherine's later ministry, the family's social and economic status helped to define the content and constituency of that ministry. The Livingston children were reared in a religious environment that meshed quite nicely with the social position appropriate to the New York upper class. Deeply pious but avowedly nonevangelical Christians, the family worshiped in their mother's somber Dutch Reformed congregation during the summers in Rhinebeck, and in the Judge's refined Anglican church while wintering in New York City. This religious ethos suited the life-style of a genteel family: Calvinist ethics and Anglican traditionalism combined with Enlightenment rationalism to support a family religion of biblical but politely reasonable piety. Moderation in language and behavior was requisite, and enthusiastic religious exercises were considered distasteful and faintly repulsive. Wealthy people simply did not have evangelical conversion experiences; having been born once into the dynasty of the Livingstons, a concomitant birth into the kingdom of God was assumed.

Catherine, however, was of a different mettle. While a young woman, a constellation of personal tragedies, coupled with the horrors of the war, precipitated a long period of anguished although sporadic uncertainty about her previously unruffled faith. Within a calamitous three-week period in 1776, her grandfather Beekman succumbed to a long-anticipated death, her adored father died suddenly of a stroke, and her favorite brother-in-law, General Richard Montgomery, was killed in battle in Quebec. "Thus in the short span of 3 weeks three heads of families were cut off [leaving] 3 surviving widows," Catherine recalled years later. "When the last death was announced I wildly ran out of the House impiously exclaiming 'What have we done, to merit such afflictions!'"[3]

Life in the middle of a war zone in turn fostered unrelieved anxiety. Writing to Mercy Otis Warren, Catherine described the ghastly human cost of this unpredictable war:

> I join with you my dear Madam in wishing with ardor that the tumult of war was no more. The inhabitants of our frontiers are flying down in droves before an enemy we are yet too weak to oppose. A few days since, a large tract of country was laid waste; men women & children wantonly murdered, and the few unfortunates that escaped exchanged affluence and ease for unsheltered poverty and wretchedness.[4]

Catherine knew intimately the terrors of forced flight and the frightening destruction of personal property. The Livingston women had been compelled to evacuate their home minutes before it was torched by the British in 1777, and had returned months later to begin the painstaking and hazardous task of reconstruction. The events of the war and the losses she sustained permanently shattered the security that had once characterized Catherine's life. She would never thereafter entirely forget the ephemeral nature of earthly existence, where beloved relatives could be snatched away without warning and precious possessions could vanish into ashes.

The end of the war in 1783 in no way inaugurated a return to normalcy for the nation. Uncertainties about the experiment in democracy, rumblings of incipient economic chaos, and the radical reconfiguration of social roles all undermined the exhilaration of victory. For persons like the prodigiously wealthy and politically savvy Livingstons, however, the declaration of peace ushered in a delightful resumption of pre-war activities, and without hesitation the Livingstons flung themselves into the glittering round of parties and balls and entertainments.

But for Catherine, the events of the war had set into motion her own interior uncertainties and rumblings and reconfigurations. Even as she danced and played and flitted about, she questioned the very meaning of these frivolous engagements: "If the smiles of the world and the pleasures of it could have bestowed happiness," she later remembered, "I should certainly have enjoyed it, but no, there was something wanting, and a dear friend . . . and myself would sit up after returning from brilliant balls, and gay parties, and moralize on their emptiness, till it really became burdensome to accept of invitations."[5]

The shallow quality of this vapid life incrementally gnawed away at her ability to participate in it happily. In 1785, the death of a sister-in-law, who was not much older than she, pushed Catherine "to withdraw from company, and read the Word of God with more attention." One day, while reading in the Gospel of John Christ's question to Peter, "Lovest thou me?" Catherine had an embryonic conversion experience and "determined to give myself to this Jesus."[6] But her good intentions were quickly sabotaged by her sense of social obligation and her commitment to proper and polite Livingston behavior; she mortgaged her tentative peace by capitulating to the pressure of family and friends eager to sweep her back into the whirl of their world. Catherine long remembered and ever regretted the ease with which the wealthy managed to accommodate, compromise, and ignore the conflict between the values of evangelical Christianity and those of secular culture.

In 1787, death once again caught her unprepared, and this time the landscape of her soul was permanently altered. Her dearest friend, Mary Rutherford, died suddenly and unexpectedly. Rutherford had been Catherine's closest spiritual companion, a young woman who had been her lone partner in the quest for deeper values and religious meaning. Her reflections about Mary's death suggest that Catherine realized, in a most profound way, that absolutely nothing in the world was reliable or stable. Mary had been as wealthy as she, and now she lay "moldering into dust." Catherine had loved her as deeply as a friend could love, and now "the lovely lily has been torn away."[7] Enormous wealth and tender relationships could not fend off death; they could not even keep human beings safely anchored in happiness.

Wondering whether she herself was prepared to die, aching with grief and depression, and mired in perplexity and yearning, Catherine withdrew into solitude and prayer and meditation on the scriptures. On October 13, 1787, the day before her thirty-fifth birthday, the years of disquietude found resolution. While reading (and praying) the liturgy in the Anglican *Book of Common Prayer*, she was irrevocably converted. (See document 1.)

Catherine's conversion was, predictably, not well received by her family and friends. Not ever inclined to cast a favorable eye upon evangelical ardor, the Livingstons may have hoped that Catherine would get over this unfortunate phase and become her old self again. The problem, of course, was that she had become—to her own understanding—an utterly new self. Her immediate shift from a generic evangelical faith to Wesleyan Methodism only made matters worse. That she was introduced to the teachings of Wesley by her mother's housekeeper was scarcely a favorable recommendation to the Livingstons, who were notoriously clear about the unbridgeable distance between the servants and the served. Moreover, of all the sects squawking for attention in the evangelical barnyard, none was more personally, socially, politically, or theologically obnoxious to this family than The Methodist Episcopal Church. The Livingstons were wealthy, slaveholding, aristocratic, patriotic Calvinists. Their Catherine had joined herself to a church that controverted every one of those qualities: The largest audience of this church was found among the lower classes; the church had publicly denounced slavery; its preaching lifted up the equality of all persons; its founder was a British reactionary; its preachers had been jailed for pacifism during the Revolution; and its theology was unabashedly Arminian.

Had Catherine merely acquiesced intellectually to the tenets of this irksome religion, the family might well have accommodated itself to her eccentricity. There were, after all, plenty of peculiar personalities perched on other branches of the family tree, and the Livingstons could, albeit regretfully, have accepted her unpleasant theology. But Catherine's entire sense of self had changed, and she plunged herself into a devotional piety and radical asceticism that stood in obstinate opposition to the values, the principles, and the life-style of the Livingstons and their social circle. Catherine reoriented her life completely in this conversion. Prayer and meditation became her primary activities, and scripture and theology were her invariable topics of conversation. Fasting and weeping replaced card-playing and flirting, and the theater and the ballroom would soon be abandoned for sermons and class meetings. In 1789, Catherine testified to this fundamental redirection in a dream:

> I was wandering with one of my brothers in a large building; after passing through many strange scenes, he took me to a trunk where he said he had a nest of birds' eggs. I took one of the eggs, and while in my hand, the most beautiful bird came out I had ever seen. Its size was that of a blue bird, the plumage like the peacock, but the colors rich and more bright. After looking at it some time, I went to the door and gave it liberty, which it unwilling received. I returned to the nest, and found a wren just bursting its shell; here all my interest was at once fixed. I watched and as soon as it was disengaged I put it in my bosom. There were more birds, but I felt no interest in any.[8]

The ostentatious feathers of the Livingston peacocks had been exchanged for the sober demeanor of a fledgling Methodist wren.

But in Rhinebeck, for the first few years after Catherine's conversion, the Methodist flock was perilously sparse. Indeed, organized Methodist preaching in the Hudson River Valley did not commence until the autumn of 1788—a full year after Catherine's momentous emergence into an evangelical (and Wesleyan) identity. At the Conference in October 1788, the Reverend Freeborn Garrettson, an experienced and energetic Methodist evangelist, was appointed to take charge of the entire territory of New York. In June 1789, Freeborn rode into Rhinebeck to preach there for the first time, staying for the duration at the home of Catherine's sister and brother-in-law, Margaret and Thomas Tillotson. Freeborn's reception by the intractable Dutch Calvinists of Rhinebeck was barely lukewarm, and the initially cordial welcome of the Livingston clan froze into glacial hostility within a matter of months. To the horror of her family, Catherine and Freeborn had fallen quickly and deeply in love.

Four years of unspeakably painful conflict followed. Catherine's mother and all her relatives (with the exception of the Tillotsons) stood adamantly opposed to her desire to marry the appalling Methodist preacher. Margaret Livingston levied preposterous accusations about Freeborn's intentions, claiming that he was nothing more than a conniving fortune hunter; given the size of Catherine's projected inheritance, Margaret's fears were credible. But the fundamental issue at the heart of this battle was a violent clash of values. Freeborn himself was a living icon of the very qualities of Methodism that the Livingstons found most offensive: He was a former slaveholder, who had upon his conversion freed his slaves and signed over to them his property; he had been beaten and jailed for his pacifism during the Revolutionary War; he preached a liberating gospel of the grace of Jesus Christ, declaring it freely available to all persons who would accept it; and he insisted that Christian faith demanded a radical reconstruction of heart and life. By proclaiming her love for Freeborn, in whom she had found her soul's partner and spiritual friend, Catherine planted herself resolutely in Methodist ground, claiming in her public and private life a non-negotiable adherence to a theology and an ethic that stood incontrovertibly opposed to everything that the Livingstons represented.[9]

The conflict within the family lasted until 1793. The strain on Catherine during those years was nearly unbearable, and in desolation she left (or was forced to leave) her mother's home in 1791. Although the cultural mores would have permitted—if not encouraged—her to marry without parental approval, Catherine was determined to wait out her obstinate family. Her profound love for her relatives, her conviction that she was called by God to serve as an evangelical witness and converting instrument to her family, and her assurance that God had providentially willed her marriage to Freeborn Garrettson all conspired to keep her rooted in Rhinebeck. These were years of barren isolation; Freeborn was continually on the road planting new Methodist churches, and the Methodist Society in Rhinebeck comprised only a handful of believers. During this period of enforced solitariness, Catherine poured herself into a disciplined and structured life of prayer, introspection, meditation on the scriptures, and theological reading, much of which she recorded meticulously in a spiritual journal.

The pain, conflict, and loneliness of those years became the loom upon which Catherine's richly textured spirituality was woven. The very oppression and isolation that generated her deepest unhappiness also, paradoxically, created the environment that nurtured her most profound religious experiences. Her anguish drove her to an intensely interior life, a life that took very seriously the Wesleyan theology of perfection and those spiritual practices that supported the believer's progress toward perfect holiness. Wesleyan spirituality was particularly attuned to the movement of the soul in response to God's endlessly graceful invitations. Early Methodist spiritual disciplines encouraged that dynamic process by focusing believers on the states of their souls and by directing the attention of believers toward the immediate and concrete acts of God's grace in their individual lives. Catherine immersed herself in such disciplines. Her prayer, her reading of scripture, and her journal were aids to the practice of holy discernment. No event, no feeling, no thought was left unexplored. She sought relentlessly to lay bare her own nature and sinfulness with scathing scrupulosity, to expose the devious machinations of Satan as he tempted her to disobedience and doubt, and to discover the presence, providence, and love of God in every moment of her life.[10]

Catherine desired only to grow in grace. But her concentrated devotional practices, her rigorous piety, and her passionate sensibilities combined to engender something far deeper and far more vast. Her progress toward perfection, while always sustaining its Wesleyan language and Methodist scaffolding, began to bear a striking resemblance to the classic stages of the Christian mystical tradition. Her self-scrutiny and ascetic disciplines translated easily into the way of purgation. Catherine's heightened sensitivity to God's intimate affection for her and God's energetic presence in creation bore clear likeness to the state of illumination. Her years of wandering in a barren wilderness of bleak despair, feeling that God had abandoned and withdrawn from her, were without question a dark night of the soul. And in March 1793, Catherine's highly charged and intensely focused spirituality ignited in a series of extraordinary visions and overwhelming experiences of mystical union with God.[11] (See document 2.)

The subtly (and sometimes heatedly) erotic language that Catherine used to narrate her experiences of union with God betrays three significant characteristics of her mysticism. First, the experiences themselves were, by her own admission, indescribable; nevertheless, she seized the imagery of erotic and marital love and used that language to give utterance to her experience of God's consummate love for her. In this she stands firmly in the tradition of many Christian mystics, who abduct the symbol systems of common human relationships and apply them to their ineffable experiences of union with God.

Second, Catherine's mysticism—and indeed, the whole of her spirituality—was clearly bound up with her relationship with Freeborn. We are not talking about sublimated sexuality here. But in ways that are far too mysterious for a historian's understanding, Catherine's love for Freeborn was inextricably entwined with her love for God, and the ebb and flow of her intimacy with God converged in a breathtakingly noticeable manner with the rhythms of distance and closeness in her relationship with Freeborn. For instance, as soon as the date of the wedding was set, Catherine's experiences of union with God blossomed; after her marriage, she had no more ecstatic visions but understood herself to be continually happy in the presence of God; and after Freeborn died in 1827, Catherine not only grieved his loss but also plummeted into a spiritual mourning, feeling that God once again had completely withdrawn from her. This inescapable pattern seems to suggest at the very least that, for Catherine, God's love and Freeborn's love mediated each other. The ramifications for her own later ministry are suggestive. Whether or not her culture served to restrict her vocational options, this woman of necessity would have created a ministry that wove itself tightly into the structure of her marriage. (See document 4.)

Third, and also important for her own sense of vocation, Catherine's mystical experiences were almost exclusively visions of love: God's tender love for her, God's outrageous love for creation, God's sacrificial love for all humankind. In Catherine's view, such abundant love demanded a prodigious human response. All persons were called to answer God's inviting love by turning from sin and flinging themselves into holy lives of love for God and for neighbor. The alternative was inevitable damnation. Catherine's own experiences and visions of God's love generated within her an irrepressible desire to convey the truth of that love to every single person she encountered. God's unanswered love for her unregenerate family and friends made them infinitely more precious in Catherine's sight, and the threat of their eternal damnation pressed upon her with mounting urgency.

Healthy Christian mystics are never inclined toward self-absorption; the vibrant power and wild delight of their love for God propels them into actions of love and service. Catherine was no stranger to such impulses, and the Methodist emphasis on social holiness compelled her to search for ways to serve God. "Lord make me a profitable servant," she wrote in 1792. "Set me upon some work. I long to be doing something."[12]

But in the 1790s there were virtually no ecclesiastically or socially sanc-tioned opportunities for women to be "profitable servants" anywhere out-side the home. Wesley's own cautious support of women in public ministry had found little favor in The Methodist Episcopal Church, and by this period in the United States women were no longer even functioning as class leaders.[13] Catherine herself never overtly articulated any desire to engage in a public ministry of preaching or evangelism. Indeed, she took some pains to defend herself to the contrary. Writing to another Methodist woman in 1791, she commented: "The applause of man I desire not, it would be irksome to me. The good of souls I wish, because I feel they are most precious. . . . I hope you do not think I have any desire to become a public speaker. Ah! No. I want to do all the good I possibly can before I go hence, and am no more seen, both to the souls and bodies of men."[14]

But it is equally clear that she had both the talent and the energy to be a preacher and an evangelist, had that avenue been open to her. She was well-read, articulate, thoughtful, and persuasive. Her letters and diaries evidence an astonishing command of scripture, an incisive ability to argue doctrine, and a powerful eloquence that—had she been in the pulpit—would have driven unbelievers to their knees. And on some level she must have known and felt that truth about herself. Several of the dreams that she recorded during this period place her in roles that are undeniably pastoral, priestly, and kerygmatic. (See document 3.) Those yearnings could find neither expression nor fulfillment within The Methodist Episcopal Church of her time. But both church and culture were starting to betray considerable tension over women's roles. The democratic assumptions implicit in both Methodist theology and repub-lican rhetoric were beginning ever so tentatively to liberate women from older constraints, and irresistibly to beckon women into more public forms of ministry.

Catherine and Freeborn were married in June 1793, having outwaited and outwitted the longstanding opposition of the sundry Livingstons. Their marriage provided a socially acceptable and personally fruitful set-ting within which Catherine fulfilled her desire to be a profitable servant. Freeborn exuberantly continued his itinerant ministry, riding the circuits to check up on the preachers under his charge and traveling for weeks at a time engaged in the work of building a denomination. For a good while Catherine traveled with him; within two weeks of their wedding they were off to Philadelphia, where Freeborn had been appointed Presiding Elder. But the two returned to Rhinebeck the following spring. Catherine was pregnant, and she and Freeborn purchased an old Dutch farmhouse close by the other Livingstons. Here she settled while Freeborn went off further-ing the work of the Lord's kingdom, and Catherine gave birth to their only child, Mary Rutherford, in September 1794. In 1799, the Garrettsons built a larger home in Rhinebeck on a tract of land known locally as Wildercliffe. Bishop Asbury bestowed upon the home the winsome name "Traveler's Rest." This house served, of course, as a resting place for Freeborn on the rare occasions when he was not off doing God's business. But it also became the place out of which Catherine attended to her own branch of God's business. Traveler's Rest quickly turned into the center of Catherine's ministry of hospitality and the headquarters for her evangelistic endeavors.

Although no personal records indicate how the pattern of pilgrimage began, Traveler's Rest readily grew into a retreat center (nearly a Christian hostel) for exhausted itinerant clergy, peripatetic ecclesiastical dignitaries, and any other persons who happened by the house needing a comfortable place to stay. And comfortable it was indeed. Catherine's inheritance provided more than enough funds to build and maintain the home, furnish it graciously, decorate it tastefully, and add continually to the exquisite (and morally improving) library. One historian describes Traveler's Rest as "one of organized Protestantism's more elegant asylums."[15] The comfort of the place, though, accounted for only part of its attraction. The keystone of this ministry of hospitality was the hospitable minister herself, Catherine Garrettson.

Traveler's Rest was, of course, very much a public household: Men and women, clergy and laity, famous personages and common folk were continually trekking in and out of this home. Catherine, though, saw this as a private household, with herself as the wife and mother, and as a good early nineteenth-century matron she took charge of the moral and religious life in her domestic sphere. Within this home that was both public and private, Catherine constructed a ministry that was entirely acceptable as a feminine enterprise and yet as vibrantly pastoral as any man's ministry. She organized and presided over regular services of worship (barring only the celebration of the sacraments); she taught Bible and theology to children, young people, and adults; she mobilized and conducted prayer groups; she expounded the scriptures within the setting of home worship; she solicited testimonies of salvation and encouraged unbelievers to repent; and she functioned, both in person and in correspondence, as a pastoral counselor and spiritual director for a great variety of persons. She was in practice a preacher, teacher, evangelist, and pastor. (See documents 5 and 6.)

Unquestionably, these very roles were nurtured in the bosom of the Methodist class meeting; the exercise of those skills invited women of later generations to envision themselves in ordained ministry. For women of Catherine's age and era, though, God's call to ministry was answered more subversively, although no less honorably. By remaining within her home and serving her household in precisely the way that every good Methodist mother was expected to serve, Catherine satisfied the propriety of her time and respected her sense of her own feminine identity. Every pious evangelical mother understood herself to be completely responsible for the moral nurture, the religious education, the spiritual guidance, and the devotional practices of every person within her household. And so Catherine attended to exactly those areas in the life of her household. That her household consisted of constantly shifting configurations of clergy, scholars, politicians, and prominent laymen, along with friends and family and servants in residence, simply escaped her notice. While functioning effectually in ministerial roles, Catherine shyly pictured herself as an unassuming wife and mother in an ordinary Methodist home.

Traveler's Rest was also conspicuous in the Methodist colonization of Rhinebeck and the Hudson River Valley. Catherine's view of the strength of the Methodist foothold in the area was somewhat jaundiced even toward the end of her life; nothing would have satisfied her short of a unanimous emigration of all those stony Calvinists to the Methodist camp. But Catherine's own conversion helped to pry open the stiff doors of the Hudson River mansions, and with her the Methodist witness stole across those thresholds. For all that her evangelical ardor embarrassed and dismayed her peers, the character of Catherine's life bore singular authenticity and power. She never betrayed her faith by compromising her values or adjusting her understanding of the gospel to suit her carnal needs. But even though her adherence to Methodism was unremitting—even relentless—she was nevertheless gentle in her judgments, liberal in her compassion, and tender in her relationships. Having been a belle of society and a beneficiary of its delights, Catherine's urgent testimony to the people of the upper classes assumed a credibility not ever accorded to the word of an ordinary (and lower-class) Methodist preacher. She knew full well the seductive attraction of money and status and power, and she understood clearly the debilitating price exacted by accommodation to the values of the world. In her own family she saw constantly and intimately the consequences of human addiction to wealth and position. Her brother Edward, for instance, went bankrupt and thereupon lost his political office, his economic viability, and his social prestige; more important, in Catherine's view, Edward's emotional and spiritual security was shattered because he had identified himself too fully with his possessions and reputation. (See document 7.)

Catherine's conversion and later mystical experiences demanded that she speak the urgent biblical word of salvation to every person she encountered. The Hudson River Valley became her evangelistic field, and rescuing the souls of Rhinebeck became her particular mission. Letters to unconverted family members (and not many remained in that precarious state for long) give us some clues about her unyielding and eloquent insistence that God had a claim on each human life and that each sinner could and must make a free and responsible decision to turn to Christ and begin a new life of humble love. Catherine and the Methodists were not as resoundingly successful in Rhinebeck as the denomination proved to be elsewhere, but the conversion of the Hudson River Valley aristocracy (including a large number of Livingstons) was notable. Once again, Catherine never conceived herself in any public role as evangelist or exhorter; rather, she simply visited and testified and conversed within the bounds of her domestic circle. That these friends and relatives included senators and Supreme Court justices was quite beside the point. The only relevant concern for Catherine was her abiding responsibility to speak God's word and extend Christ's invitation to all the people of her world, just as every faithful Methodist woman rejoiced in doing.

When Catherine died in 1849 at the age of ninety-six, she ended a life that had been historically congruent with enormous transitions in gender roles within church and culture. Born into a colonial society in which women were legally mute and politically invisible, she lived through a revolution whose philosophical rhetoric sparked a slow but comparable revolution in women's self-consciousness. Heady with the public stances they had assumed during the war and thoughtful about the implications of democratic ideology for their roles in the new nation, some women began to chafe under the constraints of their truncated citizenship and to marshal arguments in favor of fuller legal rights.[16] Women's dissatisfaction rippled more widely throughout the first decades of the early republic, and by 1848, the penultimate year of Catherine's life, women young enough to be her great-granddaughters were congregating in Seneca Falls for the first women's rights convention.

Similar changes raked the ecclesiastical terrain. In 1752, Catherine was born into a culture that was still trembling from the jolt of the First Great Awakening. Within that set of circumstances, women had claimed their voices as they narrated conversion experiences (under the watchful eyes of their male pastors) and directed domestic piety (under the technical guidance of their male relatives). But unless a woman were eccentric enough to ally herself with a marginalized and unsocialized sect, virtually all public religious arenas and positions were closed off to her.

During the near-century bracketed by Catherine's birth and death, however, evangelical Christianity seeped and then surged through American culture, leaving the wreckage of older gender roles bobbing in its wake. In its Methodist incarnation, evangelical theology translated readily into a dramatic grammar of liberation, inadvertently reformulating women's roles and identities in startling ways. In a nation intoxicated with the notion of democracy, Methodist preaching inculcated the infinite value and radical responsibility of every single person. Inherent in this structure was an awesome assumption: Like her brothers, each woman was individually accountable to God and eternally obligated to respond to God's grace and to honor God's demands. In the scheme of salvation, only two voices mattered—God's and one's own.[17] It would not be long before women discovered just how compelling God's voice could be, consecrating women to tasks of questionably feminine character.

The institutionally sanctioned spiritual disciplines of Methodism blithely supported the theological empowerment of women. Evangelicals charged all believers to be tireless evangelists, inveterate missionaries, doctrinal disputants, and moral arbiters. Those expectations nurtured an unprecedented expansion of women's vocational possibilities. Trained in the evangelical arts of public testimony, group leadership, biblical study, and moral governance, women began—at first diffidently and then resolutely—to exercise their gifts in more public ways as they responded to God's call to Christian discipleship. By 1849, as Catherine lay dying, faithful women were emerging in the most unexpected places and joining their brothers in the work of the Lord as lay preachers, itinerant evangelists, social reformers, popular theologians, and eloquent visionaries.

Catherine herself came to maturity just at the edge of those transformations, and her ministry flourished in an awkward but curiously comfortable environment for women in early American Methodism. Questions about woman's place in ecclesiastical leadership were barely percolating at the time of her conversion, and a desire to serve in professional ministry never consciously surfaced in her thoughts; the very notion was unspeakably preposterous. But the spiritual experiences that arose in concert with her increasingly refined Methodist theology were all too compelling, transforming, and liberating to go unnoticed; it would have been inconceivable, irresponsible, and impossible for Catherine to smother her witness and stifle her testimony. In faithful conformity with her culture, in logical agreement with her background, and in complete harmony with her own sense of self, Catherine Livingston Garrettson created the space—interior and exterior—within which she could fulfill a ministry that honored her call without disrupting her world view.

Catherine's "father in Christ," John Wesley, had earlier declared that the world was his parish. It was only reasonable that his American daughter chose to live by an equally generous vision of the boundaries of her household.

DOCUMENTS

1. Conversion Narrative from the "Autobiography," 1817. Like many of her contemporaries, Catherine composed an autobiographical memoir, narrating in exemplary Methodist style the providences of God in her life. It is avowedly a spiritual autobiography, and not surprisingly the story of her conversion is its centerpiece. In this extract, Catherine describes her capitulation to worldly influences after her early awakening, and then carries the narrative to its triumphant conclusion with her conversion at Clermont on October 13, 1787.

In the city I found many interruptions. I therefore determined to go and spend time with my sister [Gertrude] Lewis, a mile out of the bustling busy town. There I spent a most delightful fortnight in the enjoyment of God and the impartation of His peace, and had a most remarkable answer to prayer. But alas! alas!—Cards went out from my sister Lewis's for a private ball. My particular friends and favorites were asked. Good manners I thought demanded my presence. Other inducement I had none, and I was so ignorant on the subject of my new attainments that I saw not the gulf into which I was about to precipitate myself. That worldly wisdom which brought me into such company obliged me to dance, but it was all dull work. The same carriage that brought my sisters from town to the ball took me back with them to the city house. And thus ended my present journey in the paradise of peace and heavenly mindedness. I was left in darkness, in dullness, in heaviness. I might no doubt have regained my peace had I pursued right methods, but I consulted no one. All was locked up in my own breast. Retirement no longer yielded me peace or pleasure, and by degrees I forsook it for the world and its polluted enjoyments, and was content with a form of religion, such I mean as passes current in the present day. I could go to public amusements, not a week before but a week after the sacrament with a good conscience. Twice dead. What a mercy that in this awful state the Lord did not cut off the withered branch. . . .

In the summer we retired into the country, and blessed be the Lord He did not leave me to my own ruin. He visited me, and I had many serious reflections; but on my return in the autumn to the city, hurry, fashion, and company spoiled all again—but I was to be brought in only by affliction and humiliation, and they were preparing for me. . . . Another afflictive stroke followed, in the loss of a most dear friend, for whom I had the tenderest affection. Her death was a solemn warning not only to me but the whole city. On Saturday she was well; on Sunday at 2 o'clock I saw her a pale corpse. And the hopes of parents, husband, friends all blasted in a moment. . . . I soon after left New York for Clermont. . . .

Friday and Saturday, October 11 and 12th, 1787, were two dismal days. I took a retrospective view of my life; it seemed crowded with painful circumstances. My convictions were deep. I felt pained beyond expression. On Saturday night I sat up in the dining room at my brother Chancellor Livingston's till all the house were in bed and asleep. I then in anguish of heart walked softly upstairs, and casting myself on my knees, prayed fervently. My plea was, Lord thine arm is not shortened that it cannot save, nor thine ear heavy that it will not hear. A gleam of light broke in upon my soul, and a measure of confidence and peace sprung up into my heart. It seemed to be said to me, Lie down and take your rest. I did so. My mind was sweetly composed and I fell asleep and did not awake till morning.

On Sunday, October 13, 1787, I arose early with a heart full of expectation, came down to breakfast, took a cup of tea and then retired to my room, bolted the door and opening my prayer-book (for we had then, only preaching once in three weeks) I read over the Church Service on my knees with clasped hands and uplifted eyes. I prayed, "By Thine agony and bloody sweat; by thy cross and passion; by Thy glorious resurrection and ascension; and by the coming of the Holy Ghost." Scarce had I pronounced those words, when I was received and made unspeakably happy. A song of praise and thanksgiving was put in my mouth—my sins were pardoned, my state was changed; my soul was happy. In a transport of joy I sprang from [my] knees, and happening to see myself as I passed the looking glass I could not but look with surprise at the change in my countenance. All things were become new.

2. Diary Entries, 1793. About six weeks after her conversion, Catherine began to keep a diary "for the sole purpose of seeing what advances I make in the divine life." Catherine continued this vital Methodist spiritual discipline for the next sixty-two years, recording the intricacies of her interior life with variable regularity. The first six diaries, which conclude at the time of her wedding, reflect her movement toward mystical union with God. Her visions began sporadically in 1792, and by March 1793 she was being flooded with overwhelming experiences of God's presence. These diary selections evoke some of the power of those ecstatic periods.

I went to bed and awoke with such a glorious view of the millennium, as I have not had in all my life before or since. This view was accompanied by such power, and such sweetness, and such peace as I cannot describe. . . . My peace flowed like a river, and I had blessed hopes for all my relations. My capacious soul was enlarged with divine love, and had hope for all the world. I saw plainly nothing was too hard for God. I was happy all the next day in the great scenes of future glory. The next night, perhaps at the same hour, I had not yet been asleep, when I was favored with such a visitation as I had never had before. I felt for some moments that my soul was drinking in holiness. And then followed such a shedding abroad the love of God in my soul, that it appeared to me I was all light, fire, and power. [March 1793]

I prayed in faith, nothing doubting, but that my precious Lord was nigh. When I had been near two hours in these acts of devotion, I arose, and after one, prepared for bed. I was in peace and my mind hushed so that I was near falling asleep, when I was aroused with a visit from my blessed Lord. I could compare it to His coming on the mountains of spices. He filled me with His blissful joyous presence; I could cry out, I am the temple of the Holy Ghost, I am espoused to Jesus and in Him united to the glorious trinity; His visits were not short; for hours I could say His left hand is under me and the right hand of His power is over me, to defend me from all evil. I was lost. I found myself a drop in the ocean of love. . . . I was now led to Calvary. I saw the God of the whole universe veiled in human nature and making expiation on the cross. I contemplated His wounded hands, His side, His feet—I saw the necessity—the wisdom—the love and mercy of this glorious sacrifice—I adored at the foot of the cross, and desire often to contemplate this wonderful and blissful subject. God is love—I feel it—I know it. I taste and can and do daily and hourly rejoice in God my Savior. [March 11, 1793]

I was taught by the Spirit to look into the heights, the length, and breadth of the love of Christ, but found it too, too high for the most soaring mind to have equal conception of—I saw clearly that the length and breadth was sufficient to encompass the whole race of fallen Adam. Boundless love never sent a single soul upon the earth, to damn it to all eternity. It cries aloud "Turn ye, turn ye, why will you die." Ah! let me echo the sound, why will you die. God is love, the Son is love—the Holy Spirit visiteth the sons of earth on errands full of love—O come, taste and see that the Lord is good, supremely good. Ah! who that loves can love enough. Ah who that knows thee, can be satisfied with inferior enjoyments. Lord lead me on to higher views. And after teaching me, enable me to teach others. [April 9, 1793]

3. *Dream Narrative, Spring 1789.* Although Catherine never expressed any desire to be a preacher, a number of her dreams place her in clearly pastoral roles. In this narrative, recorded in a journal devoted only to her dreams, Catherine interprets scripture, elevates a eucharistic chalice, distributes sacramental wine, and speaks a kerygmatic word to the people.

I dreamed I was riding in a high open carriage with an old man, who I believe is a child of God. I saw a bird of a very large size; it had six wings, and passed in the air very high. While I was looking at it as a very uncommon phenomenon, this thought struck me, that something similar was related by Daniel. I saw a stream issuing from it, which I was anxious to catch. I flew out of the carriage and ran with a tumbler in my hand, time enough to receive this precious liquor: on looking at it, I found it was wine of the purest, the most lovely color. I drank part of it, commending it in the highest terms to all around me, and looking with transport at it. I thought I had a daughter of seven years old. I called her over to me and gave her some of this wine, which appeared to me sacred.

4. *Letter to Catherine Rutsen, March 7, 1794.* Catherine engaged in regular correspondence with a network of Methodist women in the New York area. Catherine Rutsen Suckley, a neighbor, was one of the first persons to join the society in Rhinebeck after Catherine Garrettson had paved the way. In this letter, written a few months after her wedding, Catherine makes one of her rare comments on the question of "woman's sphere," a

concept that was soon to become a hermeneutical principle for the discussion of gender roles in American culture.

> I bless God I find my soul on stretch for more of the mind of Christ. I want a constant uninterrupted breathing after God, a praying without ceasing and in everything giving thanks. I dare not say that I am more devoted to my good God than I was before I married; but I can truly say He has no rival in my heart, and if it was His will to call me hence, there is no created object has power to excite a longing lingering look behind. Of the cares attending married life experience has taught me nothing yet. I think it enlarges a woman's sphere of usefulness and enables her to bring more glory to God than in single life she has the opportunity of doing. But in all things this must be kept in view; Lord, not my but Thy will be done.

5. *Letter to Anne (Nancy) Van Ness, January 13, 1810.* Anne Van Ness, a prominent figure in the New York social scene, was another link in the Methodist sisterhood. In this letter, Catherine betrays her own intellectual interests, her doctrinal biases, her organizational flair, her pastoral inclinations, and her evangelistic zeal.

> We are employed in the same profitable work, that of reading Mr. Fletcher. I am better and better pleased as I advance. Never was controversy carried on with more spirit, and a better spirit. The saint, the zealous Christian shines in every page; light and conviction flashes from his pen. When I am reading I pray to the Lord to incline those that are in error only to read, that they may see and think aright. I have besought my friends, but generally find them opposed to controversy. . . . I cannot bear to think of my friends continuing Calvinistic while I see something in religion on such a broader, grander scale, and that brings so much more glory to the gracious redeemer. . . . I had a letter from our dear Eliza a few days since. She has need of much grace, and if she will understand her privileges, she will find that there is a fund in Jesus sufficient to bear her up under any difficulty, and open her way as she goes forward. I shall write again soon, and have thought when I go to town, to endeavor to set up a weekly prayer meeting with some friends, where she might find freedom to join. Mrs. Few will I know be ready to unite in such a labor of love. My dear Nancy, let us cry night and day to the Lord to give us gifts, and grace to use them to His glory and the good of poor perishing souls. If God in infinite mercy should bless our well meant endeavors, think what our rejoicing will be in time and in eternity. . . . Continue my dear, pray for me, and add that God would be pleased to make use of me instrumentally in my family. Oh! What great need is there for them to be awakened and stirred up to pray. Time is making such rapid strides. Eternity is heaving in view. Alas! Alas! My heart is sometimes rent with sorrow.

6. *Letter to Catherine Few, June 13, 1812.* Catherine maintained an energetic correspondence with both Anne Van Ness and with Catherine Few,

another member of the New York aristocracy; letters were exchanged among these women over almost half a century. Catherine's own letters speak volumes about the relationships among evangelical women: She bares her soul in confession and thanksgiving, dispenses spiritual counsel, offers emotional support, and comments perceptively and astringently on the religious health of the people she knows and loves. This letter trenchantly probes the question of Christianity and wealth, and insightfully describes the difficulties that assault the upper classes, who are least able to hear the gospel.

> I have always had but one view of an unconverted ministry; and the splendor of talents and rhetorical abilities, while they please the ear and delight the understanding, mislead the heart and deaden it to the simplicity of gospel truths. This is one cause that so few of a certain class embrace religion. Pure religion requires more sacrifices than they are willing to make. To sit at the feet of an unlearned holy man who is taught of God, and thrust forth into His vineyard to call sinners to repentance. How hard to those who can attend the word in elegant houses, and never have their ears grated by a rough word, or their feelings roused by a suspicion of their safety. Thus thousands live and are hushed asleep till they awake to a sense of their true situation in an unchangeable eternity. I would not my friend wish you to misunderstand my expression. I meant not that experimental religion was confined to any class of society; but that we must be brought down to the gospel standard, and embrace truth for its own intrinsic worth.

7. *Letter to Edward Livingston, January 4, 1809.* No community of sinners was more precious to Catherine than her unregenerate family, and her correspondence is permeated with concern for the salvation of the Livingston souls. The letters to her siblings are pointedly evangelistic, and she unabashedly raises issues of money, status, and power as she exhorts her brothers and sisters to reorder their priorities. Edward, the youngest brother, was admittedly Catherine's favorite, and when financial and political disaster loomed in 1809, she spared no efforts to help him see this tragedy in its proper light. At once tender and bracing, vulnerable and stern, Catherine challenges her brother in this letter to be honest about his condition, to wean himself from worldly attachments, to see God's saving hand in these circumstances, and to turn to a merciful Jesus who is both friend and comforter.

> Last night when every eye was closed in sleep, my heart went out in prayer to God for you my dear Edward. I reflected deeply on your worldly concerns, and the many trials and mortifications you had passed through within a few years. You must always keep in mind my dear that man is prone to sorrow, that this lower world is nothing more than a passage to another existence, where all is durable, all is eternal. Adversity is a school in which we may

learn lessons that will make the soul joyful in time and through a glorious eternity. To have a sensibility of the depravity of the human heart is no mean knowledge. This will lessen our dependence on vain man. When we see the insufficiency of created things to tranquilize the mind, we are taught to look up to the only pure source of happiness. And when we can come like the humble self-convicted publican with a Lord be merciful to me a sinner, Jesus Christ the friend of the broken hearted will rectify with a word, a look, all this misery; heal the wounds which sin has made; and give a peace, a sweetness, a holy calm which will rejoice the soul more than when oil and wine increaseth. Our way my brother is often made rough in mercy to our immortal spirits, because there is no other treatment will make us acquainted with the fallacy of human dependence. We are by nature and practice rebels to God and our own souls. The things of time occupy all our thoughts till disappointment shows we have been building on a sandy foundation. God is desirous we should be happy, but this must be in His own way. O! listen my brother, and pursue the only path that can ever lead you to peace and permanent enjoyment. A holy life makes a happy death, and furnishes a hope full of immortality. You are frequently in my thoughts, for the love I have always borne you is not small—You were my little darling, when in prattling infancy I often pressed you in my arms with almost maternal fondness, and under your afflictions and embarrassments I have all along had a secret hope that yet all these things might work together for good, and lead your heart to its great author. I have for a number of years tried hard to find satisfaction in worldly pursuits. God in mercy disappointed my hopes, and I thank Him. I did not let go my hold till conviction of my folly flashed upon me, and I was pointed by the servants and the spirit of God to Christ the only refuge. In Him I found that full and free redemption which by His blessing I still enjoy and now recommend to you and my sister as the only good worth pursuing in this life. Retire my dear friends often where no eye but God's sees, and there pour out your whole heart in prayer. He will hear; He will answer you; He will bless you, and place your feet upon the rock from whence you (if faithful) shall never be moved. Can we possibly value the favor of God too highly? If God is for us, what can man do against us. Do not be cast down my dear brother; make a friend in heaven, and all will yet go well—your light afflictions which are but for a moment will work out for you a far more exceeding and eternal weight of glory.

Eliza Garrett

CHAPTER 2

ELIZA GARRETT

To Follow a Vision

ILA ALEXANDER FISHER

When Augustus Garrett settled in Chicago in 1835 and sent for Eliza, his wife, at her family farm in Newburgh, New York, neither of them realized the far-reaching consequences of the step they were taking. After several years of accompanying Augustus in sad adventures in far-off cities, Eliza had been forced to return to her family farm. Now rejoined in Chicago, the Garretts had finally reached a place in which their talents and hard work could bring them success. Augustus at thirty-three years of age was beginning to build a fortune, and he was twice elected to serve as mayor of the growing hamlet of Chicago.

Even though Eliza, following her husband's death in 1848, made decisions of long-lasting significance, there is little material specifically about her life. In 1855, the year of her death, she became the founder of Garrett Biblical Institute, the second institution for theological education of The Methodist Church in this country. In order to trace the development of this venture in Eliza's mind, we must rely for the most part on references to her in the writings of others who knew her.

Born Eliza Clark in Newburgh in 1805 into a strong Christian home, Eliza had been reared with the ideal that "none of us liveth to himself, and no man dieth to himself."[1] Although her family was Presbyterian, she is thought to have been a probationary member in the local Methodist Episcopal Church. Eliza and Augustus were married in 1825, and four years later they decided to head west. They, like many other ambitious young couples, saw no future in debt-laden farms shared with their siblings. Augustus described it: "I left my country, the land that gave me birth . . . that my Father and my Mother inherited for a long while. With all I left behind an aged Father and Mother and so did my wife which caused her to weep for many salutary hours to seek an asylum in a new country amongst strangers."[2]

The years before arriving in Chicago were times of poverty and grief for the young couple. Upon leaving Newburgh in 1829 they settled in Cincinnati. Augustus wrote, "My losses in Cincinnati were great. Sued and prosecuted . . . I had to pay them all [the creditors] to a cent."[3] It appears that it was out of necessity that Augustus and Eliza left Cincinnati and headed for New Orleans. Imogene, their four-year-old daughter, died of cholera in 1833 as they traveled along the Mississippi and was buried in an unmarked grave along the river, soon to be followed by Charles, who died in Natchitoches, Texas. All biographies list two children born to the Garretts, but the Garrett monument at Rosehill Cemetery (in Chicago) also lists a third child, John, who appears to have died shortly after birth. The exact dates of the children's births and deaths cannot be determined. The monument is heavily weathered, making it impossible to decipher the death or birth dates. The city of New Orleans attracted adventurous people drawn by a desire to speculate and grow wealthy. These adventurers joined an established population of more than 30,000 in which the French and the Creoles held growing power. It was when Augustus again experienced overwhelming failure that Eliza returned to her parents' home waiting for her husband to achieve some manner of economic stability so that she could join him again.

Augustus arrived in Chicago in 1834 alone and in debt. The village of Chicago had scarcely more than 400 residents, but the population grew to 4,100 by 1837. When Augustus began speculating in real estate in 1845, the population was 12,000; and in 1856, shortly after Eliza's death, it had soared to 86,000. In contrast to the East where wealth was mostly inherited, fortunes were quickly gained and lost. The social structure changed rapidly; even the wealthy were likely to have experienced poverty in the recent past.[4]

Chicago had been a small trading post until the building of the Erie Canal transformed it into an important transportation center, especially for the transportation of wheat. As late as 1817 Fort Dearborn, located in what is now downtown Chicago, was destroyed in a raid by Native Americans. The rebuilt fort was soon joined by some small wooden cottages and rooming houses. In the span of one lifetime, the small hamlet of Chicago grew into a city of one million residents.

Since there is a paucity of firsthand information about Eliza, it is necessary to come to know Augustus in order to become acquainted with her. Augustus, "a jolly man, full of wit and pranks," had developed an act by the time he reached Chicago as a commercial real estate auctioneer. He was accustomed to sending out a black man, George White, dressed in scarlet, carrying a scarlet flag, and riding a horse with a scarlet harness, to announce the details of the day's auction.[5] Chicago was the right place for Augustus to find success. In the year 1835, the year in which he sent for

Eliza, he sold real estate valued at $1,800,000. He also sold marine and fire insurance (the latter a crucial item for a new city plagued with fires). He was also part-owner of a company, Seaman and Garrett, which brokered the purchase of goods from New York, and then bought back the goods of stores that had declared bankruptcy.

A contemporary commented that Augustus enjoyed greater business success after Eliza arrived. "The two together made speedier and greater financial gains than the one had done alone. They became prominent among the Methodists, but Mrs. Garrett mostly looked after his interests in that direction, while he sold lands and acted politics."[6] Mrs. Garrett appears to have had a good grasp of their real estate business, for after Augustus died in 1848 she continued to negotiate on behalf of Bishop and Mrs. Hamline on residential land in Chicago they were buying. As late as 1853 Eliza was caring for the Hamline's real estate interests in Chicago.[7]

In this aggressive society Augustus was drawn into politics. Eliza retained her ideals, even as she entertained Augustus' political and business cronies. In 1843 Augustus served as the seventh mayor of Chicago. Although he was elected again in 1844, the election was contested. He lost the rerun election, only to win again in 1845. As mayor he took decisive steps for public vaccinations during the cholera and smallpox epidemics, which were sweeping the country. He arranged for financial support for the Chicago battalion in the Mexican War.[8] Augustus' acerbic wit was evident in some of his pronouncements. When a large public school was built, he commented that it should be turned into an insane asylum since the people of the city were clearly insane to want such a large school.[9]

In 1839 Eliza and Augustus were converted under the preaching of Peter Borein, the pastor at Clark Street Methodist Episcopal Church, now Chicago Temple. The influence of Peter Borein, his regret at his lack of a formal education, and his determination to rectify that deficiency made a permanent impression on Eliza and alerted her to the need for an educated ministry.

Peter Borein was born to rough, illiterate farmers in 1809 in Sinking Creek, in east Tennessee. In his early teens he was converted at a revival and was called into the ministry. Since his father was violently opposed to his entering the ministry, Peter went to live with his uncle, who soon moved to Jacksonville, Illinois. Although he had not even known the alphabet, Borein was an eager and bright student for the two years he spent at Jacksonville College. He was driven by the need for knowledge commensurate with his call to preach. Peter's preaching abilities and enthusiasm quickly attracted the attention of the Methodists in northern Illinois and it was then that he was called to Clark Street Methodist Episcopal Church.

Borein was a captivating preacher, using "word pictures" as he dramatized the Bible.[10] His preaching attracted large crowds. He resolved to teach himself Hebrew, and he often voiced his convictions about the church's need for training schools to equip clergy for effective ministries.

Clark Street Church had been isolated geographically and socially with meager leadership—Grant Goodrich being a notable exception—until Borein arrived and began his series of revivals. The strong churches and the residential area had moved south leaving The Methodist Episcopal Church stranded in the north on the "wrong side" of the river.[11]

In spite of its less than favorable location, the Clark Street congregation grew rapidly during the two years Borein served as its pastor. In his last year on earth, 1839, Borein brought the Garretts into the church. When he was only thirty, typhoid entered his home, taking the life of his young son. Shortly thereafter, Peter himself died.

Eliza faithfully attended Clark Street Methodist Episcopal Church from the time of her conversion until her own early death. She pursued the life of a Christian despite her contact with "worldly" people as the wife of Augustus Garrett. Her contemporaries said that whenever the doors were open at the church, she was present. A young man who had been a member of D. M. Bradley's class along with Eliza testified later that she never missed a meeting.[12] Yet Eliza was always seeking further Christian growth. (See document 3.)

Eliza's struggle for faith was a solitary one, for Augustus appears to have had difficulty retaining his Christian commitment. He underwent as many as twenty additional conversions in the nine years following his initial conversion experience under the ministry of Peter Borein. In many services he confessed his failings and prayed to change his ways. His contemporaries blamed it on his "vicious" and "prodigiously wicked" habits.[13] An "Old Timer" who wrote a column in the newspaper wrote of him in 1893, "If there ever was a man in whom the spirit was willing but the flesh weak it was my late old friend, Augustus Garrett. He was after all a man of generous impulses and good intentions, but like many a better man, the world, the flesh and the ancient Edward fought against him and too often conquered."[14]

In his business letters Augustus revealed a strong motivation to retain an honest name and to earn a reputation for being trustworthy. Garrett was a complex person. On the one hand he was vulnerable and eager to enhance his reputation; yet typically he at the same time was boastful and irreverent in his manner of speaking. He bragged, for example, that he could "ruin any man alive." The "Old Timer" reported that in his first inaugural address he declared, "Boys, if there is any stealing to be done this year, I propose to do it." (*The Chicago Democrat* newspaper altered his statement to read, "I shall have discharged my duty . . . by performing conscientiously and rigidly all the duties of a faithful public servant.")[15]

Chicago was filled with young men, talented but poor, who arrived from the East to make their fortune. Commerce provided quick fortunes and corresponding risks of losing everything through speculation. Often those who became wealthy were the ones who left commerce while relatively young and went into commercial real estate.[16] As a wholesaler to Chicago merchants, Augustus felt that he was ruining his health and not enjoying life, so in 1845 he ventured into real estate on a larger scale. He complained, "I am in a stew all the time. What is the use of living unless you can enjoy life a little."[17] Augustus purchased commercial real estate not only in Chicago but also in the Wisconsin territory and Ann Arbor, Michigan.

Perhaps in an attempt to atone for his acknowledged lapses in the moral life, Augustus considered with Eliza how he might contribute to the church by founding a Christian institution. Since Augustus' business consumed most of his time and interests, they also discussed the possibility that his energy and intellect might be challenged by establishing such an institution. Shortly after her husband's death in 1848, Eliza wrote in a letter to "Brother and Sister" Hamline: "I had prayed and hoped that he would live to do some little good in the world before he should have been called to give up his account. . . . I am sorry to say that he has left nothing satisfactory in regard to the future." (See document 2.)

Although Augustus expressed his desire to establish a Christian institution, he was reluctant to donate money to an existing Methodist school. He had been asked by Clark Street Church, particularly Grant Goodrich, his lawyer, to give a subscription to Rock River Seminary. Garrett apparently thought he was investing in a profit-making enterprise and suggested that some business associates do likewise. He was livid with anger when he discovered that his "investment" had been received as a donation. He claimed that Goodrich had deceived him and demanded his money back. He described himself as "persecuted" and "falsely and scandalously" used.[18] In light of this incident there is a certain irony in Eliza's use of Garrett's estate, with the counsel and guidance of Goodrich, to establish another Christian school.

From incidents such as these, we discern some idea of the strength of Eliza and her ability to withstand submission to a willful husband. Augustus Garrett's business correspondence from 1843 to 1845 yields further insights into Eliza's personality and spirit. (See document 1.) She often sent messages to the wives of Augustus' associates through his letters. In the letters we find some indication that their marriage brought a measure of happiness to her as well as a number of challenges. Garrett in one letter relates to John Seaman, his partner, their simple joy in watching hyacinths they had been given as gifts for New Year's Day grow on their mantel. In the same year he gave Eliza two canaries whom she named Robe and Kate after her good friends. He teased her that she had nothing else to do but play with them.[19] Inasmuch as he appears to talk satirically, one is never sure whether or not he is serious. Whatever the case, Augustus usually spoke of his wife in respectful terms. (See document 1.)

We have another glimpse of their life together from their social life. When Eliza learned that Augustus and the governor of the state would be riding together in a carriage, she proposed that they hold a reception for the governor. It is clear that Augustus bristled at the idea. He writes, "I tell her that I have nothing to do with her affairs, that she must attend to hers, and that I will attend to mine."[20]

It would be assumed that one of the wealthiest—if not the wealthiest—of couples in Chicago would have owned their own home. This would especially seem true for a man who served two terms as mayor and was involved in the real estate business. However, the 1844 city directory lists the Garretts' residence as the Sauganash Hotel, which they owned.[21] By 1855 Garrett Biblical Institute had become the owner of the land upon which the hotel had stood, and in 1860 the Wigwam building was built on this site. It was in this building that Lincoln was nominated for the presidency of the United States. In one of his 1844 letters, Augustus discussed the acquisition of mahogany doors and household items for the house he said Eliza wanted. He wrote to their families requesting that Eliza's bedding, linens, and silver be sent out. He also asked his old partner, John Seaman, to find him some clean secondhand furniture because Eliza was urging him to buy a house for them. Yet within a year he was complaining that it was very constraining to own a house and that he just might sell it.

When Augustus wrote his will, he stated that he was leaving *his* house, as well as *his* bedding, linens, and silver to Eliza. In his will he also left her a house on Franklin Street.

Augustus' obituary reports that he died in the Sherman Hotel. We do not know whether he was living in the hotel at the time of his death or whether he moved there in order to ease the burden on his wife when he became seriously ill.

Although Augustus appeared to be gruff, his letters reveal anxiety on his part about his health and a fundamental fear of being ill and dying alone. He mentioned in detail friends who were ill and did not send for him. Augustus said he hoped to be "where God has reserved for just men." In 1848 he had been ill for only six days when his life was ended by congestion in the brain. During a part of that time Garrett's mind wandered, but he also had moments of clarity. While still lucid he designated what Eliza was to do with his belongings and requested an Episcopal funeral to be conducted in Clark Street Church. Even when facing death, Augustus did not make a decision to establish a Christian institution, even though he often had planned to do so. (See document 2.)

The nineteenth-century Methodist historian Abel Stevens wrote of Augustus Garrett that "he knew his duty, but he did it not."[22] He who had so strongly needed someone to console him in death left no consolation behind him. However, Eliza felt, as she put it, "the necessity of a deeper worke of Grace in my heart. I try to pray for it as well as I know how." (See document 2.)

Augustus left Eliza half his fortune. Though he owned more commercial property than anyone else in Chicago, he did not have many liquid assets. Chicago was plagued with fires at this time, and the Garrett property was not immune to this peril. As he wrote in one of his letters, "This being rich without money is not all it is cracked up to be." Life often seemed overwhelming. His will contained an elaborate system of paying off his debts before property could be sold. Eliza was left an allowance of $1,000 a year until all the debts were resolved. However she soon placed herself on a $400 a year budget to free her estate more quickly for the benevolent uses she was anticipating. She gave half of this $400 for benevolent causes.

After Augustus' death, Eliza moved into the home of the W. S. Gurnees, political friends of Augustus. Some contemporaries described the Gurnee home as the most handsome house in Chicago. In response to a letter in which Eliza had voiced the need for experiencing the Holy Spirit in her life, Melinda Hamline suggested that she move in with some Methodist friends. Eliza, however, defended the Gurnees who, she said, had gone out of their way to make her comfortable. If she would receive any religious benefits from living with Methodists, she insisted, she would not hesitate to do so, but the Gurnees were "tried and true friends." (See document 3.) Perhaps this living arrangement was the means enabling her to live on the minuscule annual budget of $200.

Eliza also found a home in the Clark Street Methodist Episcopal Church. It was a liberal and socially active church for its time, and it was in this milieu that Eliza formed opinions and built friendships.

From two episodes recorded during this period, we learn that Clark Street Church had among its congregation at least two freed or escaped slaves. Many members were sympathetic to abolition and later became friends and supporters of Abraham Lincoln. One of the members of the church was a black man, Edwin Heathcock. One day in 1843, while Heathcock was working in his fields, he got into a quarrel with another worker. The man reported him to the authorities as a runaway slave. Edwin Heathcock was placed in prison, and notice was given that he was to be auctioned and sold as a slave. When that day arrived, the sheriff brought him forward to a quiet, hostile crowd. No one offered a bid, so the sheriff, very uneasy in his unpopular role, finally announced that if no one would buy the man he had no choice but to return him to prison. Thereupon, Mr.

Mahlon Ogden bid twenty-five cents and claimed him with the words, "Edwin, I have bought you. You are my man, my slave. Now go where you please."[23]

One of Eliza's friends in the Clark Street church and her personal attorney was Grant Goodrich. Goodrich was an abolitionist, a friend of Lincoln, and a visionary leader in establishing Northwestern University and Rush Hospital. Scrupulously honest, he lost $60,000 (virtually all his wealth) in the financial collapse in 1837. He spent his next twenty years paying back his debts with interest. Goodrich again lost everything in the Chicago fire of 1871. After five years of intense effort in his profession, he was forced to retire because of nervous exhaustion.[24]

Since she was in frequent contact with the progressive thought of the people at Clark Street and with the concerned group of Methodists who were later involved in the establishment of the biblical institute, Eliza would certainly have been conversant with the needs of the church to serve the westward expansion of the country. Her particular concerns were the need for an educated clergy and for educational opportunities for women.

Eliza recognized the benevolent uses that could be made of her wealth, and she set about exploring exactly what provisions she could make for these funds that would advance the Christian cause. She was a determined, strong person who moved decisively toward her goals. She wanted her money employed in ways that would bring the greatest good to society, and she decided that higher education was essential for progress in the rapidly expanding frontier. Remembering Peter Borein, she focused on the value of a theological institute for training pastors. But she also remembered her concern for the higher education of women. While the need for women's college was beginning to receive attention in other parts of the country, there were no such institutions in the Chicago area. When she discussed the possible uses of her money with Grant Goodrich, he encouraged the founding of a theological institute in the Chicago area. She replied that that was in her thoughts as well. She received the same affirmation when she consulted her pastor, John Clark, and her former pastor, Harry Crews. In 1853, she wrote a will leaving the bulk of her fortune to a biblical institute, but she added the request that any money left over from the biblical institute be used to start a female college. She planned for her estate not only to underwrite the building and staff for the school but also to provide free tuition and rooms for the students.

The Chicago coterie of Methodists with whom Eliza was associated had already begun the development of Northwestern University in 1850. Attracted to land north of Chicago because of the distance from the temptations and unhealthful conditions of the city, they were looking for an inland site. John Foster, however, noticed a grove of ash trees on the banks of Lake Michigan, and he considered this a favorable site for build-ing Northwestern University and the new biblical institute. Throwing his hat in the air he shouted, "We found it. This is the place!" They bought sixty-six acres of farmland for $25,000, land upon which both the univer-sity and the seminary are now located. Soon Northwestern had the begin-nings of a faculty, a fund-raising president (Hinman), and a drainage committee.[25]

In 1853 John Dempster came through Chicago on the way to Blooming-ton, Illinois, where he planned to establish a Methodist biblical institute for the developing West. He had already founded the Biblical Institute of New England in Vermont, which later evolved into the Boston University School of Theology, the initial school of what is now Boston University. Upon arriving in Chicago he discovered that the Chicago Methodists had already conceived the idea of a biblical institute and that Eliza Garrett had established the financial foundation for such an institution in her will.[26]

At a meeting on December 26, 1853, "The Friends of Biblical Learn-ing," a group including Grant Goodrich, Philo Judson, Orrington Lunt, John Clark, and John Evans, organized to explore the establishment of such an institute. Although Eliza Garrett was the primary financial backer of the proposed seminary, she was apparently not present at this meeting. Without her financial support, her imagination, and vision, this meeting could not have taken place. Frederick Norwood states, "She was the deci-sive factor in the birth of Garrett."[27] Among all these founders we find a strong sense that their venture was blessed by providence. They decided to build the biblical institute on the land purchased for Northwestern but to keep the schools distinctly separate.

Even though Eliza's money was not immediately available, these men, "The Friends of Biblical Learning," thought it prudent to begin organiz-ing the seminary immediately. It would be five years before Eliza's prop-erty would yield any earnings, so they borrowed $4,000 to initiate this new educational enterprise. "The Friends of Biblical Learning" reasoned that since Eliza was still young and healthy, it would be a long time before her money from her would be available. Augustus had put a clause in his will mandating that Eliza's money be returned to the estate if she remarried. They were also moved to act promptly lest the group in Bloomington, Illi-nois, attempt again to locate a biblical institute in the Bloomington area. Dempster himself had set a two-year deadline for establishing the Chicago biblical institute. Many in the church were suspicious of the effect of learning on its pastors and might yet be moved, so "the Friends of Biblical Learning" thought, to sabotage efforts to establish the school. Dempster, drawing from his experience in New England, felt that this opposition would diminish as soon as the biblical institute became a fact.[28]

With these reasons in mind they set out in 1854 to find a small faculty, to build a temporary wooden structure, and to gain official approval from the state and church. Dempster arranged minimum salaries for the faculty, who would live, along with the Dempster family and the three beginning students, in the building later called Dempster Hall.

It is not known why Eliza's name was never mentioned in relation to the founding of the biblical institute. In the articles in the *Northwestern Christian Advocate* until about the time of her death her name is not mentioned. The school was alternately called Methodist Episcopal Biblical Institute or Northwestern Biblical Institution. The General Conference had been disturbed by the lack of communication concerning the biblical institute. However, it was necessary to move quickly and quietly because of the competing site at Illinois Wesleyan (Bloomington, Illinois) and because Dempster himself was urging prompt action. Finally Eliza was persuaded to let her name be used when the supporters of the school appeared before the 1854 General Conference of The Methodist Episcopal Church to gain authorization. The fact that she was supporting this undertaking in such a generous fashion not only quelled the opposition but won approval for the biblical institute by the Conference.

The report to the Conference began: "Your Committee regards this enterprise as the offspring of a special Providence. The fact that a wealthy individual in Chicago, should make known the purpose of providing an ample endowment for an Institution to improve our Junior Ministry, at so opportune a moment, cannot fail to arrest our attention, as a Providential interference." The report suggests that without the Garrett money the school would not so easily have been accepted. "Thus are the Directors not only exculpated from all censure, but entitled to the warmest praise."[29]

The school opened at the start of 1855 with four students, three faculty, and the benefit of the Northwestern Drainage Committee. New Year's Day, 1855, was a glorious day. The group from Chicago drove in sleighs out to Evanston for the opening of the Biblical Institute. Frances Willard says that this was the only occasion upon which Eliza visited Evanston.[30] President John Dempster gave an inaugural address, and Dr. John Evans spoke on the benefits of an educated ministry. None of the ministers responsible for the instituting of the school had had the benefit of attending such a seminary. The resolutions passed included one that referred, though not by name, to Eliza Garrett, lauding "with abiding gratitude, the unobtrusive benevolence of the kind lady who has chosen a method of permanently blessing her race which has called this Institute into being."[31]

Although she was not named in newspaper accounts of the event, it was reported that Eliza Garrett participated in the service. *The Chicago Democrat* reported, "The company from the city arrived home, early in the evening, highly delighted with the Biblical Institute . . . and feeling that they had

had a 'happy New Year.'"[32] Evanston was a unique home for the biblical institute. It might even be called a Methodist town. Originally called Ridgeville (presumably for the three ridges that were dry enough for use in farming), the town was given a new name in honor of John Evans, a physician, educator, religious leader, later governor of the Colorado territory, and one of the "Friends of Biblical Learning." Before the entry of the university and the biblical institute, the town was a farming community. Today several national United Methodist agencies have located their headquarters in Evanston. Evanston was the home of Frances Willard, and the city still serves as the headquarters of the Woman's Christian Temperance Union. Many street names reflect the United Methodist influence on the history of the city. They include Wesley, Asbury, Dempster, Simpson, Hartzell, and others.

Before 1855 people of all religious denominations had worshiped together in the one-room log schoolhouse. After 1855 and the founding of the seminary, the cotton work bonnets of the farm women mingled with the fashionable hats of those women connected with the school. At the same time the first temporary structure was being built for the biblical institute, many faculty and trustees were building homes for themselves in Evanston and thus building a strong supportive community for the students.

Eliza died before she could become part of this Methodist venture. On the evening of November 18, 1855, Eliza attended Sunday evening services as usual. The following account was written to Professor Daniel Kidder by Goodrich shortly afterward.

> The next day at noon, she was taken with the bilious colic, which resulted in congestion of the bowels, and she died on Thursday about 3 o'clock, as the good always die. . . . She was calm and serene at the approach of death as if meeting a friend. The young man who had been with her since her husband's death was with her . . . the morning she died. . . . She turned her eyes toward him and said do you think I am past hope of recovery. He said she was very sick and they feared so, and wept bitterly. . . . She said you ought not to weep for you know I am prepared to die. I [Goodrich] came shortly after, although she could hardly speak, I suggested an alteration in her will which I knew she wished. She directed I make a sign on it. She lifted up her hands and exclaimed "Bless the Lord, Oh my soul," and gave into the Spirit without a struggle.[33]

The following was on the first page of the *Weekly Chicago Democrat:*

DEATH OF AN ESTIMABLE LADY

Mrs. Garrett had so endeared herself to all who came within the sphere in which she moved by her excellent qualities of head and heart, by her amiable smile, and lady like deportment; by her gentleness of disposition, and her wide-spread charities, and, above all by a meek and Christian spirit which seemed to pervade not only her disposition and character but every act of her life. Her loss will be most severely felt as well as deeply deplored. . . . The disease made such rapid progress, as to baffle the skill of the first physicians in the city. Mrs. Garrett made her home since the death of her husband, at the residence of Hon. W. S. Gurnee of the city, and from whence her remains will be taken to the Clark Street Methodist Church at 10 o'clock tomorrow (Sunday) where funeral services will take place. Mrs. Garrett leaves a portion of her large property to the Garrett Biblical Institute and which had been named in compliment to her. [See document 7.][34]

Eliza had left the theological institute in a secure financial position through the provisions of her will. The Garrett property had suffered loss because of fire, but its value in recent years had increased to the point that there was confusion in reports as to its monetary value at her death. It appeared that eventually her bequest, along with support from the church, would be adequate to pay for the biblical institute.

The unresolved issue was whether or not there would be money available for a female college. Dr. Kidder, Professor of Practical Theology in the first permanent faculty in 1856, had discussed this issue in several letters to Goodrich, as early as October 22, 1853, before Eliza's death. He suggested that the finances for the Biblical Institute were too insecure to take on another school. Moreover, since Garrett Biblical Institute would be the only school of its kind west of the Allegheny Mountains, it would influence the whole theological character of the West. He concluded: "For while the demands are so great for the Biblical Inst. they can hardly be considered urgent for the establishment of a Fem. College."[35]

Obviously others agreed with him, because there was no strong support from the trustees to found the women's college. It is unclear in this file of letters, primarily between Kidder and Goodrich, how much Eliza was aware of the tentative nature of the commitment of her executors to the women's college. That year Northwestern did establish a women's college, but it was not founded with the assistance of the Garrett estate. On the day in 1855 when they laid the cornerstone for the first Northwestern building, a similar one was laid not far away for the Female College. It appears there was real interest in the Female College, for during its first year it enrolled 84 students, while Northwestern enrolled only 10. On the other hand, Kidder was correct in his prophecy that there was available from other quarters financial support for the Female College.

In founding the Garrett Biblical Institute, Eliza used her resources to be a change agent in society. Her means of benevolence, that of providing financial aid to this significant extent while she was still living, provided a model for future gifts in such institutions. (See documents 5 and 6.) Her dedicated mode of giving provided an example of a woman helping to shape the future. Indeed, although she hoped that the school would bring Christianity to the West, she did not know that it would influence the frontier of other areas as well. Before long the school was not only having an impact on home missions, there being no Methodist Episcopal Church in the vicinity of the school at its inception; it also had a global outreach through its preparation of missionaries for overseas service.

Eliza Garrett established a new model for women's ability to shape and initiate institutions. Indeed Garrett Biblical Institute and its successors reflect the strong hand of women throughout its history. Women's societies furnished the rooms in the enlarged Dempster Hall. President Dempster sent out requests asking that sewing circles donate the bedding and furniture at a cost of about $50 a room. When the school built a larger, more permanent dormitory, Heck Hall, its cost of $60,000 was raised by the American Methodist Ladies' Centenary Association. This dormitory was named in honor of Barbara Heck, often designated "the mother of both American and Canadian Methodism." It appears that Eliza's act motivated other women to support theological institutions as a means of participating in the mission of the church. The tradition continued and expanded as women began attending as students in 1874.

The Chicago Training School for City, Home, and Foreign Missions, which later became part of the Garrett Biblical Institute, was founded and run by a woman, Lucy Rider Meyer. Nellie Huger Ebersole, an admiring student at C.T.S., said of her, "When Lucy Rider Meyer prayed it was like you took the hand of God and talked to him yourself." Nellie Ebersole regarded it as a cherished honor to have sung at Lucy Rider Meyer's funeral.

The tradition of women's participation in benevolent giving has continued to the present day. Nellie Huger Ebersole might be called a present-day Eliza Garrett. While in C.T.S. Nellie Ebersole worked with delinquent girls at the stockyards, but most of her life was spent serving the church through music. She studied Sacred Music from Union Theological Seminary. On returning to her home in Michigan, she founded the Waldenwood Summer School of Sacred Music, which she directed for twenty-two years. For years she directed choirs, performed on radio and television, and served as a diligent evangelist in the church.

Nellie Huger earned a Ph.D. degree from the Detroit Institute of Musical Art and taught there until she married Dr. Amos Ebersole, a professor of church music at Heidelberg University in Ohio. Dr. Amos Ebersole and Dr. Nellie Ebersole established the Art Center Music School in 1952 where Nellie remained director until 1988, at the age of ninety. Seventy-five percent of the students were from minority groups. Still concerned with developing sacred music for the church, Dr. Ebersole sought to accumulate as much money as possible in order to found an educational center for sacred music. When it became apparent that her health would not permit her to establish the school herself, she made arrangements in her estate to support a sacred music program at her alma mater, Garrett-Evangelical Theological Seminary. The Nellie Huger Ebersole Endowment in Church Music at Garrett-Evangelical Theological Seminary now supports a program in sacred music conducted jointly with Northwestern University and Seabury-Western Theological Seminary.

Reminiscent of Eliza, Nellie Ebersole denied herself in order to save money for her benevolence. Dr. Ebersole bought her clothes at rummage sales and her furniture at secondhand shops. While she was still able she bought her vegetables at closing time from the open-air markets, when produce was sold for less. At her death on April 30, 1991, Dr. Ebersole contributed $250,000 to Garrett-Evangelical Theological Seminary, to endow the program in sacred music. By her beneficence churches will experience the love and inspiration of God through music.[36]

Eliza Garrett grew up on a stable and secure farm in New York. As a young woman, she experienced the dangers of the frontier. She used the circumstances of her life to change not only those around her but also those in different times and distant places. She did not live to herself, nor did she die to herself. She saw the beginning results of her vision and philanthropy while she was still alive.

Eliza Garrett established a tradition for women (and men) in later years to emulate. The institution that names her as founder, Garrett-Evangelical Theological Seminary, has benefited from a long line of women who by their generosity and vision have brought opportunities for growth to those who will serve the church.

DOCUMENTS

1. Eliza's Social Life. Many of the events of Eliza's life are known only through the letters of other people. The business letters of her husband between the years 1843 and 1845 contain several references to some of the events in her life, and they disclose hints about the personalities of Augustus and Eliza.

In these letters we find some clues to their home life and their relationship to each other. Eliza was an active worker in charities, but she served as one of a group and deflected attention from herself. The following excerpt is taken from a letter written by Augustus in April, 1844, to Jerry, apparently Eliza's brother. This incident, reported derisively by Augustus, was something less than an overwhelming success for Eliza.

Eliza was elected Treasurer of the Ladies benevolent association but there were so many different religions mixed up in it that she was afeared there would be a burst in it. [She] resigned and it turned out just as she expected for they have commenced grumbling already the Methodist complain of the Presbyterians and the Presbyterians of the Baptists and they of the Episcopalians and they of the Catholics and so it goes.

2. *The Death of Augustus Garrett.* These letters to Mrs. Hamline are the only personal writing by Eliza we have. Through them we find revealed how she felt about life and religion.

Chicago Jan 29th 1849

Brother and Sister Hamline

Dear friends,

Your very kinde . . . letter came . . . for which I return you my thanks, affliction has indeed come upon me un-expectedly. Death has taken from me my husband and protector and almost I may say my only Earthly relative, I had prayed and hoped that he would live to do some little good in the World before he should have been called to give up his account but God's ways are not our ways. I feel to say thy will O Lord be done.

Mr. G. was sick only six days with part of that time he was not considered dangerously ill, he conversed with me on the subject of his death and directed what disposition to make of his wardrobe . . . requested the Church of England service at his Funeral which was performed by an Episcopal clergyman in Clark St. M. Church, the last three days of his life his minde was wandering moste of the time. [He] spoke of the vanity of this world and how little we know what a day would bring for the pain. He was not afraid to die although he knew that he had not lived as he wished he had done, (I am sorry to say that he had left nothing satisfactory in regard to the future). I feel that I am indeed afflicted but I know that it is my benevolent Father that has done it and as he has since, that he afflicted not willingly the children of men but for their good. I am constrained to believe that it is for my good that these afflicted me. I wish to be benefitted by this dispensation, although I feel alone in the World so far as my earthly friends are concerned still I feel that I have a kinde Father in Heaven who has said that not a sparrow falls without his notice . . .

My dear Friends I have often thought of your kinde admonition, and feel that they have been a greate help to me in striving to live a Christian. . . . Pray for me.

Respectfully and affectionately your friende
Eliza Garrett

3. *The Search for Assurance.* Despite her active, loyal participation in church, Eliza was searching for further assurance of God's grace. Note the refer-

ence to the Hamline property in Chicago, which Eliza was apparently managing.

Chicago March 21st 1850

My Dear Sister Hamline,

Yours of Dec 10th came duly at hand I have delayed this long in answering your welcome letter. . . . We have been holding a series of meetings in Clark St. Church during the winter. They commence on the first of Jan. have been kept up every evening until this weeke, over one hundred have involved their names on the records of Clark St. Church. Some that experience religion among the Methodist have connected themselves with other branches of Christ's Church. The Church [is] seeking for a deeper Baptism of the Holy Spirit, [some] few people to have experienced this much to be desired blessing. I am sorry to say that I am not of the happy number although I have not experienced this greatest of all blessing still I have some of the comforts and sweets of Religion and am fully determined to push my way on to know more of that love which passeth . . . knowledge. Pray for me . . .

When you are happy in the enjoyments of religion remember your friend

P.S. all dues on your Property are paid.

Eliza

4. *Importance of Christian Relationships.* From this letter it is evident that Mrs. Hamline served as a spiritual confidante to Eliza.

Chicago Feb 21st 1852

My dear Sister Hamline

Your kind and affectionate letter of Jan 20th is received. It gives me great pleasure to hear from you, and receive your advise and encouragement to help me on my Christian journey, I feel that I need Christian sympathy and advise, for me to know that I am not forgotten by my Dear Christian friends is a great consolation. In relation to myself I still feel to trust in my Saviour. I know that he is able to keep and sustain me under all circumstances. I bless his Holy Name for the comfort that religion affords me. I feel like pressing my way on toward the land of rest . . .

Affectionately yours,

E. Garrett

5. *Vision for Education.* Eliza did not appear to want her name used in planning the Garrett Biblical Institute. She seemed very modest about her

benevolence. However she was aware of the importance of working strategically in a church that was suspicious of theological education. When it became evident that there would be opposition to the school because of its costs, she let it be known that she was supporting it financially. This quelled the opposition.

Abel Stevens wrote:

> She [Eliza] believed that future of the Church and the country demanded the thorough intellectual training of the young under the auspices of Christianity.
>
> It was precisely at this point that the superior sense and character of this excellent woman were displayed. Methodism had always favored education; it was at this moment in advance of most, if not all other, religious denominations of the country in the number, if not the effectiveness, of its colleges and academies; but it was yet generally prejudiced against institutions expressly for ministerial education. . . .
>
> Eliza Garrett's thoughtful intelligence and piety placed her, in this respect, in advance of her people. She saw that Methodism sustained an immeasurable responsibility for the moral and social training of the whole republic, as it was the predominant popular faith; she perceived also that its advancement thus far in educational provision had prepared the way for this further advancement, and that God had placed in her hands the financial means of initiating it in the general Church as it had been attempted in a locality. And such was the result; for when her proposition came before the General Conference, that body saw that it could not disregard so remarkable a providential opportunity, so munificent an offering. It may well be doubted whether the session which accepted and approved her overture, and thereby settled the policy of the denomination on the question, would not have rejected any less providential appeal to its opinions; and to Eliza Garrett, therefore, belongs the credit of turning the whole Church into this new career of ministerial improvement.
>
> Her sober wisdom was also shown in the fact that, in laying such ample and stable foundations for this great interest, she placed her plans under the guardianship of the General Conference.[37]

6. Eliza's New Vision of Philanthropy. Eliza Garrett pointed the way to a new form of philanthropy for the wealthy families in the nation. With her advisors she planned for the Biblical Institute to set up temporary classrooms and living quarters while she was alive, even though the bulk of the money was to be available only through the will.

Charles Wesley Buoy wrote in *Representative Women of Methodism:*

> In 1848 she was bereft of her husband, the Mayor of Chicago, and one of its most successful merchants, and in 1853, after remembering those in her will whom nature had made dependent upon her, she resolved to make the

Church of her choice the recipient of the estate, and prepared to hand over to its care what, at that time, was the largest gift ever bestowed in our nation for higher education. This woman turned the thought of the wealthy of the nation into the highest channel, creating a new ambition, unknown and unrecognized before—not the creation of a family name by perpetuating wealth, but diffusing her benefaction for the good of society. She linked her name to posterity, and, in honoring her Church, lives today in its highest ministry. She leads in that form of benevolence which conserves most strongly the interests of a nation.[38]

7. The Death of Eliza Garrett. Eliza died after an unexpected short illness. Even as she knew the end was near she went over her will with her lawyer, Grant Goodrich, to assure herself that her gift for Garrett Biblical Institute was properly cared for in her will.

She faced death with the same courage and clarity with which she had faced life. *The Northwestern Christian Advocate* gave the following account of Eliza Garrett's funeral:

"Mrs. Garrett has so endeared herself to all who came within the sphere in which she moved, by her amiable, mild and lady-like deportment; by her gentleness of disposition, and by her widespread charities, and, above all, by a meek and Christian spirit."

"Mrs. Garrett leaves a portion of her large property to Garrett Biblical Institute and which has been named in compliment to her."

The above is a just tribute to very high Christian worth, from the *Daily Democrat* of this city. The funeral of Sister Garrett occurred on Sabbath last, from Clark Street Church as announced. The crowd was immense, and the whole church, of which the deceased was so highly esteemed and beloved a member, bent weeping before the stroke of bereavement that had fallen so suddenly upon it. Among the persons, we noticed the agent, and some members of the Northwestern University, and the entire faculty of the Biblical Institute, the venerable president, Dr. Dempster, sharing in the services. The funeral sermon was preached by the pastor of the deceased, Rev. H. Crews, and was admirably calculated to make a deep and salutary impression. The procession to the cemetery, was one of the longest that ever moved from our city, to make another lamented deposit in its solemn vaults. As the long line of carriages, preceded by the sabled hearse, moved slowly forward on its sad mission, we felt that a century would elapse, ere Providence repeated again to the church in Chicago, the blessing which he had so suddenly removed from it, in the person of this amiable, godly, and public-spirited woman. But her works and her name will survive her forever, in that "school of the prophets," the monument of her benevolence. Her last words were "Bless the Lord, O my soul, and forget not all his benefits."

She said this and in a moment was with her Savior. The property left the Biblical Institute consists of $100,000 in real estate in the city; the proceeds of which are to be appropriated forever to that institution. . . . We are most happy to state, that at the death of its benevolent founder, the school is in a condition of great prosperity. A class of thirty young men are in attendance.[39]

Amanda Berry Smith

CHAPTER 3

AMANDA BERRY SMITH

A *"Downright, Outright Christian"*

NANCY A. HARDESTY AND
ADRIENNE ISRAEL

An ex-slave and washerwoman who traveled on four continents preaching holiness and sanctification, Amanda Berry Smith may well have been "one of the most powerful evangelists and effective missionaries of the nineteenth century."[1] A contemporary described her as "a monument of God's wondrous grace, a polished shaft in his quiver, his image 'carved in ebony.'"[2] In the introduction to her inspirational *Autobiography*, Methodist Episcopal Bishop J. M. Thoburn, who knew her from their work together in India and the United States, said she "possessed a clearness of vision" and a "rare degree of spiritual power" that he had seldom found equaled.[3]

During her forty-five-year ministry, Smith rose to prominence as a campmeeting preacher and teacher, revival leader, vocalist, and temperance worker. In her later years she organized an ill-fated orphan home and school for black children. Known for her powerful contralto voice and ability to render poignant slave spirituals, she was also a master of Methodist hymns and a renowned prayer leader, who inherited the slave tradition of long, fervent prayer from her mother and grandmother. A tall woman who appeared to be nearly six feet in height, Smith was a "commanding presence,"[4] whose life influenced thousands as an advocate of sanctification and holiness during the Methodist-led era of campmeeting revivals and evangelical reform in the late nineteenth century. Smith told her own story in *An Autobiography: The Story of the Lord's Dealings with Mrs. Amanda Smith, The Colored Evangelist, Containing an Account of Her Life Work of Faith, and Her Travels in America, England, Ireland, Scotland, India, and Africa, as an Independent Missionary* (1893).

In 1837, Smith was born Amanda Berry on a farm in northern Maryland.[5] Her father bought his family's freedom and moved them to Pennsylvania where they settled in York County, an abolitionist stronghold heavily influenced by Quakers. Denied a formal education, she learned to read and write from her parents, and as a teen worked as a domestic in the homes of wealthy whites.

Her vocational vision was initially shaped in a series of religious experiences. Her first experience took place at age thirteen during a revival in a Methodist Episcopal Church in Pennsylvania (p. 27). Although her devotion was sincere, the demands of her employers that she have dinner on the table at a certain time and the prejudices of her class leader who talked with all the whites before he would talk with her forced her to choose financial security over spiritual growth. From the beginning she had to struggle between nurturing her own spiritual life and conforming to the limits of a racially stratified society.

In September 1854, at age 17, she married Calvin Devine. She notes in her *Autobiography* that "he believed in religion for his mother's sake. . . . but when strong drink would get the better of him, which . . . was quite often, then he was very profane and unreasonable" (p. 42). With the outbreak of the Civil War, her husband enlisted in the Union army and never returned.

For Smith, religion was ever part of the cosmic struggle between God and the Devil, both of whom often spoke directly and audibly to her. Although from early childhood she wanted to be a Christian, pride held her back. In 1856 a revival at the Baptist church in Columbia, Pennsylvania, touched off a struggle in her soul: "The Devil told me I was such a sinner God would not convert me. When I would kneel down to pray at night, he would say, 'You had better give it up; God won't hear you, you are such a sinner.'" She decided that she needed to find "somebody that had always been obedient" to intercede with Jesus on her behalf. And she began to pray, "O, Sun, you never sinned like me, you have always obeyed God, and kept your place in the heavens; tell Jesus I am a poor sinner." In between her domestic duties, she would slip into the yard, look up to the moon and stars, and pray: "O, Moon and Stars, you never sinned like me, you have always obeyed God, and kept your place in the heavens; tell Jesus I am a poor sinner." Finally on Tuesday, March 17, 1856, even though the Devil was saying, "He won't hear you," she went down into the cellar, got down on her knees, and prayed, "O Lord, have mercy on my soul, I don't know how else to pray." After an intense spiritual struggle, she prayed, "O, Lord, if Thou wilt help me I will believe Thee," and "in the act of telling God I would, I did." Peace and joy flooded her soul, the burden rolled away, and a flood of light and joy swept through her soul (pp. 43-47). She was soundly converted.

In the 1860s Amanda and her daughter, Mazie Devine, moved to Philadelphia, where she met James Smith, a local preacher and ordained deacon in The African Methodist Episcopal Church. She told him that since her conversion she had felt it her duty to be an evangelist, and he told her that he was preparing to go into itinerant work. Like many a woman before and since, she "had seen and known the influence of a minister's wife, and how much she could help her husband or hinder him to a great extent in his work. Mr. Smith said that was just the kind of a wife he wanted" (p. 58), and so she agreed to be married. "After I had given my consent I went to the Lord to have it ratified, but not a ray of light came," she admitted (p. 58). When conference time came, she went to hear the appointments read at Bethel African Methodist Episcopal Church in Philadelphia. James Smith's name was not on the list. He had only feigned interest in order to win her hand (pp. 57-59).

In 1865 the couple moved to New York City but lived apart most of the time. James found employment that required him to live in Brooklyn, while Amanda lived in a tiny Greenwich Village apartment with Mazie, took in laundry, and did domestic day work.

Central to her vocational vision was her own experience of sanctification or holiness. One day in September 1868, she felt compelled to go and hear Holiness preacher John Inskip at the Green Street Methodist Episcopal Church in New York City, even though she was a member of nearby Sullivan Street Bethel A.M.E. Church. She went seeking the experience of perfection or holiness, and she found it (pp. 73-79).[6] She wanted to shout, but being "the only colored person there," and having "a very keen sense of propriety," she heard the Devil say, "Look, look at the white people, mind, they will put you out" and "No one knows you here, and they will think you are drunk" (pp. 77-78). Finally during a closing hymn, she shouted "glory to Jesus," and felt "a mighty peace and power" take possession of her (p. 79; see document 1).

Within the Protestant tradition, and particularly within black churches, vocation to ministry must be rooted in call. Amanda Smith's call and ministry developed over time. As she explains, "The Lord made this clear to me, that I was to have a prayer meeting at my room for those who wished to draw nearer to the Lord. I never expected to do anything more than this. But after He had sanctified my heart it was beginning at Jerusalem; so at Jerusalem I did begin" (p. 130). She began by holding a regular prayer meeting for a small group of women in the tiny apartment she shared with Mazie.

All four of her sons died in infancy and her husband was claimed by stomach cancer in 1869. These family tragedies freed Amanda to pursue the religious vocation that eventually took her to England for two years, India for about eighteen months, and Africa for another eight years.

Initially she began to receive invitations to work in churches roundabout—Brooklyn, Harlem, Jersey City—among her own people. Then in November 1869, the same month her husband died, she received a direct commission from God. In prayer she asked God to teach her what to do, and she felt a conviction to leave New York and go to Salem, New Jersey. God assured her, "Go, and I will go with you" (p. 132). She asked God to provide a pair of shoes and two months' rent to secure her apartment in her absence. God provided and she went. She was gone for seven months.

Then in November 1870, as she sat in the Fleet Street A.M.E. Church in Brooklyn, her eyes closed in prayer, she saw a large letter "G." Thinking God had a message for her, she asked, "Lord, do you want me to read in Genesis, or in Galatians?" Then she saw the letter "O." "Why, that means go," she thought, and she said "What else?" A voice distinctly said, "Go preach" (pp. 147-48; see document 2). Even though she had the offer of a very good situation as a live-in servant with a godly family, she turned it down. She speaks of this period as "when I left my home at God's command, and began my evangelist work" (p. 152).[7]

Amanda Smith deeply cherished the religious traditions inherited from the slaves who had preserved portions of their African spiritual heritage. North American slaves came from West Africa where women were priestesses, diviners, midwives, and herbalists. Consciously or subconsciously, the slaves transferred African religious practices into Christian worship. As a result, slave communities allowed and often expected women to exercise spiritual authority. Some slave women preached in secret church services held out of sight and earshot of slave owners and other whites.[8]

Most of these preaching women remain anonymous, but during the antebellum period, three free black Methodist women in the North left a public record that paved the way for succeeding women to preach.

Between 1809 and 1816, Jarena Lee tried to secure a license to preach from the African Methodist Episcopal Church in Philadelphia, which was subsequently Amanda Smith's church body. On both occasions, founding A.M.E. Bishop Richard Allen refused her ordination, but he finally permitted her to speak officially as an exhorter. Ordained or not, Lee preached to both black and white in the mid-Atlantic states and the Northeast, and ventured west to Ohio. In 1839 she temporarily teamed up with Zilpha Elaw, and the two of them preached together in western Pennsylvania.

Elaw, also a Methodist, had failed to secure any type of denominational sanction for her activities. Nevertheless she traveled extensively as an evangelist, going into the southern states in 1828 and to England in 1840.

A third black Methodist woman preacher of the early nineteenth century, Julia Foote, began to "proclaim the wonders of sanctification to others in the [A.M.E.] church" when she was only eighteen.[9] Despite opposition to women in the pulpit, she preached sanctification throughout New England, the mid-Atlantic states, and as far west as Cincinnati. All three of these forerunners of Amanda Smith wrote brief autobiographies.[10]

Cheryl Townsend Gilkes speaks of "the four pillars of the Afro-Christian religious tradition" as "preaching, praying, singing, and testifying."[11] Amanda Smith's vocational vision was shaped by and nurtured within these parameters.

The first of these, preaching, is most often associated with males and the authorization of ordination in both black and white churches. As Gilkes notes, "Preaching is the most masculine aspect of black religious ritual" and "preaching remains overwhelmingly a form of male discourse."[12]

That did not deter Smith or her sisters—black and white—within what is now called "the Sanctified church," those churches historically linked to the Holiness and Pentecostal movements.[13] They had role models and mentors in such women as Phoebe Palmer, Julia A. J. Foote, Martha Inskip, Zilpha Elaw, Hannah Whitehall Smith, Mary Boardman, and Jarena Lee, as well as two tactics to make their voices heard. The first tactic was "Bible reading." Women, and some Holiness men, would read through a Bible passage, commenting on the text and making applications along the way. (Somehow this was quite different from taking a text and preaching on it. Women were not allowed to preach, but this they could do.) Their other tactic was to begin with testimony—an appropriate religious expression for women since it was encouraged during the Second Great Awakening by Charles Grandison Finney, whose *Lectures on Revivals of Religion* defined the movement. Gilkes says that in the Afro-Christian tradition praying and singing by women often framed the preaching event, and testimonies were not only resources for preaching but sometimes correctives to it.[14]

Smith's ministry drew on all these tactics and resources. She speaks occasionally of attending the Tuesday Meeting for the Promotion of Holiness, in which the founder of the "Holiness Movement," Phoebe Palmer, was active until her death in 1874 (pp. 119, 193). Much of Smith's ministry was among white folk, often at Holiness campmeetings from New Jersey to Maine. She had apparently met Hannah Whitehall Smith, Mary Boardman, and Martha Inskip, all leaders in the Holiness Movement, at those meetings. Amanda renewed her acquaintance with Hannah Smith and Mary Boardman in England, where they eased her entry into Keswick circles (pp. 256ff.).[15] Keswick, named for a prominent British meeting site, came to denote a more Presbyterian form of Holiness teaching sometimes called the "Higher Life."

While attending campmeetings at Ocean Grove, New Jersey, in the early 1870s, she met local leaders of the Woman's Christian Temperance Union, the forerunner of more militant women's suffrage groups of the late nineteenth and early twentieth centuries. Among the early WCTU leaders she met were Annie Wittenmyer and Mary C. Johnson. Smith joined the WCTU in 1875, and Mary Johnson financed her first voyage to England.

At campmeetings Smith primarily found opportunities to speak in the testimony meetings following the preaching. In a typical description from her experience at the Keswick conference in England, she stated that "I felt the Lord laid it on me to give a bit of my own personal experience, how God converted and sanctified my heart, so I spoke and the power of the Spirit seemed to come mightily upon all the people" (p. 261). When she was asked to lead meetings on her own, she most often called it simply "talking," although she sometimes described it as "preaching" or a "Bible reading."[16] She seldom described what she said in these talks, preferring to dwell on the consequences evidenced by those at the altar afterward.

Smith launched her ministry in the New York area among A.M.E. churches. Since the A.M.E. Church did not license women to preach, the pastor of Sullivan Street, her home church, "found a way to preserve the order of the church, while he at the same time loosed Sister Smith and let her go. He gave her a letter of recommendation to any pastor who would be willing to accept her services. She speedily found more calls for service than she was able to fill, and had little use for the recommendation given her."[17]

Although she seldom described her ministry as preaching, usually calling it "talking" or "Bible reading," as her career unfolded she was more and more called on to conduct services and to lead revivals—in fact, to engage in preaching.

In 1876 Anna Oliver, a young pastor of a Methodist Episcopal church in Passaic, New Jersey, invited Smith to help build the membership of her floundering congregation. A local newspaper reported that "Passaic is having a lively time; what with stirring up sinners and Christians on one hand, and on the other two women in the pulpit, and one black, the buzzing grows apace!"[18]

She was given opportunity to preach in a formal setting in Liberia, where, she says, "Rev. Mr. Richards . . . pastor of the Methodist Church. . . . asked me if I would take the service on Sabbath morning. I chose the words for the basis of my remarks, 'Awake thou that sleepèst and arise from the dead, and Christ shall give thee light.' . . . The Lord helped me to deliver the message and blessed the people" (p. 339).[19]

In another spot she notes that the pastor "spoke fifteen minutes, but said nothing! At half past seven I take the service—a Bible reading" (p. 341). During her overseas travel, she was once asked to lead a shipboard service, somewhat as a novelty or entertainment. She began, "I will not preach, but I want to talk a little from this dear old chapter" (John 14), and so she "talked on for over half an hour with perfect liberty and freedom" (p. 252).

Although some were beginning to speak of women's ordination during this period, Smith did not seek it. When the A.M.E. Church decided to hold its General Conference in Nashville, she noted that she was known by only a few of the brethren, and then "as a woman preacher, which was to be dreaded by the majority, especially the upper ten" (p. 199; see document 3).[20] Though Smith did not seek ordination, she was always ready to defend the practice of women's preaching, because God called them to this witness (p. 321; see document 4).

Gilkes' second pillar of the African American Christian religious tradition is praying. Smith was an exemplary "prayer warrior" in private and public.[21] Her life was one of constant prayer, and she made no move without discussing it with God in prayer and receiving divine direction. Her account of how she came to write her *Autobiography* is typical. After a number of friends had suggested the project, she said:

> I began to think of it more seriously and prayed much over it, asking the Lord, if it was His will, to make it clear and settle me in it, and give me something from His Word that I may have as an anchor.
>
> Asking thus for light and guidance, I opened my Bible while in prayer, and my eye lighted on these words: "Now, therefore, perform the doing of it, and as there was a readiness to will, so there may be a performance also out of that which ye have," (2nd Cor. viii: 11.). [p. iii]

Prayer and Scripture were her spiritual foundations. Prayer was also her financial foundation. Smith never asked for money, nor was she ever supported by a church or denomination. Her work in India and Africa was financed by small gifts from British and American friends (p. 337). She lived by faith and on the basis of gifts given her by friends and the congregations to which she ministered. Many times she was virtually destitute, but she prayed and God provided for her needs.

Prayer also played a significant role in her public vocation. Her first public act, already noted, was to organize a small prayer meeting in her home and invite friends. She was always available to pray with friends and acquaintances experiencing difficulty. Prayer, coupled with preaching and testimony in services, and prayer during altar services, was an important component of Smith's ministry.

Singing was also a key element of her ministry. Concerning her early ministry, she noted, "In those days I used to sing a great deal, and somehow the Lord always seemed to bless my singing" (p. 194). For example, at the Sing Sing (New York) Campmeeting as she walked the grounds on a Sunday afternoon, someone asked her to sing. A deacon called upon her to stand up on a stump so that people could hear better. Soon a crowd of about four hundred persons had gathered around. After she sang several songs, the same brother said, "Sister Smith, suppose you tell the people your experience; how the Lord converted you." She notes that the "power of the Spirit rested" upon her, "and many of the people wept, and seemed deeply moved and interested" (pp. 174-75).

Another telling example is found in her account of the A.M.E. General Conference in Nashville. She came as a visitor, rather than a delegate. As a single woman plainly dressed in Quaker garb, she stood out from other women who came in their finery as wives of pastors and bishops. She felt very lonely until she was noticed by one of the Fisk University Jubilee

Singers. During a meeting, the director came down, took her by the hand, and escorted her to the platform. After he asked her to sing and led the Jubilee Singers in joining her in the chorus, people welcomed her (pp. 203-4; see document 3). Her *Autobiography* is interlaced with lines from her favorite hymns and songs.

During her ministry Smith earned the title "the Singing Pilgrim." She sang frequently at WCTU conventions. She continued to mount the platform and give stirring renditions of black spirituals into the final years of her life.[22]

Smith's vocational vision was grounded in her mature spirituality, a definite sense of call, and the Spirit's continued guidance, and these also combined to give her a strong sense of self that sustained her in the midst of hostility from both blacks and whites. She notes early in her *Autobiography* that she "had become a speckled bird" among her own people "on account of the profession of the blessing of holiness" (p. 108). Later she noted, "My people often called me 'White folks' nigger'" (p. 453). She said, "I had much to suffer, in and with my own people—for human nature is the same in black and white folks" (p. 146). Initially she was afraid of whites. Her deliverance from that fear was part of her experience of holiness. (See document 1.)

She saw the cure for racism in the sanctifying power of God, but she admitted that "some people don't get enough of the blessing to take prejudice out of them, even after they are sanctified" (p. 226). Occasionally, however, it worked. She told of how at one campmeeting "the Lord cured a good old brother, Jacob C., of prejudice." He had come to the meeting seeking the blessing, and whenever an invitation was given, he would go forward and kneel. "But then the black woman would be in every meeting; would sing, or pray, or testify. He could not get on." Finally, he gained the victory while praying alone in the woods. The first thing he saw when he came into the afternoon meeting was "the colored woman standing on a bench with both hands up, singing 'All I want is a little more faith in Jesus.' And he said every bit of prejudice was gone, and the love of God was in his heart, and he thought [she] was just beautiful!" (pp. 184-85).

Being black and carrying out much of her ministry among white people was not an easy calling. Smith noted that white people often said to her, "How nicely you get on, Mrs. Smith; everybody seems to treat you so kindly." Her reply was "Yes; that is what you think, . . . but I have much more to contend with than you may think. . . . I think some people would understand the quintessence of sanctifying grace if they could be black about twenty-four hours." Other whites asked her if she would rather be white. She noted, "We who are the royal black are very well satisfied with [God's] gift to us in this substantial color. I, for one, praise Him for what He has given me, although at times it is very inconvenient." She then gave several examples of Jim (and Jane) Crow indignities that she had suffered.

But, she concluded, "Yes, thank God, I am satisfied with my color" (pp. 116-18). In several places she spoke of "belonging to royal stock" (p. 118) and being "of the royal black" (p. 248). She intuitively linked her African heritage of women as queens and priestesses and her Christian identity as a daughter of King Jesus and a member of the priesthood of all believers.[23]

Smith had a strong sense of herself as a woman and as a keen observer of women's roles in the countries she visited. (See document 5.) Once in West Africa she witnessed the ordeal of a queen who had been condemned as a witch when a small child died after being bitten by a snake. Smith described her as "not very tall, but very black, beautiful limbs, beautifully built, small feet, as a lady would have, and beautiful hands and arms; her head was shaved and something black rubbed over it" (p. 387). The woman was led to the place of execution, and then, in a ceremony reminiscent of Numbers 5:11-31, she was forced to drink "a liquid decoction" including bark from the sassy wood tree. If the woman were to throw up the potion, she would be vindicated, so Smith prayed, "Lord, do make her throw it up." When the woman vomited the liquid, Smith said she wanted to shout "Thank God," but she "didn't say it very loud," for the woman's accusers looked vengeful and she feared they would drive her away (pp. 386-89).

In addition to evangelism, Amanda Smith was especially concerned for children and their education. When Smith heard talk of missions to Africa at the Sea Cliff Camp Meeting in July 1872, she thought, "Lord, I am too old to learn now, but if you will help me I will educate my daughter, Mazie, and she can go" (p. 216). She managed to send Mazie to Oberlin for a year, to a school in Xenia, Ohio, for a year (p. 217), and eventually to a school in Baltimore, but was very disappointed when the young woman decided to get married and settle in her own home rather than go to Africa (pp. 218-20).

In Africa Smith adopted a young woman named Frances (p. 392, possibly after Frances Willard) and a young man named Bob (pp. 393ff.). Eventually she saw to it that Bob received a full education in England. In Liberia she became very concerned about education. Although she was unable to continue the work, she did try to start a school of her own (p. 335). She was impressed with the schools the English had started in Sierra Leone. (See document 6.)

Upon returning home to the United States in 1890, Smith eventually settled in the temperance community of Harvey, Illinois, a southern suburb of Chicago. Beginning in 1895 she acquired land in order to build an orphanage, which opened officially in 1899. She was particularly concerned about the education of young men. (See document 7.) Eventually the orphans' home was granted a state charter and became known as the Amanda Smith Industrial School for Girls. It was the only Protestant institution for African American children in Illinois at the time. The school was destroyed by fire in 1918, three years after Smith's death.

As C. Eric Lincoln and Lawrence H. Mamiya note in *The Black Church in the African American Experience,* "As a gifted singer, preacher, evangelist, and missionary, Amanda Smith helped to pave the way for hundreds of black women who also felt the call to preach and found their own independent, 'sanctified' storefront churches during the great urban migrations of the twentieth century."[24] Smith herself outlined her goal in rather simple terms:

> I tried my best to be as unselfish as I could, and show in every possible way that I was a Christian and had no other object than to help everybody I could, in every way I could. I did not advocate a new doctrine, or start a new church. I told the people this was not my errand in Africa. There were churches enough already. All that was needed was the spirit of full consecration to God, and a baptism for real service. [p. 437]

Within her *Autobiography* Amanda Smith emphasized the spiritual aspects of her life and work—her commitment to Christ, her striving for holiness, for entire sanctification in the sense of both complete consecration to God and as empowerment for service. Within the *Autobiography,* and certainly beyond it, one can find ample evidence of her commitment to social justice. She clearly believed that attainment of holiness should result in the breaking down of racial prejudice and barriers. And certainly at the turn of the century the Holiness and Pentecostal movements were the most integrated sectors of the Christian church. Smith consistently challenged all that would limit her ministry, whether based on race or gender. She confronted both the leaders of her own church and those of the Holiness Movement. She vigorously opposed all forms of segregation.

Smith also worked for justice in society. In all her travels, she promoted both the temperance and the reform work of the WCTU. In testimony before a committee of the U.S. House of Representatives in 1891, she denounced the liquor traffic by white merchants in Africa.[25] When she was refused admission to a restaurant in Cincinnati in 1872, she picketed in front of the establishment, passing out tracts. She declared in letters to the *Christian Standard and Home Journal,* a publication of the National Camp Meeting Association, that she was able to receive specialized medical treatment in England that she would have been denied in the United States on the basis of her race.[26] She established the Industrial School in an effort to better educate African American children. In later years in Chicago she worked with Ida Wells-Barnett in the women's club movement and has been linked to the founding of the National Association for the Advancement of Colored People (the NAACP).[27]

Smith's ambition was simply "to be a consistent, downright, outright

Christian" (p. 494). For her that meant a seamless blend of personal holiness and social responsibility.

DOCUMENTS

1. Entire Sanctification. Seeking sanctification, Smith decided to go one Sunday morning to John Inskip's Green Street Methodist Episcopal Church. Despite incessant nagging by the Devil, she got the blessing (*Autobiography,* pp. 77-80).

I wanted to shout Glory to Jesus! but Satan said, "Now, if you make a noise they will put you out."

I was the only colored person there and I had a very keen sense of propriety; I had been taught so, and Satan knew it. . . .

I did not shout, and by-and-by Brother Inskip came to another illustration. He said, speaking on faith: "Now, this blessing of purity like pardon is received by faith, and if by faith why not now!"

"Yes," I said.

"It is instantaneous," he continued. "To illustrate, how long is a dark room dark when you take a lighted lamp into it?"

"O," I said, "I see it!" And again a great wave of glory swept over my soul— another cooling draught of water—I seemed to swallow it, and then the welling up at my heart seemed to come still a little fuller. Praise the Lord forever, for that day!

Speaking of God's power, he went on still with another illustration. He said: "If God in the twinkling of an eye can change these vile bodies of ours and make them look like his own most glorious body, how long will it take God to sanctify a soul?"

"God can do it," I said, "in the twinkling of an eye," and as quick as the spark from smitten steel I felt the touch of God from the crown of my head to the soles of my feet, and the welling up came, and I felt I must shout: but Satan still resisted me like he did Joshua. . . .

Again I yielded to the tempter and did not shout. . . .

And when they sang those words, "Whose blood now cleanseth," O what a wave of glory swept over my soul! I shouted glory to Jesus. Brother Inskip answered, "Amen, Glory to God." . . . I don't know just how I looked, but I felt so wonderfully strange, yet I felt glorious. One of the good official brethren at the door said, as I was passing out, "Well, auntie, how did you like that sermon?" but I could not speak; if I had, I should have shouted, but I simply nodded my head. Just as I put my foot on the top step I seemed to feel a hand, the touch of which I cannot describe. It seemed to press me gently on the top of my head, and I felt something part and roll down and cover me like a great cloak! I felt it distinctly; it was done in a moment, and O what a mighty peace and power took possession of me! I started up Green street. . . . Just ahead of me were three of the leading sisters in our church [Sullivan Street Bethel A.M.E. Church]. I would sooner have met anybody else than them. I was afraid of them. Well, I don't know why, but they were rather the ones who made you feel that wisdom dwelt with them. They were old leading sisters, and I have found that the colored churches were not the only ones that have these leading consequential sisters in them. Well, as I drew near, I saw them say something to each other, and they looked very dignified. Now, the Devil was not so close to me as before; he seemed to be quite behind me, but he shouted after me, "You will not tell them you are sanctified."

"No," I said, "I will say nothing to them," but when I got up to them I seemed to have special power in my right arm and I was swinging it around, like the boys do sometimes! I don't know why, but O I felt mighty, as I came near those sisters. They said, "Well, Smith, where have you been this morning?"

"The Lord," I said, "has sanctified my soul." They were speechless! I said no more, but passed on, swinging my arm! I suppose the people thought I was wild, and I was, for God had set me on fire! . . .

Somehow I always had a fear of white people—that is, I was not afraid of them in the sense of doing me harm, or anything of that kind—but a kind of fear because they were white, and were there, and I was black and was here! But that morning on Green street, as I stood on my feet trembling, I heard these words distinctly. They seemed to come from the northeast corner of the church, slowly, but clearly: "There is neither Jew nor Greek, there is neither bond nor free, there is neither male nor female, for ye are all one in Christ Jesus." (Galatians 3:28) I never understood that text before. But now the Holy Ghost had made it clear to me. And as I looked at white people that I had always seemed to be afraid of, now they looked so small. The great mountain had become a mole-hill.

2. *Call to Preach.* Smith labels this incident "My Last Call" (*Autobiography*, pp. 147-48).

It was the third Sunday in November, 18[7]0. Sister Scott, my band sister, and myself went to the Fleet street A. M. E. Church, Brooklyn. It was Communion Sunday. Before I left home I said to Sister Scott: "I wish I had not promised to go to Brooklyn." She said, "Why?"

"Oh, I feel so dull and stupid."

We went early, and went into the Sabbath School. At the close of the Sabbath School the children sang a very pretty piece, I do not remember what it was, but the spirit of the Lord touched my heart and I was blessed. My bad feelings had gone for a few moments, and I thought, "I guess the Lord wanted to bless me here." But when we went upstairs I began to feel the same burden and pressure as I had before. And I said, "Oh, Lord, help me, and teach me what this means." And just at that point the Tempter came with this supposition: "Now, if you are wholly sanctified, why is it that you have these dull feelings?"

I began to examine my work, my life, every day, and I could see nothing. Then I said, "Lord, help me to understand what Thou meanest. I want to hear Thee speak."

Brother Gould, then pastor of the Fleet Street Church, took his text. I was sitting with my eyes closed in silent prayer to God, and after he had been preaching about ten minutes, as I opened my eyes, just over his head I seemed to see a beautiful star, and as I looked at it, it seemed to form into the shape of a large white tulip; and I said, "Lord, is that what you want me to see? If so, what else?" And then I leaned back and closed my eyes. Just then I saw a large letter "G," and I said: "Lord, do you want me to read in Genesis, or in Galatians? Lord, what does this mean?"

Just then I saw the letter "O." I said, "Why, that means go." And I said "What else?" And a voice distinctly said to me "Go preach."

The voice was so audible that it frightened me for a moment, and I said, "Oh, Lord, is that what you wanted me to come here for? Why did you not tell me when I was at home, or when I was on my knees praying?" But His paths are known in the mighty deep, and His ways are past finding out. On Monday morning, about four o'clock, I think, I was awakened by the presentation of a beautiful, white cross—white as the driven snow. . . . It was as cold as marble. It was laid just on my forehead and on my breast. It seemed very heavy; to press me down. The weight and the coldness of it were what woke me; and as I woke I said: "Lord, I know what that is. It is a cross."

I arose and got on my knees, and while I was praying these words came to me: "If any man will come after Me let him deny himself and take up his cross and follow Me." And I said, "Lord, help me and I will."

3. Women's Ordination. **Although Smith was a faithful member of the African Methodist Episcopal Church, she was never accepted as a pastor of the church or invited into the inner circle. Her visit to the church's General Conference in Nashville is typical of her reception (***Autobiography***, pp. 198-200, 202-4).**

In May, '70, or '71, the General Conference of the A. M. E. Church was held at Nashville, Tenn. It was the first time they ever held a General Conference south of Mason and Dixon's line. I had been laboring in Salem, where the Lord first sent me, and blessed me in winning souls; the people were not rich; they gave me a home, and something to eat; but very little money. So, before I could get back to New York, my home, I took a service place, at Mrs. Mater's, in Philadelphia . . . while her servant, Mary, went to Wilmington, to see her child; she was to be gone a month, but she stayed five weeks; and now the Annual Conference was in session, at the A. M. E. Union Church, near by where I was, so I had a chance to attend.

The election of delegates to the General Conference the next year was a very prominent feature of the Conference; of course every minister wanted, or hoped to be elected as delegate. As I listened, my heart throbbed. This was the first time in all these years that this religious body of black men, with a black church from beginning to end, was to be assembled south of Mason and Dixon's line. . . .

. . . Oh, how I wished I could go; and a deep desire took possession of me, but then, who was I? I had no money, no prominence at that time, except being a plain Christian woman, heard of and known by a few of the brethren, as a woman preacher, which was to be dreaded by the majority, especially the upper ten. . . . I ventured to ask one of the brethren, who had been elected delegate, to tell me how much it would cost to go to Nashville; I would like to go if it did not cost too much.

He looked at me in surprise, mingled with half disgust; the very idea of one looking like me to want to go to General Conference; they cut their eye at my big poke Quaker bonnet, with not a flower, not a feather. He said, "I tell you, Sister, it will cost money to go down there; and if you ain't got plenty of it, it's no use to go;" and turned away and smiled; another said:

"What does she want to go for?"

"Woman preacher; they want to be ordained," was the reply.

"I mean to fight that thing," said the other. "Yes, indeed, so will I," said another.

Then a slight look to see if I took it in. I did; but in spite of it all I believed God would have me go. He knew that the thought of ordination had never once entered my mind, for I had received my ordination from Him, Who said, "Ye have not chosen Me, but I have chosen you, and ordained you, that you might go and bring forth fruit, and that your fruit might remain." . . .

I was quite a curiosity to most of the visitors, especially the Southern brethren, in my very plain Quaker dress; I was eyed with critical suspicion as being there to agitate the question of the ordination of women. All about, in the little groups that would be gathered talking, could be heard, "Who is she?"

"Preacher woman."

"What does she want here?"

"I mean to fight that thing."

"I wonder what day it will come up?" . . .

I would walk out in the afternoon alone, and to and from church alone. Several times I got ready in time and called at the parlor and asked if any of the ladies were ready; "not yet," was the usual answer; so I would walk on. After awhile, in the greatest style, would come these ladies with the good brethren. . . .

. . . Carriages were engaged [one afternoon to take delegates to Fisk University]; I offered to pay for a seat in one, but there was no room; I sent out and ordered my own carriage, and paid for it myself.

While I was getting ready, a certain brother took a lady and put her in my carriage; when I went out to get in, he said, laughingly, "Mrs. Smith, Miss So and So and I want to go, and as you have room in your carriage, I thought we would get in;" but neither of them offered to pay a cent. I had half a mind not to allow it; but it was a good chance to return good for evil. . . .

The meeting was opened in the usual way—an address by one of the bishops, then a song by the choir [the Jubilee Singers], singing as they could sing. Miss Sheppard spied me in the audience, and told Prof. White. He looked and looked, and could not see me at first. Then he went and spoke to Miss Sheppard again. Then she pointed out the plain bonnet. Then he spied me and quickly came down and shook hands, and was so glad. They all looked astonished. Holding me by the hand, he escorted me to the platform and introduced me to the large audience, who, in the midst of overwhelming amazement, applauded. Then the good professor told how they had met me in Boston, and how I sang the grand old hymn, "All I want is a little more faith in Jesus," and what a burst of enthusiasm it created. And of all the surprised and astonished men and women you ever saw, these men and women were the most so.

While he was making these remarks, I prayed and asked God to help me. Then he said, "I'm going to ask Mrs. Smith to sing that same song she sang at Boston, and the Jubilee Singers will join in the chorus."

If ever the Lord did help me, He helped me that day. And the Spirit of the Lord seemed to fall on all the people. The preachers got happy. They wept and shouted "Amen!" "Praise the Lord!" At the close a number of them came to me and shook hands, and said, "God bless you, sister. Where did you come from? I would like to have you come on my charge." Another would say, "Look here, sister, when are you going home? God bless you. I would like to have you come to my place." And so it went. So that after that many of my brethren believed in me, especially as the question of ordination of women never was mooted in the Conference.

But how they have advanced since then. Most of them believe in the ordination of women, and I believe some have been ordained. But I am satisfied with the ordination that the Lord has given me.

4. *Women's Preaching.* While in India, Smith met with opposition from a group of Plymouth Brethren, a growing British millenarian group of the period (and one that eventually greatly influenced American Fundamentalism). These comments appear to come from her diary for January 25, 1881, while she was in Bangalore (*Autobiography,* p. 321). She conducted meetings there at the local Methodist church.

The good Plymouth brethren were much disturbed, because I was a woman, and Paul had said, "Let your women keep silence in the churches." So they had nice articles in the daily papers; then they wrote me kind letters, and bombarded me with Scriptural texts against women preaching; pointed out some they wished me to preach from. I never argue with anybody—just say my say and go on. But one night I said I would speak on this subject as I understood it. Oh, what a stir it made. The church was packed and crowded. After I had sung, I read out my text: "Let your 'men' keep silence in the church," quoting the chapter and verse (1 Cor. 14:28) where Paul was giving directions so as not to have confusion—one to speak at a time, while the others listened. And then one was to interpret, and if there was no interpreter, they should keep silence in the church. So I went on with my version of it. We had an excellent meeting and the newspaper articles stopped, and the letters stopped, and I went on till I got through.

I have wondered what has become of the good Plymouth brethren in India since the Salvation Army lassies have been so owned and blessed of God. Their work has told more practically on the strongholds of heathenism than all that holy conservatism would have brought to bear in a thousand years.

Oh, that the Holy Ghost may be poured out mightily! Then shall the prophecy of Joel be fulfilled. For are we not living in the last days of this wonderful dispensation of the Holy Ghost?

5. *Women's Plight.* As Smith traveled the world, she noted the circumstances of women, through American eyes of course (*Autobiography,* pp. 389-90, 392):

> The poor women of Africa, like those of India, have a hard time. As a rule, they have all the hard work to do. They have to cut and carry all the wood, carry all the water on their heads, and plant all the rice. The men and boys cut and burn the bush, with the help of the women; but sowing the rice, and planting the casava, the women have to do.
>
> You will often see a great, big man walking ahead, with nothing in his hand but a cutlass (as they always carry that or a spear), and a woman, his wife, coming on behind, with a great big child on her back, and a load on her head.
>
> No matter how tired she is, her lord would not think of bringing her a jar of water, to cook his supper with, or of beating the rice; no, she must do that. A great big boy would not bring water for his mother; he would say:
>
> "Boy no tote water; that be woman's work."
>
> If they live with missionaries, or Liberians, or anyone outside of their own native people, then they will do such things; but not for one another.
>
> The moment a girl child is born, she belongs to somebody. The father, who has a son, makes it the highest aim of his life to see that his son has a wife; so he settles, and begins to pay a dowry for a girl for this son. Sometimes they are but a few months old, when you will see them with their betrothal jewels on.
>
> If the fellow who buys the girl is well off, she will have about her little waist a thick roll of beads; sometimes five or six strings together; or she will have bracelets on her little wrists, sometimes of brass, sometimes only made of common iron by the native blacksmith; she will have the same on her ankles, with a little tinkle in it, like a bell, so it makes a noise when she walks.
>
> As they grow up, they have their tastes, and their likes and dislikes. The marriageable age is from thirteen to fourteen, and sometimes younger. All these years the boy's father, or the man himself, is paying on the girl. That is why it is hard to get the girls. It is the girls that bring big money; so the more girls a father has, that much richer he is.
>
> Girls who are bought with a bullock are high toned; that is about the highest grade. Then the next is brass kettles, and cloth and beads. The third is more ordinary; tobacco, cloth, powder, and a little gin is not objectionable. To all of these he can put as much more as he likes; but what I have named are the principal things used in buying a native girl for a wife.
>
> Poor things, they are not consulted; they have no choice in the matter. If they don't like the man, they are obliged to go with him anyway, no matter how illy he may treat them; and sometimes they are cruelly treated. But their

own father could not protect them. The laws in this are very strict. A man's wife is his wife, and no one dare interfere.

One morning in Sinoe, about six o'clock. . . . I heard someone crying most piteously in the street, and there seemed to be a number of voices shouting and talking; but mingled with all I heard this deep, piteous crying.

I went and looked out of the window, and there was a poor girl, I suppose about fifteen or sixteen years of age, and as pretty a colored girl as I ever saw; she had a dark brown skin, was of medium size, and beautifully formed; her hair was done up prettily, as they can do it, and her hands and arms were as plump and as delicately shaped as if she had been born a queen.

There were five or six men, and the same number of boys. The old man was as ugly as a monkey; he was her husband; he had hold of her arm, and was jerking her along, and beating her; then the boys would run up and give her a slap on her bare shoulders. . . .

I ran down stairs and called Mr. R., and begged him to go and see if he could do anything for the poor thing. He said it was a woman palaver, he supposed, and that is the biggest kind of a palaver in Africa, and nobody can help settle them, but themselves. However, I begged him so hard that he went.

He came back in about an hour, and said she was the wife of this horrid, old man, and she had run away from him because he had beaten her, and had been gone several weeks; and these other men had found her, and had held her for the old man, but she did not want to go to him.

"Well," I said, "can't anything be done to help her?"

"No," he said, "there is only one thing; if some one of these younger men would coax the old man to sell her, and he consented and they paid him a good dowry, they could have her. But if the old man was contrary, and should refuse, he would torture her to death right in the presence of her own father, and he could not help her." . . .

Now that is the reason it is so much better for the missionary to buy the girls, at the price of a bullock, which is twenty or twenty-five dollars; that is the price of a girl. And they are very honorable in this. If a girl has been bought by a missionary, she is free as long as she lives; no one will ever claim her; but if otherwise, she can be claimed years after, by anyone of her people who chooses to make trouble. Even if she was married and settled it would not save her, if she could not say she was bought.

I was not asked to pay anything for my Frances, a Bassa girl, though that was their custom. Her father gave her to me, and so did Mrs. Brown, to whom he had first given her, without any dowry. Her mother died, and I told Mr. Brown if her people wanted her, they must pay me two bullocks; for it had cost me that with the care and trouble I had had with her. After that I never heard any more about it.

The boys are free; no dowry for them. They can go and live with missionaries, marry and settle, just as they like.

6. Education in Africa. In her *Autobiography* (pp. 421-23), Smith expresses great concern about the state of education in the African nations she visited. Here she reflects on schools in Sierra Leone:

Formerly they had good schools in Freetown. This is one thing I admire in the English government; she generally looks well after the education of her colonists. Of course there is room for much improvement, even in Sierra Leone and Lagos.

All up and down the coast, wherever you go where the English flag waves, and there has been any civilization at all, you will find scores and hundreds who have a liberal education, and are fitted for most all professions and callings.

The Wesleyan Girls' High School, at Freetown, was once a beautiful building, with well furnished dormitories, and a staff of first-class teachers; but it has seen its best days, without a great change takes place. For several years it has been sadly declining in power and influence, being almost entirely under the control of one or two parties. I was told that when it was first founded, it was under the management of white people; the lady principal and teachers were all white, and they did a grand work. And then the boys' high school, which I also visited, and had the privilege, through the invitation of the principal, Mr. M., of addressing, was not what it once was, or should be. The Episcopal school, both for girls and boys, is good. The boys have a fine, large, commodious building, and a good staff of teachers.

Several of the Liberian families, who have not been able to send their sons and daughters as far as England to be educated, sent them to Freetown. I had the pleasure of going all through this building, on the day of the dedication of the new dormitory and recitation rooms, which had been added to the main building, accommodating, I think, probably two hundred in all. His lordship, the Bishop, was in the chair, and gave a most excellent address, as did also Mr. N., who, I think, at that time had charge of the theological department, and who was a noble, Christian gentleman. His sister was the lady principal of the girls' high school, which I also visited, and had the pleasure of speaking a few words to the young ladies. Everything was in good order.

I was greatly delighted with this school, especially the housekeeping department, where, in connection with their studies, each girl took her turn in the sweeping, dusting, making bread, biscuit, pie, or cake, and in washing dishes and attending the dining room. This, it seemed to me, was the most essential of all; it would certainly be one of the "one needful things." For if, having the intellectual qualifications, the girls in Africa are remiss in this, the former is as good as lost, to a great extent, as their homes would not be what they might be otherwise.

Then, there are private schools. I visited a Mr. Leapol's school, which was a very nice school for boys. I suppose he accommodated about forty. Mr. L. was a very high type of a Christian gentleman; I think a West Indian by birth. This school was of the higher grade. Teachers and helpers, I believe were all colored.

There was a good government school, which, according to my American ideas, should have continued to exist. But when the new Bishop came, he, being a very conservative English gentleman, and invested with power, thought it best, as I was told, to disband the government school, and build a large parish school. So that many of the poor children, who were not able to pay, were shut out. This opened a good harvest for the Roman Catholics, which they lost no time in securing.

I am often asked if I think that missionary work in Africa prospers and develops better when under the entire control of colored people, or do I think it better under the control of white people.

To answer this as best I can I will give my experience and observation at the several places I have been.

The schools at Old Calabar under the Scotch Presbyterian Missionary Society, and the schools and missions at Lagos, and the Episcopal, Baptist and Wesleyan Schools in the Republic of Liberia, and then in Sierra Leone, the United Free Methodists, the Episcopals, the Lady Huntington Society, the U. B. [United Brethren] Mission, and the English Baptist Mission, all were established, supported, and superintended by white missionaries; but just in proportion as they have died, or on account of poor health have had to retire from the work, the schools and mission property have declined.

Many of them in the work have developed good native teachers and preachers, who are loyal, and faithful, and true; and the white missionary feels that he, or she, could not do without these native helpers. But when the whole work is left to them the interest seems to flag, and the natives themselves seem to lose their interest, which the teacher feels, but cannot help.

I do not attempt to make any explanation of this; I simply state the facts as I met them. . . .

Then, the white missionaries, as a rule, give better satisfaction, both to the natives and to the church or society which sends them out.

I suppose no church or society ever gave a salary to a colored man, no matter how efficient he was, as large as they give to a white man or woman, no matter how inefficient he or she may be in the start; and I think they are generally expected to do more work. This I think is a big mistake.

7. The Education of Boys. This statement is found in *The Helper,*[28] the periodical Smith founded to publicize the work of her orphanage in Harvey, Illinois.

A philosopher has said that education of boys is to "teach them what they ought to know when they become men."

First—To be true and to be genuine. No education is worth any thing that does not include this. A man had better not know how to read and be true in action rather than to be learned in all sciences and in all languages and be at the same time false in heart and counterfeit in life. Above all things teach the boys that truth is more than riches, power or possessions.

Second—To be pure in thought, language and life—pure in mind and body.

Third—To be unselfish, to care for the feelings and comforts of others, to be generous, noble, and manly. This will include a genuine reverence for the aged and for things sacred.

Fourth—To be self-reliant and self-helpful even from childhood, to be industrious always and self-supporting at the earliest possible age. Teach them that all honest work is honorable; that an idle life of dependence on others is disgraceful!

Frances Willard

CHAPTER 4

"MY OWN METHODIST HIVE"

Frances Willard's Faith as Disclosed in Her Journal, 1855–1870

CAROLYN DE SWARTE GIFFORD

In 1888 during an impromptu address before the International Council of Women, Frances Willard, president of the Woman's Christian Temperance Union and a reformer of international reputation, spoke of her strong attachment to the faith which had nurtured her throughout her life. "I will tell you how it is with me," she declared.

> I go like a bee into the gardens of thought; I love to listen to all the voices, and I go buzzing around under the bonnets of the prettiest flowers and the most fragrant, just like this bee, and when it is a lovely life and a sweet life, like the lives of those who have spoken to us today, [referring to several prominent women attending the Council meeting who had given their religious views preceding Willard] it seems to me I get a lot of honey; but I have a wonderful bee-line fashion of carrying it all home to my own Methodist hive. I couldn't do any other way. I am made that fashion; it is part of me. It is worked into the woof and warp of my spirit, the result of the sweet old ways in which I was brought up.[1]

Willard's clear statement about her Methodist loyalties suggests very strongly that those of us who attempt, a century after her death, to re-create her life and the meaning of that life for her time look closely at her faith, taking seriously her self-identification as a Methodist.

Frances Elizabeth Caroline Willard was born in 1839 into a western New York farm family. After a brief period in Oberlin, Ohio, the family moved in 1846 to a southeastern Wisconsin farm. Willard spent the years from 1846 to 1858 in Wisconsin, reveling in a carefree, country existence. She received much of her three-and-one-half years of formal education during this time. Although her parents were originally Congregationalists, sometime during their Wisconsin years they became Methodists.

In 1858 the Willard family moved to Evanston, Illinois, where Frances

Willard attended the North Western Female College, a Methodist girls' school, graduating in 1859. For almost a decade Willard taught school, except for a year, from 1865 to 1866, when she was the Corresponding Secretary of the American Methodist Ladies Centenary Association. Though she enjoyed teaching, Willard had long wished to travel abroad and she was able to do so from spring 1868 through summer 1870. When she returned home, she accepted the presidency of Northwestern University's newly founded Ladies College. She remained the head of the school until spring 1874 when she resigned in a disagreement with Northwestern's president over the governance of the Ladies College.

During the winter of 1873–74, a women's crusade against liquor dealers had begun in Ohio and spread rapidly through the northern United States. By summer 1874, a permanent organization, the Woman's Christian Temperance Union, had been launched. Willard was elected Corresponding Secretary, with the task of traveling throughout the country, speaking and establishing local unions. She rapidly became a power within the organization and was elected president in 1879. She continued to lead the WCTU until her death in 1898.

Frances Willard's journal—forty-nine volumes amounting to several thousand pages, recovered in 1982 after being lost for half a century—gives rich and extensive evidence of the "Methodist hive" in which she grew to maturity. The volumes written during her sixteenth to thirty-first years (from 1855 to 1870) yield a vivid account of what growing up meant for a mid-nineteenth-century Midwestern Methodist woman.

The journal is not merely a chronicle of events, as many journals and diaries are, but rather, like diaries of eighteenth and nineteenth-century Puritans and Evangelicals, a means for reflection as she struggled toward the development of character. In her struggle, she was representative of American Victorian society and the culture fostered by that society with its pervasive sense of moral earnestness, its striving for a virtuous life exemplified by doing one's duty. Very early in her journal-keeping, Willard announced her intention to use it for the improvement of her character. It was, she observed, a place to tell the truth, particularly about her success—or lack of it—in the maturing of character.[2]

On the front and back pages of her journal volumes, she often inscribed short mottoes (her own inventions or quotations from her current heroes) to remind her of her goal and the rigorousness with which she would pursue it. Written along the margin of an 1861 journal, for example, emphasized with underlinings, flourishes, and capital letters, is this statement: "*My word*—than any other word more *Royal*—CHARACTER."[3] Six years later, she boldly inscribed on the front page of her twenty-fourth journal volume this stern reminder: "We can hardly be too severe in judging ourselves, or too lenient in judging others."[4]

Occasionally, her energy for this moral pursuit waned. In the summer of 1860, when she was twenty, she confided to her journal: "I almost despair sometimes, of ever coming to be a noble and finished character, and I would rather be this than any or all things else in the world."[5] But perseverance and steadfastness were part of the cluster of virtues which, along with truthfulness (sincerity, integrity), magnanimity, charity, calmness, patience, geniality (kindliness, pleasant disposition), generosity, and sensitivity to suffering humanity, made up what Willard believed to be "a noble and finished character," and so she persisted. Although she often described women who exhibited her ideal of character as "womanly," the ideal was not strictly gender-based, unlike the dominant ideals of femaleness and maleness of the time. Willard admired generous, patient, sensitive, and magnanimous men and termed them "manly." For her, the terms "true womanliness" and "true manliness" applied to those persons— women and men—who exemplified character.

For Willard, as for the evangelical world in which she lived, a moral life was synonymous with a holy life, one lived in conformity with God's will and with God's aid. Acquiring character was a Christian aim sought by the converted. During the summer of 1859, at age nineteen, she was in the grip of a life-threatening bout with typhoid fever. Willard underwent a religious experience she vividly re-created thirty years later in her autobiography. As she awaited the crisis point of her illness, which she had overheard her doctor predicting, her soul was torn by an accompanying crisis of faith:

> Two voices seemed to speak within me, one of them saying, "My child, give me thy heart. I called thee long by joy, I call thee now by chastisement; but I have called thee always and only because I love thee with an everlasting love."
>
> The other said, "Surely you who are so resolute and strong will not break down now because of physical feebleness. You are a reasoner, and never yet were you convinced of the reasonableness of Christianity. Hold out now and you will feel when you get well just as you used to feel."[6]

Willard reported that the struggle between the two voices seemed to last a long time, although looking back on the event she acknowledged that "in my weakness such a strain would doubtless appear longer than it was."[7]

The crisis was resolved, at least momentarily, when her soul responded to what she perceived as the warm, comforting call of God rather than to the cold, dismal voice of reasoning skepticism. She wrote: "At last, solemnly, and with my whole heart, I said, not in spoken words, but in the deeper language of consciousness, 'If God lets me get well I'll try to be a Christian girl.'"[8] At the urging of the voice of God within her, Willard called to her mother, watching in the room next door to hers as she lay ill.

"Mother," she announced weakly, "I wish to tell you that if God lets me get well I'll try to be a Christian girl."[9] Her mother received the announcement with tears and prayers, holding her daughter's hand while she slept, Willard having been exhausted by the resolution of both her spiritual crisis and the physical crisis of her illness.

Through the late summer and fall of 1859 she attempted to carry out her resolve to "be a Christian girl." Her journals document regular participation in Sunday worship, attendance at sermons and lectures on Christianity, the study of a variety of literature on Christian faith and life, and discussion about the topic with family and friends. But once again she was troubled by a tension within her, this time between her intellectual knowledge of Christ and her continuing inability to transform that knowledge into the trusting certainty of his presence, which others had described to her. Such certainty seemed to her a prerequisite for becoming a Christian. She was convinced that she must feel Christ in her heart as well as comprehend his Person and meaning with her mind. But to her great sorrow, she did not know how.

In December 1859 her church held a revival preached mainly by Methodist Bishop Matthew Simpson, whom Willard admired greatly for his personal holiness. As she attended the revival she struggled over whether she could and would obtain the personal experience of Christ's love, that feeling which would propel her forward to the altar in public affirmation of her faith. Bishop Simpson preached a sermon that offered to Willard a way out of her dilemma by reordering the sequence of moments in the spiritual event of entry onto the path of a committed Christian life. She wrote in her journal: "He told us that it was idle in an unconverted person to wait for *feeling* before he attempted to become better. He said you might as well tell a frozen person to feel warm as a frozen heart to melt. First the sinner must commence to do what his reason taught him was best, and in the act of striving for the right, feeling would come."[10] Bishop Simpson's simple, straightforward advice had the effect of removing a roadblock on the spiritual path Willard pursued. Though she still did not feel converted, she was certainly able and willing to employ her intellect to discern what was righteous and just, to seek a moral course for her life. Three days after the bishop's moving sermon she came forward to the altar and made a public affirmation of faith. The following year, when she was twenty years old, she joined the Methodist Episcopal Church on probation. Five months later, in May 1861, Willard was baptized and received into full membership. (See documents 1–8.)[11]

As Willard persevered in her efforts to acquire character, her Methodist environment provided her with a lively and intense spiritual community of intellectual and moral striving, a series of settings and groups of companions designed by Methodists to encourage and support the intense intellectual and moral self-examination in which Willard participated. These two aspects, intellectual and moral, were integrally connected. For Willard and her community, the intellectual life without an accompanying moral life was impermissible; and a moral life without an intellectual aspect to it was an impoverished life.

Family worship was an important center of the spiritual life of the Methodism of Willard's time. Indeed, the home became a "little church" for mid-nineteenth-century evangelicalism, complete with a family altar, religious pictures and mottoes, Bible stand, and a miniature organ or melodeon. Willard family worship assumed a variety of forms, which come vividly to life on the pages of Willard's journal. They assembled regularly for morning prayers and held informal Sunday evening gatherings in the living room to sing their favorite hymns together. From time to time, at moments of particular emotional strain in family relationships, special evening prayers and Bible reading strengthened and sustained those participating and made them more bearable to one another. Deaths of family members became worshipful events, with the dying person recapitulating her or his "religious history" and hopes for heaven, as relatives and friends took turns reading the Bible, praying, and singing the dying one's best-loved hymns. Willard's journal is punctuated throughout with detailed descriptions of many such worshipful events shortly after they happened or of fond, nostalgic reminiscences of them long after they had occurred.

Willard thought of her formal education as a spiritual and moral quest as well as an intellectual process. The North Western Female College in Evanston, Illinois, which she attended from the spring term of 1858 until her graduation in June 1859, was an important component of the community of intellectual and moral striving. After small beginnings as early as the second decade of the nineteenth century, Methodist educational institutions had proliferated by the 1830s, 40s, and 50s. Among these were a number of female seminaries (the equivalent of high schools). Methodist activity in higher education reflected an increasing national interest in universal education with both public and private school systems developing in the middle decades of the century.

The Methodist education system also signaled a shift in the denomination's understanding of what made a good Methodist. As the Methodist movement rapidly spread over the country from the 1780s to the 1830s, enthusiastic but often uneducated itinerant preachers had accompanied equally uneducated pioneers onto the frontiers. As the members of the denomination became settled, some leaders began to push for a better-educated ministry and laity. The cluster of Methodist higher education institutions, of which the North Western Female College formed a part, was the direct result of the wish to create a more learned church. "The regenerate heart [long the mark of a Methodist] must be accompanied and directed by an enlightened intellect to give man the full image of his Maker," stated a memorial to several Methodist Annual Conferences in the Old Northwest requesting the founding of Northwestern University, another part of the cluster.[12] Garrett Biblical Institute, the third part of the Methodist educational cluster, and North Western Female College could also have claimed the statement as their goal, as could Willard herself.

The Willard family's move in 1858 from a Wisconsin farm to Evanston, Illinois, a newly founded village just north of Chicago and the site of the cluster, was a calculated relocation in order to live in a center of Methodist education and acquire for their children "enlightened intellects" capable of directing "regenerate hearts." The Willards' son, Oliver, enrolled at Garrett preparing for the Methodist ministry, and his sisters, Frances and Mary, entered North Western Female College. When the entire family was seated in its assigned pew at the Methodist Episcopal Church for Sunday morning worship, it was surrounded by neighbors and friends, many of whom were professors from Northwestern and Garrett with their families and their students alongside them. They were joined by rows of young women from North Western Female College, who had walked in procession from their dormitory to the church led by their teachers. In this company, the Willards truly felt that they were at the center of a powerful community of intellectual and moral striving.

Many of the same friends, neighbors, and teachers Frances greeted at Sunday morning worship she also saw in a round of events throughout the week, which had as their purpose strengthening the desire to lead a Christian life as the fruit of a regenerate heart: Sunday school and missionary meetings, class meetings and reading circles, and public exercises of the colleges and the seminary featuring addresses on aspects of moral philosophy. She chose her friends on the basis of their ability to become partners in the moral quest of developing character. Much of her reading matter was selected on a similar basis. Her journal continually served as a vehicle for self-examination on moral progress. As one reads through the journal, a certain rhythm of self-scrutiny emerges: The sabbath, of course, was a time of self-assessment, as was mid-week class meeting. Her birthday and New Year's Eve were often occasions for a long journal entry reviewing her character development over the preceding year and pondering her future.

In 1859, when Willard was nearly twenty years old and her formal schooling almost finished, her moral quest also became a vocational one. Focusing her rather vague intentions to do something good and be somebody, she began to think seriously about the kind of useful work she could do. Like most middle-class girls of her time she perceived only two possibilities: marriage or teaching. She had no prospects of marriage at that point. Further, with a decidedly independent disposition, she was not sure she was suited for marriage. She therefore considered teaching.

Her short time at school had been for Willard her first glimpse of an exciting world of ideas, culture, and friendships. It was a great disappointment that her parents would not allow her to continue for another year by enrolling in her school's classical program. But if she could not continue as a student, she could aspire to be a teacher. With the help of neighbors and friends connected with public school systems in the Midwest, she began applying to teach. Though reluctant to leave her family and friends, she was determined to become fully independent and self-reliant, to earn her own living, and place herself in a situation where she could test her endurance through a new, difficult, and lonely task.

Over the next nine years Willard taught in both public schools and Methodist female seminaries. In both settings she endeavored to re-create a community of intellectual and moral striving and took responsibility for setting up and maintaining a discipline of character development for her students. She worked to foster an atmosphere she would later refer to as "moral horticulture," in which teachers acting as moral examples, friends, and confidantes, would guide students toward self-discipline and imbue in them a desire to "be good and do good," a desire she herself continually recorded in her journals until the close of her life.

Moral horticulture had as its aim the goal that Willard had set for herself in her early twenties, that the moral life become, as it were, second nature.

> When I see that what was irksome becomes pleasant—that what I did as a duty . . . I come to do naturally & unconsciously; when I see my self forbearing as a matter of course, and patient and kindly as a spontaneous thing, then I believe God's spirit is within me. Only so far as it comes directly down into my Life—into its smallest action & most trivial word, do I trust to religion as connected with me. . . . When . . . I find my Life quite pure and patient, I look up so thankfully to God & Christ, & pray for more of that Love in my Heart which makes the Life right without our watching it—which "makes no duty seem a load," "no worship prove a task."[13]

Willard sought for herself and, later, for her students a moral life, which might at first be a duty but would eventually become, through God's Holy Spirit, a joy.

Willard's desire to do good became increasingly focused on what she could do for the "cause of woman." From the time she was in her teens her journal contained occasional sharp comments on the dependent position of women in American society. By 1867, when she was twenty-eight, Willard decided that her vocation was to become more actively involved in enlarging woman's sphere and women's possibilities. The following year it became much clearer to her just what it was she wanted to do for women. In Evanston, preparing for a two-year trip to Europe and the Middle East, she and a friend, along with many other Evanstonians, attended a lecture, "The American Woman," by Theodore Tilton, popular women's rights lecturer and newspaper editor. Much discussion of woman suffrage followed in the wake of the lecture, and Willard decided that she supported it. As they packed their trunks for Europe, Willard's friend enthusiastically read aloud John Stuart Mill's speech to the British parliament on women's rights, with which the two young women strongly agreed.[14]

Arriving in France for six months of study and museum touring, Willard wrote in her travel notebook of her intention to study the woman question in the countries she visited, planning upon her return to the United States to assess the situation there, and then

> *talk in public* of the matter, & cast myself with what[ever] weight or weakness against the only foe of what I conceive to be the justice of the subject—unenlightened public opinion. Sometimes I feel "the victory in me"—often I do not. Always, I have clearly felt it to be "my vocation" but a constitutional dread of criticism & love (too strong) of approbation have held me back.
>
> With encouragement I believe myself capable of rendering services of some value in the word-&-idea battle that will only deepen with years & must at last have a result that will delight all who have hastened it.[15]

Many journal entries throughout her two-year trip record extensive conversations with a variety of people in France, England, and Italy about the situation of women, meetings in Paris with American and French women's rights advocates, and observations about women's position in the Middle East. There are also a small number of notations on *how* she would present the cause of woman, which give valuable indications of her concern from the beginning that her advocacy be conducted in what she considered a "Christian, womanly way."[16] Exactly what she meant by this is not entirely clear from her journals, but there are a few clues. In Italy during fall 1869, she wrote that she hoped to "write or utter some earnest words for evolution, not revolution; for *womanly* liberty not . . . wild license."[17] A hastily scribbled note, written while she was en route through Palestine in spring 1870, gives a further clue: "I will cater to the peculiarity—Instead of 'Woman's Sphere'—it shall be 'Ladies Orbit'—instead of taxation without representation—women's rights—&c.&c."[18]

Like most evangelical women's rights reformers and members of the burgeoning women's foreign and home missionary societies, Willard considered Christianity to be the largest single cause of women's emancipation; thus her work for women would issue from her Christian faith. Although she might—and, in fact, did—attempt to reform the church's attitude toward women, she would never renounce her faith as a few radical women's rights advocates did, since she believed that women's greatest hope for liberation lay with a reformed Christianity.

Willard's idea of what constituted a noble Christian character included strong notions of geniality—especially the wish not to offend anyone needlessly. Thus she would endeavor always to couch her defense of women's rights in language carefully constructed so as not to frighten or alienate audiences who, she felt, needed only to be gently led to see the justice of her subject. Then, she assumed, they would support it. This seems to be, at least in part, the meaning of her statement "I will cater to the peculiarity." It also probably indicates Willard's realization that her first audiences would come most naturally from her Methodist community, some of whom might likely be supporters of the cause of woman, but not of what they, like Willard herself, perceived to be the combative attitudes and aggressive strategies of the more radical faction of the women's rights movement. This faction was often accused of being unwomanly because it was thought bold, confrontational, and argumentative. None of these traits was included in Willard's ideal of character she labored to nurture in herself. Nor would such traits be apt to attract most evangelical women in the 1870s when Willard launched forth on her career as a women's rights speaker. On her return from her two-and-one-half-year European trip, she gathered together her notes on the situation of woman and gave her first public address on the subject before Chicago area Methodists at Centenary M.E. Church in spring 1871. (See document 9.)

From that time until her death in 1898 she never deviated from her vocation to serve the cause of woman. Whether as the president of the newly established Evanston Ladies College (the female department of Northwestern University) during the early 1870s or as the Corresponding Secretary and longtime President of the WCTU, which she built into the largest women's organization of its time, Willard advocated energetically and unceasingly for woman's self-development—her right to be and do whatever she believed she was called by God to do. (See document 10.)

She insisted as well upon women's responsibility to participate in the process of creating a moral nation, one that would embody the ideals of justice and care her Methodist community of moral striving had imparted to her. In an often-repeated aphorism: "Woman will bless and brighten every place she enters, and she *will* enter *every* place!" she urged her followers to pursue their self-development in order to become reformers—to bring into reality the ideal world of truth, justice, mercy, and compassion she had heard preached from the pulpit in her young womanhood, been taught by her teachers, discussed with her class meeting, and been nurtured to believe in by her parents, relatives, and older friends.

Willard's struggle to build her character and discern her vocation is richly documented on the many thousand pages of her journal. Thus the journal is an invaluable source for tracing the link between the spirituality and social responsibility of this remarkable nineteenth-century reformer, who understood her faith as the core of her being—her "own Methodist hive"—a faith that grounded her life, yet impelled her always outward and onward toward a broad social vision.[19]

DOCUMENTS

In December 1859 when Frances Willard was twenty years old she came forward during a revival at the Methodist Episcopal Church in Evanston, Illinois, and publicly affirmed her faith. It was but one moment, albeit a highly significant one, in her lifelong spiritual journey, which was characterized by her striving always to translate her good intentions into moral action. Her understanding of faith was that it must issue forth in deeds of righteousness; thus she was quintessentially a reformer. Documents 1 through 8, a series of journal entries from 1859 to 1861, show the spiritual events surrounding her decision to declare herself a Christian before her Methodist community. They also give the reader a good idea of Willard's theology: her notion of God, her relationship to Christ, her understanding of the work of the Holy Spirit, the place of the Bible and the church in her life. Although she continually studied theological treatises and maintained a lively interest in attending sermons and lectures by leading pastors and scholars, her personal faith was an uncomplicated one, focused on the simple goals of "being good and doing good."

For the most part, the transcriptions below retain Willard's spelling and punctuation. Her use of dashes to indicate a new paragraph has been replaced with indentation.

1. Journal Entry: October 23, 1859.

Ever since I was sick, I have thought much of Religion. I wish that I stood in right relations to God. I wish I could practically apply the intellectual belief I have in Christ. I wish I could trust in him whom I have not seen, as I trust even in my friends on the earth who are tangible to me. I wish when B[isho]p. [Matthew] S[impson] says "Leave it all to Christ" "Give him your heart, just as it is, with all its sins upon it," I knew how to give it him. I wish I could *feel* my sinful condition—I see it, I acknowledge it, intellectually, but I don't *feel* it. O, Christ and Heaven seem to me *afar off*, and my conscience is very quiet, seared by my long neglect of its admonitions. Though not an "outbreaking" sinner, yet I have been a fearful one. My influence has been all wrong, my purposes intensly selfish. I have sinned in the broad light of noon day. How carefully have I been reared—how diligently have I been instructed; how have I been shielded from the evil influences that are in the world! Yet I have disregarded it all. And I sit here, surrounded by mercies and blessings, and love and kindness; I sit here bathed in the sunshine of this hallowed and beautiful day, and write all this with perfect calmness, nay, almost with serenity! I am indeed, very, very far astray. But I shall not give it up. I intend immediately to be a Christian. For Christ's sake, I ask Thee, O Lord, to spare me until then. Divest me of all false pride, let me *feel* as I *see*, how glorious a thing it is to be at peace with Him by whom I was created, by whom I am preserved. Let me truly repent, and help me to please Thee, and to be useful in the world, I ask it very humbly and sincerely, *only* for Christ's sake.

2. Journal Entry: December 12, 1859.

Yesterday Bp. Simpson preached in the evening. He feels what he says. He is, I think, the most holy man I have ever seen. I would give much to have him pray for me to God. Several went forward to the Altar for prayers. I shall go when I feel impressed with a desire, a need, a necessity to go. I shall not go before. I hope I may feel on *The* Subject. But certainly—I almost fear to say it—I never felt more fiendish indifference than I did last night. God help me—God forgive me!

3. Journal Entry: December 14, 1859.

Last night attended church. Bp. Simpson preached. His sermon was—as I think—the most movingly practical of any I have ever heard. A few things that he said, I will write here for the truth and value that is in them. He told us that it was idle in an unconverted person to wait for *feeling* before he attempted to become better. He said you might as well tell a frozen person to feel warm as a frozen heart to melt. First the sinner must commence to do what his reason taught him was best, and in the act of striving for the right, feeling would come. He said these three things were what a seeker after Righteousness should do: 1st. Read the Bible. (The New Testament.) He would not attempt to say how it was, but in reading God's Revelation to man there was great benefit—even when it was read coldly by the unconverted. 2nd. Asking God to show you the true meaning of what you read, and to impress it upon your mind. 3d. Reflecting upon Life, Death and Eternity and our relation to things Past, present, & to come. . . . About going forward to the altar for prayers, I have always had doubts. Friends of mine who are Christians have advised me not to do so, and I have thought it unwise to do so. Bishop Simpson presented the matter in a new light. He said we had sinned publicly. We had not been careful to do evil and say evil in private. But now we think we must repent in secret places. He said, "My dear friends, you have thought it a little thing to sin publicly, and it is just and right that you *publicly* declare by your actions if not by your words that you intend to stop sinning—that you intend with Christ's help to be reconciled to God."

This seemed to me reasonable. I wished to go—I was very much agitated—I could see my heart beating—and yet I stood there apparently calm and careless & *resisted*. No, I did not go, I did not try for forgiveness as I have often thought I would. I stood in my place very quietly. Fool! Fool! I shall never again think it idle to openly declare oneself on the Lord's side. I think I will go tonight. And yet I may not. I cannot tell.

4. Journal Entry: December 16, 1859.

I have commenced! O Lord! I am trying to redeem the solemn promise I have made to Thee. I have publicly declared my determination to forsake my sins—to seek forgiveness for the past and help for the future; to endeavor with Christ's help,—always with Christ's help, to live a good, true, valuable life—a life that shall glorify God and be a blessing to my fellow toilers and sufferers on the earth.

I have not yet the change of heart that Christ has promised to those who ask Him rightly, but I expect it.

I feel inclined to do right more than I ever did before; it is easy for me to be obliging and patient today, and it was never *easy* before. This is not of myself. I know that the *third person of the Trinity* is helping me, even as Christ has said.

I will never stop trying. I have not commenced in my own strength—I never could have done so—nothing is more distasteful to my *nature* than what I did last night—and yet, I found it easy, for Christ—the Christ part of God—was helping me!

[Written along the left margin in large letters covering the length of the entry for December 16, 1859:]

The Day that Stands Alone!

5. Journal Entry: December 22, 1859.

Though I have yet no evidences of that change of purpose—that reconciliation to God—that active Peace—which I believe accompanies conversion, I am not discouraged. I see many reasons to hope that gradually I shall come to be "in the light as He is in the light." I enjoy reading the Bible, and I used to dislike it; I am willing & glad to talk with my friends about the Interest of all our lives, and I used never to mention it; I find it today comparatively easy to be silent when angry—not as easy as it was on one day I have referred to—a day that stands upon my calander alone in its purity, but yet, not as hard as it is usually. I believe that if I pray earnestly for Christ's sake & if it be God's will,—for more light;—if I read the Bible thoughtfully, and reflect upon what the Past has done, the Present is Doing & the Future will do for me, I shall "through the forbearance of God" come to be a child of His. There are several chapters in the book of Romans that help & comfort me, and anything that Christ has said I love to read & think about. O! how kind and loving and gentle was Christ! He never was harsh; he never was severe; He "knew our frame, he remembered that we are dust." He had sympathy and pity and compassion for us always! He never was impatient, He never was tyrannical; He was tempted even as we are tempted, and yet, without sin! How forgiving was his spirit, how tender! What a Heart was that which beat in the bosom of the Christ—God! What a great, yearning, pitiful Heart! What comforting words He left for us, before he went back to His "Father's house" to plead for the children of men as long as one shall remain upon the earth who is unforgiven! What a message is this that has gone out into all the world: "Come unto me, all ye that labor and are heavy laden, and I will give you rest; take my yoke upon you & learn of me, you shall find rest for your soul." I have come to believe that in one way or another, every human being is "weary, and heavy laden." We try to disguise it, but we are tired and faint in our hearts; we find it not a little thing to live bravely and well; we find that toil is our portion; labor of body or of brain; labor in the heart, aye! in the heart—how very cheering then are Christ's words. And these, "In the world ye shall have tribulation, but fear not, I have overcome the world." O, Thou who art so kind, help me to see the glory of Thy character! Help me to serve Thee, and to *strive* always to be like Thee!

6. *Journal Entry: December 29, 1859.*

I am trying to do right. I feel very differently from what I did a month ago. I see every day how helpless I am of myself. I can will to be kind and forgiving; to possess all the Christian graces, but I lack executive ability. I am learning better every day that "of myself I can do nothing." And I am finding out that in proportion as I *ask* with sincerity & earnestness for aid, Christ aids me.

7. *Journal Entry: May 4, 1861.*

Tomorrow morning I expect to be baptized & received into "full connection" with the Church. Mr. Bibbins [the pastor of the Methodist Episcopal Church Willard attended in Evanston, Illinois] will lay his hand upon my forehead, & say the solemn words: "I baptize thee in the name of the Father & of the Son & of the Holy Ghost." . . . O God! make me better—more worthy to call myself Thy child. May I be in earnest, & though in great humility, may I try to live worthily in the world.

The vows I shall voluntarily make tomorrow, may color my whole destiny. Help me to appreciate what I shall promise then. May I be more watchful, thoughtful, prayerful, henceforth.

I have no wish so great as that I may be better. No prayer so earnest, O! Father in Heaven, as that Thou wilt "*make me right.*"

8. *Journal Entry: May 5, 1861.*

An eventful day to me.

Mary [Willard's younger sister] & I publicly declared our determination to endeavor—with God's help—to live as *Christians;* we were baptized, received into the Church, & Communed.

Those were solemn vows we made!—I almost trembled as our voices mingled in the responses to the questions that were asked us. I felt how solemn a thing it was—how awful the responsibility that would thence-forth rest upon us.

And yet, the ceremony seemed very beautiful to me. We knelt there at the Altar, *we* whose lives & hearts & thought have been *one*. It was eminently fitting that we should in this, as in every thing, be together. I think God looked on us kindly, & Christ loved us, with His infinite, condescending love, as we promised, publicly . . . to serve and honor Him always. I know that I will try. I prayed so earnestly for help & strength to keep the promises I made, as the hand of our Pastor trembled while it rested on my head, and he baptized me.

And I felt some strength—some quietness. O! so much more than I deserved!

I will write faithfully here, of my failures or successes. Christ pity me & make me strong. . . .

I know that there is nothing in Life that does not seem trivial to me, compared with God's approval. I know that there is nothing I would not sacrifice for this; no desire that is not insignificant, compared with this. And yet Life looks rich & beautiful to me—full of joy and blessedness. I think only too much about it, & with all this, I feel that no *purpose* is so deep & all prevading with me, as the purpose to live for God in the world, & no desire is so strong as the desire to have Him smile upon me here, & take me to Himself *at last.*

9. *From "The New Chivalry; or, the School-Mistress Abroad."* [20] When Willard returned to Evanston from her European and Middle Eastern tour in the fall of 1870, she spoke to the local Women's Foreign Missionary Society about her experiences abroad. She described her observations on what she felt to be the deplorable condition of women in the countries she visited, drawing on the extensive notes she had documented in her journal. She was invited by a prominent Methodist layman to deliver a paid lecture at Centenary M.E. Church in Chicago. Willard spent three weeks preparing her one-and-a-half-hour talk and gave it on March 21, 1871, before an audience she described as "the elite of the West Side, with many from the North and South Sides [of Chicago]." [21]

Although Willard had spoken for almost ten years before her Sunday school classes and her public and private school pupils on a variety of topics and testified on the state of her soul before large gatherings at church revivals and campmeetings, she considered "The New Chivalry" her first *public* lecture. With this speech, she launched her reform vocation, working in her own distinctive way for "the cause of woman."

"The New Chivalry" is typical of Willard's speech-making during her nearly three decades as a reformer. The talk is sprinkled with classical and literary allusions likely to be unfamiliar to modern readers, and filled with flowery descriptive passages which would seem excessively wordy and trite to a late-twentieth-century audience. Yet Willard's contemporaries reported being thrilled by her words and convinced of the justice and rightness of her position.

The following excerpt illustrates one of her favorite ways of presenting ideas she believed might be unwelcome to at least some of her audience. Taking a traditional concept, in this case "chivalry," and redefining it less conservatively and more attractively for her American listeners, she assumed that her audience would want to join her in what she believed to be a crucial part of America's mission as a "Christian nation": to be a shining example of a new equality for women and men.

> Let me, then, invoke your patience while together we review the argument from real life which has placed me on the affirmative side of the tremendous "Woman Question"—while we consider the lot of woman beyond the seas, and then contrast this with her position, present and prospective, here in America, and while we seek the reasons of this amazing difference. Or, as I like better to express it, let me try to picture the position taken by the *New Chivalry* of our native land in contrast with that of the Old Chivalry in the old world. And by this term, "The Chivalry," for I do not use it as a dictionary word, I mean to denote (sometimes sincerely, and sometimes sarcastically) the sex now dominant upon this planet.

The body of Willard's speech details the understanding of women's status she had gained from her observations in Egypt, Italy, France, Germany, and England. She concludes:

> The Knights of the Old Chivalry gave woman the empty husk of flattery; those of the New, offer instead, the wholesome kernel of just criticism; the Knights of the Old Chivalry drank our health in flowing bumpers; those of the New invite us to sit down beside them at the banquet of truth.
>
> "By my lady's bright eyes," was the watch-word of the Old; "Fair play for the weaker," is the manly war cry of the New! Talk about the Chivalry of Ancient Days! Go to, ye medieval ages, and learn what that word meaneth. Behold the sunny afternoon of this nineteenth century of grace, wherein we have the spectacle, not of lances tilted to defend the *prestige* of "my lady's beauty," by swaggering knights who could not write their names, but of the noblest men of the world's foremost race, placing upon the brows of those most dear to them, above the wreath of Venus, the helmet of Minerva, and leading into broader paths of knowledge and achievement, the fair divinities who preside over their homes.
>
> No picture dawns upon me so refulgent as this Home that yet shall be the gift of this Better Age to the New America, in which a *three-fold tie* shall bind the husband to his wife, the father to his daughter, the mother to her son. Religion and affection—as heretofore in all true homes—shall form two of the strands in this magic three-fold tie; the third this age is weaving, and it is

intellectual sympathy, than which no purer or more enduring bond survived the curse of Eden!

Whoever has not thought thus far, has failed to fathom the profoundest significance, or to rise to the height of the noblest inspiration, which our new ideas of woman's privilege infallibly involve.

10. From "The Woman's Cause Is Man's." [22] In 1892, more than twenty years after Willard gave her speech "The New Chivalry," the reform journal *Arena* published her article "The Woman's Cause Is Man's," an excerpt from which appears below. By this time, Willard was a world-famous reformer who spoke hundreds of times a year, from many and varied platforms, to audiences numbering in the thousands. But her message was still essentially the same call for equality for women and men. Each person—whether male or female—should be able to develop his or her talents to the fullest extent, so that all could work together for a better life for everyone. For Willard, as for many nineteenth-century women's rights reformers, the equality of women was not an end in itself; it was, rather, a necessary step toward the ultimate goal of reforming the world.

The noblest way in which to think of men or women is to think first of their more enduring nature, their spiritual part, that which all human beings have in common, and by which they are separated from the lower orders of creation. The more we can think of each other on this plane the nobler will be our treatment of each other, because we cannot help reverencing the spiritual for the reason that it is the highest, it is the most enduring, it is the most godlike. All else will some day fall away from us, but spirituality is an undying characteristic. To legislate for a woman first of all as a being endowed with intellect, sensibilities, and will, is the truest way to legislate. To educate her because she has these characteristics is the noblest way in which to give her an education. To think of her in these categories helps him who thinks more than the thought of her can help him otherwise. The whole intention of the woman movement is not to declare the rights of women, or to usurp power, or to alienate men, but on the contrary it is to unite men and women on the most enduring plane; to study the harmonies between them; to prove that their interests are indissolubly linked; and it is a far more scientific, sensible, and Christian way of dealing with one half of the human race, because it is equally in the interest of the two halves.

These are the two lines along which the great argument proceeds: Conservatives say, "Let man have his virtues and woman hers;" Progressives answer, "Let each add to those already won the virtues of the other." Man has splendid qualities, courage, intellect, hardihood; who would not like to possess all these? What woman would not be the nobler and the greater if they were hers? And what man would not be grander, happier, more helpful to humanity, if he were more patient, gentle, tender, chaste?

The frowns of fate are but the smiles of God. Woman's high development is impossible except through the struggle not only to be but to become. She has always excelled in being; she is learning that becoming is part of the price and well-nigh all of the power. She is learning the greatness and sacredness of power, that there is nothing noble in desiring not to possess it, but that to evolve the utmost mastership of one's self and the elements around one's self that can be is, to the individual, the highest possible attainment, if only these forces are used in the spirit of the utmost beneficence toward whatever has life, no matter if it be as lowly as a blossom or as high as a seraph, for life should have as its ultimate to bless all other lives.

Jennie Fowler Willing

CHAPTER 5

SHARED FIRE

*The Flame Ignited
by Jennie Fowler Willing*

JOANNE   CARLSON   BROWN

James Wm. McClendon, in his book *Biography as Theology*, speaks of the importance of having a singular or striking life available to truly understand and be able to examine the convictions of a community or group. These striking lives serve to embody the communal convictions while at the same time pushing those boundaries.[1] So it is with the continuity between spirituality, activism, and vocation. Many women could be used as an example of this union of faith and action, but none perhaps has the breadth of experience of Jennie Fowler Willing, a committed Methodist and reformer. Willing is a significant representative to examine because she was active in almost every important reform movement of the late nineteenth century, wrote many books and essays, and was acknowledged during her lifetime as a spokeswoman for Methodist women.

Frances Willard, one of the most famous Methodist women and long-time president of the Woman's Christian Temperance Union, wrote of Willing: "The life of aimless reverie must be replaced by the life of resolute aim—so said a teacher once, addressing her girl pupils. If I had chosen to bring forward an illustration of the last half of the antithesis, I could not have done better than to name the gifted woman whose pen and brain picture I here present."[2]

Jennie Fowler Willing was born January 22, 1834, in Burford, Canada West, what is now Ontario, and died October 6, 1916, at the age of eighty-two. She was one of three children born to Horatio and Harriet Ryan Fowler. Because of Horatio Fowler's involvement in the Papineau Rebellion, her family had to flee Canada, finally settling in Newark, Illinois. Willing was largely self-educated because of ill health, which plagued her from childhood.

In 1853 Jennie married William Crossgrove Willing, a Methodist Episcopal pastor. They moved to New York to begin their ministry in the

Genessee Conference. William and Jennie viewed their marriage as a partnership of equals. He supported Jennie in all her endeavors. William wrote to his wife, expressing these very modern observations:

> We men are a selfish lot. Everyone of us will avail himself of the help in evangelistic or temperance work that some other man's wife can give, but it is quite another thing when it comes to having our comfort interfered with. We may say the Lord's Prayer till we are black in the face, but until we are ready to sacrifice our own heart's joy for his work the kingdom will not come. We hang back, like great babies and make it wretchedly hard for the women who are called to public service. Everybody pities me because you leave me alone so much. I don't know whether they think I'm too delicate, or that I can't be trusted to stay alone. If I were a bishop, or a brakeman on a freight-train, or anybody between the two, I might leave you months at a time, and nobody would make a fuss about it.[3]

This realized ideal did much to shape Jennie's thought and work. William and Jennie were caught in the holiness battle, which erupted in the Genessee Conference in the 1850s between the Free Methodists of Benjamin Roberts and the Buffalo "Regency" which upheld the status quo. The Willings both professed conversion and sanctification, but this seemed to place them on the side with the Free Methodists, a place they did not want to be. Worn out by the controversy, they transferred to the Rock River Conference (Illinois) in 1860.

Jennie became publicly active in church work and reform first through the mission movement. In 1869 she was chosen as one of the first corresponding secretaries of the Woman's Foreign Missionary Society of The Methodist Episcopal Church, a post she held for fourteen years. She was responsible for organizing and coordinating the work of the society from the state of Ohio to the Pacific Ocean. Willing was enormously successful in this task. By the end of her fourteen years as secretary every district had at least one WFMS. She was also a devotional leader and consummate fund-raiser for the society. She wrote regularly for the society's paper, *The Heathen Woman's Friend.* (See document 1.)

While she was actively working as corresponding secretary of the WFMS, a second calling claimed her. Her lifelong study and writing had earned her the reputation of being a very learned woman. Even though she had no college degree, Jennie was awarded an honorary Master of English Literature in 1867 by Jennings Seminary in Aurora, Illinois, and an honorary Master of Arts by the Evanston College for Ladies at their first commencement exercises in 1872. In 1874, Willing was named Professor of English Language and Literature at Illinois Wesleyan University in Bloomington. William was presiding elder of the Rockford district, which enabled them to be together. At Wesleyan she helped organize the Women's Education

Association. Its purposes were to raise funds for an endowed chair to be filled by a woman and to provide a home where inexpensive board and a safe atmosphere could be given the women who were studying at the university.

While Willing was teaching at Wesleyan, the temperance crusade reached Bloomington. Although reluctant at first because of the time constraints, she joined the crusade.

> I was teaching in the Illinois Wesleyan University in Bloomington when the crusade struck that city. My Great Heart came in one day with a strange gladness in his face, a gladness touched by apprehension, as if he shrank from what it all might mean to that particular household. "The crusade is here at last," he said in his strong, quiet way. "The ladies are to have a meeting tomorrow, and they want you to come."
>
> I laughed a little, somewhat nervously, at the preposterousness of my going to any sort of meeting outside of the college. I, who had not time to get a dress or a pair of shoes fitted, except by proxy, with all the English in the University on my hands. How could I have anything to do with this grand crusade? In spite of my laughing, the tears would come. "No I can't go. Oh, if only I could, for God is in this work!" "I wouldn't give up yet," said my brave, self-giving friend. "I do hope you can have something to do with this wonderful work of God. He can make time for it if He wants you to have a little part in it."
>
> And He did. I led a temperance meeting every day for weeks until we carried the town, or city of 10,000 for no license. And then we organized the State Union and at Chatauqua we issued a call for the Cleveland Convention and organized the NWCTU. All this was brought about by a few women who knew themselves to be nothing, but who trusted God to take the things that are not to bring to naught the things that are.[4]

Willing was elected president of the local woman's temperance league. Under her leadership the league helped carry Bloomington for "no license." She was invited to deliver an address on women and temperance at the Chatauqua Assembly Grounds in August of 1874. Many present were moved to start a national society to work for temperance. Willing chaired those early organizing meetings, which issued the call for women to gather in Cleveland in November 1874 to constitute the new group. Presiding at the November meeting where the National Woman's Christian Temperance Union was formed, she declined national office but agreed to edit the Union's first paper, *The Woman's Temperance Union*. At the end of a year, with the paper firmly established, Jennie handed over the editorial reins to Margaret Winslow. She remained active in the Union all her life and left half her estate to it.

But no matter what else she was involved in, Willing's concern for mission work was ever present. She was not among the initial founders of the

Woman's Home Missionary Society but was hired in 1884 to be the General Organizer of the Society. She was the only salaried officer and was paid $1,000 a year. Holding the post for two years, she then moved to abolish the position because the auxiliaries were now capable of doing the work. Jennie became a vice-president, and was later named Secretary of the Bureau for Spanish Work from 1886 to 1890 and then Secretary of the Bureau for Immigrants from 1890 to 1894.

Jennie not only worked to organize mission work, she was also actively involved in it. The Willings left Bloomington in 1876 to focus more fully on mission work. They served several charges in Chicago. In 1890 they followed the call to further service, which guided them to New York City. William died four years later. In 1895 Jennie opened the New York Training School and Settlement House in Hell's Kitchen. It was financed completely with her own resources. There Willing could combine all her causes—temperance, missions, education, and holiness. She taught, preached, wrote, and edited a magazine called *The Open Door*. The Training School was closed in 1910 when the property was leveled to build the Pennsylvania Railroad Station.

Little is known of the last five years of her life. She remained in New York and continued to write, though her output slowed considerably. At the time of her death at the age of eighty-two, Willing was president emeritus of the 18th Street Methodist Episcopal Church WFMS, president of the Frances Willard WCTU of New York City, and organizer for the New York State WCTU. Her obituary appeared in the *New York Times* and in the *Christian Advocate*. Dying on October 6, 1916, Willing was buried beside her "Great Heart" in Greenwood Cemetery in Brooklyn under a simple stone that bears only her name and dates.

Jennie Fowler Willing was a woman of sincere convictions, boundless energies, and an intense desire to make the world a better place in which to live. Her driving force was her undivided commitment to her Lord Jesus Christ. She was aided in her work by this commitment, the influence of her parents, and the support and encouragement of her husband. She put her energies into writing, preaching, speaking, teaching, and organizing movements that would aid her goal of bringing in the Kingdom. For Willing the questions of what to do, what to feel, what to teach, and how to teach were inseparable.

Willing was a Holiness Methodist, reflecting that movement's theology in all she wrote and did. She emphasized complete surrender to a loving God who in return would infuse one with the energy, strength, and courage needed to work to transform the world into what God created it to be—a place of freedom, justice, and equality for all people. Willing believed in Entire Sanctification and Christian Perfection. Willing took these concepts from John Wesley, and her understandings of these experiences were representative of Methodists of the day. By sanctification and Christian perfection, Willing meant that a person's will was one with God's will so that the person would do and be what God wanted the person to do and be without needing to think about it. It was Wesley's concept of faith and holy living. One is grasped by the radical love of God and there can be no other authentic response but love of God and of God's people in return.

Willing urged people to strive for sanctification, and she claimed it for herself and others whom she knew. (See document 2.) Jennie recognized that sanctification was not a permanent state but something to be worked for every day.

> Tempted? Why I thought you people who profess to be fully given to the Lord were a way beyond that. If you think, my friend, it is possible to get out of reach of temptation, this side of the world of glory, you can't have read your Bible to very good purpose.[5]

Willing believed that every reformer had to have a clear conversion. Through this "heart purity," the reformer would discern God's will and gather strength from which to act. It was impossible not to respond to the needs once one had been "awakened." Willing used the parable of the good Samaritan to illustrate the principle.

> The lesson of social obligation taught in this parable may be formulated something in this way: the knowledge of need and the ability to meet it lay upon one a responsibility commensurate with his power to serve. It is not optional with us to help those who need our aid. There is an obligation upon us as sacred and binding as it is possible for any to be, because it is one that grows out of the nature of our relation to others, and it is laid upon us by God himself.[6]

Willing's reforms and work were scripturally and theologically grounded. She wanted all people's work to be so based. Willing was a folk theologian; that is, she did not create new and different theologies. Rather she took the basic doctrines of Holiness Methodism and interpreted them to the folk, the laypeople who she thought were the real church. Jennie emphasized Christ's role as the only Lord and Master of anyone's life. The importance of millennial ideas and convictions is evident all through her writings. The Bible was an essential tool and guide for all Christians. Although she held to the inerrancy of scripture and rejected biblical criticism, Willing interpreted passages according to her beliefs and for her own social purposes. Her main concern was that all people know and understand the tenets of the faith. Only then could they truly have the conviction of their faith to help God in bringing in the Kingdom. (See documents 3 and 5.)

Kingdom-building was behind her stress on education. Willing was not interested in education for education's sake. Nor did she urge women to obtain an education merely to get ahead. As people became informed and educated, they would be led to a firmer conviction of the needs of the world and a stronger commitment to their task of fulfilling those needs. This stress is demonstrated in her introduction of the monthly reading circles in the WFMS. The more people knew, the better off the world would be.

Willing worked for education not only as a teacher but also as a writer, editor, and speaker. Writing allowed her to reach many more people than she could touch personally. She could bring the full weight of her literary reputation to bear on the problems of society. As editor and publisher of *The Open Door,* she brought together all her causes in one magazine for a combined frontal attack on the evils of this world. Jennie was in great demand as a speaker and evangelist. It is impossible to make a distinction between these two roles in Willing's life. Every day of her life was dedicated to serving God as God saw fit. Her messages, whether dealing with temperance, slums, missions, or women, had as their base her Lord Jesus Christ.

Willing wanted the world to be better, but she had her own ideas on how that could happen.

> The subject race must be made to comprehend its own dignity. The principle violated in human servitude is the inherent greatness of humanity, and they who are under can be trusted to rise to equality or superiority only as they apprehend this principle. Without that apprehension, a change of position would be only a change of tyrannies. To lift up a man or a race, one need not trouble himself to make the oppressor understand the worth of the slave. Let him teach the slave his own dignity and trust him to make his master comprehend that lesson. The liberator must also see so plainly the tremendous import of human life, that he will go down among the oppressed and share the obloquy of their wrongs, sustained by his belief in the intrinsic human royalty.[7]

She worked for justice, equality, and freedom for all, but believed that these would come only through adhering to Protestant American virtues and beliefs. Willing's was not an irrational prejudice. She attacked groups such as the Mormons, Catholics, and foreigners because of the inhumanity and inequality she perceived them to foster. Her main criterion for judgment of a society or group was the position of women. She could be withering in her critiques, of foreign nations such as India for example, for their treatment of women, but she rarely turned that same sharp critique on Protestantism or America. She occasionally admitted that all was not perfect in this nation, "God's last great hope," but she blamed this imperfection on the lack of purity of heart in the land, not on intrinsic deficiencies in either Protestantism or American ideals.

Willing viewed herself as a "Social Christian," championing the poor and urging the rich to right use of their wealth.

> Let all come to the plain, simple, unostentatious style of living that becomes the true followers of the crucified Nazarene, and temptations to over-eat, over-work, over-reach, and oppress the poor, sins that drive people into dishonesty and ruin, would be easily overcome. . . . Social complications, wrongs, and outrages are the rule among the unsaved, take them from ocean to ocean, and from pole to pole. If everyone would "walk worthy of the Lord, unto all pleasing" loving his neighbor as himself, Christian Socialism would bring in at once the blessed universal truce of God.[8]

Jennie worked for temperance because she saw the misuse of alcohol as a significant cause of poverty and abuse. When challenged on why she concentrated on temperance when there were so many problems, her response was that intemperance was the basis of all other crimes. "All the people who live by the vices of others depend upon liquor to draw their victims into their power. If we can conquer this, we may be able to manage the rest."[9]

Reformers like Willing have been criticized for their work on issues such as temperance and evangelism because these issues seem to be such "conservative" or traditional causes. Women religious reformers are specifically cited in these critiques, accused of sacrificing their cause on the altar of "true womanhood." Ann Douglas is a good example of this kind of critique. In her book, *The Feminization of American Culture*, Douglas raises this question: "Both exalted and ignored, was the lady the saving of her nation or the slave to an unappreciative master?"[10] Douglas is not speaking specifically of Willing but does refer to the group in which Willing would be classified. Willing would have responded with a resounding "yes" to the first option and a resounding "no" to the second. Willing did not condone women being slaves to anyone or anything. She worked to free women from the bondage of custom and caste.

Willing affirmed that women were capable of running their own benevolences and resisted the efforts to subordinate the women's societies to the general church (male-led) societies. Women had only one Lord and Master and that was Jesus Christ. No man had jurisdiction over any woman. Women were to be obedient to only one call—that of God and Christ. "The creator alone has authority to limit 'the sphere' of the attainment or activity of any human being. To His bar alone, all may appeal. 'Whom the Son maketh free, is free indeed!' That is the measure of the woman's liberty!"[11]

Willing emphasized the importance of each individual woman. No woman should shrink back because of lack of self-confidence or because it was not fitting for women to work openly and in public. She was very effective in this aspect of her work. The women and groups she addressed, whether in person or in writing, were urged to recognize the responsibilities and obligations each woman bore. No one else would do the work if she did not. Willing stressed each woman's capability and responsibility. Each woman was needed. Her technique was to combine this individual effort with group effort in such a way that the individual was not lost. The nation needed saving and women were the ones who would save it. Women were the slaves of no master, not even an appreciative one. They were free workers for and with their Master—Mary's Son—the best friend women had.

Willing was a grass-roots organizer. All people had to be reached and had to feel the need to work. It was more important for 5,000 women to give two cents a year than for one woman to give a hundred dollars. Organizing helped the people to whom the efforts were directed and also helped the women who were organizing. It gave them a sense of themselves, their capabilities and strengths, and also nourished a "sisterhood of shared fire" available nowhere else. "The pledge to band praying women together, helps all concerned. . . . The women who have joined hands for special prayer, bearing one another's burdens, are freer to pray for those to whom they are not personally related . . . we never get greater blessings from God, than when we are trying to help others walk more closely with him. All social reforms are wrought by this rule."[12] (See document 4.)

Jennie Fowler Willing was many things—an organizer, a reformer, an educator, a social commentator, a writer, a speaker, and an editor. All these facets of her life are important. One role, however, far outweighs the others. Willing was first and foremost a Christian. All of her other activities were based on her Christian conviction and her call from God. This overriding principle guided all her life, shaping her work, her outlook, and, through her, the society in which she lived.

Willing wrote advice on many subjects. A great deal of it stemmed from her own personal experiences. Early in her career she wrote an article on how to succeed and achieve. This article was written in 1868, a year before she began her active involvement in any of her causes. It is fitting to use the criteria of the young Willing to evaluate her life and career. Willing listed four elements that aided success and achievement:

1. Think out something that the world needs. The more you help, the more you will be thought of. Do not overlook it because it is so simple.
2. A prime element of success is work.

3. Forget yourself in your effort. Keep yourself safe from silly sensitiveness.
4. You must trust God to make way for you.[13]

In all that Willing did she held these principles before her. Her work for missions, both foreign and home; her work for temperance; her labor for women's rights; and her concern for better conditions for the poor—all these were things the world needed. Through each of these causes, reformers worked for the betterment of humanity. And for Willing each of these efforts was God-led and, indeed, God-demanded. She responded and worked, not shunning simple or lowly tasks, and she urged others not to either. The work at hand was to bring in the kingdom of God. All had to work for this goal or the Kingdom would be delayed in coming. Willing put many hours and days and years into her work. Her family life was important to her but her Lord and Master had the higher claim. In all her work she did not seek to further her individual importance. Each and every worker was essential—none better and none worse than another. The cause, the work, was supremely important. One did what one could, where and when one could, not shrinking from a task because of its lesser importance. Willing's highest principle, the one that overshadowed all others, was the absolute need to put complete trust in God. Anything was possible with God's guidance and aid. "Either God's will can be done, or it cannot. If it is done arbitrarily, we are free from responsibility; and there is nothing for us, but the moral helplessness, and imbecility of perpetual babyhood. If power can be given us to co-operate with the Divine will, let us see to it that we begin at once to 'mend our ways.'"[14] Willing firmly believed that all the goals of her causes were attainable if all those involved placed themselves completely in God's hands in trust and love.

Jennie Fowler Willing had a strong impact on society and yet she was all but forgotten by history. There are several possible reasons for this. Willing was not "the" dominant personality in any of the organizations in which she worked. That style of leadership was antithetical to everything she believed. She also worked in some causes that are almost an embarrassment to modern church people: mission work, with its connotations of cultural genocide; temperance, which many look upon as a prudish, unrealistic attempt to dictate one's own morals to others; and the Christian Socialist movement, with its emphasis on the kingdom of God to be realized here and now; and an idealistic view of humanity, accused of being naive. But all of these were causes appropriate for a nineteenth-century woman in a society that had not achieved for women the full equality and freedom and respect Willing knew God intended. Moreover, she did her work well. It was her unassuming style of leadership that proved unable to excite extended historical comment. Willing has slipped into what Horace Bushnell, in *Moral Uses of Dark Things,* called the dead history of oblivion.

"Dead history consists of those deeds and people which live on in their unrecognized influence rather than in the articulated memories of their fellows."[15]

Willing was known and respected by her peers. But that remembrance died with her generation. Still, she represents an important segment of Methodist and women's history. She had a decided influence on those around her and the society in which she lived. She and the women and men whom she influenced shaped the society in which we live. We cannot afford dead history.

Willing was aware of her debt to God and to the ones who had gone before. She helps awaken us to our debt, exhorting us to affirm the continuity between spirituality and activism. And she has provided us with the perfect metaphor for this bond—shared fire. It embraces her vocational vision, a vision of transformed people working together and with God to transform the world. In true Methodist calling it is a vocational vision of spreading scriptural holiness to reform the nation.

> There may be cases of spontaneous combustion in missionary zeal, but the rule is that we must borrow fire. One has to kindle another. The more we lend the more we have left. Nothing warms us up like trying to warm those who are chillier than ourselves. They may not want us to bother them. We dislike to crowd people in matters of conscience, so the work is not done. We grow selfish. The poor perish. Christianity is neglected. The Spirit is grieved. God's work suffers irreparably. The neglected women of our land will not be saved till every Christian woman does her best. Somebody must crowd into favored homes and let fortunate women know how the others live. . . . When we lend our fire . . . it is hard to tell which burns most brightly, the lender or the borrower.[16]

In Jennie Fowler Willing's vocational vision and faith, the continuity between spirituality and activism is a fire-bond, which will set the world ablaze for justice if we will but learn from our foremothers and sisters and share the fire.

DOCUMENTS

1. A Call to the Church. Jennie Fowler Willing was active in the Woman's Foreign Missionary Society of The Methodist Episcopal Church from its beginning. Not only was she Corresponding Secretary, but she wrote much of the material for the Society's magazine, *Heathen Woman's Friend.* This selection is from the first year of that magazine and reflects not only her attitude toward women's vocation but also calls on the church to let the women work. It is also a clear reflection of the commitment she had to the Methodist church.

The Church and the world are infinitely indebted to Methodist women. The mother of the Wesleys has been called the Foundress of Methodism. She guided the hand of her son, helping him mould this immense enginery of salvation. Her intellectual culture and religious independence gave her decision and firmness, specially fitting for her work. When Wesley's imperious regard for Church precedent was likely to lead him to harm Christ's cause, she planted herself in his way, like the angel before Balaam. Lay preaching has been the driving wheel of Methodist machinery. Coming home from one of his tours, Wesley found that one of his laymen had been preaching at the Foundry. "Thomas Maxwell has turned preacher I find," he said to his mother with unusual abruptness. "Take care what you do respecting that young man" was her reply; "he is as certainly called of God to preach as you are." Thus she held him from throwing the band off the driving wheel. She approved his field preaching, when the authorities of the Church condemned it. She stood by his side, on Kennington Common, while he preached to twenty thousand people.

Selina, Countess Huntington, stood next to Susannah Wesley in influence upon the mighty revival of evangelism that swept over the British empire. She had access to the nobility, the court, and the royal family; and it is impossible to estimate the result of her work for Christ.

It was the hand of a Methodist woman that launched the Sunday-school craft. Robert Raikes' name wears the honor of originating this work, but Stevens gives it to Hannah Ball, a young Methodist woman, who established a school in Wycombe, England. Twelve years after, another, afterward the wife of the celebrated lay preacher, Samuel Bradburn, suggested the Sunday-school work to Raikes, in Gloucester, and helped him form his first school.

Barbara Heck opened the Methodist campaign in the New World. Phoebe Palmer has led thousands of souls to Christ, and helped the Church immeasurably in the higher life. The best the Church can give women, in return for this zeal and sacrifice, is a chance to work.

How can Methodist women live indolent, muck-worm, fashion-enslaved lives, with such examples before them, and such opportunities to do good as crowd upon them? Opportunity makes obligation. We cannot innocently be idle. God will require at our hands the blood of those who perish for lack of knowledge.[17]

2. What Consecrated Women Are Doing. The *Guide to Holiness* was a magazine founded by Phoebe and William Palmer to further the cause of Holiness throughout the land. In the 1890s Willing was asked to write regular columns for the magazine, having been a popular contributor for years. One of her regular columns was "Woman in Gospel Evangelism." She took as her overall theme for this column Joel 2:28-29. She selected topics relating to women and their work for the church and the world. She lifted up historical and biblical women as examples and exhorted her contemporaries to follow suit, to heed the call of their Lord and Master, to pick up their vocational vision and walk. The following selection is from the first of these columns.

It was a wise thought, and so of God, for the Editor of this time-honored magazine to set apart two pages of each number for a glance over the fields where women are at work for our Lord.

It will be a pleasant duty to speak to the sweet and gentle, the queenly and strong who are giving their very life's life to hasten the Coming of the Kingdom.

This will not be done to give the workers due recognition. That is a paltry reward in a world that shouted "Hosanna" one day, and "Crucify Him" the next. There is risk that one may work a life-time, and not hear a single "Bravo," but there is greater risk of the woe that is threatened when all men speak well of you.

We hope this writing will inspire new workers to trust for the "greater things." Seeing what was done when the way was rougher, and the obstacles more obdurate, they will seek to be filled with the Holy Ghost and with faith, that much people may be added to the Lord. Many a young woman in the repressed, isolated life of a country home, will turn over the pages of the *Guide* to this department. She will hardly sleep for joy when she reads how the Lord took Phoebe Palmer from her quiet, busy life and many family cares, as He took David from following the sheep, and made her a teacher of millions. Many a frail, timid woman will take heart when she sees how Catherine Booth, in delicate health, with a nestful of little children, and narrow means, became through perfectly obedient faith, the greatest human being of the century, more honored of God than any other in the salvation of the neglected. She will set her needle more steadily at her Sysiphus task of mending and hold her soul more firmly to its consecration; for no one can tell what God will yet do by her.

The women who read what has been done will see by the light that flares out against the darkness that a thousand times more help ought to be given to those who perish in their sins. Finding that there remaineth so much more land to be possessed they will gird on their armor and take the sword of the Spirit, determined to make every hour of time, every dollar of money, every ounce of strength, all talent, culture and influence tell in bringing this lost world back to God.

It will glorify our Lord who has counted women worthy, putting them into this service. It will help the silent two-thirds of the Church to see that there is a place for them in the ranks. It will call this reserve corps into active duty. It will relieve the overtaxed one-third, those who are expected by our social customs to exhaust their brain on business cares, leaving only outworn energy to give to great benevolent and philanthropic schemes. It will help women who grieve over the heavy burdens that are bound on their husbands' shoulders, burdens that they themselves have not dared to touch with one of their fingers; it will give them the hint to put aside some of the petty exactions of society and level up the loads of benevolence by sharing their weight. There may be less mince pie to tear to tatters [as] the household slumbers, but there will be more drunkards and heathen saved, and more homes held in comfort by keeping the wage earners from premature breakdown.

All this in obedience to the Lord's command, "Pray ye therefore the Lord of the harvest that He would send forth laborers into His harvest." With this belief I gladly set pen to paper, trusting God to make this department a great blessing to the consecrated women who are the majority of the readers of the *Guide*. Will not every woman whose eyes rest on these pages pray that this effort may help thousands "out into the work."

The woman who received the miraculous supply of oil with which to pay her debt, was told to borrow vessels of her neighbors. As long as she furnished vessels the oil flowed. If she had arranged for a succession, and her successors had kept on borrowing, perhaps the oil would be flowing yet, and all the world would be filled with its richness. Phoebe Palmer and Catherine Booth were not content to get a supply for themselves and their own families, their faith and love took in the whole earth. At the noon hour of prayer let us ask our Lord that the holy anointing may be given to all consecrated women the world over, and that each may do her very best for God.[18]

3. Woman and the Pentecost. Willing was a Holiness Methodist. She believed deeply that people who had been grasped by the love and the spirit of God were transformed. They had "heart purity." This would lead them into service for their Lord. For Willing this was especially true for women. Willing felt that the Bible was women's Magna Charta and that Jesus was the best friend women ever had. But to whom much has been given, much is required. In an article appearing in the *Guide to Holiness*, Willing makes this position clear as she calls women to recognize their gifts and their responsibilities, to hear their call to work for the church, the world, and the coming of the Kingdom. This call will also enable women to challenge unjust societal restrictions on their activities. The love of God restores all to their rightful place—on equal footing—knowing their own worth and value and vocation.

Our Lord said, "It is more blessed to give than to receive." It is not in human nature to desire always to take and never to give. It is not in regenerate nature to receive great benefits, even from God, without making some effort at return. Divine love must move one to want others to become partakers of like precious faith. The grace that has saved us from ten thousand sorrows will save in like manner all who sit in the region of the shadow of death. One who has received that grace can do no less than desire that all be lifted to the joy of self respect and Divine fellowship.

A woman may look out hopelessly over the wide sea of great endeavor, and say in her helpless sorrow, "If I were a man, I might row out into the teeth of the gale and rescue the perishing; but what can I do now?—a woman fettered and hampered by unjust restrictions. I see small chance to use the ability I do have. I could not attack the great evils that are in the way of Christ's Kingdom."

This writing may not be in vain if it serves to strengthen the weak hands and confirm the feeble knees. . . .

Women are seeking broad opportunities and setting their earnest, loving hearts against the world's great need. Their day has dawned at last. The battles that are now to be fought are in the moral realm. The weapons we use are not carnal, but spiritual. They are in reach of the weakest hand, and are mighty through God to the pulling down of strongholds.

No one can deny women the privilege of living in such union with Christ that they may ask what they will and it shall be given them. In filling this pitiful world with Pentecostal light and glory, each may bear her full, unhindered part.

Each must begin by living the Pentecostal life. Women are one-half the human race. Christian women are more than one-half of Christendom. If they could be brought to receive the full enduement of Divine power, the weight of Christian influence would be thrown at once upon the side of holy living. . . .

We complain of the coldness of the Church. Yet each of us is responsible for the spiritual condition of one Church member. If every woman who desires the prosperity of Christ's cause would go at once to Him and receive the enduement of power, at one stroke two-thirds of the Church would be brought into the full fellowship of the Holy Spirit. Let the two-thirds of the Christian Church who are now regarded as the most devout and reliable be brought into the Pentecostal life, and the whole body would be lifted to a higher plane.

In these later and wiser days hundreds of thousands of women are working in religious and philanthropic societies. Their achievements for missions, temperance, purity, and kindred causes during the last quarter of a century read like a fairy tale. If one had prophesied forty years ago of all this work which has now become as commonplace as the steam cars and telegraph, he would have been set down as a first-class fanatic.

All the great organizations of women have grown out of the Pentecostal power falling on little companies who are ready to risk everything for the salvation of souls. Each began with the baptism of the Holy Spirit. Let the thousands who are now at work in them receive the anointing that forgets all in earnestness for the Lord, and the advance of the work will be immeasurable. The power that carried the machinery of these societies through the slow, timid, difficult movement of getting under way, would increase its present efficiency a thousand fold. Those organizations seem sometimes to yield to the general human tendency to drift away from the first deep spirituality that gave them birth, and become worldly, selfish, and bigoted. The Church has had to be taken through terrible persecutions to keep it clean and humble.

When the conversion of Constantine made Rome the world's ecclesiastical capital, the Church lost its simplicity, lowered its standard of holy living, and began to cater to the tastes of the rich and great. Its decline in spiritual life emphasized the universal human trait. Women are human, so they are not exempt from the general risk of failure through prosperity.

Just as we feel that the Church needs a general Pentecostal revival, so are we sure that missionary, temperance and all other women workers must have the outpouring of the Spirit of the Lord to help them know their hour of opportunity and measure up to its possibilities.

It is quite right for us to seek the broadest fields of service; but let us see to it that we are faithful over a few things. Then we can safely be made rulers over the many . . .

Since women owe everything to the Pentecost, not one of them ought to do less than use all energy and strength to win every soul the wide world over to know and trust the Holy Spirit for the fulness of His power to save.[19]

4. The Reapers. Willing followed this general call with specific articles on how women needed to work, and, by focusing on specific women, such as Susannah Wesley, she illustrated this Pentecostal life and fire. Willing was a progressive and as such was convinced that the nineteenth century was God's best century, particularly for women. In this article, Willing runs through a sweep of history to show how we have arrived where we are today as consecrated women and to point out what our duty is because of this activity of God working on behalf of women and their full participation in the work of the Kingdom.

The women who are doing strong work for Christ have been sent into the field by the Lord of the harvest during the closing years of the last best century . . .

Among the organized bodies of women working for Christ, it was most fitting that the Woman's Foreign Missionary Society should lead the van. At great cost to themselves, and without fee or reward, the "missionary women" set about letting Christ's light in upon the darkness of their heathen sisters, and unexpectedly to themselves, they greatly increased their own privileges. They worked night and day, and often with great self-denial, to gather the facts that had lain about unheeded, setting forth the pitiful condition of pagan women, and to pick up the "two cents a week," that would give the Gospel of Christ's freedom to the poor, trampled, hopeless creatures. All doors flew open before them. Every noble, greathearted pastor welcomed them into his pulpit to arouse the women of his congregation to care for the women of heathen lands.

After thirty years of simply gleaning after the reapers, they are able to face a pledge to raise half a million for their work in the first year of the Twentieth Century. Their workers are treated with the utmost attention and respect by all who appreciate good Christian service. . . . The gracious, unselfish work for the salvation of the hopelessly oppressed, that the missionary women have done has greatly broadened their own field of activity.

The same may be said of the Woman's Home Missionary Society, The Woman's Christian Temperance Union, the Young Woman's Christian Association, the Woman's Sabbath Alliance, the King's Daughters, the Mother's Clubs, Assemblies and Congresses, and all the rest. Each of these great organizations originated in the earnest purpose of a few godly women to so save time, strength and money, that their beautiful, blessed home work might be even better done than before, while all the small economies of talent, means and opportunity might be brought to bear, in the name of the Lord on some gigantic evil. It is the old story of the shepherd boy and the Philistine champion. In the "name of the Lord of Hosts" they have done exploits. They have helped hundreds of millions into a better life, and this work all within thirty years, wrought by those who have done not only "what they could," but "what they thought they couldn't." . . .

The broadening of the field and increase of activity bring added ability. So all this new work by new workers has multiplied greatly the effectiveness of the Lord's force. We live in practical days. The question is not how exquisitely, or how magnificently one may do a thing, but does it bring anything to pass that gives plain plodding common sense the advantage in the race with butterfly sentimentalism? . . .

Large-souled, thoughtful women may now consecrate themselves fully to the Lord and be filled with His fulness. They will find their usefulness as wide as their ability: the approval of good people as genial as the Master's love: their sense of glad service as sweet as His smile: and the eternal fruitage as glorious as Paradise.[20]

5. *Dorcas, the Friend of the Poor.* A number of people in the nineteenth century wrote books about women in the Bible. Willing's contribution to this literature is similar to the majority of these in that it selected specific women from the Hebrew and Christian Testaments to use as examples on which women should pattern their lives. Willing's examples are used to demonstrate the need to be about the work of God in the world despite worldly or church prejudice. She uses her women to exhort others to learn from their foremothers how to be faithful to God's call even in a hostile environment. The following selection is taken from her chapter on Dorcas. Willing uses Dorcas as an example of an ordinary woman who did not want or seek leadership but quietly worked in her own way for the poor, God's people. She exemplifies, for Willing, the task of the majority of Christian women—staying at home and responding to the needs around them. In this selection, Willing's vocational and spiritual values and goals are prominent.

Dorcas was the happiest of women. She was not called to long, hard voyages, like Phoebe, nor to difficult teaching, like Priscilla, nor to evangelistic work, like Philip's "four daughters which did prophesy," nor to the tremendously heroic deeds required of the good women of the Old Testament. She could stay at home, in her own town, among her own people, and use her needle for the poor. . . .

Possibly Dorcas had disturbing dreams of broader usefulness when she heard how wonderfully God used others for the salvation of souls; but she settled back to her needle, and her poor folk, with a belief that she was in His hands, and He had put her to work where she was most needed; she was content to do His will, and leave Him to make the most of her small service.

She was always busy. Idleness is a cruel enemy. It leaves one at the mercy of every one who would get her into mischief. It is so great a comfort to be always active, and so to seem of some account, that people have even been known to bustle about, hither and thither, under the pretense of great activity, when in reality, they were of small use in the world, because they did not make the most of themselves for the sake of others. . . .

She had no time for the "blues"—another name for self-pity. So many needed her help, it left her no time to worry about herself, because she could not do, be, have this, that, and the other fine thing; but she flew around from morning till night, lifting burdens, and scattering blessings—a joy to see.

Her work was appreciated, even by worldly people. They pitied the poor enough to give a trifle of their abundance; and they were glad that Dorcas made it go as far as possible. Their social functions were so many, so exhausting, and so expensive, they could not worry themselves with personal attentions to the unfortunate. They never missed their small contributions; and they were ready to pat Dorcas on the shoulder, for using the self-sacrifice that was not at all to their taste for themselves.

The church thought well of her. It began its work among the lowly, and it succeeded in proportion as it cared for those whom God had chosen, the "poor of this world, rich in faith." Most of its membership were from among the neediest who were glad to get the little upward lift, and the help of a woman like Dorcas . . .

A poor woman said to one of our Hell's Kitchen Settlement workers, "It isn't so much food and clothing that we want, as it is folks." When Dorcas came into their cabins, they felt that a friend had come, one who did not look at them mechanically, as so many census items, "cases" that had to be dealt with; but one who loved them as if they belonged to her; weeping with those who wept and rejoicing with those who rejoiced. She was one of their "folks." . . .

Dorcas did her work for love of the Lord; and the Book has plenty of promises for those who care for the poor, for Christ's sake. She did not work by proxy, supporting some one to do what she, herself, needed to do for the good of her soul, not giving a dollar now and then, while she spent thousands in luxury and display; but for love of Christ, and in His name, doing to others, as she would have them do to her, if circumstances were reversed, as they might be, any day, if an earthquake or a great fire came along.

There was hardly the weary lifting of an eyelid in self-pity, when Dorcas had gone through a heavy day's work, for our Lord had seen it all, and knew that every stitch had been for Him. She had been doing what He bade, and as He had ordered, hoping to receive nothing in return. It was all set down in the Bank, to the "Inasmuch" account.[21]

Anna Oliver

CHAPTER 6

EVANGELISM AND SOCIAL REFORM IN THE PASTORAL MINISTRY OF ANNA OLIVER, 1868–1886

KENNETH E. ROWE

Many remember Anna Oliver (1840–1892) as the first woman to graduate from a North American theological seminary (Boston University School of Theology, 1876) and as the woman who led an unsuccessful campaign for ordination in The Methodist Episcopal Church in 1880. Few know that before receiving her divinity degree Oliver had undertaken significant "ministries" in Connecticut, Georgia, and Ohio, and after her graduation and without ordination she pastored significant congregations in New Jersey and New York. Throughout her pioneering ministry her commitment to holiness theology, which stressed personal purity, did not preclude attention to matters of social reform and transforming unjust structures. This essay aims to tell that story.[1]

Anna Oliver was born near New Brunswick, New Jersey, April 12, 1840.[2] Oliver was not her family name; it was Snowden. Baptized Vivianna Olivia Snowden, she changed her name to Anna Oliver in the early 1870s so as not to embarrass her family when she decided to enter the ministry.[3] Her mother grew up in a Fifth Avenue mansion and received an upper-class education. Her father was a prosperous dry goods merchant in the small city in central New Jersey. When she was three years old, Snowden moved the family business to New York City to take advantage of an expanded clientele. His large family (four girls and two boys) took up residence first in Harrison, New Jersey (near Newark), and two years later in Brooklyn. Anna received a good education in Brooklyn's public schools. Her family attended an Episcopal parish church.

The Snowdens contemplated teaching as a career for their precocious daughter and sought to send her to college. The demand for female education coincided with rapid growth of common schools in the Northeast. Women were generally thought better suited than men to teach the young, and they would do it for less money. Together with Mt. Holyoke in

Massachusetts and Oberlin in Ohio, Rutgers Female College in New York City was the college of choice for women of the Northeast's elite. Anna and her family chose Rutgers, the school closest to home.[4] Anna completed the college course in 1859 and stayed on to take a Master of Arts degree with honors the next year, 1860. During her college years in New York City, Anna was introduced to the women's rights movement. She devoured the steady stream of feminist publications and attended public lectures by the movement's leaders.[5]

CONNECTICUT

In 1860 Arthur Snowden moved the family to a handsome suburban estate named "Cliffwood" in South Norwalk, Connecticut. Upon graduation Anna rejoined her family there and taught in an elementary school nearby. In addition to teaching, she took an active role in women's suffrage and dabbled in temperance work in her adopted state for the next eight years.

GEORGIA

In 1868 Anna volunteered to teach black children in Georgia under the auspices of the American Missionary Association, one of several secular and denominational societies providing education opportunities to freed men and women during the critical years following emancipation. Teachers were most often young, single, and from farming or professional families. The majority were women. Anna fit the AMA's profile for recruits—northern, white, young, female, educated, Protestant, self-sacrificing with antislavery and reform background. The society's hope was that black education would be a force to "northernize" the conquered South. Its curriculum sought the "improvement" of the blacks as people, emphasizing industry and self-reliance. Dedicated to traditional education, its staff also considered the "practical" disciplines essential for the black community. The "black curriculum" of the 1860s also contained propaganda for its sponsors' Unionist and civil-rights ideas.[6] Anna found racial integration a delicate question in her work. Believing that true "freedom" and "civilization" would depend on evangelical Christian content and direction, Anna energetically threw herself into her new assignment in the Storrs and Ayers schools in Atlanta.[7]

Conditions were horrifying: disease, malnutrition, poverty, critically insufficient funds, and inadequate facilities. And the hostility of southern white opposition was formidable. The Continental Insurance Company in New York declared AMA schools "hazardous" and refused to insure them because they were so frequently the target of arsonists. Some black students carried guns for self-protection, and the AMA actually shipped rifles to Talladega.

Two disappointments marred Anna's missionary endeavor—one pedagogical, the other personal. First, Anna had taught in Connecticut schools several years before going south. She filled her letters to the AMA headquarters with intricate descriptions of her attempts to employ the latest pedagogical techniques in her southern schoolroom. Although primitive facilities and a domineering male supervisor limited her success in this area, she demonstrated the type of self-confidence that comes from both specialized training and practical experience. Second, the society, always pressed for funds, paid female teachers less than men who did the same work. It opened no leadership positions to women in its southern schools or its New York City headquarters, and rationalized its position by stressing that teaching was missionary work. The women who wanted to join the cause should concentrate on "moral reform" and leave administrative matters to the men. The evangelical emphasis of the AMA only served to reinforce prevailing attitudes toward women as highly emotional, sensitive, and religious beings who by virtue of their maternal instincts were specially suited to teach young children. The association's call for "self-sacrificing" young females implied that these women should put the interest of "their work" above their own interests.

But Anna's idealism and firm conviction that she had a "great work" to do gave her a self-conscious, if not self-righteous, zeal that exacerbated the whole problem. Her sense of mission encouraged her to act with deliberation and speak out with conviction. Like other nineteenth-century female reformers, she sought to express herself within the boundary of benevolent activity and the womanly function of teaching. But, as Nancy Cott has suggested of female missionaries in general, "Religious commitment . . . proposed a submission of self that was simultaneously a pronounced form of self-assertion," and therein lay one source of conflict between men and women in freedmen's work.[8] This tension inspired a variety of group and individual responses on the part of the women, including refusals to obey guidelines that infringed on their ability to run their own classes as they saw fit and demands for salaries equal to those of male teachers.

There were considerable internal and other problems as well for the AMA educational mission in the post-war South. The AMA believed in racially inclusive institutions, but blacks preferred their own teachers, which placed them in agreement with southern whites who could not stand to see blacks and whites living, eating, and working together. The AMA was committed to interdenominationalism, but was pressured by supporters who wanted to see Congregational churches founded. The AMA wanted to focus on teaching teachers, but until the Reconstruction legislatures established public school systems, they had to provide for education at all levels. Perhaps the greatest internal problem, however, was the attempt of middle-class northern whites to impose their values and way of life on southern black communitarian folk culture. In speaking of the black churches, Joe M. Richardson points out that AMA workers never fathomed that the religion of the ex-slaves was about "joy and collective hope rather than personal guilt and self-denial."[9]

The grit of Yankee teachers like Anna bent on their "civilizing mission" made it possible for them to endure great hardship, but it had its negative side. Together with her supervisors and sister teachers, Anna's unreflective assurance in knowing what was right and the unstoppable compulsion in doing it were marred by human insensitivity and made her oblivious of the sin of self-righteousness.

Recent scholarly judgment on the appropriateness of the whole enterprise is mixed. Some interpreters, like Robert Butchart and Ronald Morris, are highly critical of the methods and motives of the northern educators.[10] More positive in their evaluation of the AMA's mission are Jacqueline Jones, Joe Richardson, and Allis Wolfe.

In her 1980 "collective biography," *Soldiers of Light and Love: Northern Teachers and Georgia Blacks 1862–1875,* Jacqueline Jones suggests that there is value in comparing the position of northern white women to that of newly freed black women and men in the South. Careful not to imply that sexism was, or is, analogous to racism, Jones does, however, raise the issue of the possible significance of "the similarities and differences between the two groups in their struggles to free themselves in this period of social dislocation, their roles within the Northern-sponsored educational bureaucracy, and their rather ironic confrontation with each other."[11] White women like Anna Oliver represented the strength of the teachers corps in Georgia and yet lacked real power within the strictly male-dominated educational hierarchy. Anna faced discrimination in salary and work responsibilities, as well as enduring social and physical privations in order to carry out her mission. Jones shows that white women employed many different tactics (some to great effect) to challenge the prevailing notions of their proper "place" in the educational world. The important question of whether there was a perceived connection between the struggle of white women and the struggle of freed men and women remains obscure. Did Anna react to the passage of the Fifteenth Amendment and the resultant enfranchisement of her older male students? Jones suggests that white women working in Reconstruction Georgia as schoolteachers made their contribution to the women's movement by breaking away from the "cult of domesticity." That seems fair enough, but I suspect that there was more than coincidence to the collapse of Reconstruction and the renewed call by suffragists in 1877 for a Sixteenth Amendment to the Constitution.

AMA paternalism, however well-intentioned, often replicated the superior-inferior color relationships of the larger society. And northern whites seldom understood or appreciated the richness and vitality of black culture, especially as it was manifested in the black churches. Despite the ambiguities and its cultural imperialism, the AMA made a great and lasting contribution. African Methodist Episcopal Bishop Henry McNeal Turner said there would be no public schools for blacks in Georgia were it not for the AMA.[12] And W. E. B. DuBois, no flatterer of white people, spoke eloquently of that "wonderful call which sounded in the ears of the sons and daughters of the North in the later sixties [which] was a call to far greater heroism and self-sacrifice than that which called them earlier through the smoke of Sumter."[13]

Near the end of her first year in Atlanta, October 1869, Anna protested the AMA's policy of paying women teachers smaller salaries than those paid men. Her harried Atlanta supervisor denounced her as an "impulsive troublemaker" and requested that she be transferred to another school. Two months later she saved the AMA some paperwork by leaving the field willingly. In a stinging December letter of resignation, she suggested that "in this day of the discussion of human rights, work and wages, it is well to look into things." She highlighted the discrepancy between the responsibilities and salary ($800 a year) of a male superintendent and the exhausting duties and little pay ($135 a year) of the women who worked under them. The issue transcended the "equal pay for equal work" argument, for women did a much greater amount of work than their male superiors, she contended. AMA officials failed to gauge the extent of teacher discontent on the matter, for Snowden concluded her letter with the assertion, "I am not speaking for myself, but for my sisters."[14] (See document 1.) The Atlanta superintendent who worked with Snowden showed little sympathy for her or for her arguments. Her final communication was ridiculed as a "smashing letter."[15] Superintendent Smith lived up to his reputation as a resourceful AMA official by reminding the New York office that a Connecticut congregation had donated money to Atlanta in Snowden's name. He suggested that it be collected immediately.

Anna packed her bags in Atlanta and headed for Connecticut where she rejoined her family, resumed her interest in women's issues, especially temperance and suffrage, and took up painting. One year later (1870) she headed west to Ohio, partly because Cincinnati was a center of the new landscape art she wanted to study and partly because the women's rights movement in Ohio was more advanced than in Connecticut.

OHIO

Anna enrolled in the University of Cincinnati. For two years, 1872 to 1873, she studied art in the university's McMicken School of Design.[16] Her work was of such high quality that nine pieces were selected for a show at the Cincinnati Museum of Art in 1873.[17] During these years Anna supported herself by selling newly fashionable landscapes for the parlors of Cincinnati's rich and famous.

Anna also learned the art of public speaking and politics in her adopted city. Cincinnati in the early 1870s was the storm center for the Ohio Woman's Crusade. The crusade marked the beginning of a new period of development, organization, and expansion for the temperance movement, one that led directly to the formation of the Woman's Christian Temperance Movement and indirectly to the victory of national Prohibition half a century later. Begun in earnest as a Christmas Eve pray-in at a saloon in Hillsboro, Ohio, within four months 30,000 women in more than 300 Ohio communities were participating in saloon pray-ins. Anna Oliver was one of them.[18] A baptism into the power of liberty for women, the protest spread to many communities from Maine to California, with only the Deep South left untouched. Within a year the Woman's Christian Temperance Union had been organized.

Most historians of temperance credit the Hillsboro incident as the starting point for female dominance of the temperance movement in the last quarter of the nineteenth century. The crusade achieved its spectacular intensity because a cluster of southwestern Ohio communities organized prayer bands all at once, attracted significant newspaper attention, and proselytized their success, so that instances of praying crusades suddenly began to snowball. Crusade tactics were best suited to smaller communities where the psychological, social, and economic pressure they exerted could have a strong effect. Eventually, the enthusiasm of the Crusade spread to large cities: Praying bands appeared in Springfield, Columbus, Dayton, Cleveland, and Cincinnati in Ohio as well as Chicago, Pittsburgh, Philadelphia, and Boston. In March 1874, Cincinnati Methodist Episcopal clergy took the first organizational step—they sponsored a mass rally. After a prayer meeting, 120 women marched to the city square where mass arrests took place. Forty-three women were jailed for obstructing sidewalks.

More than anything else the Crusade was a public theater of propaganda, aimed at stopping social drinking of its growing respectability within the middle class. It also forged a spiritual, and later organizational, link between women throughout the country who had been fighting isolated skirmishes against the drink trade in defense of their families since the 1850s.

During her stay in Cincinnati in the early 1870s when she was in her early thirties, Anna felt called to the ordained ministry. After hearing her temperance talks in Ohio churches, town halls, and YMCAs, several persons—lay and clergy, women and men—encouraged her to think about becoming a pastor. A marvelous autobiographical account of her call to the ministry has been preserved thanks to an enterprising reporter for the *New York World* who published a transcript of a lengthy interview with the by then Passaic, New Jersey, pastor in February of 1877.[19] (See document 2.)

> You know, I believe I was called by the Lord to study for the ministry. I told the Lord that no seminary would admit me; if one did, perhaps I would not be successful, and would only bring myself into unpleasant notoriety, and be abused by my enemies and rejected by friends. I was not anxious to be a martyr. I brought every conceivable argument against it I could find, but the Lord overturned all and bid me to go on.

In time Anna inquired about enrolling in the theological school at Oberlin. Despite Oberlin's pioneering spirit in coeducation, Anna felt second-class in its theological school. Antoinette Brown, first woman ordained in an American denomination, had felt the same oppression when she tried to study theology at Oberlin in the early 1850s.

Oberlin made contributions to the women's movement, though it resisted much of the women's rights crusade. It was the first coeducational college, a step that met much resistance. But opinion divided on whether women should speak in public, even though Finney's revival techniques had been a strong influence in opening up this possibility. Asa Mahan, Oberlin's president a decade before Anna arrived, supported the women, especially as his own daughter neared the time for her commencement oration, but was unable to carry a majority of the faculty. Antoinette Brown had been permitted to attend theological lectures only "unofficially." But she did attend and did complete a theological education. And the education that Oberlin provided laid the foundation for moving beyond Oberlin's position. Oberlin graduated some of the most radical feminists of the era. Among them were Lucy Stone, whose name became the household expression for a woman who kept her maiden name in marriage, and Betsy Cowles, president of the second National Women's Rights Convention.[20]

Despite assurances from Oberlin's President Fairchild, Anna Snowden experienced a less than warm welcome from Oberlin's theological faculty and student body when she enrolled in the fall of 1873.

> First from one thing and then another, I was debarred until, for all that I was getting there [she later told an interviewer], I might as well have been taking private lessons in Hebrew and Greek. Of course, I remonstrated, and quoted President Fairchild's words, and there were many interesting scenes between the professors and me which should not be repeated.

Anna pressured the faculty to state the terms on which she would be able to continue in the ministerial training program. In a formal letter they told her she would be admitted to classes, assemblies, and chapel, but "feminine propriety" forbade her to speak publicly in any of them. Yet during the Ohio temperance crusade, she chuckled, "The carriages of the Faculty, with their wives, would stand before my room every day to take me to some small town to speak—it might be in the street, or in a saloon where a bottle of whiskey might be flung at my head. That was in accord with feminine propriety."[21] Determined to find a more friendly environment to continue theological study, Anna decided to look elsewhere.

BOSTON

Letters of application to fourteen theological seminaries produced three acceptances.[22] Anna decided to test Boston University, founded in 1870 and by charter coeducational in all of its schools. With little money to her name she made the long journey from Oberlin to Boston at the end of the summer of 1874, determined to earn the Bachelor of Divinity degree, and that fall enrolled in the University's School of Theology. Tuition was free for all theological students female and male, but accommodations for room and board at the school could not include a woman. In order to pay for food and her off-campus room, at first she tutored students. Word spread among Methodist women of her oratorical abilities and soon she was earning her keep by giving public lectures—"the easiest way of making money I know," she later said. Lecturing left more time for her studies, in which she excelled. Still she had difficulty making ends meet. She sold some of her jewelry to buy books and often lived on six cents of porridge for a week.

In a long letter published in May 1875 in Lucy Stone's *Woman's Journal* Oliver wrote:

> Women have so long been treated as of secondary or no consequence, that it is impossible for us to believe in a moment that we shall receive equal consideration with men. Besides, we have trusted elsewhere, and found our confidence betrayed. We have relied on pledges only to learn that words mean one thing when spoken to men, and quite another when addressed to women; only to be told, "Yes, we make you that promise, but we meant merely as far as accords with feminine propriety—we men, being judges of said propriety."[23]

Asked by many whether there were differences between women and men in the Boston University School of Theology, Anna answered, "Nothing short of a microscope will detect any difference." At Boston University she confidently reported, "Women are still hampered. But a good time is coming, and the Boston University is the star that heralds the dawn of a brighter day."[24]

Anna was one of four students chosen to give an address when she graduated in 1876. Her achievement made the headlines. The *Boston Globe* commented favorably on her commencement oration, "Christian Enterprise, Its Field and Reward":

> Miss Anna Oliver, who has the honor of being the first woman in America to receive the title of B.D., made a very pleasing impression. Her manner was marked by a quiet earnestness, which was very effective: and the appeal for individual effort in the cause of Christ was made with a pleasant absence of all straining after effect or attempt to imitate masculine gestures or information.[25]

PASSAIC, NEW JERSEY

Anna Oliver was not only the first woman to receive a theological degree; she was also one of the first women to lead a mainline Protestant congregation. During the summers of 1875 and 1876, Anna preached for six weeks at First Place Methodist Episcopal Church in Brooklyn and occasionally at summer assemblies and campmeetings on Long Island and the New Jersey shore. But not until the fall of 1876 was she able to take on full pastoral duties of the First Methodist Episcopal Church in Passaic, a thriving factory city in northern New Jersey.

Several "wealthy and prominent gentlemen of Brooklyn" had offered to fund an independent church and call her as pastor. Oliver refused the offer on the grounds that it was premature. She wanted to test the Methodist bishops and conferences on the matter of ordination and a regular parish appointment of a woman. She also deemed the offer unmissionary. Fearing those who joined her church would leave another, she told her would-be benefactors she preferred to gather in new members rather than steal sheep from other flocks.

In April of that year the five-year-old St. George's Methodist Episcopal Church in Passaic ("a handsome Gothic structure which cost nearly $100,000 and whose towers and gables would not demean Fifth Ave," according to a New York reporter) became victim of the stock market crash of 1873 and the depression that followed. The church was sold under foreclosure. Four months later, August 1876, the church was reorganized under the name First Methodist Episcopal Church of Passaic. The church building was bought back, a much reduced mortgage was assumed, and a parsonage was rented. Too late for a regular ministerial appointment from the Newark Conference of The Methodist Episcopal Church, the congregation was without a pastor until the end of the summer when the church's official board decided to call Anna Oliver as interim pastor. Was it because they supported women in the pulpit or to save money on the pastor's salary?

Oliver preached her first sermon to her Passaic flock on the third Sunday in September, 1876. Her first sermon, titled "Singleness of Aim," was delivered to a congregation numbering only fifteen out of a total membership of twenty-five; only three persons showed up for Sunday school. Within weeks, a New York newspaper reported: "Her eloquence has filled the church to overflowing; her combined tenderness and power have won for her numerous admirers from all denominations who profess themselves willing to follow her into any church she may occupy."[26] Oliver was a determined pastor and kept a dizzying pace as she tried to put First M.E. Church in Passaic on a firm footing financially and spiritually. To raise money, pews were rented at from five to fifty dollars a year. During the spring of 1877, she held a series of highly successful revival meetings paired with a popular Wednesday evening lecture series to which she invited a number of distinguished friends from the New York area as speakers.[27] Offerings received more than met expenses for the meetings. Although not ordained, Anna performed several baptisms as well as marriages and burials, as the church's surviving register attests. However, she called upon a former pastor and ardent supporter, the Reverend John M. Howe, to celebrate the Lord's Supper for her flock. The young pastor also called for assistance from the best-known black woman evangelist, Amanda Smith. "Between them [the city's weekly newspaper reported] Passaic is having a lively time; what with stirring up sinners and Christians on the one hand, and on the other, two women in the pulpit, and one black, the buzzing grows apace."[28] During 1876–1877, Oliver also gave a series of lectures at New Jersey's Methodist woman's college (Centenary College for Women) in Hackettstown, New Jersey.[29]

Passaic was then in its prime as a manufacturing city noted for its cotton and wool mills. In a widely publicized sermon, "The Needs of Passaic," delivered March 18, 1877, Oliver indicated the broad range of her ministry. In her sermon she reminded those living in the golden age of foreign missions that it was not necessary to go to the ends of the earth. The mission field was at hand—Passaic, she said, was ripe for harvest. She cited a religious census commissioned by several churches in the city the past summer which indicated several thousand families were unconverted and unchurched. Even more alarming, claimed Miss Oliver, were the rapidly increasing crime rate, broken families, and unwanted children, which led to overcrowded prisons and burgeoning welfare rolls.

Anna had a special passion for the plight of women and children in her adopted New Jersey city. She proposed a three-point program for social reform: (1) Because she traced the roots of Passaic's most pressing problems to alcohol, she proposed to close the liquor traffic, a standard Victorian answer to society's ills.[30] (2) She called for reform of Passaic's public school curriculum to include vocation training. "Let us demand of our government a compulsory law that shall teach not grammar and arithmetic only, but some trade or skilled occupation by which every boy *and every girl* shall be able to earn a support." (3) To relieve the problem of homeless children she called on Passaic's residents to adopt "the little ones into Christian households, training them in the love of Him who said 'of such is the Kingdom of Heaven.'" She concluded her sermon:

> In the work of drilling the new recruits among children we need no police stations, penitentiaries, nor gallows; but with the love of Christ in us, we will storm the citadels of these little hearts, give these busy fingers skill, with which to answer their daily prayer for daily bread, and then win our enemies in society over, and with all united we will fall into ranks and march together toward the great goal God *wills* for our race.[31]

Not all members and friends of the church approved of her style and methods. Nevertheless the church prospered. After only four months the back interest on the mortgage was paid and the current operating expenses were met. Although "the slight dark-eyed pastor with short black curls" could report to the Newark Methodist Conference in April of 1877 a membership increase of more than 500 percent, the bishop refused to recognize Anna even as an interim pastor and quickly replaced her with a newly ordained male pastor from nearby Drew Theological Seminary.

Through the busy months in Passaic, Anna lived with a female companion ("a young lady who looks after the inner woman") in a "stately" parsonage three doors away, surrounded with her paintings and drawings. Occasionally Anna received invitations to preach throughout the New York area, but no Methodist bishop offered to ordain her or give her a parish appointment. When her health failed, she entered the Jackson Rest Home in Dansville, New York, well known for their success with water cure, and as the home of Civil War heroine Clara Barton.[32]

BROOKLYN

Upon recovering her health, at age thirty-seven, Anna Oliver expected to "go west and build up a Church from the beginning," she told a *New York World* reporter in 1877. Two years later, in the spring of 1879, she went east to become pastor of a Methodist Episcopal Church in bustling Brooklyn.[33]

In March of that year, a heavily mortgaged Wesley Methodist Episcopal Church building was sold at public auction. A small group of members and friends purchased the large church in April for $14,000, and requested Miss Oliver to be their pastor and to hold the property in her name.[34] Fearing the worst from the male-dominated New York East Methodist Conference in which they were situated, the group drew up the deed without the usual Methodist trust clause, lest the conference claim the property and appoint a male pastor.[35]

The congregation divided: Some transferred their membership to nearby Green Avenue Methodist Episcopal Church; others agreed to stay and reorganize themselves into a new Methodist Episcopal parish on the basis of five general principles:

1) Preach and teach holiness. A brief excerpt from the writings of the leading woman Protestant (Holiness) theologian Phoebe Palmer was adopted as the church's doctrinal statement. "There is but one way from earth to heaven and the Lord has given that one way a name. Isaiah 35:8-9. And a highway shall be there, and a way and it shall be called, '*The Way* of Holiness.'"[36] Following Palmer's "shorter way," the road to holiness of heart and life was neither lengthy nor complicated. A clearly defined, step-by-step procedure of giving up one's idolatries and consecrating oneself wholly to God is outlined:

> The Bible teaches progression. Men are first justified and then sanctified wholly. We believe also in the direct witness of the Spirit. If justified in the sight of God, it is the privilege of the believer to have the witnessing Spirit, assuring him of the fact that he stands justified before God.
>
> We believe, and also teach from the Scriptures, that if sanctified wholly, the Holy Spirit beareth witness with the spirit of the believer, that the work is wrought. "We have received of that Spirit, whereby we *know* the things freely given to us of God."
>
> We earnestly press upon all believers, as an immediate necessity—an endowment of power available to all, by an *act of faith,* that must be obtained by all who would be true to their heavenly calling.

2) Trust God in financial matters as well as in spiritual. "If the Lord needs a church, and the church does the Lord's work, He will just as surely give it the money to meet its current expenses as He will give it the Holy Spirit to lead its meetings." So no

> church fairs, festivals, oyster suppers, charades, tableaux, cantatas, wax works or any other numerous projects gotten up by churches in order to meet their expenses, and which turn the Lord's sanctuary into a playhouse or an eating saloon or a house of merchandise. Our method of raising money is to ask people to give it in return for the profit they derive from the church services.

3) Develop an educational program to advance "the sanctification of believers and the conversion of sinners." So in addition to Sunday services morning and evening and Sunday school in between, weekdays at Willoughby Ave. church were filled with a nursery school and a music school; weeknights with prayer meetings (Wednesdays), class meetings, lectures, concerts, spelling bees, history examinations, and debates.

4) Abstain from beverage alcohol. So temperance lectures and lessons were regularly given, and the temperance pledge was constantly upon the altar table. More than one hundred persons signed the pledge during the year 1880.

5) Practice gender inclusiveness. So, for example, their pastor was a woman, eight women served on the church's eighteen-member "Official Board" for 1880–1881, and two served on the board of trustees.

The congregation took a new name, Willoughby Avenue Methodist Episcopal Church, and services of public worship began April 6, 1879. Oliver's opening sermon to what she knew was a risky experiment was titled "Brethren, Pray for Us," an exposition of 1 Thessalonians 5:25. Oliver promised a full Methodist program—preaching services Sunday mornings and evenings and Sunday school in the afternoon, prayer meetings on Wednesday nights, class meetings Tuesday and Thursday evenings and Friday mornings, and regular sacraments.[37] She began at once to receive new members, baptize babies, marry couples, and bury the dead on her own, but called on ordained male pastors to help celebrate the Lord's Supper. She was not without clergy friends in the New York East Methodist conference. A strong setback occurred three months later. The church was stripped of its furniture—pulpit, pew cushions, carpets, gas fixtures (lights), even the Sunday school library—by Mr. Thomas Nostrand, who held a mortgage on the church and parsonage furniture. Oliver refused to purchase the church or parsonage furnishings on the ground that the $2,200 price was too high.[38] Despite the setback, membership climbed from the original thirteen to more than seventy by the end of the summer. With donated pulpit furniture and borrowed communion ware, services continued. A year later (April 1880), Anna's flock multiplied to more than a hundred, and she presided over a Sunday school "womaned" by thirty-six teachers with an average attendance of two hundred.

That same year Miss Oliver and friends launched a spring offensive on The Methodist Episcopal Church, hoping to press a test case on the ordination of women. The church's General Conference, the highest legislative body with authority to change the church's book of discipline, would meet in Cincinnati in May. Oliver had already been recommended as a suitable candidate for ordination from a Boston-area Methodist church and the board of ordained ministry of the New England Conference of the church. When the bishop presiding at the April meeting of the New England Conference refused to present her to the conference as a candidate for ordination or to ordain her, several clergy appealed the bishop's decision to the forthcoming General Conference.

Oliver made the long journey from Brooklyn to Cincinnati hoping with others to press her case. Despite many petitions favoring the ordination of women and their appointment to parishes, and much debate, the conference resolved not to ordain women, barred them from receiving a "local preacher's license" (the first step to ordained ministry in the M.E.C.), and declared null and void all licenses that had been given to women.[39] A large number of Methodist women including Miss Oliver had received such licenses since the middle 1860s. Records show that Anna's own license continued to be renewed annually from 1876 through 1883 by the annual meeting of the Jamaica Plain, Massachusetts, Methodist Episcopal Church.

Oliver returned to her flock in Brooklyn with little hope of ordination and regular appointment to a parish in the near future, but with much courage to continue her ministry. In December of 1880, the church published an impressive *Annual* outlining an ambitious program, with "Rev. Miss Anna Oliver, Pastor" in bold type on its cover along with a sketch of the imposing Gothic Revival church drawn by the pastor. In the church *Annual* she renewed her dedication to lead its ministry:

> I commenced this work feeling that it was of the Lord, and I have been more and more convinced every step of the way. The trials of the past have increased our faith in God. We have confidence in the captain who takes us safely through a storm. These trials have also bound us together in the tenderest love; and I here and now pledge myself anew to my beloved people to the most entire consecration in the work of the Lord with you.[40]

She also joined the circle of New York women working for women's issues—suffrage, temperance, health care, and dress reform. She regularly welcomed women in the temperance and suffrage movements into her pulpit, along with colaborers in the struggle for women's rights in the churches.

Despite gifts from friends from Kansas to Massachusetts, nonrecognition by the denomination and "persecution" of clergy and lay supporters by the Methodist hierarchy finally conquered the pastor and remaining members of the Willoughby Avenue church experiment. Four years after the church was begun, in April of 1883, the church was abandoned and Miss Oliver resigned. In her parting statement she assured her supporters that she was not abandoning the pastoral ministry. After much needed rest and relaxation, she vowed to return to the New York area ready to take another parish assignment.[41]

Oliver spent the summer resting in the Catskills, traveled through Europe in the fall, studied art in Italy in the Spring, and visited Egypt and the Holy Land the next summer. She returned to Brooklyn in the fall of 1884 accompanied by a young Swiss girl, whom she "adopted" and supported through nursing school. Without a pulpit of her own, she was dependent on invitations from sympathetic pastors in the New York area, which continued to come her way until the early 1890s. During this time she also took an active role in the local chapter of the Woman's Christian Temperance Union. When in 1886 Brooklyn's Methodist mayor was pressured by the liquor industry to overturn a rule requiring alcohol education in the public schools, Oliver helped draft a WCTU memorial asking the mayor to enforce the instruction rule, appoint teachers and school board members in sympathy with the rule, and appoint women to the city school board.[42] Oliver also took leadership in the suffrage movement and in the drive for dress reform for women, using a doll to demonstrate the advantages of new attire for women in her lectures.[43] Expanded health-care services for women and children were another cause to which she devoted her attention in her later years.[44]

In 1886 Anna went to Europe to recover her health. Little is known of her last years. She died November 21 in 1892 in Greensboro, Maryland, during a visit to the home of her brother Arthur. Anna Howard Shaw delivered a moving tribute to her departed "clergy" colleague at the National Woman's Suffrage Association convention in Washington, D.C., in January 1893:

> Miss Oliver was not only the minister and the minister's wife, but she started at least a dozen reforms and undertook to carry them all out. She was attacked by that influential [New York] Methodist paper, *The Christian Advocate,* edited by the Rev. Dr. James M. Buckley, who declared that he would destroy her influence in the church, and so with that great organ behind him he attacked her. She had that to fight, the world to fight, and the devil to fight, and she broke down in health. She went abroad to recover, but came home only to die.[45]

Throughout her ministry Anna's favorite biblical text was Revelation 3:8 (KJV): "Behold, I have set before thee an open door, and no *man* can shut it." Although official doors to the Methodist ministry were closed to her—no Methodist bishop would ordain her, no Methodist conference would admit her—she found other Victorian doors to ministry wide open—teaching white children in South Norwalk and black children in Atlanta, protesting the evils of alcohol in Ohio, assailing sexism in Passaic, railing against the women's restrictive dress code in Brooklyn, preaching holiness on the Jersey shore. It was Anna Oliver's way of reminding folk in the golden age of foreign missions that ample opportunities for evangelism and social reform awaited committed Christians at their church door. By opening her home as well as her pulpit to a growing stream of women who were pioneering ministerial roles in Victorian churches, she became a respected mentor and model.

DOCUMENTS

1. Letter of Resignation to American Missionary Association.

December 22, 1869

Rev. E. P. Smith

Dr. Friend,

Allow me to resign my position under the Amer. Mis. Asso. My reasons, briefly: I returned to Atlanta believing that I was to retain the little room I occupied last spring & summer. I had written asking it of Miss Fitch. She did not reply. Objected on my arrival. I offered to the A.M.A. through Mr. Ware &c. the value of several hundred dollars in salary, scholarship, &c. for the use of the room. Mr. Ware, Miss Fitch and Mr. Cravath decided that a spare room is not ideal. I feel that in using the best of their judgment, these friends have done perfectly right. I am *entirely satisfied* and leave here friendly and pleased with all the family, and every one.

I view it simply as a business transaction. I made an offer which they saw fit to decline—

I was told that above 500 women stand ready to come down and teach the freedmen at $15 per month. I am, therefore, not needed. I hope to find some good work for which no willing hands are waiting.

More interested in the Freedmen than ever before, & just beginning to understand what is needed & how to do it, I would regret to leave did I not feel that it would be sin to remain. Should the time ever arrive when your 500 "waiting" women are unemployed, & you have work that stands waiting, I will be happy to serve the cause to the utmost of my ability—*provided you offer the same remuneration that you do to men for the same work.* I am not saying that I will accept any compensation at all, any more than at present. But in this day of the discussion of business rights—"work & wages"—it is well to look into things.

If the Minister here receives $1,000 salary & house and board for himself & wife, that is more than New England ministers receive. He could lay up a good sum yearly—a thing hardly expected in missionary life, while the ladies receive $15 per month and board for one! Exactly the wages, if I remember, of our cook at home! I have heard of Mr. Bassett in Augusta receiving $20 per month as *assistant* teacher, while the teacher received $15—the teacher a woman. Ought those things so to be? I've grown "strong minded" under the fostering influences of the A.M.A.

You will probably laugh, Mr. Smith, when you read this letter but I am in earnest. I am not speaking for myself but for my sisters.

I remain Respectfully & Truly

Yours in the love and work of Jesus.
Anna O. Snowden,
Atlanta, Ga.[46]

2. *"Rev. Anna Oliver's Story, How She Was 'Called' and the Trouble She Had in Being 'Chosen,'"* New York World, *February 23, 1877, p. 2. Reprinted in the* Weekly Item *(Passaic, N.J.), March 24, 1877, p. 1.*

The invitation extended to the Rev. Anna Oliver, the only licensed female preacher in the United States, to address the Methodist ministers at their next Monday's meeting but one, has been received with great interest, not only by Miss Oliver's own congregation at Passaic, but by her neighbors of other congregations and churches, to whom the woman preacher has been a puzzle and the topic of unremitting conversation since she first occupied the First Methodist [Episcopal] Church pulpit in that overgrown Jersey village.

Miss Oliver's revival meetings, which have been in progress since the week of prayer, have been crowded to overflowing from out the various ranks of Passaic. One member of her church said yesterday: "This place has not been so stirred up since I lived here, and that is fourteen years." And another: "There has not been so much of a revival in Passaic for twenty years." A gentleman of the congregation remarked: "Since the existence of the Church it has not been in as high a state spiritually as at the present time." And a lady adds: "No one but a woman could have brought this Church into such harmony; all the members working together for Christ. This Miss Oliver has accomplished only as a pastor."

Another member regrets that her congregation have no hopes of keeping Miss Oliver, as the Church is so built up that the conference will send them a [regularly ordained male] pastor, since there are more preachers now than places for them.

In addition there is a "Woman's Christian Temperance Union," and no little enthusiasm over the success of its work, and a lecture course under her auspices towards the filling of the church's coffers. Matters are thus wrought up into that interesting pitch that while one side are devotedly singing praises at the change coming over Passaic's dream, the other are avowing that "really the goings on over at Miss Oliver's church are becoming scarcely decent."

The parsonage is three doors away. It is a modern home, made stately with a Mansard roof and bay windows, where in its commodious rooms, neatly furnished by the Church, and adorned by Miss Oliver's paintings, drawings and gifts, dwell snugly the Rev. Anna with a young lady who looks after the inner woman. At this parsonage Miss Oliver was yesterday found and asked how she happened to study for the ministry:

"But it's such a long story," protested the grand-daughter of Robert Bogardus.

"Never mind. Go on."

"You know, I believe I was called by the Lord to study for the ministry," lifting her black eyes. "I told the Lord that no seminary would admit me; if one did, perhaps I would not be successful, and would only bring myself into unpleasant notoriety, and be abused by my enemies and rejected by friends. I was not anxious to make myself a martyr. I brought every argument against it I could find, but the Lord overturned them all and bid me go on. You remember Gideon demanded of the Lord two signs when he wanted to know whether the Lord wanted him to go out and fight the Midianites. Like him, I asked of the Lord a sign. I wanted it to be so clear that whatsoever might come I should know I had obeyed the voice of the Lord. So I said, 'Lord, if any one suggests such a thing to me, which is the most improbable thing in the world, since no theological seminary has ever admitted a woman or given any intention that one will, I will accept that as a sign.' I was then in Cincinnati studying art, with the intention of making it my profession, so I went on with my pictures without bothering any more about it. About a week after, early one morning Mrs.—— called, a lady I had met but casually two or three times. She began apologizing for her early call, saying for a week she had me on her mind, and begging I would take kindly to what she had to say. I knew in a moment what it was, though I said nothing. She began: 'Do you know, Miss Oliver, I think you ought to prepare yourself for the ministry by taking a theological course.' I could not keep from laughing. I begged her to please not mention what she had said to me, as it would injure me in my work, and I was then painting some portraits. But I was not satisfied; I wanted it still clearer, so I asked of the Lord another sign. 'If any minister should suggest my going to a theological seminary I would accept it as final,' I said to myself. Nothing seemed more unlikely than that. I went on with my work as before, and about a month after I met the Rev.——" (naming a well-known minister in Cincinnati) "on the street, and he said to me: 'Miss Oliver, I heard a little sermon you preached one evening at the Young Men's Christian Association meetings' (I often spoke at them, not preached, and among the friends,) 'and I've had you on my mind for a month. Do you know that every one would say to you if you were a man: "Go fit yourself for the ministry." But I say to you, Do it, though you are a woman. Now, what do you say to that?' I immediately urged again that no theological seminary would admit me, and all that I had urged before, but he advised my applying to the Lane Seminary of which he seemed to know much.

"I doubted no more, but began to put my affairs in order. In the meantime I made application to Lane Seminary and received no answer; then I wrote again with like result. That was the only seminary, in fact, that was not polite to me, and they treated me with contempt. Then I applied to Oberlin. To be sure I had no money, but I said: 'Lord, all the money in creation is thine.' I knew if he meant me to study for the ministry he would provide; and he did, bless his name. Well, President Fairchild told me in answer that Oberlin would admit me, and that no difference should be made between me and the other theological students. I have reason to know those words by heart, for, first from one thing and then another I was debarred, until, for all that I was getting there, I might as well have been taking private lessons in Hebrew and Greek. Of course, I remonstrated, and quoted President Fairchild's words, and there were many interesting scenes between the professors and me which should not be repeated. Finally, I went to Cincinnati, talked with some friends, and made another application to Oberlin for admission, saying I supposed I had been admitted to the seminary, but it seemed I had not, &c. Then they drew up a letter—I wish I had it here to show you—in which they set down what they considered in admitting me was in accordance with feminine propriety and what was not. For example, for me to get up and say anything in a parlor full of my classmates and the Faculty and some of their wives was not in accordance with feminine propriety; but, at the same time, it afterwards happened that during the Ohio [Temperance] Crusade, the carriages of the Faculty, with their wives, would stand before my room every day to take me to some of the small towns to speak—it might be in the street, or in a saloon where a bottle of whiskey might be flung at my head. That was in accord with feminine propriety, for one of the professors most bitter against me said if ever the hand of the Lord was shown, it was in the Ohio Crusade.

"At Oberlin it is about like this: a cat or Balaam's ass, a little boy like Samuel, or even a woman may be called of the Lord, but you don't send cats, or asses, or little boys, or women to theological seminaries. Some of the trustees of Oberlin are officers of the American Missionary Association, whose teachers in the South preach regularly, as at Andersonville, but Oberlin would not prepare them to do it. They think a woman can do by instinct what it takes a man three years to learn.

"The conclusion of the matter was that one day I sent out letters of application for admission to fourteen theological seminaries. To Princeton I wrote, stating that my grandfather, the Rev. Samuel Snowden, and his six brothers had been educated there, both in the college and in the seminary, for the ministry. I would like to have gone there. I received polite answers from every one of the fourteen presidents. Some urged that their charters would not permit—Yale, I think, did that—others that they were not prepared to take such a step, but three consented to receive me, though at Oberlin they had always said that they were doing more than any other seminary could do. I decided finally to go to Boston. To be sure I only had five dollars at the time, but it was six months until I went, and the Lord knew better than to let me have the money until I needed it. I always had supposed that I would teach, and when I went to Boston I began to consider getting scholars. But as it happened one day a gentleman called and said he was getting up a lecture course, and asked me to put my name down for one lecture. I suppose he had heard of my speaking during the [Ohio] Crusade, for I had never lectured or thought of such a thing. But I thought: 'Now, there is an opening for me to pay my expenses,' so I said I would lecture for him. Then he asked me for my subject, as he was going to get out the circulars that afternoon. Subject! and I hadn't any. I told him I would let him know at 2 o'clock. During the conversation he remarked to a minister who happened to be in the room that he believed in living and helping people to live. 'There!' thought I, 'is a subject.' And so I gave it to him in the afternoon: "Live, Let Live and Help Live." In the end the lecture proved very successful. I delivered it twelve or thirteen times at different places. In fact, it is the easiest way of making money I know, and it left me time for my studies.

"Then when I had money I boarded very comfortably. When I had but little I boarded myself. One week it was very little; I had but 10 cents, and I lived a whole week on 9 cents' worth of brown meal and some salt that I had, which I made into porridge."

"How did you feel at the end of the week?"

"Very weak. I really suppose I might have gone on starving without realizing it. I had things, too, I might have sold, but I never thought of it. I sold a bracelet afterward for $30 and got those Commentaries out of the proceeds. But no matter what I had or didn't have—I never went in debt. Neither was it so very discouraging, for even in my many efforts to make money I always had a good time. Then they were so very kind to me in Boston. The seminary gave me every privilege it gives to men, and I was one of the four chosen to speak when we graduated.

"But it's all over now," said Miss Oliver, leaning back and clasping her hands over her head. "My only trouble is that I am so tired. For four years I have not had one day's vacation, though I have often planned them; the work has always gone along. First, there was the Ohio Crusade, then the last two summers I preached in Brooklyn. But in April I will have a rest."

"Won't you apply to Conference?"

"No, I think not. I want to go West and build up a Church from the beginning. But that's all in the Lord's hands."

"You don't wear overskirts, do you?"

"No, I gave them up some time ago. But you see I have the back breadth puffed in, and it doesn't look bad, with the side plaits below; and then people wear everything so plain in front. Oh, I have learned many little ceremonies in dress in these past years, you may believe."

"However, this has nothing to do with how it happened that Passaic was called upon in an untimely and sudden hour to sit upon the case, [Saint] Paul vs The Rev. Anna Oliver."

Ida B. Wells-Barnett

CHAPTER 7

BECAUSE GOD GAVE HER VISION

The Religious Impulse of
Ida B. Wells-Barnett

E M I L I E   M.   T O W N E S

Ida Bell Wells-Barnett (1862–1931) was an active participant in the various movements for social changes of her day. Wells-Barnett responded to her era as well as shaped it. Her greatest contributions to United States society were her untiring work in the anti-lynching movement and her vocation as a journalist and social justice advocate. The political, social, cultural, and economic movements of her day shaped her work in this movement. She attempted an integrated analysis of discrimination and violence and sought to call the nation to task for violating its social principles on race.

Her rebellion against the traditional roles assigned to women emerged in her career as activist and newspaper journalist. She negotiated societal conventions surrounding domesticity and took time away from the sociopolitical world to rear her children, returning to her work as quickly as time and circumstance allowed. Her concern for decent jobs and wages for African Americans found voice and action in the Negro Fellowship League. (See document 9.)

Born in 1862, Wells-Barnett spent most of the first three years of life in slavery in Holly Springs, Mississippi. She was the oldest child of Elizabeth and James Wells. Her father was politically active during Reconstruction and exposed young Ida and the rest of his family to leading black political figures of the day such as Hiram R. Revels and James Hill.[1] The ten years following the Civil War featured an outpouring of African American political, economic, and social participation in the public sphere. This initial period of black participation in the public realm dampened by 1875. In this thirteenth year of Ida B. Wells' life, white Mississippians resorted to armed violence to drive the Republicans from power and to reestablish white hegemonic rule in the South. However, in an ironic twist, the federal Civil Rights Act, which outlawed segregation on a national scale, passed in this same year.

In the midst of this mixed but worsening climate, James Wells provided a comfortable home for his family, and all attended the local Methodist Episcopal church. He was a carpenter and used his skills to buy a home and to send young Ida to Rust College.[2] Ida progressed from the elementary department to the college department.

Her school days ended tragically in 1878. A yellow fever epidemic killed her parents and one younger sister. Wells, at age sixteen, became the sole support for five brothers and sisters. She provided for her siblings and herself by teaching in Memphis, Tennessee. Because of her status as a teacher, Wells became a part of the small, emerging black middle class in Memphis. She discovered her writing ability through her participation in a literary society, which met weekly to sponsor exercises that included recitations, essays, and debates.

The literary society's meetings ended with the reading of the *Evening Star,* which Wells described as a "spicy journal," by the editor of the paper. When the editor left Memphis to return to his previous job in Washington, D.C., Wells was elected to replace him. Under her editorship, the paper grew in popularity. One of the men who came to hear it read aloud was the Reverend R. N. Countee, publisher of the weekly newspaper the *Living Way.* He asked Wells to write for his paper and she accepted. Using the pen name Iola, she used the format of letters to observe the condition of the schools and churches and other general concerns of blacks in Memphis. Through these columns, Wells created a standard for herself, her people, and United States society. She forged a deep and abiding spirituality rooted in the black church of the South. (See document 1.) Her earliest writings reflect a woman with a strong sense of Christian duty. Wells' understanding of Christian duty emerged from her belief in an immanent God in Christ. The mission of her Jesus was to offer salvation for the sinner. (See document 2.) She stated much of her personal theology in commenting on Dwight Moody's preaching at a revival held in Memphis. Beginning with the observation that Moody's style was such that it was both simple, plain, and natural, Wells noted that Moody did not "preach a far-away God—a hard to be reconciled Savior but uses a natural earnest tone and tells in a natural way without long drawn doctrine or finely spun theology or rhetoric the simple truth that Christ Jesus came on earth to seek and save that which was lost."[3] But Wells could not accept segregated worship. In the same diary entry, she wrote of her intention to write Moody to inquire why pastors "never touched on that phase of sin—the caste distinction—practiced even in the churches and among Christianity." Wells also noted that pastors accepted segregation as a matter of course and in doing so "tacitly conniv[ed] at it . . . instead of rectifying it."

Wells' understanding of God and Christ was typical of both slave and free blacks who saw God as personal and just. Writing after a New Year's Eve watch meeting at one o'clock in the morning in 1886, she painted a lucid picture of her intensely personal experience of God in which she "felt lifted up," thanked God, "and told of His wonder mercies to me and [my] heart overflowed with thankfulness." In Wells' estimation, the office of ordained minister entailed a serious commitment to adhere to the word of God and to be a model for the worshiper. She extended her personal high standards of moral rectitude farther for the preacher than for the layperson.

She was biting and uncompromising in her estimate of a young preacher she described as a "very slender, puerile-looking, small specimen of humanity occupying the pulpit."[4] She returned that evening to hear him *preach* (her emphasis) and reached a conclusion about his fitness for the ordained ministry. Her evaluation was negative and to the point. She found his discourse to be "a constant arraignment of the negro as compared to the whites, a burlesque of Negro worship, a repetition of what he did not believe in, and the telling of jokes." Further, Wells found him lacking in stability and reverence. She believed both characteristics to be essential elements in the composition of a preacher. She ended her entry with the observation that the young preacher had "a disregard of the Father's command to 'take off thy shoes; for the ground on which thou standest is holy.'"

As biting as she could be in her condemnation, she could also be magnanimous in her praise. Writing more than a year later, she delighted in the preacher of her church. She found him to be "the most energetic man I know. He has made the waste places blossom as a rose and the church is beginning to look up." Wells marveled at his ability to handle difficult congregants and keep them involved in the life of the church. She ended this entry with the observation "He is certainly a splendid judge of human nature."[5]

Wells' words reveal her standards for leadership. Ultimately, the preacher needed to be a good judge of human nature who could lead the church in its mission. The preacher must show stability to provide the members of the church with a firm model of moral agency. The preacher could not shy away from belligerent behavior. He must address it directly while bringing the difficult person or persons into fellowship with the whole church. Wells held the ordained minister in high regard. Her personal code of moral conduct demanded much of others and herself.

Her diary entries of January 1887 reveal a fully developed and unequivocal understanding of moral action and Christian duty. Wells decided to teach a Sunday school class to begin to work for God, who had done much for her. She found fault with the way the Bible was taught and preached and hoped to influence her charges "in a small degree to think of better things." She concluded her entry with a covenant plea and commitment to be a Christian in all her acts and a "master in the way of good works." Wells also asked for better control of her temper and told God that she felt "Thou art with me in all my struggles." (See document 5.)

By January 18 of that same year, she had organized a class of young men who promised to come regularly on Sundays. Throughout her adult life, Wells taught young men's church school classes. She understood the moral and vocational development of young men as crucial to the social uplift of the African American community. However, her relationship with her brother was strained. Some of the difficulties she would encounter in later life, as she tried to work with others toward her understanding of justice and moral rectitude, are revealed in her analysis of her relationship with her brother. Wells understood that she alternated between harshness, indifference, and repulsion in his regard. She asked, "God help me to be more careful and watchful over my manners and bearing toward him. Let not my own brother perish while I am laboring to save others!"[6] (See document 6.)

Again in 1887 in another set of entries recorded in February, Wells encountered her humanity and her responsibility in a direct manner. After asking God to bless her in her undertakings and guard her against evil, she was brought up short by a severe lecture on going to the theater. In reflecting on herself as a leader and a role model—and the implicit vocational message therein—Wells revealed her humility and her resolve to put teaching and deed in harmony: "I had not placed so high an estimate on myself. [God] certainly gave me food for thought and hereafter when I grow weary or despondent and think my life useless and unprofitable, may I remember this episode, and may it strengthen me to the performance of my duty."[7]

Later, as Easter neared and she heard a sermon on the cost of religion, she resolved to put away her plans for fun and pleasure during the Easter season. She would fast for her "many sins of dereliction and remain home to work, watch and pray, and praise for the wonderful goodness of my Father to an unworthy servant."

In an entry near the end of this diary, Wells reflected on her life and her future as she celebrated her twenty-fifth birthday. She found herself falling short of the mark—particularly with her education. She noted her "hunger and thirst after righteousness and knowledge" but felt that she was not as persistent as she should be in her pursuit of both. She asked God for the "steadiness of purpose" to acquire both and hoped that ten years hence she would be "increased in honesty and purity of purpose and motive!"[8] (See document 6.)

Wells' early diary reveals her growing concern against lynching and the brutalization of blacks by whites. Her diary entry for March 18, 1885, contains her reflections on the shooting of thirteen black men in Carroll County, Mississippi. Her plea, "O, God when will these massacres cease" is followed by her observation that the black men probably had just cause for attempting to assassinate a white man. She ends the entry with the remark, "Colored men rarely attempt to wreak vengeance on a white one unless he has provoked it unduly."

A year and a half later, Wells expressed her outrage at the lynching of a black woman accused of poisoning a white woman for whom she cooked. The black woman was taken from the jail, stripped naked, hung in the courthouse yard, riddled with bullets, and left for the people of the town to see. Wells wrote with anguish, "O my God! can such things be and no justice for it?"[9] The only evidence against the black woman was the coroner's discovery of arsenic in the stomach of the dead woman and a box of "Rough on Rats" found in the black woman's house. Wells continued in this diary entry, "It may be unwise to express myself so strongly but I cannot help it and I know not if capital may not be made of it against me but I trust in God." (See document 3.)

In the face of this growing onslaught against the humanity of African Americans, Wells rejoiced at the growing unity she perceived forming among blacks of that period. In 1887, she wrote that blacks were beginning to think and recognize that strength can only be found in unity. She also revealed her penchant for action, noting "the men of the race who do think are endeavoring to put their thoughts in action for those to inspire those who do not think." For her, African Americans had to unite if they were to survive. The most effective spokespersons for black people were those blacks who evaluated what needed to be done and then drew a blueprint for action.

Buttressed with this interior world, Wells' public career began as Reconstruction came to a dramatic halt for black people. Black voters were driven from the polls and black lawmakers lost their seats in southern legislatures and in Congress. In 1883, the Supreme Court ruled the 1875 Civil Rights Act unconstitutional. The new laws barred blacks from restaurants, parks, cemeteries, and required railroads and steamboats to provide separate but equal accommodations for the two races. The response of T. Thomas Fortune, founder of the Afro-American League in Chicago, revealed the frustration of countless black Americans as he described legalized discrimination on the railroads, in hotels, and in theaters: "The colored people of the United States feel as if they had been baptized with ice water. . . . One or two murders growing from this intolerable nuisance would break it up."[10]

Barely six months after the Fortune editorial, Wells boarded a train for the ten-mile trip from Memphis to Woodstock to join her family. As was her custom, she seated herself in the women's car. The conductor refused her ticket and ordered her into the smoking car with other blacks. Wells refused to move, and it took three men to pry her from her seat and throw her off the train when it stopped at the next station. As she tumbled down the stairs to the platform, white passengers stood up and applauded.

The same Supreme Court that had ruled the 1875 Civil Rights Act unconstitutional advised blacks to apply to state courts for redress of maltreatment. Wells took this to heart, hired a lawyer, and sued the railroad for damages. She was awarded $500 in damages and the railroad appealed the decision. The case of *Wells versus Chesapeake, Ohio and Southwestern Railroad* was the first heard in the South after the demise of the Civil Rights Act. The leading newspaper of Memphis, the *Memphis Daily Appeal,* ran the headline "A Darky Damsel Obtains a Verdict for Damages Against the Chesapeake & Ohio Railroad" on Christmas Day, 1884.

One of her first published articles was a "write-up" of her suit for damages against the Chesapeake and Ohio Railroad. In the article, she told blacks to stand up for the rights granted to them in Reconstruction legislation.[11] Wells soon found that retrenchment and repression were monolithic. The judge who originally awarded damages to Wells was a former Union Army soldier. The Supreme Court that heard the appeal was composed of southern men. Their ruling was in concert with the general mood of the South: "We think it is evident that the purpose of the defendant was to harass. Her persistence was not in good faith to obtain a comfortable seat for the short ride."

The verdict was devastating to Wells. She had placed her faith in law and in justice but neither was served. Her cry of bitter disappointment, "O God is there no redress, no peace, no justice in this land for us?" reveals the depth of her disillusionment. Yet as she voiced her frustration, she appealed to God to "show us the way, even as Thou led the children of Israel out of bondage into the promised land."[12] (See document 4.)

The reader may deem Wells naive. However, as late as the 1880s, most blacks believed that racial injustice was the work of the lowly white person and a changeable aberration. African Americans had faith in the system, which had allowed economic gains for many after the war and education for more than a quarter million blacks in more than 4,000 schools. The court decision prompted Wells to reexamine her expectations and to cast a critical eye on the events happening to and around blacks.

Over time, other newspapers carried Wells' articles in the *Living Way.* She became a spokesperson for the women of her period. Wells adhered to the ideal of the cult of true womanhood and its emphasis on virtue for women. She recorded a defense made by the editor of one of the local Memphis papers, the *Scimitar,* on behalf of "respectable" black people and added that his defense included black womanhood: "It was not now as it had been that colored women were harlots etc., whose virtue could be bought, that there were as decent [women] among them as among their own race [the white race]; that there were some who were disgraces to their race [the black race], but that the white race had no room to talk, the same was true of them."[13]

Although she was intolerant of immorality, Wells defended the reputation of a "silly woman" who had engaged in an extramarital affair with an "equally scatterbrained boy" who boasted about their relationship. The young man was killed by the brother of the woman, and Wells wrote: "It seems awful to take human life but hardly more so than to take a woman's reputation and make it the jest and byword of the street; in view of these things, if he really did them, one is strongly tempted to say his killing was justified."[14] Wells equated murder with the sullying of a woman's reputation. She hedged somewhat on vindicating the actions of the outraged brother. Her general tone was sympathetic toward the woman, less so for her unfortunate lover.

Like many women of her day, Wells utilized her strong sense of Christian duty and vocation in the public realm. She did so from the understanding that women must be in the world of thought and action. When she was called to respond to the theme of women and journalism at a black newspaper convention, she regretted her neglect to recognize the male editors' acceptance and praise of the work done by women journalists. She realized that she might "never have a more favorable opportunity to urge the young women to study and think with a view to taking a place in the world of thought and action."[15] Wells' fame as an honest and candid journalist grew, and she received letters from black editors across the country asking her to write for them.[16]

By 1891, Wells was a regular correspondent for the *Detroit Plaindealer, Christian Index,* and the *People's Choice.* In addition, she was the editor of the "Home" department of *Our Women and Children* and a regular contributor to the *New York Age, Indianapolis World, Gate City Press* (Missouri), *Little Rock Sun, American Baptist* (Kentucky), *Memphis Watchman, Chattanooga Justice,* and the *Fisk University Herald.*

In the midst of this notoriety, Wells lost her teaching job after a particularly pointed article on the inequities of the black schools in Memphis. She then bought a one-third interest in the *Free Speech* and devoted her energies to turning it into a profit-making newspaper to support herself and her two new partners. Her efforts took her throughout the South, where she found the position of black people growing worse.

Wells' editorials reflected her concern about the tense racial climate in the South. The number and frequency of white mobs lynching black men, women, and children was increasing steadily. Yet Memphis African Americans did not believe that the injustice of the lynch law would cast its shadow on their thriving community—not until the illusion was shattered by the 1892 lynching of Wells' dear and close friend, Thomas Moss.[17] The lynching also served to launch Wells into national and international prominence as she became a key leader in the anti-lynching crusade in this nation.

Moss's lynching did not stem from the charge of rape. As one of the growing number of blacks who were beginning to make economic gains in the South, Moss and his business partners had opened a grocery store and were selling at prices competitive with those of the white store owner across the street. Their crime was that they were successful, black, and chose to defend their store against attack by whites rather than allow it to be ransacked and destroyed. The lynching of these three leading citizens of Memphis was not carried out by a few lower-class whites. Members of the respectable white establishment of Memphis composed the lynch mob. Wells wrote, "The more I studied the situation, the more I was convinced that the Southerner had never gotten over his resentment that the Negro is no longer his plaything, his servant, and his source of income."[18]

The black community of Memphis was devastated. They had believed that lynching would never become part of their lives. Wells saw their only recourse to be boycott and exodus. No attempt was made to punish the murderers, whose identities were known. She echoed Tom Moss's last words and urged the blacks of Memphis to leave that city for the West.[19]

Wells viewed the anti-lynching struggle as a moral one. Her strong religious and moral stance was evident to the Reverend Norman B. Wood writing in 1897. Wood described Wells in biblical terms as a modern Deborah "whose voice has been heard throughout England and the United States wherever it was safe for her to go, pleading as only she can plead for justice and fair treatment to be given her long-suffering and unhappy people." Wood compared Wells to Lincoln and Grant but ended his description of Wells with a direct appeal to the prophet Isaiah of the Old Testament that she might "cry aloud, spare not, lift up thy voice like a trumpet, and show my people their transgressions and their sins."[20]

Wells was confident of the power of truth. She called on the reader to look at facts and persuade "all Christian and moral forces" to pass resolutions against lynching. In addition, she urged her readers to bring to the attention of southerners that businesses refused to invest capital in areas where mob violence ruled. She did not allow the North to escape its own complicity in the anathema of lynching: "Is not the North by its seeming acquiescence as responsible morally as the South is criminally for the awful lynching record of the past thirteen years?"[21] Wells noted that, while northern papers published, without question, southern press stories that black men assaulted white women, they refused her request and other requests by blacks to print their responses and accounts of the horror and facts of lynching.

Wells could not tolerate apathy or indifference by African Americans any more than the apathy toward the religious institutions of her day. (See document 5.) In 1893 as the toll for lynching mounted, Wells did not disguise her outrage and anger with the lack of unity or protest by blacks. She could not understand why blacks sat by and did not speak out against the atrocity of lynching. Wells noted that blacks did little "except to doubt the expediency of or find fault with the remedy proposed, [there being] no plan of raising money by which the things can be investigated."[22] The proposed remedy was the creation of a federal commission to study the lynch law and to make recommendations for its eradication. Wells was a supporter of this plan and used her column to give it a national voice among the black presses of her day.

Wells evaluated the nascent black accommodationist movement and what she termed its call to "sacrifice [the race's] political rights for the sake of peace."[23] She did not believe in the accommodationist position that blacks should ready themselves for responsibility, prove their abilities, and wait patiently that such a display of talent and patience would remove any objection for black political participation. Wells noted that this sacrifice did not remove the trouble or move the South to do justice. "One by one the Southern states have legally disfranchised the Negro."

Her estimate of the effectiveness of the accommodationist stance is clear from the passage. Wells saw nothing beneficial that could result from the forfeiture of rights or dignity. She was unwilling to deem the position a result of a lack of thought, but wished to point out the bankruptcy of such an approach.

Unequivocal in her judgment of the motives of white lynchers, Wells noted that "white men down there [the South] do not think any more of killing a negro than they do of slaying a mad dog." The lynching she referred to in this particular article involved the lynching of black men charged with burning barns. The incident proved that the lynchings of blacks were for crimes other than rape or alleged rape of white women. She closed the article, "An excuse is made by the whites for the purpose of shielding themselves and leaving them free to murder all the negroes they wish."[24] Further, Wells saw lynching as representing "the cool, calculating deliberation of intelligent people who openly vow that there is an 'unwritten law' that justifies them in putting human beings to death without complaint under oath, without trial by jury, without opportunity to make defense, and without right of appeal."[25]

Lynching was also an act of political and economic repression in Wells' eyes. She did not believe that the problem of lynching was due to poor education. Her study of 728 lynchings revealed that only a third of those cases contained any charge of rape. However, the charge of rape against black men was leveled so consistently that the whole nation took it to be true to some extent.[26]

Wells' attack on the rape myth was an attack against southern sexual mores. The South contented itself with the illusion that any liaison between an African American man and a white woman must be an involuntary one for the woman. Wells was quite clear that such liaisons were ill advised, but she was candid about the willingness of white women. In one instance Wells obtained the sworn statement of a mother whose son had been lynched after he was swayed by the advances made by the daughter of his employer. Wells states that the unfortunate youth "met her often until they were discovered and the cry of rape was raised." Meanwhile, white men seduced and raped black women and girls with impunity.

When Wells suggested in an editorial that women were responsible agents in interracial liaisons, this created a firestorm in Memphis among the whites.[27] Luckily, she was attending an African Methodist Episcopal Church General Conference in Philadelphia and went on to New York. The office of the *Free Speech* was broken into, vandalized, and destroyed. Her co-owners fled Memphis and she was threatened with lynching. T. Thomas Fortune met her at the ferry landing in Jersey City with a dispatch from the *Daily Commercial*. The *Commercial* charged Wells with being a black scoundrel and lauded southern patience with "such loathsome and repulsive calumnies."[28] It warned that southern white men would only tolerate so much of Wells' allegedly "obscene intimations" and ended with the comment, "We hope we have said enough." Wells responded to the *Commercial* with her June 5, 1892, seven-column article in the *Age* on black lynching, written in exile. It contained names, dates, places, and circumstances of hundreds of lynchings for alleged rape. The response was overwhelming, with 10,000 copies of the issue sold, 1,000 in Memphis alone.

In one of her columns for the *Age*, Wells gave another detail of that fateful night when Moss, McDowell, Stewart, and other black men defended the People's Grocery. One of the men escaped with his wounds. He was found three days later some twenty miles from the grocery store scene. He told his captors that Dr. Elbert, a black physician, had taken him away in his buggy, tended his wounds, and given him money. This had taken place the day before the lynching. A black woman heard a group of white men declare they were going after Dr. Elbert late on Tuesday night. She warned him and he left on the ten o'clock train. Wells concluded, "It is currently believed that this is the only thing which prevented his being the fourth man lynched on March 9, in Memphis, Tenn."

Wells was aware that her message was not reaching the white newspapers. She believed that ruling-class whites were the key to social change, and her desire was to manipulate their self-interest to effect that change. Wells' appeals focused on the powerful groups outside the South, which she believed had moral and economic authority, but they were not listening. Her dilemma was how to reach those key leaders. Non-southern whites, both in this country and in England, were the key Wells saw to halt lynching.

Wells carried this analysis with her to England in 1893. She believed that England's role as a leading importer of United States cotton gave British views additional weight in the affairs of the United States. Her analysis of lynching and her demystification of the political motives behind the manipulation of both black male and female and white female sexuality led to confrontations with women like Frances Willard of the Woman's Christian Temperance Union, who was also in England on an international temperance campaign. Willard considered herself progressive, but she was unable to see lynching as an institutionalized practice. Willard's inability to see led to their clash in England and in the United States.

The events at the October, 1890, WCTU national convention helped set the stage for the confrontation between Wells and Willard. This was the first time that the WCTU had held a national convention in the South. In the *Red Record,* Wells writes that the southerners set out to win the northerners over. The northern members of the WCTU did not seek the black viewpoint of conditions in the South. Wells was biting in her assessment of the work of the WCTU when she noted that it was "only after Negroes are in prison for crimes that efforts of these temperance women are exerted without regard to 'race, color, or previous condition.'"[29] However, it was Willard's remarks in an interview that put the two women in open confrontation.

In an interview with the *New York Voice,* a temperance newspaper, Willard described the southern black as a "great dark faced mob." Her most inflammatory statements described blacks as multiplying "like locust of Egypt. The grog-shop is its center of power. . . . The safety of women, of children, of the home is menaced in a thousand localities so that men dare not go beyond the sight of their own roof-tree."[30] These remarks created a firestorm of protest by southern African American leaders who quoted and criticized the interview. Many black journalists, including Wells, and readers sent Willard marked copies of their journals. However, Willard neither retracted nor explained her interview. Willard's position against the federal Election Bill to give the federal government control over national elections was also troubling to Wells.[31] Willard's hesitant and equivocal stand on lynching and her defense of the southern record fueled her response to the bill. She defended the South as being wronged in northern public opinion and noted the number of "alien illiterates" and drinkers who vote in the North with what she believed to be less than desirable results. She concluded: "It is not fair that they [alien illiterates and drinkers] should vote, nor is it fair that a plantation Negro, who can neither read nor write, whose ideas are bounded by the fence of his own field and the price of his own mule, should be entrusted with the ballot."[32] Wells' reply to this was to note that in the ten years of lynching, the WCTU had "never suggested one plan or made one move" to prevent the slaughter of black men, women, and children.

In the ensuing bitter public debate between Wells and Willard in the British press, Wells eventually won the sympathy and support of the British populace. Before she left in July, the British Anti-Lynching Committee formed, with British notables among its members. Wells now had access to white groups in the United States previously closed to her. British opinion broke the silence of many United States leaders such as Richard Gilder, editor of *Century* magazine, and Samuel Gompers.

However, the confrontation between Wells and Willard continued into the fall of 1894 and the WCTU convention in Cleveland, Ohio, in November. Some convention delegates made an effort to secure the adoption of a resolution to protest lynching. Willard gave them assurances that such a resolution would be adopted but then attacked Wells in her annual address. Willard declared that Wells had sullied the reputation of white womanhood by suggesting that white women were willing participants in "nameless acts between the races." She found Wells' charges to be "wholly without foundation . . . [the] unanimous opinion of the most disinterested and observant leaders of opinion whom I have consulted on the subject."[33]

Wells' response to the charges was swift. Wells maintained that only "when the facts were plain that the relationship between the victim lynched and the alleged victim of his assault was voluntary, clandestine and illicit" did she mention the exact nature of the interracial relationship. In a *Cleveland Gazette* article, Wells wrote in a similar vein, "We did not expect this from one who has stood so long for humanity. We have to give the facts. In giving them [the facts] no imputation is cast upon the white women of America and it is unjust and untruthful for any one to so assert."[34]

Wells challenged Willard on her negative statements in a private talk. Willard's response was that someone in England had told her it was a pity that Wells attacked the white women of America. Wells' response was measured, but to the point: "Oh, then you went out of your way to prejudice me and my cause in your annual address, not upon what you had heard me say, but what somebody had told you I said?"[35] Willard's reply was less than satisfactory. She declared Wells "must not blame her for her rhetorical expressions—that I had my way of expressing things and she had hers." Wells' response to this explanation was piercing. She did not believe that when the lives of black men, women, and children hung literally in the balance and "when the inhuman butchers of innocents attempt to justify their barbarism by fastening upon a whole race the oblique of the most infamous of crimes" that so vapid an explanation could explain fully Willard's rhetoric. Wells termed it just short of "criminal to apologize for the butchers today and tomorrow to repudiate the apology by declaring it a figure of speech."[36]

When the committee on resolutions for the WCTU convention reported their work, no protest was made concerning lynching. A resolution against lynching was introduced from the floor of the convention, but it did not receive the needed support. Wells wrote that the convention "wholly ignored the seven millions of colored people of this country whose plea was for a word of sympathy and support for the movement in their behalf."[37]

Disappointed but undaunted, Wells' continued her crusade against injustice. Her contribution to the anti-lynching campaign was crucial. She spoke out when few voices challenged the horror and injustice of the lynch law. Her research, writing, and public speaking articulated the truth and brought the facts before the public. She was convinced that once the facts came to light, the acknowledged atrocity of lynching would be the antecedent of its demise.

Wells did not confine herself to agitating for the end of lynching. She organized the first black woman's club in Illinois at the end of the controversial Columbian Exposition of 1893 in Chicago. This club was also the "mother of the woman's clubs" in Illinois. The club met every Thursday to hear music and lectures, and to discuss current topics under Wells' leadership. One of the early projects of the club was to raise money to prosecute a police officer for killing an innocent black man on the west side of Chicago.

When Wells was in England in 1894, the club took out a charter and assumed the name of its absent president. Wells remained as president for five years until the demands of caring for two young children prompted her resignation. The club was instrumental in establishing the first black orchestra in Chicago and opening the first kindergarten for black children. It was also a charter member of the Cook County Women's Clubs, stopping the color line in clubs.

Strong of character though Wells was, she remained wedded to the ideal of the cult of true womanhood. She believed, as did countless black and white women of her day, that women were the repositories of moral integrity and virtue. In a February 18, 1888, article for the *New York Age,* Wells painted the picture of the ideal southern black woman cherishing and protecting her virtue and good name as akin to a miser hoarding his gold. Wells suggested that black women scorn "each temptation to sin and guilt." Wells was aware that blacks "as a whole, are charged with immorality and vice" and "that it depends largely on the woman of today to refute such charges by her stainless life." For Wells, black women must encourage black men to be "honest, noble and manly." She captured the ideals of the cult in these few lines: "a woman's virtue and good name, a woman's responsibility to be the paragon of moral conduct, her duty to encourage men to a higher moral life."

In June of 1895, Wells married Ferdinand L. Barnett, a lawyer in Chicago. Together they parented five children.[38] She believed that marriage and motherhood signaled her retirement from public work. Her marriage drew protest from various social reform groups, including African Americans who felt she had abandoned the struggle against lynching and other forms of injustice. However, she was enticed out of retirement by the Women's State Central Committee of the Republican Party, which wanted her to travel the state on a speaking tour. They also promised to hire a nurse for her six-month-old son.

More than thirty years after the 1888 *Age* article and a life of public social activism, Wells-Barnett continued to espouse the ideals of the cult. She passed them on to her two young daughters, Ida and Alfreda, who were "true to me, to themselves and their God wherever they are, and my heart is content."[39] She believed both to be "shining examples of noble true womanhood. And so mother's heart is glad and happy when she thinks of her daughters, for she knows that wherever they are and whatever they are doing they are striving to please her and reach the ideal of true womanhood."

Wells-Barnett blended the strong influence of the cult of true womanhood with an equally strong sense of Christian duty. Her views on motherhood reveal the strong influence of the ideals of the cult. Writing after the birth of her children, Wells-Barnett recognized the wonderful place of women in creation. She believed that it fell to woman to share in "the work of creation."[40] She wondered "if women who shirk their duties [childbearing and childrearing] in that respect truly realize that they have not only deprived humanity of their contribution to perpetuity, but that they have robbed themselves of one of the most glorious advantages in the development of their own womanhood."

Later, she wrote with pride of Madame C. J. Walker, who amassed a fortune selling black hair-care products. Wells-Barnett was originally among the doubters when Walker predicted success in the hair-care industry. Wells-Barnett noted Walker's meager education, but also that Walker "was never ashamed of having been a washerwoman earning a dollar and a half a day. To see her phenomenal rise made me take pride anew in Negro womanhood."[41] The impact of the cult notwithstanding, once out of her brief retirement Wells-Barnett continued her tireless agitation for social change and civil rights. In 1900, she again appealed to the national character and the Christian and moral forces of the nation. She pointed out that blacks were denied access to newspapers, religious periodicals, and magazines to refute the slander that appeared on their pages from white authorities from the South. She even noted that the "leading pulpits of the country are open to stories of the negro's degradation and ignorance but not to his defense from slander."[42] (See documents 7 and 8.)

Wells-Barnett was clear about the locus of leadership in the African American community. She commissioned black preachers, editors, and teachers to "charge themselves with the responsibility" of agitating for a restoration of the peace and due process along with their white counterparts. She placed responsibility squarely in the hands of white leaders, as they worked within their spheres of influence, as black leadership worked within its domain: "Not until the white editors, preachers and teachers of the country join with him [the Negro] in his fight for justice and protection by law can there be any hope of success."[43]

Wells-Barnett could not tolerate Booker T. Washington's model of leadership. She decried his proclivity for telling "chicken jokes," which she and other black leaders felt was detrimental to black social uplift. When Julius Rosenwald asked Wells-Barnett if African Americans had accepted Washington as their leader, she responded that, although he was respected, not everyone agreed with Washington's accommodationist position. She likened Washington's remarks to Rabbi Hirsch, a Jewish leader of Chicago, telling Gentile audiences stories about Jews burning down their stores to collect the insurance. She ended their exchange, "I am sure you would not, and a great many of us cannot approve Mr. Washington's plan of telling chicken-stealing stories on his own people in order to amuse his audiences and get money for Tuskegee."[44]

In a 1903 lecture entitled "The Colored Woman, Her Past, Present and Future," delivered to the Political Equality League, Wells-Barnett noted that "there was little employment for the Negro, and the average Negro scarcely exceeded the domestic scale."[45] After the white listeners responded with expressions of sympathy, Wells-Barnett answered, "We ask only that the door of opportunity be opened to us."

During the 1908 Springfield, Illinois, riot, Wells-Barnett organized the young men of her Bible class at Grace Presbyterian Church of Chicago into what evolved as the Negro Fellowship League. The League established a Reading Room and Social Center for men and boys at 2830 South State Street. Wells-Barnett ran the League until 1920 when her health required an operation and a long confinement in the hospital and later in her home.

In 1909, Wells-Barnett led the fight against the reinstatement of Frank Davis as Sheriff in Alexander County, Illinois. Davis had allowed a black to be lynched in Cairo, Illinois. Under Illinois law this was neglect of his duties. After investigating the incident in Cairo, Wells-Barnett brought out the facts of the case and, in a bitter fight, presented her case to Governor Charles Deneen. He subsequently refused to reinstate Sheriff Davis despite heavy political pressure on Davis' behalf. Wells-Barnett was succinct in stating her conclusion of the effect of the case: "From that day until the present there has been no lynching in the state."[46]

Wells-Barnett was staunch in her mission. She used lecture podiums and newspaper articles to bring the injustices and outrage of bigotry before the public eye in an uncompromising and clear manner. Wells-Barnett was present for the founding of the National Association for the Advancement of Colored People in 1909. When she and other more militant African Americans were not seated on the Committee of Forty to form the permanent organization, Wells-Barnett withdrew her time and interest from the organization. Although eventually added to the Committee, she felt betrayed by W. E. B. DuBois. Without consulting Wells or any others present at the meeting, DuBois had removed her name in favor of a representative from his Niagara Movement.

In addition to these activities, Wells-Barnett was active in the women's suffrage movement. She formed the Alpha Suffrage Club, Illinois' first black woman's suffrage organization, in 1914 when the Illinois Legislature passed a law allowing women the vote in local elections.

Wells-Barnett attacked discrimination wherever she found it. In 1915, she confronted President Woodrow Wilson for his tacit approval of segregation within his administration. When African American soldiers in Houston, Texas, were provoked to violence against local citizens in August of 1917, Wells-Barnett vigorously protested the summary court martial and execution of the soldiers.

She traveled to East St. Louis, Illinois, to get the details of a riot in which more than forty African Americans died the same year as the soldiers in Houston. Wells-Barnett was in Chicago during its 1919 riots trying to set up a Protective Association and find out the facts of the situation for the investigation to follow. Later that year, she traveled to the scene of a riot in Phillips County, Arkansas, to gather information needed for the release of seven black prisoners called "black revolutionists" by the white power structure of the county.[47] (See document 8.)

School teachers, press, and pulpit provided the key leadership positions in United States society. Wells-Barnett believed earnestly that persons in these areas of leadership must unite in a "vigorous denunciation of all forms of lawlessness and earnest, constant demand for the rigid enforcement of the law of the land."[48] Wells clearly saw moral agency and justice as the responsibility of leadership. Any one or any group that did not have as part of its agenda the dignity of the person and respect for the law could not provide valid leadership.

Wells-Barnett never slowed her pace. In 1930, only a year before her death, she was a candidate for the state senate. In March of this year, she spent time "reviewing [her] campaign and urging women voters to do their Christian duty and vote for race women on Primary Day April 8th."[49] She yoked Christian duty and womanhood with justice, moral agency, and vocation. True womanhood meant virtue and right action in both the private and public realms. Wells-Barnett did not believe that woman's moral influence had any limits. A woman must never content herself with her own salvation. She was responsible for her race as well. Wells-Barnett lost the campaign, in which she had run as an independent. With her usual candor, she noted that "the independent vote is weak, unorganized and its workers purchasable."[50] She attempted to forge an active and effective independent movement when the democratic and republican parties dominated Chicago politics. Her effort was doomed from the beginning. Wells-Barnett had alienated many potential supporters with her penchant for unilateral action and impatience with those who would debate or make resolutions without taking informed action. From her early days as a young school teacher in Memphis to the last, Wells-Barnett *lived* out her faith and sense of vocation. At times she was able to work effectively with coalitions, but more often she could not. Her high social, moral, and religious standards demanded a just society. Unfortunately her strong sense of Christian duty and moral action precluded her effective involvement in the various groups engaged in social reform. Wells-Barnett blazed the trail for others to follow.

When she died of uremic poisoning on March 25, 1931, the obituary in the *Chicago Defender* captured the essence of Wells-Barnett: "Elegant, striking, and always well groomed, . . . regal though somewhat intolerant and impulsive."

DOCUMENTS

1. Diary Entry: January 3, 1887. Ida B. Wells-Barnett kept a diary from 1885 to 1887. This surviving diary reveals a young woman immersed in an intense inner-religious experience, if not awakening, on the brink of her public career as a crusader for justice.

In the seven months before her twenty-fifth birthday, her diary entries reveal some of the passion of her struggle. This evangelical impulse, which wedded head and heart, evolved from a drive to shape a disciplined self.

In the entry for January 3, 1887, Wells takes this drive farther and acknowledges a demand to move beyond herself and to help shape the moral character of youths younger than she by leading a Sunday school class. Her concern is to lift up the truth of the biblical message. Yet she is ever vigilant to maintain and improve her moral character.

> Was at Cong. Church yesterday and took sacrament. While there I reviewed my last year of existence and I am so overwhelmed with the little I have done for one who has done so much for me, and I resolved to connect myself with the S.S. forthwith and work for the master. I think I shall ask for a class of youths and see if I can not influence them in a small degree to think on better things. The Bible and its truths are dealt with too flippantly to suit me. God help me to try. I shall begin this year with that determination, so that another year may find me with more to offer the master in the way of good works. God help me to be a Christian! To so conduct myself in my intercourse with the unconverted. Let it be an ever present theme with me, and O help me to better control my temper! Bless me for the ensuing year; let me feel that Thou art with me in all my struggles. May I be a better Christian

with more of the strength to overcome, the wisdom to avoid and have the meekness and humility that becometh a follower of Thee.

2. Diary Entry: May 28, 1887. Once again, Wells appealed to God to strengthen her and keep her mindful of the demands of faithful living. The rhetoric of her entry from March 28, 1887, is not unusual for the African American religious expression of the day. African Americans engaged in a constant attempt to yoke personal spirituality and social responsibility. The Christian vocation was to improve self and to improve others.

In the following passage, Wells provides a clear example of the concern for self in a drive for discipline and perfection. She also appeals to God to aid her attempts to influence her Sunday school class for the higher, nobler life found in God.

> Went to meet my class in S.S. at Avery at one o'clock. Father help me to have some influence over them and use that influence for good! I want to be of use to them, show me the way, I beseech Thee. Mr. Ames preached about our religion costing us something and I thought of the beautiful Easter time coming, that my thoughts had strayed away from the true significance of the time to less important matters of dress; that I have made no preparation for an Easter offering, but must do so and instead of spending my holiday in fun and pleasure for myself will fast for my many sins of dereliction and remain home to work, watch and pray, and praise for the wonderful goodness of my Father to an unworthy servant.

3. Diary Entry: April 11, 1887. Although Wells won her suit against the railroad for throwing her off the train when she refused to move to the smoking car reserved for African American passengers, the Supreme Court of Tennessee ruled in favor of the company on appeal.

Wells had a lifelong belief in the law and the truth. She felt certain that the rightness of her cause would prevail over the forces of injustice.

In her columns for the *Living Way,* Wells exhorted her readers to use the legal system to gain their rights. She believed in the words "the land of the free and the home of the brave." This entry reveals the depth of her despair and is poignant in its grief and disappointment. Yet Wells continued to turn to God for sustenance and the ability to persevere.

> The Supreme Court reversed the decision of the lower court in my behalf, last week. Went to see Judge G. this afternoon and he tells me four of them cast their personal prejudice in the scale of justice and decided in face of all the evidence to the contrary that the smoking car was a first class coach for colored people as provided for in that statute that calls for separate coaches but first class, for the races. I had hoped such great things from my suit for my people generally. I have firmly believed all along that the law was on our

side and would, when we appealed to it, give us justice. I feel shorn of that
belief and utterly discouraged, and just now if it were possible would gather
my race in my arms and fly far away with them. O God is there no redress,
no peace, no justice in this land for us? Thou hast always fought the battles
of the weak and oppressed. Come to my aid at this moment and teach me
what to do, for I am sorely, bitterly disappointed. Show us the way, even as
Thou led the children of Israel out of bondage into the promised land.

4. Diary Entry: July 16, 1887. Near the end of this diary, Wells included an
entry on her birthday, July 16, 1887. The themes of earlier entries are
brought together in both a testament of hope and a commitment to moral
discipline and living. She credited her spiritual growth and maturity to the
foregoing ten years of her life. During this period, she became the sole
support for her brothers and sisters and grieved the loss of her parents
and a younger sibling.

Through it all, Wells praised God. She acknowledged God's steady presence in her life and God's willingness to provide for her and her family.
However, she remained critical of her ability to embody her faith. She
again appealed to God to strengthen her resolve and to provide a firmer
foundation as she continued to improve herself spiritually, morally, and
intellectually.

This morning I stand face to face with twenty five years of life that ere the
day is gone will have passed by me forever. The experiences of a quarter of a
century of my life are my own, beginning with this, for me, new year. Already
I stared upon one fourth of the extreme limit, (100 years), and have passed
one third of the span of life which, according to the Psalmist, is allotted to
humanity. As this day's arrive enables me to count the twenty fifth milestone,
I go back over them in memory and review my life. The first ten are so far
away in the distance as to make those at the beginning indistinct; the next 5
are remembered as a kind of butterfly existence at school, and household
duties at home; within the last ten I have suffered more, learned more, lost
more than I ever expect to again. In the last decade, I've only begun to
live—to know life as a whole with its joys and sorrows. Today I write these
lines with a heart overflowing with thankfulness to my Heavenly Father for
His wonderful love and kindness; for His bountiful goodness to me, in that
He has not caused me to want and that I have always been provided with the
means to make an honest livelihood. And as I rehearse these measures my
soul is singing the glad refrain "Bless the Lord O my soul and all that is
within me, Bless His Holy name for all his benefits." Then I turn to sum up
my own accomplishments I am not so well pleased. I have not used the
opportunities I had to the best advantage and find myself intellectually lacking. And excepting my regret that I am not so good a Christian as the goodness of my Father demands, there is nothing for which I lament the wasted
opportunities as I do my neglect to pick up the crumbs of knowledge that
were within my reach. Consequently I find myself at this age as deficient in a

comprehensive knowledge as the veriest school-girl just entering the higher course. I heartily deplore the neglect. God grant I may be given firmness of purpose sufficient to essay and *continue* its eradication! Thou knowest I hunger and thirst after righteousness and knowledge. O, give me the steadiness of purpose, the will to acquire both. Twenty-five years old today! May another 10 years find me increased in honesty and purity of purpose and motive!

5. *From "Lynch Law in America."* Wells-Barnett began her public speaking career February 3, 1893, in Washington, D.C., at Metropolitan Church.[51] However, she was best known through her newspaper articles and pamphlets. Throughout the 1890s, Wells-Barnett's reputation grew as her work for social justice increased. In her most systematic article on lynching, "Lynch Law in America," Wells-Barnett paints a vividly gruesome picture of lynching, citing facts and figures gathered from the *Chicago Tribune* in 1892.

Throughout her career, Wells-Barnett always sought out the facts of any social issue she addressed. She was well known for arriving at the scene of a lynching or sending a detective to gather testimony. She went to the scenes of urban riots and interviewed the people and authorities involved. Wells-Barnett was meticulous in her information-gathering. This care for detail and honesty made her articles and pamphlets bitter pills for those who would continue to sow the seeds of injustice.

The following article is rich in detail and provides the reader with a graphic picture of the unwritten law of lynching and the people who carried out this law.

Our country's national crime is lynching. It is not the creature of an hour, the sudden outburst of uncontrolled fury, or the unspeakable brutality of an insane mob. It represents the cool, calculating deliberation of intelligent people who openly avow that there is an "unwritten law" that justifies them putting human beings to death without complaint under oath, without trial by jury, without opportunity to make defense, and without right of appeal . . .

But the spirit of mob procedure seemed to have fastened itself upon the lawless classes, and the grim process that at first was invoked to declare justice was made the excuse to wreak vengeance and cover crime. It next appeared in the South, where centuries of Anglo-Saxon civilization had made effective all the safeguards of court procedure. No emergency called for lynch law. It asserted its sway in defiance of law and in favor of anarchy. There it has flourished ever since, marking the thirty years of its existence with the inhuman butchery of more than ten thousand men, women, and children by shooting, drowning, hanging, and burning them alive. Not only this, but so potent is the force of example that the lynching mania has spread throughout the North and middle West. . . .

The first statute of this "unwritten law" was written in the blood of thousands of brave men who thought that a government that was good enough to create a citizenship was strong enough to protect it. Under the authority of a national law that gave every citizen the right to vote, the newly-made citizens chose to exercise their suffrage. But the reign of the national law was short-lived and illusionary. Hardly had the sentences dried upon the statute-books before one Southern State after another raised the cry against "negro domination" and proclaimed there was an "unwritten law" that justified any means to resist it. Whenever a burning is advertised to take place, the railroads run excursions, photographs are taken, and the same jubilee is indulged in that characterized the public hangings of one hundred years ago. There is, however, this difference: in those old days the multitude that stood by was permitted only to guy or jeer. The nineteenth century lynching mob cuts off ears, toes, and fingers, strips of flesh, and distributes portions of the body as souvenirs among the crowd. If the leaders of the mob are so minded, coal-oil is poured over the body and the victim is then roasted to death. This has been done in Texarkana and Paris, Tex., in Bardswell, Ky., and in Newman, Ga. In Paris the officers of the law delivered the prisoner to the mob. The mayor gave the school children a holiday and the railroads ran excursion trains so that the people might see a human being burned to death. In Texarkana, the year before, men and boys amused themselves by cutting off strips of flesh and thrusting knives into their helpless victim. At Newman, Ga. of the present year, the mob tried every conceivable torture to compel the victim to cry out and confess, before they set fire to the faggots that burned him. But their trouble was all in vain—he never uttered a cry, and they could not make him confess.

This condition of affairs were brutal enough and horrible enough if it were true that lynchings occurred only because of the commission of crimes against women—as constantly declared by ministers, editors, lawyers, teachers, statesmen, and even by women themselves. . . . Instead of lynchings being caused by assaults upon women, the statistics show that not one-third of the victims are even charged with such crimes. . . .

. . . The negro has been too long associated with the white man not to have copied his vices as well as his virtues. But the negro resents and utterly repudiates the effort to blacken his good name by asserting that assaults upon women are peculiar to his race. The negro has suffered far more from the commission of this crime against the women of his race by white men than the white race has ever suffered through *his* crimes. . . . What becomes a crime deserving capital punishment when the tables are turned is a matter of small moment when the negro woman is the accusing party. . . . [52]

6. From "The Negro's Case in Equity." Wells-Barnett was clear that the moral leadership of African Americans and whites provided a crucial piece to the eradication of lynching in the United States. She took white leaders to task for their failure to provide adequate moral leadership for the white citizenry. At the same time she challenged African American leaders to set and then uphold high moral standards for their people.

Throughout her life, Wells-Barnett could never reconcile faith without works. Wells-Barnett believed in a living God and a living faith. For her, the Christian must put his or her faith into practice and live out of that faith as fully as possible in personal life and vocationally. Her tone in this article is direct and to the point. Wells-Barnett never shied away from calling African Americans to task, but she also demanded the same high moral standard for her white brother and sister in Christ.

The Independent publishes an earnest appeal to negro editors, preachers and teachers "to tell their people to defend the laws and their own rights even to blood, but never, never to take guilty participation in lynching white man or black . . . "

For twenty years past the negro has done nothing else but defend the law and appeal to public sentiment for defense *by* the law. He has seen hundreds of men of his race murdered in cold blood by connivance of officers of the law, from the governors of the States down to sheriffs of counties. . . . All this and more the negro has seen and suffered without taking the law into his hands for, lo, these many years. There have been no Nat Turner insurrections and San Domingan horrors in retaliation for all the wrongs he has suffered. When the negro has appealed to the Christian and moral forces of the country—asking them to create a sentiment against his lawlessness and unspeakable barbarism; demanding justice and the protection of the law for every human being regardless of color—that demand has been met with general indifference or entirely ignored. Where this is not true he has been told that these same forces upon which he confidently depends refuse to make the demand for justice, because they believe the story of the mob that negroes are lynched because they commit unspeakable crimes against white women. For this reason the Christian and moral forces are silent in the presence of the horrible barbarities alleged to be done in the name of woman.

When the negro, confident in the justice of his cause and the sincerity of the aforesaid Christian and moral forces seeks the opportunity to disprove this slander, he is refused, except in very rare instances. The columns of powerful dailies, religious periodicals and thoughtful magazines have printed these charges wholesale until the civilized world has accepted them, but few wish to consider the refutation of them or give space for the possible other side. The leading pulpits of the country are open to stories of the negro's degradation and ignorance but not to his defense from slander. . . .

Notwithstanding all this is true and has been true for twenty years past, while ten thousand men, women and children have . . . been done to death in the same manner as in the late Virginia case; in spite of the fact that the governors of States, commanders of militia, sheriffs and police have taken part in these disgraceful exhibitions; and with absolute proof that the public sentiment of the country was with the mob—who, if not the negro preachers, editors and teachers, are to be credited with the fact that there are few, if any instances of negroes who have had "guilty participation in lynching white men or black?" And if all the negro preachers, editors and teachers should charge themselves with the responsibility of this one lapse after years of the greatest human provocation, should not all the white preachers, editors and teachers charge themselves with the thousands of lynchings by white men? . . . For seven years the negro has been agitating against lynching he has made this appeal to the leaders of thought and action among the white race. If they will do their duty in this respect the negroes will now have no bad examples of the lynching kind set, which in their desperation they may be tempted to follow. . . .

Not until the white editors, preachers and teachers of the country join him [the Negro] in his fight for justice and protection by law can there be any hope of success.[53]

7. *From* Crusade for Justice: *the Last Days of the Negro Fellowship League.* The Negro Fellowship League was a significant part of Wells-Barnett's life in Chicago. The League sponsored a settlement house on South State Street to help black men find jobs, provided temporary housing, offered counseling services, and sponsored Sunday worship services. The League grew out of Wells-Barnett's conviction that the church must be engaged in creating a moral and just society. She likened the work of the League to that of Jane Addams' Hull House on Chicago's North Side.

Because of failing health and lack of community support, Wells-Barnett approached The Methodist Episcopal Church for support to keep the League going and to expand its programs. She was met with male chauvinism. She faced the bitter disappointment of a fading vocational commitment, which meant fewer resources in the African American community. In the following passage, Wells-Barnett also makes a clear case for class elitism and sexism in the African American community of Chicago.

Although the Methodist Episcopal Church is one of the oldest Protestant denominations in Chicago, it has not taken the rank it deserves among colored people. Since Chicago is the headquarters for much of its auxiliary work, I felt that they would get behind the movement we had been able to build and make it the greatest social service work in the country. . . .

Coming to the North, I was greatly disappointed to find that no specific attention was being paid to the Negro communicants of the church. Even the routine church work was of very poor quality, and the leading church it had in Chicago, the Saint Mark's Methodist Episcopal Church, was worshiping in a storefront when I first came to Chicago . . .

I had a vision of building on the foundation we had already established at the reading room and social center. We had not only been the Hull House for our people on the South Side and for those who came to us from all over the country, but we had also—as Hull House had done—provided a place for practical training of young men and women who wanted to do social service work. I knew the church had money. They knew I had the vision.

Bishop Thomas Nicholson, who was then over the district, became enthusiastic over the matter, and I felt that at last I was going to see the fruit of my labor. The matter was referred to Rev. G.E. Bryant, who was then the district superintendent over the colored churches. Rev. Bryant said that it could only be done by permitting the use of the place for church service on Sunday. I told him that was just what we desired, as we had held services there every Sunday since the place had been opened.

The next report I had about the matter was that the church would take over the work provided I would step aside and turn it over to a young minister whom they had in mind; he was studying at Garrett Biblical Institute and had made a wonderful record as a Greek and Hebrew scholar at the institute. It was there decided that his qualification would make him the ideal person to take over the work. At first I was very much grieved over the thought that I was not to be permitted to continue the work I had started. . . .

I was already heartbroken over their willingness to shut me out with no consideration for my ten years' work. The chairman [of the committee that would now direct the center] said, "Why, do you know, Mrs. Barnett, I was amazed when I found out that you had no leading people of the race with you in the league." "Yes," I said, "well I would like to have had them. I certainly have done all I could to get them interested, but for some cause or other they refused to come in. But then," I said, "neither did Jesus Christ have any of the leading people with him in his day when he was trying to establish Christianity. If I remember correctly, his twelve disciples were made up of fishermen, tax collectors, publicans, and sinners. It was the leading people who refused to believe on him and finally crucified him.

. . . "The secretary of our organization is an elevator man in the Boston Store. He is not one of our 'most leadingest.' The treasurer is a redcap at the Illinois Central Station. He does not figure as one of the leading colored citizens, either, but he is faithful in his attendance and contributes his mite every Sunday. The leader of my Bible class is a rag picker. I see him every time I go downtown on the streetcar with a large bag of dirty rags on his back—junk, I take it. But he believes in the Negro Fellowship League with all his heart and is here every Sunday to take a leading part in our Bible lessons.

"It is bad enough that our leading people refuse to take part in work of this character or to know men of this type. But to me it is still worse that they not only refuse themselves to help, but they are doing everything they can to disparage and to sneer at those of us who are struggling that they may keep this effort going."[54]

8. *From* Crusade for Justice: *the Arkansas Riot.* Wells-Barnett visited the twelve African American men who were jailed, found guilty of murder in the first degree, and sentenced to death for their alleged leadership role in the Phillips County, Arkansas, riot. This riot was the result of black tenant farmers and sharecroppers attempting to organize a labor union.

When we came into the building in which these twelve men were incarcerated, we were readily admitted. Mrs. Moore, the leading spirit among the wives, who was well known because of her frequent visits, said, "Boys, come and shake hands with my cousin who has come from Saint Louis to see me." The iron bars were wide enough apart to enable us to shake hands. The one guard on duty sat about fifty feet away reading the sunday paper. When he looked up, he saw only a group of insignificant looking colored women who had been there many times before so he went on reading his paper.

When we got up close to the bars, Mrs. Moore whispered, "This is Mrs. Barnett from Chicago." An expression of joy spread over their faces, but I put my finger to my lips and cautioned them not to let on, and immediately a mask seemed to drop over the features of each one. I talked with them about their experiences, asking them to write down everything they could recollect about the rioting, and what befell each of them. . . .

Then Mrs. Moore said, "Boys, don't you want to sing for my cousin?" Whereupon they sang a song of their own composition and many others. . . . I listened to those men sing and pray and give testimony from their overburdened hearts, and sometimes the women would take up the refrain. They shed tears and they got "happy," and the burden of their talk and their prayers was of the hereafter.

Finally I got up and walked close to the bars and said to them in a low tone, "I have been listening to you for nearly two hours. You have talked and sung and prayed about dying, and forgiving your enemies, and of feeling sure that you are going to be received in the New Jerusalem because your God knows that you are innocent of the offense for which you expect to be electrocuted. But why don't you pray to live and ask to be freed? The God you serve is the God of Paul and Silas who opened their prison gates, and if you have all the faith you say you have, you ought to believe that he will open your prison doors too.

"If you do believe that, let all of your songs and prayers hereafter be songs of faith and hope that God will set you free; that the judges who have to pass on your cases will be given the wisdom and courage to decide in your behalf. That is all I've got to say. Quit talking about dying; if you believe your God is all powerful, believe he is powerful enough to open these prison doors, and say so. Dying is the last thing you ought to even think about, much less talk about. Pray to live and believe you are going to get out."

I went away and spent nearly all night writing down the experiences of the women who were also put in prison in Helena, and within two days I had written statements of each of those twelve men and the facts I had requested. It is a terrible indictment of white civilization and Christianity. It shows that the white people did just what they accused the Negroes of doing: murdered them and stole their crops, their stock, and their household goods. And even then they were invoking the law to put the seal of approval on their deeds by legally (?) executing those twelve men who were found guilty after six minutes' deliberation![55]

Katharine Bushnell

CHAPTER 8

MAN'S PRATTLE, WOMAN'S WORD

The Biblical Mission of Katharine Bushnell

DANA HARDWICK

Katharine Bushnell believed the Bible to be inspired, infallible, inerrant, and inviolable. She did not, however, hold the same reverence for translations of scripture. She said, "We hold the Bible as supreme in authority, and its text as inviolable. But we must not forget that man's prattle about it may be very foolish."[1] She was convinced that sex-biased translations were at the root of the subordination and oppression of women. (See document 1.)

> Every time there has been an opportunity for the use of option in [biblical] translation, use has been made of that option, by this or that man of learning, to build up one sex and to deprecate the other, and so the result, through the ages, has been cumulative, and that without actual intention.[2]

Katharine Bushnell lived for ninety years (1855–1946). Her life included careers as a medical doctor, evangelist, crusader, scholar, writer, and educator. Each of her careers flowed from and incorporated the ones before. Each was focused on bringing women to a clearer understanding of God's word and God's will for them as equal creatures in God's eyes.

Undergirding and guiding all of her work was a deep spiritual life grounded in prayer and study of the Bible. In her view, the attributes of infallibility and inerrancy applied only to the original texts of the Bible, and not to the translations and interpretations later applied to those texts. This led her to a lifelong study of the biblical languages and the original biblical texts. She did not look in faith to scripture and then feel the need to act upon what she saw there. Rather, action and faith were interwoven: Faith called her to serve women, and what she saw in the plight of the women she served drove her back to the Bible to find some basis for what she saw. Convinced that some passages were deliberately misinterpreted, she was driven to study these passages in the original languages. Her new interpretations called yet again for action in sharing her work with others. Talking about her faith was not enough. The talk had to be accompanied by action.

Katharine Bushnell was born in Peru, Illinois, on February 5, 1855, the seventh of nine children. After a public school education, she attended the preparatory school of Northwestern University and remained at Northwestern for two years of study in the classics. At the end of this time, she entered The Woman's Hospital Medical College, graduating when she was twenty-four. Bushnell had been strictly brought up in the Methodist Episcopal Church, and her primary motivation for studying medicine was to benefit her work in Christian mission. So even though her plan was for advanced medical training, after a residency in Chicago's Hospital for Women and Children she allowed herself to be persuaded by the Women's Mission Board of The Methodist Episcopal Church to go to Kiukiang, China, as a missionary in 1880.[3]

Believing that this was the will of God for her life, Bushnell threw herself into this missionary work. However, she was very homesick and unhappy; endless heat, primitive facilities, and never-ending work took their toll on her health. She frequently found herself performing surgery, acting as her own anesthetist, and doing all the nursing. Eventually, a former classmate, Ella Gilchrist, was sent to assist her, and with periodic retreats into the mountains for rest, Bushnell's health began to improve. However, it was during one of these mountain retreats that she fell and injured her spine, an injury that would plague her for the rest of her life. About the same time, Gilchrist contracted tuberculosis, and the two doctors returned home. Bushnell left China feeling that she had failed to fulfill God's will, that God "had branded [her] whole future 'failure.'"[4]

Forty-seven years later Bushnell would say that her work in China "was the mistake of my life, excepting that 'All things work together for good to them that love God, to them who are called according to His purpose.'"[5] Her time in China proved to have two very important influences on her life. It was in China that Bushnell first began to observe the effects a male-dominated society had on its women, and the lengths to which this domination could drive them. (See document 2.) It was also in China that Bushnell began to feel the call to deeper and more critical Bible study.

At the time Bushnell went to China, she believed "it was neither desirable nor necessary for women to preach the Gospel; it was unbecoming."[6] However, during her travels in China, she encountered a sex-biased translation of a passage in the Chinese Bible, and when she questioned a male missionary, he blamed the pagan prejudice against women in ministry. (See document 3.) It had never occurred to her that such a thing could happen.

As Bushnell began to study both the Chinese and English Bibles, her opinions as to the place of women in the gospel began to change. Her conviction grew that men's prejudice was influencing scripture translations, and the seeds were planted which would one day blossom into a ministry of teaching and a new interpretation of many biblical passages that seemed to encourage the subordination of women. (See document 1.)

After their return to the United States from China in 1882, Bushnell accompanied the dying Gilchrist to the latter's home in Denver, Colorado, and remained with her until her death. Then twenty-seven years old, she continued her medical practice but was increasingly unhappy. She became involved with the Department of Social Purity of the Woman's Christian Temperance Union (WCTU), working among Chinese women and prostitutes in Denver.[7] In 1885 Frances Willard persuaded Bushnell to give up her medical practice and to come to Chicago as National Evangelist of the Purity Department of the WCTU. For Katharine Bushnell, the WCTU was the perfect milieu in which to live out her spirituality and the action her spiritual life demanded. Prayer was a part of each WCTU meeting, and no plan for mission among "fallen" women was formulated or carried through without it.

Bushnell arrived in Chicago early in 1886 and was soon engaged in setting up reading rooms, missions, and programs directed toward the rescue of women working in prostitution. She and her corps of women volunteers actively sought out those women who were caught in the seemingly inescapable net of prostitution and vice. Bushnell and her volunteers read the morning newspapers and police records to get the names and whereabouts of offenders and searched the streets for them. They offered faith and a future by offering counseling and helping the women to find jobs and homes.

The primary aim of the WCTU was the promotion of universal temperance.[8] Katharine Bushnell's work, however, shows little interest in this issue except as it was related to social purity. Her focus was the plight of exploited women and girls. Her writing reflects that she found the cause of the degradation of women not in the abuses resulting from drink, but in the bias of both the writing and the translations of the Bible by males.[9] The abuses resulting from drink, which admittedly were many, she felt were mere symptoms of the deeper problem. From the time in China when she first realized that the bias in translation could be deliberate, Bushnell's focus was twofold: the reformation and healing of the women and the society who were victims of that bias; and the education of all women, including herself, in the Bible and the biblical languages so that the questionable passages could be reinterpreted. (See document 5.)

Bushnell began to take the message of "social purity" across the country. She was on the road for months at a time, traveling by train and living as a guest in the homes of local WCTU members. She was paid no salary, but lived on the donations and hospitality of those to whom she lectured. Her travel time was spent in Bible study and the study of biblical languages,[10] and the writing of articles for *The Union Signal* and pamphlets for the Social Purity Department.

Around this time, reports began to circulate about "white slavery" in the northern Wisconsin and Michigan lumber camps. The reports were that women and girls, some of them mentally retarded, were being enticed north by the prospect of good wages and easy work. There were even reports that some of the stockades in which the women were held were being guarded by dogs. When nobody could be found to investigate the conditions and get reliable facts, Bushnell determined to investigate them for herself.[11] Thus began the first of Katharine Bushnell's great crusades.

The Wisconsin governor's office had investigated the allegations and found them without grounds. Bushnell, however, was not satisfied, and interviewed the governor's investigator, James Fielding, herself. He admitted that he had been to only one town, had entered only one brothel, and had interviewed only the one group of inmates found in that brothel.[12] His report, published in the *Milwaukee Journal,* said that he had found no evidence of abduction, enticement, or involuntary detention of women or girls from Milwaukee and Chicago in the many brothels he claimed to have inspected.[13] He admitted to Bushnell that he had never done the investigations about which he had written,[14] but also admitted that the "dens" did exist, that women were "detained" for payment of fines levied by the house for misbehaviors of various kinds, and that their clothes and wages were withheld pending payment of such fines.

Bushnell began her own investigation. She had planned to spend only one month on her inquiries, but it stretched to four. It was at considerable risk that Bushnell entered the brothels and stockades in which women were being held. She compiled information both from those who aided women in escape attempts and from her own observations. She interviewed lawyers, pastors, doctors, as well as escapees and staff from the "infamous dens."[15] Using methods she had learned while working with prostitutes in the larger cities, she carefully compiled her report.

Having penetrated the brothels using one excuse or another, Bushnell was able by various pretexts to obtain proof of the actual conditions which existed there. She found cases of abuse, broken bones, even murder. Many of these conditions were known, condoned, and even abetted by local police.[16] Previous reports of women and girls being detained and guarded by dogs she found to be true. She made sketches from within one of the stockaded and guarded dens, and made several sketches outside the more notorious places.[17]

Bushnell was not without aid in her investigations. She found more-than-willing help from local WCTU members and pastors in the towns and villages in which she was making her inquiries. When she was in danger, there were always Christian friends or sympathetic pastors within calling distance, and she was careful to keep someone aware at all times of where she was going. In the four months of her study, she investigated nearly sixty dens and compiled information on 577 "degraded women," many of whom she interviewed personally.[18]

Bushnell's research uncovered the use of flagrantly purchased political influence to inhibit legal action. False reports were filed by politicians who owed their position and influence to men who had grown rich in this industry.[19] Many of the medical profession supported the strict "Contagious Diseases Acts" and forced examination of the prostitutes. Townspeople also supported the brothels, both for business reasons and to protect "virtuous" women from the lusts of the lumberjacks.[20] (See document 3.)

Bushnell reported these findings at a WCTU meeting in Chicago and became an overnight sensation as newspapers rushed to get in on this latest furor. Exaggerated and unsubstantiated reports of her investigations appeared everywhere, even in *The Union Signal,* organ of the National WCTU. Bushnell accused the newspapers of deliberately distorting the facts as she had presented them in order to discredit her allegations.[21]

Bushnell was accosted, verbally abused, and accused of unchastity by James Fielding, the state investigator she had discredited. Bushnell brought charges against him, and Fielding did not deny the charges. However, after a number of delays and political contortions on the part of the defense, the case was thrown out of court.[22]

Wisconsin officials denied Bushnell's reports and heaped abuse on her for slandering their state.[23] When she appeared before an out-of-session meeting of the Wisconsin legislature, she had to be protected by police from possible violence.[24] At this meeting, she was initially a bit overwhelmed by her position as the only woman in a room full of hostile men. Being a woman of prayer, she began to pray, and soon the door to the room opened to admit a number of local WCTU women who stood around her in support of what she was doing.[25]

There was other support for Bushnell. Her report was widely distributed by the Wisconsin WCTU. Resolutions were adopted all over the country praising Bushnell for her work and pledging further support, condemning those who condoned prostitution, and requesting legislatures to enact laws that would severely punish and suppress such activity.[26]

The result was the passage of a bill nicknamed "The Kate Bushnell Bill," which dealt with the issues she had been investigating. Although Bushnell says that she had no part in its drafting, the newspapers gave her the credit and the bill her name.[27]

Bushnell's popularity as a speaker exploded. However, she found her new reputation to be a hindrance to her work of evangelism. Everywhere she went, the audiences preferred the Wisconsin stories to talks on social purity. Bushnell went home to Evanston to think and to pray for God's guidance for light on the future direction of her ministry. She saw little use in continuing to speak on the social purity question until the sensation of the lumber camps died down, but she feared that the furor might have branded her message permanently. "I did not wish to keep an unhealthy sensation alive; legislation having been secured, I wished the matter dropped."[28]

One warm summer afternoon in 1890, Bushnell was seeking guidance from the Bible, and twice in a row her random selection fell on references, in both the Old and New Testaments, to Joseph's dreams. The third turning of pages resulted in the story of Peter's dream on Simon the tanner's rooftop in the city of Joppa. After saying to herself, "Why could not I be guided by a dream?"[29] she fell asleep. She records that she dreamed that she had been tossed about on the waves on a voyage to England to see Josephine Butler, the head of the Social Purity Department in England's WCTU, and to do some work for her. After some initial hesitation, she decided that God had provided the guidance for which she had been praying. She promptly wrote Butler, telling her of the dream, and since Butler "saw no reason to doubt that the vision vouchsafed to Kate Bushnell was of God,"[30] she wrote and invited Bushnell to come to England because she might have work for her in an Indian campaign for purity. This, of course, was right up Bushnell's alley.

This fell in with her plans in other ways, also. Bushnell had been chosen by the officers of the newly formed World WCTU as one of two world evangelists. She and Elizabeth Andrew, her co-evangelist for the next twenty-five years, were to travel around the world, speaking in the interests of social purity.[31] Once again, there was to be no funding, and Bushnell found it necessary to continue her public speaking. She was still willing to speak on the subject of forced prostitution in Wisconsin and to put the facts, however disagreeable, before her listeners. In December of 1890, only one month before she sailed for England, Bushnell told her Berea, Ohio, audience, "I know these facts are not pleasant to hear . . . but you *shall* hear them."[32]

When Bushnell reached England, she joined forces with Elizabeth Andrew and together they went to see Josephine Butler. Butler had been working for moral reform among prostitutes for twenty-four years, and she would work with Bushnell and Andrew in the same field for the next sixteen. The problem of immediate concern was reputed violations of the repeal of the Contagious Diseases Acts, which had provided for mandatory medical "inspection" of prostitutes who were being supplied, with government knowledge and approval, for the "requirements" of the men of the British army. Two official male British commissioners had investigated the situation, but reportedly found no wrongdoing. Although the Acts had been repealed and alleged infractions denied, rumors continued to circulate.[33]

Butler's plan was for her two new partners in reform to go under the cover of their roles as World Evangelists of the World WCTU and quietly investigate the situation in the military cantonments (compounds). Their American nationality would arouse less suspicion, and it was hoped that Bushnell's status as a doctor would gain them admission into the "lock" hospitals in which diseased women were reportedly being incarcerated.

As planned, India was incorporated into the World WCTU tour. Andrew and Bushnell left England in July, 1891, for Madeira and Capetown, South Africa, where they spoke on social purity until India's hot summer months were past. They were not permitted to speak of their Indian mission to anyone, which raised their anxiety considerably. When they arrived in India, one of the men upon whom they were to depend for assistance condemned their mission as foolish, impractical, and impossible for women to accomplish.[34] Alienated by this attitude on the part of their only source of aid and weighted down by the burden of the secrecy of their task, the two women turned to God. After a day spent in prayer and fasting (an activity to which the women had frequent recourse in the months to come), they determined to continue their mission. They interviewed endless government officials and doctors, but met only official evasions and deliberate misleadings. The next five weeks were spent in similarly futile attempts to penetrate the barriers which separated them from information about regulated prostitution in India.

Near despair, Bushnell and Andrew once again spent a day in prayer. The resulting guidance led them to a friend who had lived in India for a considerable period of time and was able to familiarize them with Indian customs and language, which made them considerably more independent. This enabled them to interview the women themselves instead of trying to get information from the evasive public officials. Through Bushnell's medical status, they gained access to the "lock" hospitals and hospital records.[35] They held religious services for the inmates of the houses and hospitals, and listened to their personal stories. They interviewed the native physicians and nurses who treated the women and the "mahaldarnis" who procured, trained, and supervised them in the cantonments. The evidence proving the military government's participation in the regulation of vice began to mount.[36]

The work was exhausting. The women traveled as "intermediate" passengers in the trains to avoid attracting attention as first-class or second-class passengers, arriving at their destinations in the middle of the night, sleeping in the ladies' waiting rooms at the train stations, eating in station restaurants. They "trusted the Lord" to save them from confrontation with the authorities, and in their travels and investigations of ten military cantonments, they were never confronted.[37] They traveled 3,600 miles, visited ten military stations, interviewed 395 prostitutes and many medical personnel.

Their investigations complete, Bushnell and Andrew wrote their report, sent it to England, and continued on their tour for the World WCTU. About their business in India, they were warned by cable, "Silence concerning India imperative," and shortly thereafter were recalled to England to appear before Prime Minister Gladstone, who had read their confidential report and was appalled.[38]

When the report became public, things in England became quite lively, with accusations and denials flying back and forth. Newspapers characterized Bushnell and Andrew as well-intentioned but ill-informed philanthropists.[39] However, governmental investigations ensued, and the allegations of the women proved correct. Lord Roberts, Commander-in-Chief of the British Army in India, who had previously denied knowledge and participation in the scandal in which he had played a leading role, wrote a letter of apology, which was included with the official report.[40]

Katharine Bushnell and Elizabeth Andrew left England and continued their WCTU work, traveling to Ceylon, Australia, and New Zealand. They eventually arrived back in the United States, where they spoke about their crusades at the international WCTU convention. They did not stay long at home, though, soon off on another worldwide tour, still speaking in the interests of social purity. More detective work awaited. The women returned to India on their speaking tour, and while in Bombay were asked to investigate the growing opium trade in the Orient. A Royal Commission had been appointed to investigate the trade. As a majority of the Commission favored continuing the trade, the initial report had given the impression that "opium was beneficial to its users."[41] Bushnell and Andrew prayed for guidance and soon went under cover again. They felt there was a strong relationship between prostitution and the use of opium, and also thought that the British and the Americans strongly supported the trade.

While Bushnell and Andrew were involved in this work, Britain's Colonial Secretary, the Marquis of Rippon, asked the women also to investigate the growing incidence of the sale of Chinese women and girls to organizations in Hong Kong, Shanghai, and San Francisco.[42] Once again the women found themselves visiting "lock" hospitals and gathering evidence of forced examination of women. They also found British government "protectors," who, under the guise of helping diseased or freedom-seeking prostitutes, actually sanctioned their continued forced labor.[43]

Bushnell was appalled at the complaisance toward forced prostitution that she found among the British government officials in China. In this she was joined by Chinese Christians who were amazed at the extent of participation by "Englishmen and Americans who called themselves 'Christians.'"[44] Men publicly recognized for their Christian acts of charity were the authors of ordinances punishing Chinese women who attempted to leave the owners who forced them to work as prostitutes. (See document 3.) Bushnell felt that the Christian nations were judged by the morals of the men who came to the Orient and set up the system of brothel slavery, domestic slavery, and coolie labor. The fact that children as young as seven were kept in training in opium dens and houses of prostitution, and that the "Christian" officers of the Protectorate would do nothing to procure the children's release, was an utter condemnation of Christianity as far as the Orientals were concerned.[45]

After giving their written report to the Colonial Secretary, Bushnell and Andrew once again continued on their world tour. In June 1894, they finally arrived back in the United States but were met at the dock with urgent requests to return to England to testify before the opium commission and to join efforts in the fight against renewal of the Contagious Diseases Acts.[46] They returned as requested and toured England for the next two years, speaking against opium and prostitution, and for social purity.

However, in 1896, Lord Roberts initiated a successful drive to have the Contagious Diseases Acts reinstated. Lady Henry Somerset, President of the British WCTU, Vice-president of the World WCTU, and very close friend of WCTU President Frances Willard, had suggested proposals in favor of mandatory examination of both men and women, and was persuaded by Lord George Hamilton, Secretary of State for India, to use her influence in the various WCTU organizations to support reinstatement of the Acts. By the end of 1896, when the dust of the ensuing WCTU furor had finally settled, the Acts had been reinstated and Somerset remained in her various WCTU offices; however, Josephine Butler, Elizabeth Andrew, and Katharine Bushnell had resigned.

Andrew and Bushnell remained under Butler's guidance during the rest of their stay in England, during which they continued to speak on social purity. Bushnell also began to lead Bible studies for women based on some of her new interpretations. The time finally came when Butler sent for them and told them their mission in social purity in England was finished. She told Bushnell that she had "a message from God" for their future.[47] When they met, Butler recommended that Bushnell turn her attention away from social purity work and toward holding meetings based on her Bible studies.

Bushnell was elated. She had had enough of the lecture circuit and had long been preparing for the work of biblical interpretation. After discussion and prayer about their plan of action, the three women agreed that "the social evil would never be got rid of so long as the subordination of woman to man was taught within the body of Christians."[48] (See document 2.)

173

The crusade for purity could never be completely successful until men and women began to see that people of both sexes were of equal value, and this would have to be proved by reinterpreting the very passages which had always been used to subordinate women. (See documents 3 and 4.)

> But place Christian women where God intends them to stand, on a plane of full equality with men, in the home and in the Church, where their faculties, their will, their consciences are controlled only by the God who made man and woman equal by creation, and who is "no respecter of persons"—then the world will become much purer than it is today.[49]

Bushnell's long years of study of the Bible and biblical languages and her experience of working for justice for women were now to be carried into that body of Christians. Shortly after this meeting with Josephine Butler, Bushnell and Andrew returned home and Katharine Bushnell began her new work.

Bushnell continued her study of the Bible and began to write. From San Francisco, she and Andrew also continued their fight against the sale of Chinese women and girls into prostitution, and reported on this and their China opium and prostitution investigations in *Heathen Slaves and Christian Rulers* (1907). Bushnell then returned to England and spent the next seven years studying in the libraries of the great English universities and publishing the first of her Bible studies. World War I drove her back to the United States, where she waged one more war against organized government support of vice, this time against the United States and its "Federal Social Hygiene programme."[50]

Once again, as she had in Wisconsin, in India, and in Hong Kong, she went into red-light districts, visited hospitals, and interviewed doctors. The report she prepared under the title "What's Going On" reflects her anger at the injustice and indignity suffered by women. To the argument that one woman could infect twenty men in a night, she replied that in such a case "there are about twenty men to one woman practicing vice; and the thing resolves itself into the simple arithmetical rule that, if one woman may do the mischief of twenty men, then twenty men may do the mischief of one woman."[51]

For Bushnell, there was no measuring the difference between the reward or punishment meted out to men or to women. The men received "early" or "prophylactic" treatment, whether or not they knew that the woman with whom they had sexual relations was infected. On the other hand, simple suspicion was enough to subject a woman to examination and quarantine. Further, since prostitutes were automatically classified as vagrants, the health officers assumed that all female vagrants were prostitutes and forced women charged with vagrancy to submit to examination and quarantine. To make matters worse, all a soldier or sailor had to do was to report any woman as suspicious, or as the source of his disease, and that woman would be picked up, detained in a hospital, and examined.[52] Bushnell deplored the flagrant injustice to women manifested in the unequal amounts of shame and punishment suffered by equal partners to the immorality. (See document 2.) Never did she condone the immoral behavior of either party to the illicit sexual act. Her desire was justice for both parties: the same punishment, the same shame to be meted out for both the man and the woman involved. She was incensed that the men would always go free, while the women lost all rights, including that of *habeas corpus* and due process of law. Under the terms and instructions of the Federal hygiene program, women were to be held and their trials postponed so that they could be examined and treated if necessary. The men were to be tried and sentenced immediately. "Men are to have their Constitutional rights respected, even to being free to infect their innocent wives and children!"[53]

Bushnell roundly condemned this program as promoting vice on the part of servicemen. As in India, she tried to show that regulation did not stop vice, but promoted it. Once again she traveled—investigating, giving speeches, exhorting—but this time to no avail. She sent pamphlets and letters to the President of the United States, his cabinet, and the Congress. Although she was supported in her crusade by the contributions of a few who concurred with her views, she found no widespread sympathy or cooperation. In the end, the great effort expended in this last and most bitter of all her crusades was in vain. Bushnell returned to her Bible study and continued writing for more than twenty-five years.

Bushnell's final crusade was waged on paper and was the culmination and justification of a life spent in the service of God and of humanity. She saw woman's need universally because she traveled the world over and was witness to the abuse of women everywhere she went. Each crusade she undertook added to her conviction of the need to have the power of the Bible behind woman's search for freedom; each mile journeyed on each crusade increased the motivation for her journey into the Bible.

The longer she worked in the mission field, the more convinced she became that the biased translations done by men were the source of the prejudice against women. (See document 1.) The longer she worked for the equality of women, the more Bushnell realized that woman's plight was rooted in the fact that the Bible was seen to support the degradation and suppression of women. Her conclusion was that the Bible needed to be reinterpreted. Her task was to devise an interpretation that would free women to seek their proper "place in the divine economy."[54] (See document 4.)

To turn to Bible study and writing from a life spent in active lecturing and on mission fields required a fundamental refocusing of Bushnell's efforts and a new understanding of her call to ministry. Bushnell maintained that it was not possible to study and write about the Bible properly without an intimate knowledge of the biblical languages. She had studied Latin and Greek in her classical course at Northwestern and she never ended her study of biblical languages and interpretations.[55] Katharine Bushnell's writings fall into two categories: reports of her crusades and Bible studies of varying lengths.

Bushnell's spirituality found expression in action—action in mission, action in evangelism, and action in teaching, writing, and interpretation. She saw herself as empowered by the Holy Spirit, and no action was undertaken without prayer. There was always an expectation that God was guiding everything that happened, and this expectation was reflected in all she did in the mission field.

Bushnell also saw divine guidance in the integration of study and service that informed her writing. In looking back over her life, Bushnell notes that "it was according to a Divine plan that the . . . investigations in the Orient should have gone forward hand in hand, as it were, with my Bible studies—for nearly every moment of my many sea voyages and railway journeys was spent in these studies."[56] A constant theme in her writing was the call for women as well as men to educate themselves in the biblical languages and take part in the work of biblical translation and interpretation so that each could serve as a buffer against the bias of the other. (See document 3.) Although she believed in the inviolability of the Bible, she felt that "criticism of a Bible exposition may be undertaken in the interests of a deeper reverence for the Word than the expositor who is criticized has shown,"[57] and she felt that this work required the united efforts of both women and men.

DOCUMENTS

1. Sex Bias in Translation. In *God's Word to Women,* Bushnell's principal work, one of her leading themes is the effects of sex bias in biblical translation. She writes of how this came to be.

It must, then, impress reasoning minds that the interpretation of Gen. 3:16 has had a history something like this: Men of old found a phrase here that seemed to have to do with woman's relation to her husband, but it was beyond their comprehension. Unconsciously these men of olden time have consulted their own ideas of what a wife *should be,* in her relation to her husband, and inserted those ideas into their interpretation. The interpretation has been accepted by other men, without challenge, because it conformed to their unsanctified wishes, and handed on from generation to generation, until it became weighty through "tradition." No effort, scarcely, has been put forth to reconcile such teachings with the spirit of Jesus Christ. A letter, relating to the passage, has come to me, during the preparation of these Lessons, from an eminent Bible scholar, to whom I suggested the need of a better interpretation. He replies: "I should hardly have thought a correction of the text was either called for or probable." Of course, our proposal had never been to amend the text, as he well knew, but the interpretation and translation. Prejudice blinds men, even in their treatment of the Word of God, if a faulty rendering coincides with their preconceptions . . .[par. 112].

It is well known that when a man gets lost on the prairie he begins to go round in a circle; it is suggested that one side (the right, generally), being stronger than the other, he pulls unconsciously with greater strength upon the corresponding guiding rein of his horse. Just so does the translator; he pulls unconsciously on the strong side of preconception or self-interest. This may not be intended, but it is none the less inevitable to the uninspired hand. For this reason, no class nor sex should have an exclusive right to set forth the meaning of the original text. It is notorious that the Samaritan Hebrew text, even, has been manipulated to a considerable extent to suit Samaritan prejudices, so that manuscript must be corrected by comparison with others before it can be trusted on points that involve Samaritan interests. The Alexandrian, or Septuagint version, shows traces of an attempt to meet the prejudices of Egyptians. What wonder that all versions, having for all time been made by men, should disclose the fact that, on the woman question, they all travel more or less in a circle, in accordance with sex bias, hindering the freedom and progress of women, since (in times past more than at present), the self interest of man led him to suppose that woman served God best as his own undeveloped subordinate? [par. 616]

2. Personal Feelings in Writings.

2. Personal Feelings in Writings. Bushnell did not write with any lack of feeling. She owned bitterness and anger when faced with the oppression and degradation of women and the investment "decent" men and "virtuous" women had in supporting such degradation.

In *The Reverend Doctor and His Doctor Daughter,* when the reverend doctor accuses his doctor daughter of speaking bitterly of the position of women forced on them by men, Katharine Bushnell speaks through the daughter's reply:

I speak as I feel. Men have taken upon themselves the task of governing, managing, and tutoring women, almost throughout the world's history. It was to be supposed that men would have modestly stood on one side and let Christ take the matter in hand, after woman alone brought Christ into the world—but no, even since then they must continue to hold the reins of government over women, just as they did when pagans. Do they not understand that there can be no morality for women apart from freedom? They understand this with their sons, and soon put them, as they advance towards manhood, on an increasingly independent footing, that the youths may develop strength of character; but their daughters, wives and even mothers, must be under perpetual management or tutelage from their birth to the grave; with no free choice between right and wrong, no free will apart from interference. After death, when all sex shall have been obliterated, then, the Church will graciously allow that women and men at that time are to be on an equality—that is, when men can no more dominate them, no matter how much they may long to do so.[58]

3. Equality and Responsibility. Bushnell's views on the complete equality of women and men were quite pronounced. The unequal status of women was a constant goad to her—to keep studying, to keep searching for biblical truth, to keep writing about her interpretations, and to keep disseminating these interpretations and the universal need for educated Bible study among all human beings, male or female. It was not a question of women being permitted the sexual freedom of men, or that all should go guiltless, but that women and men share equally the responsibility for wrongdoing and that the virtues incumbent upon women also become the standard expected of men.

> I've been brought up a straight-laced Methodist, and I have my own ideas about Universalism, but I had rather have a preacher say we can all get to heaven on an equal basis than to be told that a woman must be 100 per cent purer than a man to get there.[59]

> Women, as men's subordinates are nonentities; they cannot be reckoned as good or bad, because morality and immorality both alike have their origin in free choice. When a master robs a subordinate (as every master does, in fact) of free choice, the virtues or vices, as they may seem, in the subordinate, are the virtues or vices of the master. So a God of justice must ever reckon them. Woman in control of another is a moral cipher—unless she chooses to renounce her will for another's; then she is base by choice.[60]

Bushnell does not hold women guiltless. They are responsible for their choices. They are also responsible for rearing their sons to hold values that would preclude the degradation and oppression of women.

> That is sham virtue in woman which lends a cloak or gives stimulus to vice in man. "By their fruits ye shall know them." That which begets vice is vice. A wifely self-immolation which encourages masculine sensuality is vice. A feminine "humility" which gives place for the growth of masculine egotism is vice. Women need to ponder these things, and their responsibility (as the mothers and trainers of the men of the world), for the lack of gentleness, meekness, humility and chastity among men. Women must train their sons in all these virtues.[61]

4. "Let the Women Keep Silence." First Corinthians 14:33*b*-36 has traditionally been used to bar women from preaching and leading worship. Recent biblical scholarship has argued a "new" exegesis that this is a Corinthian slogan.[62] In 1889, an article by Bushnell appeared in *The Union Signal* arguing against the prohibition of women preaching based on Paul's words in 1 Corinthians 14:34, "Let your women keep silence in the Churches." She enlarged on this argument in many of her later works, including *God's Word to Women,* and several pamphlets. The following excerpt is from "Prefatory Note" to one of these leaflets, and the last excerpt is the article itself.

Two fixed points are required in order to determine the direction of a line. As in geometry so has it always been taught in sound doctrine. An inner Voice is not alone sufficient for guidance. The written Word must accord therewith. When these two are present then a line of conduct can be fixed upon with confidence. How are we to interpret the fact that women of holy life did speak in the public assembly both in the Old and in the New Testament times? "An exceptional call" is the usual reply. God could exceptionally call and qualify a woman to prophesy just as He bestowed exceptional qualities upon Balaam's beast of burden, so that the ass was led quite outside the "sphere" of her natural calling. We grant that: but the animal did not have to meet the difficulties of any supposed divine prohibition, and the woman must. Expositors teach us, not only that the Apostle admonished women to keep silence, but that he backed his admonition with the "as also saith the law," and added thereto the declaration that this silence was "a commandment of the Lord." The woman who goes forth to preach, then, is taught by the Church through its Bible expositors to believe that she must do so on an "exceptional call" that tramples upon Paul's admonition, defies the "as also saith the law," and disobeys the "commandment of the Lord."

But if we accept the inner Voice as sufficient, though it tramples upon the Word of God as written, we plant our feet on the broad road of fanaticism. No woman can afford to believe that she has a "special revelation" to disobey a commandment. No Church can afford to teach such a doctrine. The Church fears the preaching of woman in its pulpits lest it bring in irregularities and fanaticism. She may well fear so long as she is herself the tutor of fanaticism to women. There is no middle ground safe for the Church. She should either silence women altogether in every activity that would make her voice heard in the Church as a teacher or preacher, or else give a tardy assent to the truth of Paul's sweeping assertion that "there can be no male and female" distinctions as to call and privilege that the Church is authorized to make, or can make, without mischief, to the body of believers.[63]

Now the male commentator uses two verses in that passage that are of infinitely more importance to him than all the rest in the passage put together. They are the thirty-fourth and thirty-fifth. To maintain the dignity of his translation of these two verses, he is quite in the habit of plunging right into the middle of that section, making chaos of everything else, that he may, by sheer masculine force, keep the verses plumb to his ideas of womanly uprightness. . . . Let me illustrate my point.

Let us compare verses 31 and 34.

"Ye can all prophesy one by one." | "Let your women keep silence."

Why does not Paul note and explain the inconsistency here?

Now let us try verses 32 and 34.

"The spirits of the prophets | "Let them [the women] be
are subject to the prophets." | in subjection" [to their
| husbands].

But Paul knew and recognized *women* prophets, and women prophets in Corinth, too: see I. Cor. 11:5.

Now does Paul mean, after all, that it is the spirit of the male prophet only that is to be subject to the prophet? and that the spirit of the female prophet is subject to her husband? And, supposing, as not at all unlikely, this husband is still a heathen, and a *Corinthian* heathen at that. Then the Divine spirit in a prophetess is to be controlled and guided by the devilish spirit of a Corinthian heathen. Why does not Paul explain this great inconsistency, or even mention the fact that by prophet he means male prophet only?

Now compare verses 36 and 35.

"What, was it from you [men] | "It is shameful for a
that the Word of God went | woman to speak in the
forth, or came it unto you | church."
[men] alone?"

Let us consider the construction of this thirty-sixth verse a moment. Is there any warrant for inserting, as explanatory, the word men in two places, as I have done in this instance? I think there is, for the following reasons:

In the English language we use *alone* and *only* interchangeably (although incorrectly); not so the Greek. This word translated *only* in the Old Version is changed to *alone* in the New, because *only* could be an adverb qualifying come, while in fact the word used is an adjective qualifying men understood. Oh, how easily a preconception can introduce error into a translation of this Holy Word! This adjective is in the masculine gender—a matter of considerable import just here. It gives full warrant for the introduction of the word men as explanatory of the thought. But, you object, by such a rule of translation as that, then we would need to declare that *brethren* in the twenty-sixth verse, and *man* in the twenty-seventh, etc., relate to males only, while you are trying to show the very opposite.

I hardly admit it. Had the adjective *alone* been correctly translated as in the Old Version by *only*, such might be the case. But when Paul asks, "What, came the Word of God unto you men when you were alone by yourselves?" it is perfectly plain that in the very question he implies the presence of others besides these comprehended in the word (masculine) you. Does he refer then to Timothy, Titus, the Thessalonians, or to whom? Common sense tells us that he refers to another class *not* remote from his present consideration at all, or he would say to whom. Hence he exclaims so emphatically that the word did not come to "you" alone, he meant just what the Bible teaches, viz.: that the word came unto *women* also. [See Acts 1 and 2.]

Now let us compare verses 39 and 34 and see if they are consistent, "Wherefore, my brethren, for- | "Let your women keep bid not to speak with tongues | silence in the churches"

To what does this *wherefore* refer? and of what is it the conclusion?

It refers either to verses 35 and 36, or else to some others. Let us couple it first with 34 and 35, and see if it makes an intelligible statement:

"Let your women keep silence."

"Let them ask their husbands at home."

"It is a shame for them to speak."

"Let them be in subjection; wherefore forbid not to speak with tongues."

Well, *that* would make more sense if we made the conclusion of the whole matter be "wherefore *forbid women* to speak with tongues," and more truthful, too. Hence the "wherefore" is not a conclusion derived from verses 34 and 35.

Let us now couple this summing up of the argument to all the rest of the verses.

"All can prophesy." (31.)

"The spirits of prophets are subject to prophets." (32.)

"God is not a God of confusion, but of peace." (33.)

"The Word did not go forth from men." (36.)

"The word did not come unto men alone." (37.)

Now couple Paul's "wherefore" with each one of these verses, and we see nothing but beautiful consistency everywhere. . . . That, I admit, disjoints verses 34 and 35 from all the rest of this passage. Yes, and I believe it should be so disjointed. I believe it would have been so disjointed by male commentators had it related to limitations on the male sex. But man has invented the remarkable theory that while "God is no respecter of persons," still God does respect bifurcated garments worn by persons. Souls, God treats alike; sexes, He treats very differently.

Let us make Paul his own interpreter. Turn to I. Cor. 15: 29-34. Supposing an epicurean or an annihilist wished to establish his pet theory, he would not need to overturn the authority of as many verses to teach that we must give ourselves to eating and drinking to-day because death ends everything. I say he would not need to overturn the authority of as many adjacent Scripture verses to set up that one clause, as the male commentator must overthrow to set up as of divine authority the sentences beginning, "Let your women keep silence."

But the male commentator says: "'Let us eat and drink, for to-morrow we die,' are supposed to be the words of another reasoning with Paul."

Yes, and why not admit that the verses beginning, "Let the women keep silence," is also the voice of an objector? Haven't we some reason for so thinking, when Paul says it is the *law* saying it? He tells where the objector springs from—those sticklers for law who were always contending with Paul; and Paul declares his impatience with them by his exclamation: "What! was it from you men that the word came? isn't God's authority higher than your law? Remember that the word didn't even come upon you men alone. If you think yourself a prophet, you will be able to discern that these things are from the Lord; but if you are an ignorant pretender, you will have to remain such."

"Wherefore, don't forbid these women to speak with tongues. Let everything be done decently and in order."

Now . . . the lesson is over, excepting one question I want you to think about with me: Shall we ignore all the force there is in the admonitions contained in eight verses of these ten in the lesson, in order to force a meaning into the remaining two that will suit the male commentator? I do not think that is treating Paul and Scripture with proper reverence, do you?[64]

5. Birthright of Equality. Katharine Bushnell was far ahead of her time, and her voice speaks to women today. She stands for the freedom and equality of all women everywhere. She stands for the right and responsibility of women to take their position beside men and to be heard in every arena of life. She stands for the responsibility of women to educate themselves adequately to fulfill their responsibility, and she looks with contempt on those who would shun that responsibility.

In the final paragraph of *God's Word to Women,* Bushnell flings a challenge to all women to claim their birthright of equality.

> To which body will we belong? That is the question for each woman of us to answer to herself. This is not a matter concerning which indecision is of any avail. A great promise and prophecy—the very greatest in all the Bible—lies before us women. We cannot escape; we must either choose the best that could be, from the highest standpoint, or by failing to choose prove ourselves Esaus. God has given the challenge to our faith. Shall we despise our birthright? God forbid!

Katharine Bushnell answered her own challenge. She rejoiced in the promise and prophecy she found through her study and reinterpretation of scripture. She claimed the birthright and she fulfilled the promise, and her life and work stand as example and monument to that fulfillment.

Alice Rebecca Appenzeller   *Lulu E. Frey*

Mary Fletcher Scranton

CHAPTER 9

SISTERS IN CHRIST

American Women Missionaries in
Ewha Women's University

K Y U N G - L I M   S H I N - L E E

In the late nineteenth century, a new phase of life opened for American women. Realizing that God was calling them not only to work at home, but also to work in society, they expanded their mission fields accordingly. They started to live what they believed, rather than what they were told to live. While most women were excited about working for their town or country, some women lifted their eyes up to the world beyond the United States.

This essay focuses on American female missionaries in the Wesleyan tradition who worked in Korea, particularly for Korean women's education. As a matter of fact, official education for Korean women began with the establishment of Ewha Hak-dang, which was founded and developed by American women missionaries until Dr. Helen Kim took over leadership in 1939. The story of three women missionaries will be shared: Mary Fletcher Scranton, the founder of Ewha, the first school for Korean women; Lulu E. Frey, who built Ewha Hak-dang into Ewha College; and Alice Rebecca Appenzeller, the last, Korean-born, missionary president of Ewha College.

1. MARY FLETCHER SCRANTON

Mary Fletcher Scranton was born on December 9, 1832, in Belchertown, Massachusetts. Her father, the Reverend Erastus Benton, was a member of the New England Conference of The Methodist Episcopal Church. She married William T. Scranton of New Haven, Connecticut, in 1853. After the death of her husband in 1872, Mary F. Scranton accompanied her only son, William B. Scranton, when he moved to New York for his medical study and to Cleveland, Ohio, for his practice.

In 1884, Dr. William B. Scranton became the first appointee of the

Methodist Board to Korea. Upon learning of this appointment, the Woman's Foreign Missionary Society urged Mary Scranton, who was going to accompany her son, to accept the responsibility of being their first representative to Korea. Even though she had been Conference Secretary of the Woman's Foreign Missionary Society for some years and was very much interested in foreign mission work, she was, at first, reluctant to accept the appointment, because of her age. The next year, however, she headed for Korea as the first female missionary from the Woman's Foreign Missionary Society.

Even though the missionaries' contribution to education for Koreans, especially for Korean women, was tremendous, education was not the missionaries' primary aim. Josephine O. Paine, who was the third principal of Ewha (from 1892 until 1907), aptly expressed the aim of the missionaries at that time by saying that her only aim in life was to love God and to make God known.[1] Their fundamental aim was the conversion of Koreans to Christianity, and education was a tool needed to achieve this goal. The first Western school for boys, Pai-Jai, was founded in Seoul by Henry G. Appenzeller several months after the first Protestant missionary party arrived in Korea. The Appenzellers, along with the Scrantons, were a part of the first American Protestant missionary team to Korea. Mary Scranton concentrated on establishing a school for Korean girls.

Even though most of the girls of Korean upper-class society were privately educated at home, a school for Korean girls was beyond imagination, for neither outside activities nor association with strangers, especially foreigners, was allowed for Korean women at that time. In spite of the great hindrance of culture, Scranton was determined to provide Christian education for Korean girls. She started by making a request to the WFMS to purchase a piece of ground with nineteen straw huts for a school building. Permission for the purchase was granted, and on October 23, 1884, she wrote: "I feel like singing the 'Te Deum.' The papers are signed. The WFMS now owns property in Korea. Here we hope to have a home and school, and perhaps a dispensary combined. This buying and building for the church is a great responsibility, but I am daily, yes hourly, asking counsel from my Heavenly Father that I make no mistakes."[2]

The house that had been purchased by the American women missionaries was in no condition to be used as a school without extensive repair work. Scranton, however, could not sit and wait for the completion of renovation. She expressed her impatience and zeal for her mission work in a letter:

I am all ready to begin on the new building as soon as I know what I may do. I intend to have the timber prepared this winter, so that work can go rapidly forward in the early spring. The prices of material and labor have already advanced considerably, and I begin to be afraid the money will not hold out! . . .

Two or three weeks ago I was sure I was on the right track at last. I heard of many destitute orphans, and I said at once, I will take two into my little bit of a house immediately. I will not wait until the new house is finished, I'll begin where I am. I thought and planned, and planned and thought, until morning, and by that time had decided to crowd my accommodations to their utmost capacity, and on my own responsibility to take six instead of two.[3]

In spite of all difficulties and obstacles, the first school for Korean girls was founded in May 1886. The name, "Ewha," was given by the Queen of Korea. What made the school possible was Mary Scranton's strong conviction that the women and girls must be educated for the most speedy advancement of Korea. Scranton's participation in the childbirth of Alice Appenzeller in Korea played a significant role in her determination to work for the education of Korean women.

On November 9, 1885, Alice was born to Mrs. Henry Appenzeller, and became the first Caucasian child born inside Korea. Scranton, who lived next door and had come to Korea on the same ship with the Appenzeller family, came to help her friend. She ended by spending the entire night holding the newborn baby to keep the baby warm.

Scranton stated the purpose of beginning Ewha as an elementary school for girls: "We would emphasize . . . that our school is, first of all, a school to make Korean girls better Korean girls and true Korean women. There is no other thought when a girl or woman comes to us than that she will become a Christian and go from us to lead others to Christ."[4] She worked diligently to fulfill this goal, but found success elusive mainly because of the language barrier and her limited contact with Koreans, which prevented her from understanding what it meant to be "true Korean women."

It is unfortunate that most of the missionaries did not try harder to learn Korean. Instead they forced the students to learn English. Lucy Kim, a student from 1888 to 1897, remembers her school days: "When I first came to Ewha, the missionaries taught me the Lord's Prayer, and several hymns in English. As more teachers came, the curriculum was enlarged. A translator was not used, and everything was taught in English from the beginning."[5]

This Korean student must have been named "Lucy" by the American missionaries. As a matter of fact, many of the students were called by American names—indeed, most Korean women either retained only their last names or were called by nicknames. The missionaries would have done better had they respected the Korean culture more and encouraged Korean girls to become "true Korean girls," leaving them their Korean names instead of calling them by Christian names or naming them after their American sponsors.

Admittedly, Mary Scranton was more successful at making Korean women "true Christian women" than at making them "true Korean women." She was convinced that the most important goal was to convert them, not to educate them. Only when she detected any evidence of a woman's becoming a genuine Christian would she regard her work a success.[6] She wrote, "When I see the work which these girls of ours are doing, and doing it because the love of Christ constrains them, I believe I am the happiest woman in this world. It has paid a great deal more than the hundredfold to come to Korea."[7]

After five years of hard work for Ewha, Scranton resigned from Ewha and began to concentrate on evangelism outside Ewha. Recognizing that education was needed for the children of native Christians and others who were willing to send their children to be taught Christianity, she established Tal Syeng Day School in Seoul in 1895. To provide sufficient opportunities for Korean women, she founded the works among the women in the three large Methodist Episcopal churches in Seoul; Jung-Dong Church, Tal-Syeng Church, and Baldwin Chapel.

To win hearts, she did not mind being an object of curiosity by making a show of herself before strangers or traveling through the mountains and country. Traveling around the small towns was very dangerous even for Korean men, but she dedicated herself to making long-distance trips, one of which was four hundred miles in length. She often stayed in the country for more than a month at a time, even after she was well over seventy.[8] She was daring, dauntless, and strong enough to risk these ventures because she firmly believed that though a thousand fall at her side and ten thousand at her right hand, danger would not come near her.[9]

Scranton not only proclaimed the gospel by herself but also educated Korean women to bring other women to God, for she had learned from her past experience that "when the Korean woman once gets 'fairly started' in the good way she zealously labors to induce her friends and neighbors to become 'partakers of like precious faith.'"[10] Scranton trained many Bible women through the Training School for Bible Women. She also made herself available "to give the younger and less experienced workers the value of her counsel,"[11] in spite of her busy schedule.

In 1900, fifteen years after the missionaries began to plant the seeds of the gospel in Korea, they proudly informed the Woman's Foreign Missionary Society of the establishment of:

33 Methodist churches
more than 1,300 attending Sunday schools

six hospitals and dispensaries treating patients
25 schools in which students were learning about the world and the Gospel.[12]

If we consider the attitude of the Koreans toward foreign missionaries in 1885, no one can deny that this outcome is little short of miraculous. In a letter of 1885, shortly after arriving in Seoul, Scranton described how the Koreans responded to her appearance: "The presence of the foreigner was not desired. . . . Our presence on the street in too close proximity to the women's apartments was oftentimes the signal for the rapid closing of doors and speedy retreat behind screens, while children ran screaming with as much lung power as they could bring to bear on the occasion."[13]

Within a year, however, she was able proudly to report the change of Koreans' attitude toward them:

As I look back now over fourteen months in Korea, my heart is full of joy and thankfulness, not because any great things have been done, but because we have made a beginning. . . . But progress has been made. At first we were regarded with great suspicion; now many trust us. They know we mean good and not evil, though few understand much about our plans . . .

The house on the hill is growing. I have been very ill, and saw it for the first time this morning for four weeks. The progress made is very encouraging, and I have not much reason to find fault even with Korean slowness. We are called the "Jesus doctrine doing people," and they say my home is the place where the sacrifice is made. I rather like the name they give. I have been a little afraid that this thought might keep some timid ones away from us. But it is God's own work and he will not let it come to nought. Won't you give one of the devotional hours at executive meeting entirely to Korea? This request comes up out of the depths of my heart. It seems to me if you would then and there, pray with the earnestness you ought, for my poor Korea, and for us who are here, and for the teacher and the doctor who are to come, it seems as if the Holy Ghost would also fall on us, as it did upon the disciples at the beginning, and we should be able to speak plainly in this new tongue, and tell the wonderful story as we have never been able to tell it before, and that you would pray us into grand and glorious success.

We should have full schools and hospitals, and open doors and wide opportunities everywhere. Pray for us as you never prayed for anybody or anything before. What a good meeting you will have. I can imagine it all, and hope you will write a line as soon as it is over, to tell me that there is a doctor and a teacher and plenty of money coming to this most needy spot on earth.[14]

An article, written by the editor of the *Korean Repository* in 1898, describes the changed attitudes of Koreans toward Scranton when she left Korea on her second furlough:

Great executive ability, disinterested devotion, burning zeal, kind, thoughtful and patient, Mrs. Scranton has drawn to herself many Korean women who look to her as their best friend. Many of the men and women, church members, walked three miles to the river, crossed over in boats, and there on the sand was repeated the scene of St. Paul when he took his leave of the Elders of Ephesus, they kneeled down, prayed, wept sorrowing most of all in the thought that some of them might see her face no more. We wish her a safe voyage, a restful furlough, and speedy return to her chosen field of labor.[15]

Mary Scranton truly loved God, and she also loved and dedicated her service to Koreans with all her heart, soul, strength, and with all her mind. The Koreans knew that she was sincere. This woman, who had been a mother to Koreans and to other missionaries, died on October 8, 1909, in Seoul, Korea—the land she loved until her death. The Korean government expressed its condolence, and numerous people followed her to the burial place, Yangwha Jin. On the anniversaries of Ewha, present students still visit the cemetery in which Mary Scranton is buried, to have a memorial ceremony in front of her grave. On the seventieth anniversary, Ewha built the Scranton Memorial Hall, in memory of her love and dedication to Korean womanhood. Scranton Memorial Hall is still used by Ewha High School girls.

She was a woman of great courage and strong faith. Because of her trust in God, she was able to overcome all dangers without fear and make inconceivable accomplishments without hesitation. She started her mission work at an age when others began to retire, and she continued with her work until the last day of her life. She could not stop working. She said, "The fields, wherever I have been, are 'white.' We only lack the laborers."[16]

2. LULU E. FREY

The year 1910 was one of the most significant years for all Ewhaians and for Korea itself. Twenty-five years earlier, Ewha had begun with only one student, but in 1910 Ewha opened its doors to fifteen young girls as the first women's college. It was a historical moment for Koreans. Lulu E. Frey, the founder of Ewha College, had undergone all sorts of hardships. First of all, Ewha was not really ready to open its doors as a "college." It did not have appropriate facilities or enough students and faculty. Yet she could not just sit and wait for just the right moment. The chance of opening a women's college might never come again.

When she determined to open Ewha College, Frey had to confront strong objections from both Koreans and her missionary colleagues. The opposers were convinced that it was too early to provide higher education for Korean girls. Their objection seemed reasonable in a way, for many Ewha students had had to leave because of early marriage, without completing even a high school education. The dissident group thought that there would not be enough students or enough support. Lulu Frey had the same fear. Yet her courage was greater than the fear. She was so convinced that Korean girls must be equally educated with boys if the country were to advance that nothing could thwart her determination.

She was not intimidated by any criticism or blame, for she strongly believed that it was the missionaries' privilege and responsibility to furnish higher education for Korean girls. Yet she did her best to explain the need of higher education for Korean girls, in order to sidetrack conflict between those who felt it urgent to provide higher education for Korean girls and those who thought it was too early to take the leap. She wrote articles and made public addresses on this issue. Her main points were:

1) The Korean women's desire for learning was increasing.
2) The families' expectations for them, as mothers and as wives, were getting higher.
3) To supply leaders for Korea, Ewha must provide the highest education.
4) The best education was Christian education. (See document 1.)

Korean dissension seemed natural to Frey. Resistance from the missionaries, however, must have brought more pain and more distress to her. The missionaries held many different points of view regarding the education of Korean girls. Some of them favored extreme changes; some set their faces against any change that was not considered absolutely necessary. Many of them thought that "if changes must come they should come slowly."[17]

Throughout history, the appropriate time for changes and how they should come has always been an issue. What are the absolute necessities and what are not? Clearly, there was some divergence in opinions among missionaries. For some of them, it seemed too progressive to take down curtains, which had been used since the beginning of mission work to separate Korean men and women in churches and schools, out of respect for the Korean tradition of women's seclusion. A male missionary, who refused to reveal his name, wrote an article titled "Some Remarks on Woman's Work." (See document 2.) His general stance described in that article seems pretty progressive. Yet he said, "She [a Korean girl] may be taught to render all due obedience and submission to those over her and to be faithful as a wife and mother."[18] It must have been very difficult even for American missionaries to believe that all human beings should be treated equally and wives should not be required to obey their husbands or mother-in-laws.

Understandably, the missionaries had to be very sensitive in cultural matters. Many of them must have struggled both to respect "indigenous culture" and to make "necessary changes for the Kingdom of God." But no one makes a clear distinction between those two issues. Missionaries, in general, were accused of not having respectful understanding of Korean culture. They should have been more careful in condemning indigenous culture as heathen tradition. What would be the status of Korean women today, however, if the missionaries had not dared to make some changes, running counter to the firm tradition?

Jesus did not mind going against tradition when he healed a woman who had had a spirit of infirmity for eighteen years (Luke 13:10-17). Jesus and the woman could have waited until the sabbath was over. To others, including the woman, one more day might not have been important compared with eighteen years. Yet, to Jesus, it was. When he saw the woman suffering, he could not let her suffer any longer. He cured her immediately. To release the woman from her infirmity, Jesus broke the tradition.

To set Korean women free from the long, binding tradition of predominance of men over women, Lulu Frey dared to go against Korean tradition. What strengthened her resolve was her complete trust in God and Korean women's eagerness to learn. In one of her articles on higher education for Korean women, Frey introduced a Korean woman's story that had exerted a great influence on her determination to work for the enlightenment of Korean women:

> One night in the early days of our school work a young married woman from a non-Christian, high class home came to see us. Her application for entrance into the school had been previously refused; but, ambitious and determined, she came with her servant to plead her cause in person. The light in the lantern they brought had been extinguished. Pointing to the lantern she said, "The women in Korea are like that—dark in mind. If they know nothing, how can they teach their children?"

That Korean woman, Ran-Sa Ha, studied in America after graduating from Ewha, and made a great contribution to Ewha when she returned to Korea.

One positive contribution foreign missionaries can make is that they often notice problems and issues of which natives are not generally aware. Even though missionaries have a tendency to condemn most of the indigenous traditions and habits, which are different from theirs, their judgment needs to be taken seriously when it concerns issues of humaneness. There is no doubt that Korean women would have experienced discrimination and oppression for many more years had the missionaries not been brave enough to take the decisive steps.

Looking back on Frey's earlier life we see her decisiveness and endurance. Frey was born on March 9, 1868, in Sydney, Ohio, where her father owned a drugstore. When she was about ten years old she was converted and was baptized four years later. After graduating from Bellfontain School in 1887, she began to think about her calling and her life as a Christian, about which she had been unclear until she was moved by an article, "Why Do You Not Go?" which she read in a mission magazine.[19]

Her father was not happy about her decision, and she preferred to run a dress shop for a while instead of protesting her father's opposition directly. When she finally got her father's approval, she was able to take her education at Wesleyan University in Ohio, the Chicago Training School for Home and Foreign Missionaries, and the Moody Bible Institute in Chicago. When she completed her education, she heard of the need for a missionary in Korea from Josephine Paine, who had come to America for a vacation. Considering it God's call for her, Frey went to Korea as the youngest missionary from the Woman's Foreign Missionary Society in October 1893.

Fifteen years of experience as a teacher and as an acting administrator at Ewha during the absence of Josephine Paine made her an effective and sensitive principal. As the fourth principal of Ewha Hak-dang and the first president of Ewha College, Frey made great progress in Ewha:

1) Kindergarten, Kindergarten Training School, College, and a special adult class for married women were established.
2) Faculty, curriculum, and facilities were expanded.
3) Many extracurricular activities were introduced.
4) Various associations of students were organized.
5) The color of the school and tradition of selecting a "May Queen" were established.

Jeannette Walter describes Lulu Frey's appearance: "She was a tall, very dignified person, with blonde wavy hair and blue eyes."[20] Even though her appearance differed from that of Koreans, Lulu Frey was regarded as one of them by many Koreans. Although she was eager to go back to Korea after her furlough, she was not able to return to Ewha to finish her work. The work she started has been continued throughout the first century of Ewha. Her dedication to Ewha is aptly described in the address of the Reverend C. D. Morris given at the laying of the cornerstone of the Frey Hall: "During the difficult times of Ewha, Miss Frey insisted that education was the best way for Korean women, which is now settled as a future policy of Ewha. . . . Miss Frey is gone. Her great contribution, which was accomplished by her efforts, for Korean women in the church of Jesus Christ, will remain forever."[21] Her service has borne countless fruits, and she is still remembered by Koreans as "missionary, educator, administrator, builder, and prophet."[22]

3. ALICE REBECCA APPENZELLER

On the Monday morning of February 20, 1950, Alice Appenzeller was leading chapel for the Ewha family. As she read Matthew 7:15, "Beware of false prophets," her voice faltered and became indistinct. When President Helen Kim suggested that she take over the service, Appenzeller said, "But I have not finished."[23] Those were her last words. Without recovering consciousness, she died in the hospital at 6:10 P.M.

Alice Appenzeller, the first Korean-born American missionary, was the first child of the Reverend and Mrs. Henry G. Appenzeller, who came to Korea in 1885 with Dr. and Mrs. William Scranton and their family as the first Protestant missionary party. Alice was born November 9, 1885, eight months after their arrival in Korea. Her relationship to Mary F. Scranton has already been explained. She returned to America as a youth, receiving her bachelor's degree from Wellesley College in Massachusetts and finishing a summer session at Harvard University. With a fine education and five-year's teaching experience in the Shippen School, Lancaster, Pennsylvania, she returned to Korea in 1914 as a missionary to Ewha from the Woman's Foreign Missionary Society.

Education was an important part of Appenzeller's life. She not only educated others but also was always mindful of the need for her own continuing education. When she had an opportunity to stay in America for a while, after working hard at Ewha for some years, she spent her furlough studying at Columbia University Teachers' College, gaining a master's degree. Alice consulted with and advised other missionaries to use their furloughs to further their education:

> No matter how superior your native ability and training before going to the field, or how valuable your practical experience there, you will find that you need to get into touch with the moments of the day, from which you have been more or less isolated. You do not realize your need until you begin to study in some institution and meet people engaged in the same kind of work as yourself. . . . Furlough study is far more valuable than any pre-missionary preparation, because one knows just what one can use.[24]

She also pointed out that physical rest and spiritual refreshment were important to missionaries on furlough.[25]

During her presidency from 1922 to 1939, Appenzeller demonstrated her excellent capabilities in administration and education. She realized her dream of a new campus for Ewha by raising enormous funds, both in America and in Korea. From 1923 on, when the land for the new campus was purchased, buildings, such as a chapel, music building, gymnasium, dormitory, English House, and classrooms, were added one by one. On March 9, 1935, four hundred and fifty students and faculty of Ewha finally moved onto the beautiful and huge campus with a song and prayer of thanksgiving. "Ewha Sunday" was one of the products of this gigantic fund-raising and construction. On Ewha Sundays, all Korean Methodists prayed for women's education in general and Ewha in particular, and a special offering was taken for Ewha. Appenzeller's achievements were not limited to outward improvement. The school was also expanded inwardly by the increase of departments, curriculum, and faculty.

Most of all, Alice Appenzeller was a gifted educator. She was sensitive, not only to students' academic needs but also to their social needs. Her goal was to help the students "find true satisfaction and lasting success."[26] Stressing the fact that "the old bars are down, the clock cannot be turned back, and the old restrictions are no longer binding in many cases," Appenzeller initiated sweeping changes in the rules and policies of the school.[27] This challenge should have come long before. The rules and policies of Ewha had been very strict and allowed no freedom to the students. The rules regarding the students' relationships with outside people had been especially stringent. The college girls had been allowed to see male visitors only under chaperonage twice a week; the high school girls had been able to see only relatives, no friends regardless of gender or age. All letters had been subject to censure by a teacher. The students' social life had been extremely limited and restrained.

Fortunately, Appenzeller was very progressive and considered it a "handicap" to view and judge young people by the standards of the teachers' own "teenage" years ten, twenty, or thirty years before. To her, liberty was one of the essential elements of education. She described her understanding of the educator's job: "Our chief job is to build up controls from 'within,' to help the young people to build such character that they can use the liberty of this age not for an occasion to the flesh, but so that they may by love serve one another."[28] She also suggested some concrete tactics:

1. Lectures and talks on relationship between education and life should be given.
2. Personal talks that take so much life blood, the method that Jesus used most, should be used.
3. Short books of etiquette should be written and sold at the popular bookstores.
4. More proper places for social gathering should be provided.
5. We should try to do more to educate the parents concerning their responsibility toward their children, who too often rule them.
6. We should help the students realize that they cannot make a success of life or be happy without God.[29]

Appenzeller invited all missionaries and Christian workers to stand for the highest Christian standards. (See document 3.) She asked them to show the students that "liberty means social responsibility."[30] Her plea drew such a strong response from both teachers and students that Ewha Women's University and Ewha Girl's High School are still considered the schools in which liberty is most respected and practiced. The mottoes of Ewha Women's University are truth, righteousness, and beauty; those of Ewha High School are liberty, love, and peace.

To be a model to Koreans and students, missionaries maintained a very disciplined life. They tried not only to follow most of the rules but also to practice what they believed and what they were being taught. Most of the unmarried female missionaries remained unmarried throughout their lives, or at least, while they were in Korea. Celibacy was highly valued and even encouraged among Korean female students directly and indirectly. Even though women's celibacy was not well accepted by Korean society, there have been a good many Korean female presidents and professors at Ewha who accept the moral beliefs of celibacy and have not married.

Self-sacrifice was another distinctive feature of the missionaries' lives. God always came first, and then the people whom they came to serve. Frequently, the missionaries had no spare time for themselves. Thus, in 1932 when serious consideration was given to a large monetary cutback, all the workers at Ewha said with one voice, "Not from the College or Theological School." They would rather sacrifice their own budgets.[31] Their life-styles were generally frugal and self-giving.

One of the most outstanding contributions of Alice Appenzeller to the curricula of Ewha College was the lessons she gave in native Korean music. Since Korean music had been used primarily for entertainment and shamanistic worship and neglected by Christian missionaries, this venture must have produced a sensation. To collect Korean melodies, Alice even offered a prize for the best collection. According to her report to the Woman's Foreign Missionary Society, however, the collection chosen seemed to be limited to Korean hymns, though it seems clear that the missionaries used Korean musical instruments.[32] Considering the fact that foreign missionaries have been blamed for disregarding native Korean music, Alice's attempt should be taken seriously and seen as a positive influence on Korean music.

While making incessant endeavors on behalf of educational matters, Alice Appenzeller and other missionary teachers never treated spiritual matters lightly. Ewha would hold annual revival meetings, through which many Korean students and teachers were converted to Christianity and baptized. Revival meetings were described by Lulu Frey as times when the power of the Spirit, conviction of sin, and radical changes in the hearts and lives of all the students were felt.[33] The revival meetings were held for a week and ended on Sunday with baptism. The sermons were on texts, chosen to awaken the students to their sins and the dreadful consequences of rejecting Christ. This kind of revival meeting throughout the country greatly accelerated the expansion of Christianity.

In 1939, the Japanese government, which had control over Korea, proclaimed that no foreigners should hold the presidency of an educational institution. As a result, Appenzeller encouraged Helen Kim, an Ewha graduate, to replace her, saying, "Some are born great, some achieve greatness, and some have greatness thrust upon them. You are in the third category. You will have to take the presidency whether you like it or not."[34] Kim finally agreed to assume that heavy responsibility and became the first Korean president of Ewha College on April 4, 1939. If the transfer of the presidency from missionary to native Korean woman had been realized voluntarily, not by outside extortion, it would have been the most beautiful and meaningful moment in the history of Ewha and Korean missions.

In November 1940, all missionaries were expelled from Korea by the Japanese government. Alice Appenzeller was appointed to Scarritt College and worked there as a professor and Dean of Women until she went to Hawaii in 1943 to serve a Korean church on Oahu Island. Having been ordained in Korea, she was able to provide pastoral leadership for that church. Her constant love and deep devotion to Koreans were evident.

When she finally returned to Korea in 1946, she was greeted with a special ceremony. Until the last moment of her life, she continued to serve Ewha as honorary president. On February 25, 1950, a funeral service was held for her at Chungdong Methodist Church, which her father had founded. It was also at this church she had been baptized at the first baptismal ceremony in Korea, which was conducted by her father, and where she had been ordained to the ministry. Many people who loved her and were loved by her gathered at that church, and for those people who could not find room in the church loudspeakers were installed outside it.

Koreans loved her as a sister. Korea was not a foreign country to Alice. She rejoiced and suffered with Koreans as a Korean. Just as Koreans put their first priority on harmony, she too loved harmony and unity. Most of all, she loved Ewha. For the protection of Ewha she did not mind compromising. When the Japanese government ruled that all Koreans should worship at Shinto shrines, she did not protest in spite of the strong opposition of all Koreans, especially Korean Christians. She did not want to take the risk of having the school closed. Believing that Korea would be free from Japan someday, she rather chose to concentrate on raising leaders for the future of Korea.

Her prayer request to the Southern Methodist women in 1932 well describes the dedication of her life:

First, that the College may continue to grow in pioneering for Korean women's education, the gateway by which women enter into the paths of "abundant life."

Second, that every course and every activity taught and carried on in the College may uphold and enhance the kingdom of righteousness in Korea.

Third, that the College may discover and develop outstanding leaders whose lives and activities may count in the rebuilding of human society.

Fourth, that every student, every teacher and every worker in the College may conscientiously strive to live more like Jesus each day.

Fifth, that the new buildings may become real symbols of harmonious cooperation of the East and the West, prompted by love for humankind and zeal for the Kingdom. That every gift, however great or small in economic value, may represent the highest type of love and loyalty to the cause of women's Christian education in Korea.[35]

Her favorite motto, which is also a motto of her beloved Wellesley College in the United States, is inscribed on her gravestone: "Not to be ministered unto but to minister."[36] As Alice Appenzeller claimed right before her death, her ministry has not been finished but succeeded from generation to generation. Ewha Women's University celebrated its centennial in 1985 as the largest university for women in the world and now is looking toward a bicentennial. One tiny light kindled more than a hundred years ago has brought marvelous changes to the lives of Korean women, to the country of Korea, and now to the whole world. This transformation would not have been possible if those women, whether Korean or American, had not dared take social responsibility in accordance with their spirituality. (See document 4.)

DOCUMENTS

1. The Need for Higher Education for Korean Women. Lulu E. Frey, the fourth principal of Ewha Hak-dang, confronted strong objections from Koreans and her colleagues to the establishment of Ewha College in 1910. In response to those objections, she wrote articles on the urgent need for higher education for Korean women. The following article published in 1910 through *The Korean Mission Field* clearly expresses Frey's dedication to advanced education for Korean women as well as her self-understanding as a missionary educator.

For years the Korean woman has been content in her ignorance, for she has not known that there was any higher plane for her, but now she has begun to climb, she will not be satisfied till she reaches the top and stands beside her brother. . . . If it is true that the fate of nations rests upon woman, surely time and money cannot be better expended than in giving her a full share of educational advantages.

. . . In Seoul alone there are twenty schools for girls where less than five years ago there were none aside from the mission schools. Of course this change in public sentiment is due to the change of mind on the part of the fathers, brothers and husbands. This change seems no less marvelous to those who recall the attitude taken only a few years ago. Formerly the only way by which we could get pupils for our schools, was to take advantage of poverty, and promise to feed and clothe the girls. To-day our schools might easily be filled by those who can pay. More than that many fathers, brothers and husbands, are willing to sacrifice in order that the daughters, sisters and wives may have the advantages of education. Quite a few of the women who have been put in our school this last year are wives of men who are studying in Japan or America. They do not care to come back to live with their wives as they were, but want companionship, which of course could never be were their wives left in ignorance.

. . . We missionaries are largely responsible for the start the Korean woman has taken on the upward climb. May it not be both a privilege and a duty to further help her? Shall we let those only provide for her need, who will give her education without Christian teaching? As yet none of the non-Christian schools have graduated a class of the High School grade. The fine curriculum of one of the non-Christian schools attracted a girl in one of our primary schools, but when she applied it was found that she had already had higher work than their most advanced class, so she was obliged to seek entrance in a Christian school. Our mission schools are in advance, and surely it is of advantage to the Kingdom to keep in advance. Though educators, as missionaries, education is not our objective, and none of us would be satisfied with less than the moulding of Christian characters; without Christianity there are dangers which western learning may bring and what we desire is that they should long for, and acquire knowledge not to improve their own position alone, but to benefit others, having the power to aid and influence them for good.

It is never sentiment when we say "The hand that rocks the cradle rules the world," "A nation cannot rise higher than its mothers." If this is the demand of to-day what will be the requirements in the near future?

The government schools and private heathen schools afford us an opportunity for good. A number of our girls have taught and are teaching in these schools. In the extremity for teachers they are glad to get them though they are not our best girls, as we cannot yet spare the best from our own work.

. . . As to ways and means for Higher Education for women here in Korea, suggestions may come to our minds as to feasible ways of helping one another. Our own beginning is like the beginning along any line of purely mission work, very small indeed, but we have faith to believe that from this small beginning may develop something worthy of the name of college which will be used of God for the advancement of His Kingdom in Korea.[37]

2. Some Remarks on the Work of Women Missionaries. In 1915, five years after the establishment of Ewha College, *The Korea Mission Field* published an article written by a male missionary. This article shows what it meant for Korean women to go to a college at that time and the issues that female missionaries were confronting. It is interesting to note that this article was contributed anonymously.

> Most missionaries wisely corrected what was wrong and adopted the balance entire for the church and for Christian communities. And not only so but most of them set their face against any change that was not absolutely necessary. Taking down the curtain, wearing of foreign clothes, new styles of doing up the hair, any tendency towards freedom in the mingling of the sexes, an inclination towards western customs in engagements and marriage ceremonies, have been stoutly resisted by both a majority of the missionaries and a majority of the Korean church leadership. This has been necessary and right; if changes must come they should come slowly.
>
> And yet some missionaries are agitated needlessly over certain changes that are coming gradually and perhaps are over extreme in their opposition. Many of the Koreans also have their doubts about the new training for Christian girls. The writer knows of a well-to-do, wide awake, up-to-date Christian man who has supported the church heartily in all its educational work. He engaged his two boys, high school graduates, to two very bright Christian girls, both of them Girls' school graduates. Both are ideal young women from Christian homes and their training has not been "new fangled," and yet both are strong minded and independent and perhaps lacking in the proverbial "daughter-in-law obedience" of a Korean home. At any rate this man has a third son in a Christian academy and the report is that he has engaged this third son to a Christian country girl who has never had the sight of a Girls' school and who knows nothing except how to read her Bible and do housekeeping and sewing according to the best Korean standards.
>
> . . . It should not seem strange if Korean young women want something to say about their own marriage and they are not necessarily great sinners because they resort to some western notion and customs in the matter. If Korean women are inclined to be independent and defend their honor and liberty, as a result of a Christian training, we should rejoice. If a woman refuses to submit to her overbearing, irate mother-in-law and to the whims of a husband who still holds to his low non-Christian views of women, there is no cause for regret. At the same time she may be taught to render all due obedience and submission to those over her and to be faithful as a wife and mother.
>
> These remarks began by calling attention to the separation of the sexes common to the life of the Korean people for ages, and by assenting to the principle being carried over into the church with reservations. The remarks will close by specifying one of the reservations. It is all right to have women's Sunday Schools, Bible classes, Bible Institute, Bible Women, single lady missionaries—in short a separately organized women's work but a mistake to

have the teaching and directing done by women workers only. A safe and general law of church government is that the church governing bodies which are composed of men, and those in charge of women's work should not only welcome and seek this official direction but not feel hurt when it does not harmonize exactly with what they (the women themselves) would like to have. Part of the time Women's Sunday School classes, Teachers classes and Bible classes should be taught by men—Korean church officers, Korean pastors and missionaries. It is a mistake for male missionaries, busy though they be, not to teach in Women's Bible Institutes.

. . . . As an American I lament some of the extremes to which our American women have gone. At the same time our present standards with the extremes are much to be referred to a lifeless, willess, over-docile, idealess, temptation-resistless, uninitiative womanhood.

In short, in the development of our woman's work changes will come, problems will arise, mistakes will be made, extremes will crop out, but in it all progress will be made. But the best results cannot be obtained by maintaining a strictly separate woman's work.[38]

3. *"A Service of Personal Dedication for Ewha College Teachers and Staff."* The faculty and staff conference of Ewha College and Kindergarten-Normal Training School was held on September 3, 1932. The faculty and staff together agreed that the purpose of Ewha College would be "to provide broad foundations for the richest and fullest Christian living." Their aims and convictions are clearly conveyed in this personal dedication held at the close of the conference.

Hymn, "Take My Life and Let It Be."

Leader: To the unfailing ministry of the details of organization,
Teachers: WE DEDICATE OURSELVES, O LORD.

Leader: To the hearty cooperation in the fulfillment of the pains and policies of the school,
Teachers: WE DEDICATE OURSELVES, O LORD.

Leader: To the upholding of professional integrity and the development of professional skill,
Teachers: WE DEDICATE OURSELVES, O LORD.

Leader: To the encouragement of high scholastic standards throughout the student body,
Teachers: WE DEDICATE OURSELVES, O LORD.

Leader: To the fostering of originality and initiative in the thought and action of our students,
Teachers: WE DEDICATE OURSELVES, O LORD.

Leader: To the preservation of all that is noble in Korean culture,
Teachers: WE DEDICATE OURSELVES, O LORD.

Leader: To the appropriation, for Korea, of all that is best in Western culture,
Teachers: WE DEDICATE OURSELVES, O LORD.

Leader: To the inculcation of the ideals of Truth, Beauty, and Goodness,
Teachers: WE DEDICATE OURSELVES, O LORD.

Leader: To the development of healthy bodies, keen minds, high character, vital spirits among our students; to the upbuilding of a gracious and efficient young womanhood in Korea,
Teachers: WE DEDICATE OURSELVES, O LORD.

Leader: To the unstinted giving of ourselves, that we may enter into the lives of our students with sympathy and understanding,
Teachers: WE DEDICATE OURSELVES, O LORD.

Leader: To the ministry of patience, that awaits with confidence the full growth and fruitage in the lives of youth,
Teachers: WE DEDICATE OURSELVES, O LORD.

Leader: To the pouring out of our strength, our time, our abilities, in service to the girlhood of the land,
Teachers: WE DEDICATE OURSELVES, O LORD.

Leader: To the deepening of the spirit of love, without which our service is in vain,
Teachers: WE DEDICATE OURSELVES, O LORD.

Leader: To the renewed endeavor to follow the pattern of life, as revealed by Jesus, the Master Teacher,
Teachers: WE DEDICATE OURSELVES, O LORD.

UNISON PRAYER

O Thou God of Wisdom and Strength, Thou God of Truth and Beauty, Thou God of Love and Patient Understanding, we beseech Thy blessing upon us.

> O teach me Lord, that I may teach,
> The precious things Thou dost impart,
> And wing my words that they may reach,
> The hidden depths of many a heart.[39]

4. "Why I Became A Missionary." Jeannette Walter, the fifth principal of Ewha, was born in 1885, the year Ewha was founded. She served Ewha as an educational missionary from 1911 to 1933. Defining a missionary's life as "the gospel she or he taught," Walter brought significant changes and progress to Ewha, which she fully describes in her book, *Aunt Jean*. Her testimony on how she became a missionary is typical of many women's motives to become missionaries.

A few weeks after entering College I joined a "mission study class," and there the study of the life of Isabella Thoburn first stirred my heart along the line of missionary work. Later, the testimony of a young woman who had heard the call made me ask myself the question, "are you willing" and the answer was a decided "No." The same question repeated itself so often I was tired of hearing it. I sang, "I'll go where you want me to go, dear Lord—except across the sea—I'll be what you want me to be—except a missionary," until I felt it to be mockery, and I stopped singing that song, and one by one many other songs of consecration dropped from my list.

During the following summer before leading a missionary meeting I settled the question in this way, I'd be a missionary if the Lord called me, but I hoped He wouldn't call. I felt happy, and returned to College very soon to be almost scared out of my senses on hearing a Secretary was coming to organize a Volunteer Band. I spent many uneasy days before and after her arrival, but one day at the noon hour, I made the decision which drove every fear of mission work from my heart and joined the new band.

Years passed before graduation; Circumstances so changed that I felt at times I scarcely knew His will, and before I applied to the Board I wanted to know for myself. I applied for a school at home, all the time telling the Lord I'd do His will if I knew it. Before the contract was made, a Korean young man came to my house and asked if I would go to Korea. I said little to the man that night but to the Lord I said, "That must be the leading, I'll go," and within two weeks I was under appointment to the land where I now deem it a blessed privilege to serve! It's a happy life out here.[40]

Georgia Harkness

CHAPTER 10

GEORGIA HARKNESS—THEOLOGIAN OF THE PEOPLE

Evangelical Liberal and Social Prophet

ROSEMARY SKINNER KELLER

Georgia Harkness, the first woman theologian to teach in a Protestant seminary in the United States, was scheduled to deliver the keynote address at "Women's Night" on May 11, 1939, at the Uniting Conference of the formation of The Methodist Church. However, "Women's Night," intended to be a celebration of the founding of the Women's Society of Christian Service of the new denomination, was never held.

The historic conference finished its work of uniting The Methodist Episcopal Church, The Methodist Episcopal Church South, and The Methodist Protestant Church into the new denomination on the day before, May 10. All events scheduled from May 11 through 14 were simply canceled. Unity had been achieved, in the eyes of the delegates.

The Uniting Conference of 1939 abides in the annals of United Methodism for its creation of the Central Jurisdiction, the separate governing structure for black churches within The Methodist Church. The church maintained the administrative arrangement of the Central Jurisdiction, alongside the five geographic divisions of the church for white members, until after creation of The United Methodist Church in 1968.

The 1939 Conference is also historically significant for the formation of the Women's Society of Christian Service, which created a fellowship of women, recruited and funded women for mission fields throughout the world, and became a prime advocate for social justice within the church and the world. Georgia Harkness celebrated the founding of the WSCS. But what would she have said had she given the scheduled keynote address at Women's Night on May 11, 1939?

I believe that Harkness would not have given the expected pep rally presentation for the new women's organization and stopped with that. My speculation is based on what she said one year later in 1940, when again she was invited to be the keynote speaker at "Women's Night" at the first

General Conference of The Methodist Church. She took this occasion to address the new church on the topic "One in Christ Jesus," emphasizing to the delegates that the church still had a great distance to go to attain genuine unity. Her text was the "great Galatians text," as she referred to it: "There is neither Jew nor Greek, there is neither slave nor free, there is neither male nor female; for you are all one in Christ Jesus." Galatians 3:28 was one of the primary texts reflecting Harkness's spirituality. She challenged the church to be a prophet of unity in Jesus Christ by engaging in the battles against racism, sexism, and militarism within its own body and the world.[1]

Georgia Harkness's prophetic witness for social justice throughout her adult life was closely tied to her faith commitment as an evangelical liberal Christian. This essay traces her vocational journey from childhood to older adulthood, particularly focusing on her determinative spiritual conversion when she was fifty years old. Upheavals within herself and the world brought maturity to her experiences of personal and social transformation during these early years of her older adulthood, leading to an essential unity between her personal spirituality and her commitment to the inclusivity and equality of all persons in Christ.

Georgia Harkness capsuled her mature self-perception as a theologian shortly before her death on August 21, 1974. In the interview, which was published the following October, Harkness was quoted as saying, "I have not become a big name in theology. My talent, if I have one, lies in making theology understandable to people."[2]

Harkness understated her prominence as a theologian. She was the first woman to teach theology in Protestant seminaries in the United States, serving as Professor of Applied Theology at Garrett Biblical Institute from 1939 until 1950 and Pacific School of Religion from 1950 until her retirement in 1961. She also authored almost forty books. Her enduring contribution was not as an academic who charted new theological directions. She was a folk theologian, a synthesizer of maincurrent Protestant thought and a practical woman of faith, committed to relating thought to action. As an interpreter to both clergy and laity, Harkness was one of the most distinguished theologians of her age. She was also one of the few precursors at the mid–twentieth century of feminist scholars in higher education and seminary teaching today.[3] Not surprisingly, some scholars, particularly of the New England establishment, did not sufficiently esteem her definitive contribution.

Harkness provides initial insight into her identity as one who made "theology understandable to people" in an autobiographical sketch written in the early 1950s for the Pacific Coast Theological Group, a circle of professional theologians in which she was the only woman. Its members met regularly to share their spiritual journeys and discuss theology. Georgia began the sketch by describing her relationship to the "goodly heritage" of her historical origins, the small rural community of Harkness, New York, "a hamlet of four-corners with some houses clustered about but with most of its post-office-address population living on outlying farms." She stated: "I have no better friends anywhere on earth. These *were* and *are* my roots—and for these roots I humbly thank God. If in some measure He has been able to use my words to speak in plain language to common folk, the reason is . . . simply this—that I am one myself."[4]

What did Georgia Harkness mean in describing herself in terms we might paraphrase as a "theologian of the people"? First, in delineating her talent "to make theology understandable to people" and "to speak in plain language to common folk," Harkness correctly identified her methodology of writing and speaking. Former students, clergy, and laity consistently point to the clarity of her organization and to the directness and cogency of her words, whether presented in written or oral form. They also emphasize that she never watered down the content of her theological convictions or faith stance, but stated hard truths and challenging commitments which the Christian message called forth from people.[5]

Second, when Harkness stated that if God had been able to use her words to speak to common folk, "the reason is . . . simply this—that I am one myself," she correctly identified her roots. She remained close to those roots, as demonstrated in telling ways. In her eighty-three years of life, from 1891 until 1974, Harkness became a national and international pioneer and leader in the ecumenical church, as well as in her Methodist denomination. She witnessed her faith as a forerunner of liberation theology, focusing her commitments on pacifism and the liberation of women and racial minorities in church and society. During these same years, however, she retained her membership in the Harkness Methodist Church, which she joined at age fourteen when it met in an old schoolhouse. She was elected to the General Conference of her denomination as a lay delegate from the Troy Conference in New York, rather than from Illinois or California where she spent most of her professional career.

Never forsaking her small-town roots in terms of values, loyalties, and appreciation, Harkness wrote in the late 1950s that she found it a high and moving privilege to have preached recently at the centennial of the founding of the West Peru, New York, church. "The best part is that they welcome me, not as a theological seminary professor or the author of books, but as one of them with the mutual enrichment of common memories. They are the salt of the earth, and the salt has not lost its savor."[6]

However, Harkness's vocational center did not blossom simply out of the natural sprouting of her roots. The third and deepest meaning of her identity as a "theologian of the people" unfolds through her vocational journey, as she ventured far from home during her young, middle, and older adult years. Maturing in her spiritual development over the course of her life, she gained an essential unity between personal and social transformation.

Georgia Harkness grew up in upstate New York, an area known in the nineteenth century as the "burned-over district," to symbolize the revival fires set by Charles Grandison Finney, "the father of modern evangelicalism," which had spread over the land.[7] Her childhood revival experience was similar to that of countless other persons of the twentieth century who claim an evangelical heritage. (See document 1.) She grew up in a church-going family in which her father said grace before every meal. However, her parents were not particularly pious, and she recalled no other family prayers or Bible reading.[8]

Though well-nurtured in regular church and Sunday school attendance, Georgia yearned for a definitive conversion experience which would put the seal of authenticity on her evangelical faith. She counted on the yearly winter revival services, to which "we always went," to provide that definitive conversion. "As often as the revival came I got converted," she wrote. "Then I backslid during the summer, and was ready for conversion again the next winter. I do not know how many times this happened, but I recall that when I wanted to join the church at the age of seven, my mother, to my considerable disappointment, thought I ought to wait till I was a little older."[9]

Finally, when Georgia Harkness was in high school, her "definitive conversion" occurred. "Whether I had been a Christian before is matter of definition," she wrote when more than sixty, "for certainly I had been a religiously sensitive child and had loved the Church since before I can remember. But under the preaching of a traveling evangelist, whose name I cannot remember, I decided that the time had come to take a definite stand and join the Church."[10]

The language of conversion was completely natural to Harkness, but her own experience included no dramatic "turning around." Conversion, in Harkness's life, was a personal decision to become a member of "the Church" and to participate responsibly. She had studied the Methodist *Discipline*, learned that baptism was supposed to precede membership, and had to remind the pastor that she had never been baptized.[11] Georgia received a coveted scholarship to attend Cornell University in Ithaca, New York, graduating with academic excellence by making Phi Beta Kappa. Her strong evangelical commitment led her into the Student Volunteer Movement in college and caused her to seek a calling for her life. Along with thousands of others of her generation, she signed the SVM pledge: "It is my purpose, if God permits, to become a foreign missionary." For as long as she could remember, however, Georgia had expected to become a teacher. To be a missionary or a teacher: They were the two most accessible professions for women of her day.[12]

After graduation from Cornell, Harkness taught for two years, until 1918, in high schools in Schuylerville and Scotia, New York, close to her home. Her heart lay elsewhere, however. Reading an article in *The Chris-*

tian Advocate about a new profession for women in religious education, "I decided forthwith that if I could not be a missionary, this was my calling."[13] Two years later, in 1920, she received a double Master's degree (in Religious Education and Arts) from the Methodist-related Boston University School of Religious Education.

Before receiving her Master's degree, however, Harkness made a vocational shift to the study of philosophy. She described herself as having "fallen under the spell of Dr. Edgar S. Brightman's kindling mind" during the second year of her Master's program. Deciding that her calling lay in teaching religion to college students, "I asked Brightman if he would take me on as a candidate for a PhD. He told me that I had the preparation, probably the brains, but that I lacked the stick-to-it-iveness. I told him that if that was all, I would see to that."[14]

After gaining her Ph.D. in philosophy, Georgia Harkness spent her first sixteen years in higher education teaching philosophy and religious education. She served on the faculties of Elmira College from 1922 until 1937 and of Mt. Holyoke College during 1938. Her teaching and writing stance during these years reflected her academic training in philosophical liberalism. Harkness was introduced to idealism at Cornell by Professor James Creighton. Her work in Personalism at Boston University, primarily under Edgar Brightman, steeped her in the tradition and solidified her allegiance.

A primary quest for an ideal of philosophical objectivity to enable a person to "live religiously" defined Harkness's writings until she was almost fifty years old, when she came onto the faculty of Garrett Biblical Institute. An ideal, she stated simply, is "a conviction that something ought to be, held before the mind with sufficient power to motivate effort to bring it to pass." Most people settle or aspire in life to lesser levels of idealism, of "prudential adjustment," to live out of a proper mean, do nothing in excess, and to be a socially respectable person.[15]

In statements which had direct application to overcoming racism, sexism, and militarism in the attitudes of individuals and in the structures of society, she stated, "The Christian . . . should aspire to the highest idealism of triumphant religion," the level of active saintliness demonstrating the dynamic union of social action and social passion, sympathy for all persons and courage to serve the needy. "If our ideals are as inclusive as they ought to be, we find through them not only personal mastery but the impetus toward the creation of a society where none need be inhibited by artificial barriers from living at his best. The function of the ideals is both individual and social. In the power to live by ideals, whether directed against sin or chaos, lies salvation." Harkness's definitive statement of the Christian faith through philosophical idealism in 1937 is summarized in her words "Living in Christ, one could look the world in the face, do a mighty work, and know that nothing could daunt the soul."[16]

The pace and momentum of Harkness's rapidly escalating career brought her early success as one of the pioneer female professors of religious studies in higher education, and reflected a personal quest for religious idealism in her own life. During the 1920s and 1930s, she traveled in Europe to observe the devastation following World War I and became a pacifist, a stance she maintained for life. Harkness toured the Holy Land and Mediterranean countries, became ordained a deacon in The Methodist Episcopal Church, and took study leaves at Harvard, Yale, and Union, which enabled her to write four important books in philosophy of religion and ethics. She also "discovered the joys of writing verse," in the form of poems, prayers, and personal spiritual meditations. Devotional literature characterized a part of the scholarship of her vocational journey long after her philosophical idealism became melded with her evangelicalism.[17]

Georgia Harkness soon became distinguished as a prominent figure in international ecumenical circles. She was a consultant to the Oxford Conference of the World Council of Churches in 1937, and to the Madras Conference in 1938. The following year, Harkness journeyed to Geneva as a member of the Board of Strategy of the W.C.C. and to Amsterdam as a consultant in education at the World Conference of Christian Youth.

Her participation increased her prominence but took a heavy toll, as she stated in explaining her work at Oxford:

> I made a four-minute speech on the place of women in the church which caused quite a stir, and being cabled under the Atlantic in an AP dispatch, gave me a good deal of publicity at home. This would not be worth mentioning except that it precipitated so many invitations to speak here and there that I ran myself ragged in the attempt to keep up my school work and accept even a few of them.[18]

Harkness's rapidly escalating career brought her "outward recognition that, by the canons of the world, I had 'arrived'" when, in 1941, she and fifty-three other "notably successful pioneers" were presented with scrolls of honor by the General Federation of Women's Clubs at their golden jubilee meeting. She noted the way in which a popular church journal interpreted her selection. "The other person in the field of Religion to be honored was Dr. Hilda Ives of New England Congregational fame, and an article in *Advance* regarding this incident spoke of us as 'Dr. Hilda Ives, great organizer and worker in the church, and Dr. Georgia Harkness, abstract theologian and retiring mystic.'"[19]

Two personal events, more consequential to her vocational journey and identity for the last half of her life, from the mid-1930s until her death in 1974, were taking place in Georgia Harkness's life. They were influential in the merging of her evangelical commitment with her belief in philosophical idealism, enabling her to cultivate a witness to social justice as a public expression of her inner faith. Through them, her public image as "abstract theologian and retiring mystic" would be permanently altered and her more significant lasting distinction in church and society would be established. The first was her father's death and the second was her "dark night of the soul." Together, these experiences constitute a mid-life crisis, which in the terms of evangelical Christianity is described as the death of the old life and the birth of the new.

Georgia's father, Warren Harkness, her mentor, model, and the most influential person in her life, died in 1937, shortly before she left Elmira College. In the last hour of his life, he asked Georgia how many books she had written. She told him seven. Warren Harkness responded, "I think they must be good books. Wise men say they are. But I wish you would write more about Jesus Christ."[20]

The evangelical awakening Harkness's father's death and words instilled in her did not lead to an immediate conversion in her faith perspective or in her academic thrust from that of a philosophical idealist to a more Christ-centered approach to religious truth. Something happened—or some things happened—which, in conjunction with the loss of her father, created in Georgia Harkness an extended period of a "dark night of the soul" from the late 1930s through the early 1940s. By 1945, when her book *The Dark Night of the Soul* appeared and she had been on the faculty of Garrett Biblical Institute for more than five years, she was beyond its severely depressive effects and entering the most creative and productive period of her life, which was to gain for her the distinction as a "theologian of the people."[21]

Harkness wrote the book as a part of her recuperation and therapy from the intense depression—in her words, "as an alternative to having a nervous breakdown."[22] Little is known about the specific circumstances behind Harkness's description of the spiritual, emotional, and physical depression that led to her "dark night of the soul." From her own words, we know that she suffered severe and painful physical problems, which were exacerbated by the strain of overwork and accelerated the drive to succeed as a lone woman in a profession dominated by men.

The deepest underlying cause of her "dark night of the soul" was spiritual depression, in evangelical terminology "spiritual death," a sense of being cut off from God, of seeking but not finding the source of strength and support she most needed. A far different Georgia Harkness wrote *The Dark Night of the Soul* in 1945 than authored *The Recovery of Ideals* in 1937, when she could say valiantly out of her idealistic stance that "living in Christ, one could look the world in the face, do a mighty work, and know that nothing could daunt the soul." She was gaining a different vocational identity, one that would make her a genuine "theologian of the people" because she could identify with their experience.

Her autobiographical statement, that *The Dark Night of the Soul* "was written as an alternative to having a nervous breakdown," needs to be read along with her statement of the book's purpose in its Introduction: "It is written primarily for those who have tried earnestly, but unsuccessfully, to find a Christian answer to the problem of spiritual darkness. . . . It is these unhappy ones, who not only continue on in the 'dark night' but are plunged still deeper into it by the corroding effects of failure, who are the chief object of our concern."[23] (See document 2.) Harkness's inner spiritual journey witnesses to the evangelical experience of death and new birth in Jesus Christ within the life of an individual in mainline Christianity. It did much more, however, in expanding her evangelical dedication to social responsibility. In her mid-life and after, she described herself as an evangelical liberal and applied theological positions to the hard issues of human rights regarding racism, sexism, and militarism.

From evangelicalism she inherited the faith that new and full life in Jesus Christ can come to all persons as children of God. From the liberal tradition of philosophical idealism, she gained deeper insight into the human dignity, supreme worth, and equality of all persons simply because of their common humanity. Through liberalism, she understood that rights are not simply given by God but must be affirmed by society. Harkness emerged in middle adulthood molded by both her evangelical and liberal heritages. (See document 3.)

Georgia Harkness's distinct identity and contribution to church and society were more than simply a combination of her inherited faith and values, however. In the late 1930s and after, she devised a radical social critique which went beyond liberalism. (See document 4.) Harkness clearly saw that the attitudes and goodwill of persons in positions of power could not be trusted to elevate minority and oppressed people to positions of power equal to the dominant group in society. If all are one in Christ Jesus, if there is neither slave nor free, neither male nor female, as affirmed in "the great Galatians text" on which she preached, then the structures of society and the laws undergirding them, particularly those of the church, had to be changed.

The elimination of racism, sexism, and militarism from the church, in terms of both theological grounding and practical application, was a twofold commitment of Harkness's socially prophetic vision by the late 1930s. The foes of one were the enemies of all. Racial and sexual differences were given by God and enabled a vision of deeper unity growing out of diversity. Racism and sexism both defy the nature of a God who created humans in God's own image and values each individual.

Applying this principle specially to race and racism, Harkness wrote that the evil is "not race, which in the order of nature is ordained of God that there may be variety in the many families that make up the family of God, but racism. Racism is the perversion of this variety by the injection of enmity, superiority and contempt where there ought to be fellowship and diversity." (See document 5.) Because God created a moral universe,

"Racism cannot go on without peril to all . . . those who dominate and those who suffer from the domination of others."[24]

Harkness critiqued racism, as well as sexism and militarism, in church and society primarily through her written and spoken words. She also worked on Methodist and interdenominational agencies from the local to the international level and in specific social justice organizations related to the church, such as the Methodist Federation for Social Action, but did not take part in public demonstrations against these social evils.

The church was called to be the social pioneer in securing racial equality, Harkness contended, going out in front and pointing the way for the rest of culture. It had to understand and proclaim its gospel of unity in Christ, as stated by the writer of Ephesians 2:14: "For he is our peace, who has made us both one, and has broken down the dividing wall of hostility." However, the church must move farther than simply proclaiming the gospel, by seeking to eliminate racism from every structure of the church's life, as in the local church by integrating worship services, leading educational programs, sponsoring social fellowships, and conducting interracial ventures such as pulpit exchanges.[25]

Her prophetic stance, as applied to the national structures of her denomination, was addressed directly to the evil that had been institutionalized in the creation of The Methodist Church in 1939 through establishment of the Central Jurisdiction for all black members beside the five geographical jurisdictions for white members. Harkness believed that the entire concept of a jurisdictional system defied the church's unity in Christ. Her radical position was presented through legislation at the 1956 General Conference of The Methodist Church. She and others, including Thelma Stevens, proposed that the entire jurisdictional system of the denomination be abolished.[26]

Harkness contended that the elimination of the jurisdictional system could pioneer the church toward its self-proclaimed, but unlived, unity in Christ. The inherent contradiction lay in the governing structures of the national denomination. In reality, The Methodist Church was one church of black Americans and five churches of white Americans. Under her proposal, both black and white bishops and ordained clergy would be pastors of the entire church, subject to appointment in any area of the country, not simply within the specific jurisdiction in which they were presently located. The proposal was primarily designed to abolish the Central Jurisdiction and to break loose the closed system of the denomination in the southeastern states where racist views and policies were the rule.

The legislation had no chance of passing because it required the votes of clergy and lay delegates whose views were firmly entrenched in their racial and regional configurations. It did, however, challenge the Methodists, as well as all other denominations, to confront how far their pronouncements of "one in Christ Jesus" fell short of the reality.

The Central Jurisdiction was not eliminated until 1972, four years after The Evangelical United Brethren and Methodist denominations merged to form The United Methodist Church. The proposal for merger provided that the geographical annual conferences, presently composed only of white members, had one quadrennium to merge voluntarily with all-black conferences of the Central Jurisdiction.

Georgia Harkness opposed the merger, again out of the prophetic vision that racism must be eliminated from the structures of the new denomination before unification was effected. Formation of the new church contained a built-in conflict between the values of immediate union and racial equality. Recognizing that her opposition to the merger would puzzle persons who knew her as a "warm supporter of the ecumenical movement and of Christian unity for many years," she held that the intention of persons of goodwill to integrate all structures of the new denomination should not be trusted.[27]

"The segregated Central jurisdiction, which has existed in Methodism since 1939, is a clear contradiction of Christian morality," she stated unequivocally. "It was voted at the Methodist General Conference of 1964 *not* to carry this ubiquitous structure into the union. It appears about to be carried into it—not by name but by substance in the continuance of segregated annual conferences in some sections." Such an "interim" arrangement created a double injustice to black people, denying "to our Negro members their present opportunities of representation without commensurate gain in Christian fellowship." Harkness concluded with these strong words: "This injustice I cannot stomach and I hope my church cannot."[28]

She experienced sexism, as well as racism, at work in the history of the Methodist denominations in the United States. From the 1920s until her death in 1974, Harkness pressed for the opening of equal rights for women in executive leadership positions on boards and agencies, for their right to sit on governing boards of the church, and for ordination with full conference membership for women. (See document 6.) Her work prior to 1956, in confronting the general conferences of the denomination with the necessity to ordain women, provides a significant case study in the political strategizing essential to effecting important structural change.

Convinced that ordination of women carrying full parity with men was essential to the life of the church, Harkness wrote in 1939 that "to close the door to any persons possessing spiritual and mental qualifications is, in effect, to say that sex is a more important factor in Christian vocation than character, spiritual insight, or mental ability." The denomination had bowed to exclusion on the basis of gender throughout its history, but the position could not be maintained in light of the teachings of Jesus Christ regarding the intrinsic worth of all persons before God.[29]

Throughout the 1940s, Georgia Harkness lobbied vigorously for full clergy rights for women. However, it was not until the 1948 General Conference that enough support could be mobilized to support a Minority Report from the Committee on Ministry for "Clergy Rights for Women on the Same Basis as for Men." Harkness spoke in favor of the Minority Report. The debate on the floor took an unexpected turn after an amendment was offered to reserve full clergy rights for women in two categories, those who were single and those who were widowed. Supporters of the Minority Report disapproved of the amendment. Both the Minority Report and the amendment were defeated.[30]

Prior to the 1952 General Conference, Harkness worked with the Committee on the Status of Women of the Women's Division of Christian Service on an extensive survey of District Superintendents throughout The Methodist Church. The survey evaluated the preparation and effectiveness of women serving as Accepted Supply Preachers when ordained ministers could not be obtained to appoint to churches. Responses from the District Superintendents showed that the majority of women were as well-prepared educationally and functioned as effectively as men, while many of the women rated higher than men in each category. In spite of the tabulated results, the 1952 Conference did not vote to ordain women.[31] Thousands of petitions from Women's Society of Christian Service groups in local churches throughout the nation were presented to delegates attending the next General Conference in 1956, a part of the strategy devised by Georgia Harkness and other workers. Despite the intense grass-roots support, people expected that the Conference would endorse the amended proposal from the 1948 Conference to ordain single and widowed women. To the surprise of the delegates, full ministerial rights were granted to all qualified women.[32]

One of the clergy delegates, Lyn Corson from New Jersey, arose immediately after the vote and paid this tribute to Georgia Harkness:

> This is a day of particular triumph and significance to one of the members of this group who for so many years has been looking forward to this moment when full clergy rights for women would be voted by this General Conference. I refer to Dr. Georgia Harkness.
>
> I think it is a matter only due as a courtesy from the General Conference to express the appreciation of the Conference for this valiant fight she has waged for this cause for many years and express to her how we know that on this day she must have peculiar satisfaction in the knowledge that this fight has eventuated in final victory for her cause.[33]

The delegates of the Conference rose to their feet and gave Georgia Harkness a standing ovation. She responded with these few words: "I must have a moment to thank you for this very wonderful expression. Some of you wondered why I didn't speak this afternoon. It says in the Bible there is a time to speak and a time to be silent. I thought we would do better if we let the rest of you speak. Thank you."[34] Her words convey a touch of dry humor in expressing that others, along with herself, were responsible for the vote. However, the Conference members were clear that Harkness had made the crucial contribution.

Her rejection of militarism was as unequivocal as her positions on sexism and racism. (See document 7.) Harkness's unconditional pacifist stance was nowhere expressed more clearly than in the "Report of the Commission of Christian Scholars," in shortened form known as the "Dun Commission," appointed by the Federal Council of the Churches of Christ in America in 1950. The Commission was named to develop a Christian position regarding the moral implications of obliteration bombing and the use of hydrogen bombs for mass destruction. Serving with Georgia Harkness on the Commission were nine men, including its chair, Bishop Angus Dun, and Reinhold Niebuhr, Paul Tillich, John C. Bennett, and Robert Calhoun.

The report responded to the dropping of the first atomic bomb on Hiroshima in 1945 and the escalation in development of weapons of mass destruction during the ensuing five years. It acknowledged that "the clearest and least ambiguous alternative is that urged upon us by our most uncompromising pacifist fellow Christians," referring to two members of the committee, Georgia Harkness and Robert Calhoun of Yale Divinity School.

> Further the infinitely heightened destructiveness and the "amoral" character of modern war confirms their conviction that followers of Christ can make no compromise with so great an evil. They find themselves called to follow the way of love and reconciliation at whatever cost and to accept the historical consequences of a repudiation of armaments and of war.[35]

The committee report acknowledged that no matter what good may come of war, incalculable evil always results. "We believe," it continued, that God calls some persons "to take the way of non-violence as a special and high vocation in order to give a clearer witness to the way of love than those who can accept responsibility for the coercions in civil society." John Bennett, author of the report for the Commission, and professor of social ethics and later president of Union Theological Seminary in New York City, affirmed that we "are humbled by the faithfulness of many in bearing . . . that non-violent way."[36]

Referring then to the position on the committee held by Niebuhr, Tillich, Dun, and himself, Bennett continued, "Most of us find ourselves called to follow a course which is less simple and which appears to us more responsible because more directly relevant to the hard realities of our situation." The majority of the committee favored "responsible collective action against aggression within the framework of the United Nations." Though done in fear and trembling, "In the last resort we are in conscience bound to turn to force in defense of justice even though we know that the destruction of human life is evil." To prevent the two great dangers of totalitarian tyranny and global war, "Policies which carry the risk of global war may be necessary."[37]

The primary conclusion of the Dun Commission was that

if atomic weapons or other weapons of parallel destructiveness are used against us or our friends in Europe or Asia, we believe that it could be justifiable for our government to use them in return with all possible restraint. We come to this conclusion with loathing. But any other conclusion would leave our own people and the people of other nations open to continuing devastating attack and to probable defeat.[38]

The Dun Commission's action could well be justified in light of the practical realities of national responsibilities on a global scale. However, John Bennett, now ninety years old and in retirement at Pilgrim Place in Claremont, California, has continued to reflect on the majority report of the Dun Commission more than forty years ago. Interviewed in 1990, he concluded that had its members known how devastating the effects of nuclear warfare could be, he, and undoubtedly others on the committee, would have affirmed the position of unqualified pacifism held by Georgia Harkness and Robert Calhoun.[39]

Georgia Harkness's approach to the battles against sexism, racism, and militarism in the church continue to be relevant to full integration on the basis of equality of persons of all races and of women, and to the place of the United States in the global community. Two reasons stand out. First, in the role of the prophet, she held up to the church an uncompromising theological position of the God-given equality and unity of races and sexes in the body of Christ and of the divine mandate for nations to beat their swords into ploughshares. Second, she worked as the political activist and strategist within the church, holding the institution accountable to "repudiate these attitudes within itself and to act as the pioneer of society" by eliminating racism and sexism within its structures and daily life at all levels, from the local congregation to national and international agencies and legislative bodies. (See document 8.)

As is true of most prophets or political strategists for change, Harkness was also a product of her culture, sometimes reflecting it more than transcending it. She never favored inclusive language in regard to God or to human beings. Instead, she believed that male references were generic. Further, she did not believe a feminist theology was appropriate or necessary, but that one theological formulation could represent all persons. Though she had her blind spots, Harkness was introduced to inclusive language and feminist theology when she was eighty years old. Her past track record indicates that, had she been graced with life until ninety or one hundred years of age, she would have embraced feminist theology overtly as well as covertly.

Harkness's preeminent contribution to applied theology was as a precursor, a forerunner, who pioneered by going out in front and pointing the way for the larger numbers who would continue the battle against racism, sexism, and militarism in church and society. She did not devise a theoretical critique from the perspective of a liberation theologian, nor a feminist theological or ethical critique within that stream. However, she was not far from those visions, either in time or ideology, when she died. In her interpretation of history, her theological stance, and her practical application, Harkness stood on a threshold.

A final story illustrates the unity of Georgia Harkness's spirituality and social responsibility rooted in the Bible and growing out of her stance as an evangelical liberal theologian. She loved to tell of this encounter at a meeting of the World Council of Churches in 1948, though the theologian with whom she had been in dialogue did not enjoy the recollection as much as she did:

> One incident from the Amsterdam Conference may be worth relating. With a few other men, Karl Barth chose to participate in the section on the Life and Work of Women in the Churches. At the beginning of the discussion Sarah Chakko, the Chairman, asked me without warning to state its theological basis. I said briefly that it is the O.T. it is stated that both male and female are created in the image of God; in the N.T. Jesus assumed always that men and women were equal before God, and in our Christian faith is the chief foundation of sex equality. Barth claimed the floor; said that this was completely wrong; that the O.T. conception of woman is that she was made from Adam's rib and the N.T. that of Ephesians 5, that as Christ is the head of the Church, so man is the head of woman. Then followed a lively interchange in which I did little but to quote Galatians 3:28, but the room buzzed. Barth convinced nobody, and if I have been told he was trying to have some fun with the women, his joke back-fired. A year later when a friend of mine asked him if he recalled meeting a woman theologian from America, his cryptic reply was, "Remember me not of that woman!"[40]

DOCUMENTS

1. Recovering Her Evangelical Heritage. From the perspective of maturity, Georgia Harkness looked back on her childhood faith experiences, valuing her conservative religious upbringing with its Wesleyan emphases on revivalism and conversion. Her love of that heritage, sense of humor, and religious precociousness as a child come through in her autobiographical sketch written when she was more than sixty years old for the Pacific Coast Theological Group.

> I was about six years old when I began to say my prayers. Contrary to the usual custom, I was not taught to pray at my mother's knee. Whether my mother ever prayed vocally I do not know. My father always said the grace at table, and we had no other family prayers and no Bible reading. Who then taught me to pray? A hired girl, who soon after was summarily dismissed for adultery. I did

not know what had happened, but I can still see the blaze in my father's eyes and hear the tones of decision with which he told her to pack her satchel while he hitched the horse to the buggy, *and not come back.* I was sorry, for I liked her, and it was a bit lonesome to have to say my prayers alone.

It was customary in those days to have a revival every winter. We always went. As I recall them, the services were not very fiery, and in retrospect I honor the underpaid, often undereducated, but almost always devoted line of ministers who preached at our school-house, and who undertook the nightly long drive involved in those "special meetings" for the love of the Lord and the desire to win souls for his Kingdom. As often as the revival came I got converted. Then I backslid during the summer, and was ready for conversion again the next winter. I do not know how many times this happened, but I recall that when I wanted to join the church at the age of seven, my mother, to my considerable disappointment, thought I ought to wait till I was a little older.

Though she was doubtless right, an experience which occurred to me when I was either nine or ten has convinced me of the reality of child religion. One Sunday after church I asked my father, "Pa, what are angels?" His answer touched off a chain reaction. "Some people say that when folks die they go to heaven and become angels, but I don't know how they know it." I am sure he had no doubt of personal immortality, and this did not immediately trouble me. What got hold of me were the words, "I don't know how they know it." How did any body know that the things we heard in church were true? In the Bible, yes, but the Bible might be a made-up book, like the many I was reading by this time. And if so, why might not Jesus be like a man in a story-book? And if Jesus did not really live, how could we know that God existed? The awful possibility seized my mind that He did not exist. And if He did not, it was foolish to pray. In fact, without being sure, one could not pray. So with full consistency, I stopped saying my prayers. But this did not solve the problem. I felt alone, bereft, queer. I knew of nobody else who did not believe in God, and was too appalled at myself to talk to anybody about it. I clearly remember lying awake alone at night, sobbing because I could not pray and could have no certainty that God existed.

It was during this period that the annual revival came along. I went, but the services brought no answer. They did not touch my problem. One night, the minister said that if anybody had any questions, we might stay after the meeting and ask him. My heart leaped with hope! The minister, if anybody, should know. I sat on the front school bench, a-quiver with eagerness while Gertie Baker talked to him about something. Just as I thought Gertie was about through and my redemption nigh, my mother came and said it was getting late and we had better be starting home. Obediently, I climbed into the cutter and carried my problem home.

How did I escape from my theological dilemma? By accident—or Providence—I came upon a book entitled *Donovan* by Edna Lyell, which I have not seen from that day to this. It was the story of a young man named Donovan who went to college and came there to question the existence of God. On a right-hand page about two-thirds of the way down I came upon a word which I had never seen before, but which I pronounced "ath-eist." Yes, that was what I was! But Donovan was one also. So there were at least two of us! With an eagerness I have seldom, if ever, experienced since, I read on to see what happened to him. He went to a wise teacher, who told him nobody could prove the existence of God, but who showed him that there were many more reasons for belief than disbelief, and who assured him that the greatest and best people of all ages had lived by this faith. Donovan's troubles cleared up, and with them mine. I began again to say my prayers, and to sleep nights. The connection between this painful experience and my present profession I leave you to trace. . . .

Did time suffice, I should like to tell you more of my "varieties of religious experience" in those school-house days—of Myron Baker who taught the young people's class, who lived in a hovel but had the soul of a Christian gentleman, and who discoursed of prophets and Jesus with prophetic fire and Christian insight as strange crawling things went up and down his black Sunday coat; of Horatio Baker who was the Sunday School Superintendent for all those years, never varying once his Sunday prayer that we be delivered from the wiles of "the Evil One who goeth about like a roaring lion seeking whom he may devour," and who whenever he called on me to substitute at the wheezy organ always announced the same hymn for fear I might not know any other. It bad us to

> "Trust and obey,
> for there's no other way
> To be happy in Jesus
> But to trust and obey."

Incidentally, I still believe those sentiments to be good Christian advice! It was he also who devised the plan of having all of us when I was about ten or eleven learn to repeat the books of the Bible. I was soon repeating the Old Testament sequences so volubly that my father advised me when we got to the N.T. to keep still and give others a chance, with the result that I can now find any book in the O.T. with relative ease, while in the New I flounder beyond Corinthians.

In due course, we moved into the lovely new church at Harkness, and things became gradually more modernized, though for years we still used the David C. Cook lesson materials. But I am not aware of any element in my sixteen years of school-house religion that did me any harm, and there was much in it for which I can profoundly thank God.[41]

2. *The Dark Night of Her Soul.* Conversion was not a once-in-a-lifetime event for Georgia Harkness. Her most meaningful experience of death and new birth came when she was a mature woman, fifty years old. She shared the depth of her inward journey with her Pacific Coast theological colleagues in the selection that follows.

The next chapter I should gladly omit, but it is too crucial to do so. In the fall of 1939 my health, which up until this time had been invulnerable, began to crack. An illness resembling undulent fever, though as yet undiagnosed, put me in the hospital for awhile, though I got well enough to write the Mendenhall lectures for the next Spring and to begin teaching at Garrett first. My energy had been depleted by the strains of leading a double life, both public and intramural, at Mt. Holyoke and trying desperately not to neglect either set of duties. For several years thereafter, though I learned to say no to most of the invitations, it was a struggle to find energy enough for my work. This problem was rendered the more acute by the fact that in the Spring of 1940, an apparently minor injury to my spine precipitated several years of nagging pain and baffled all the specialists on whom I spent my money. This combination of low energy, a "thorn in the flesh" and frustration at "suffering many things at the hands of many physicians" plunged me into insomnia and acute depression. It was in these years that I learned what appeared in 1945 as *The Dark Night of the Soul.* The book was written as an alternative to having a nervous breakdown, and in those dark years God taught me much that I should not otherwise have learned. I do not wish to repeat them, but neither do I wholly regret them.

The second selection, from an essay first printed in *The Christian Century* and then republished as the first chapter of *The Dark Night of the Soul,* was addressed to a wide reading public of laity and clergy.

There were more than ten times the usual number [of letters from readers], and I am still getting them from persons who felt that their plight had been stated for them. . . . This study presents no final wisdom. . . . I should have preferred that the book be written by one who had training in clinical psychology, but it has seemed better to write than to wait. The field is open, and there is room for many. . . .

There is one assumption without which this quest cannot be undertaken. This is that there is a way forward out of the dark. One can launch forth with much tentativeness and keep going if he believes that the goal is sure. . . . Such assurance we can have through the God revealed in Jesus Christ. It is the ultimate conviction of Christian faith that there is no situation in life where spiritual defeat is final. We may be defeated, but God cannot be. It is the message of Christianity—and has been ever since the first Easter morning—that though God's victory may be deferred it cannot be lost. . . . Across the years he speaks in Christ to say to darkened spirits in our time, "Let not your heart be troubled, neither let it be afraid." In his light we can see light.[42]

3. Incorporating the Liberal Tradition. Harkness's stature as a theologian and ecumenical churchwoman, immediately before she became Professor of Applied Theology at Garrett Biblical Institute in 1939, was affirmed by the invitation of *The Christian Century* to write an article in its series, "How My Mind Has Changed in This Decade." As a mature woman of faith, she movingly brought together her evangelism and liberalism.

Ten years ago I was a liberal in theology. I am still a liberal, unrepentant and unashamed. This does not mean that I have seen nothing in liberalism that needed correction. We were in danger of selling out to science as the only approach to truth, of trusting too hopefully in man's power to remake his world, of forgetting the profound fact of sin and the redeeming power of divine grace, of finding our chief evidence of God in cosmology, art or human personality, to the clouding of the clearer light of the incarnation. Liberalism needed to see in the Bible something more than a great figure living sacrificially and dying for his convictions. It needed to be recalled to the meaning of the cross and the power of the resurrection.

These correctives have come to us. I do not think liberalism ever had as many utopian illusions as it is now customary in retrospect to attribute to it, but its self-confidence has been challenged both by events and by theological trends. With many others in America I have profited from the currents coming out of continental Europe and too superficially called Barthian. These have come to me through books, but more through the forceful personalities of Reinhold Niebuhr and Paul Tillich—men with whom I do not agree very far but by whom I am stirred to rethink my faith. They have come at Oxford and Madras through wrestling with continental theology for the liberalism which I believe to have the truth.

My liberalism is, I trust, a chastened and deepened liberalism. But I am more convinced than ever I was before that God reveals himself in many ways and that only through the spirit of free inquiry can Christian faith go forward. I believe in the essential greatness of man, in a Christian social gospel which calls us to action as co-workers with God in the redemptive process, in a Kingdom which will come in this world by growth as Christians accept responsibility in the spirit of the cross. My Christian faith has its central focus, not in Paul's theology or Luther's or Calvin's, but in the incarnation of God in the Jesus of the Gospels.

I said above that my religion was both more theological and more Christ-centered than formerly. These two movements are part of one process—a movement away from an ideal of philosophical objectivity to one of more overt Christian commitment. For many years the philosopher and the theologian in me have been, not exactly at war, but in friendly rivalry. My graduate training was taken mainly in philosophy, though in the personalistic school congenial to religion. For fifteen years I taught philosophy. My academic conscience has the conviction that philosophy should be taught philosophically, and with greater or less success I held to this conviction. But while I was teaching philosophy I was writing religion. When the opportunity came to transfer to a department of religion I welcomed it, and the change has done much to terminate the rivalry.

When I wrote *Conflicts in Religious Thought* it did not seem to me appropriate to include a chapter on Christ. I was trying to write a simple philosophy of religion which would rest the case for religious faith upon experience without theological presuppositions, and I do not think the omission wholly unjustified. But were I writing the book now, I should put in the chapter. Whatever other grounds of faith may be adduced, it is "through Jesus Christ our Lord" that the Christian finds God with life-transforming power. The manifestations of God in the order and beauty of nature, in human fellowship and progress, in the spiritual strivings of men of all faiths, are important and real. It is essential to recognize them, for nowhere has God left himself without a witness. Yet all such evidences are incomplete. Only in Christ is revelation ultimate and unequivocal.

I am not sure how long this conviction has been growing. It probably roots in the Christ-centered religion of my childhood. In recent years an awareness of the centrality of Christ has been deepened by attempts to interpret the Christian faith to students at their conferences. A fresh exploration of the Bible made in order to teach it has left the personality of Jesus high and lifted up. At Oxford the truth of the familiar words,

> The Church's one foundation
> Is Jesus Christ her Lord,

came to me with power, and this experience was renewed at Madras.[43]

4. Spirituality and Social Responsibility: United in the Passion of God. Georgia's poetry provided means for expression of her inner spirituality. This particular poem, written during the height of suffering in World War II, profoundly brings together her spirituality and social responsibility. Her faith and its call to action were rooted in the personal nature of God:

The Agony of God

I listen to the agony of God—
I who am fed,
Who never yet went hungry for a day,
I see the dead—
The children starved for lack of bread—
I see, and try to pray.

I listen to the agony of God—
I who am warm,
Who never yet have lacked a sheltering home.
In dull alarm
The dispossessed of hut and farm
Aimless and "transient" roam.

I listen to the agony of God—
I who am strong.
With health, and love, and laughter in my soul.
I see a throng
Of stunted children reared in wrong,
And wish to make them whole.

I listen to the agony of God—
But know full well
That not until I share their bitter cry—
Earth's pain and hell—
Can God within my spirit dwell
To bring His Kingdom nigh.[44]

5. Racism: Perversion of Variety in the Family of God. Harkness focused her spiritual zeal against the primary racial injustice of the treatment of blacks in church and society. In the name of the church, she also called the nation to accountability for wrongs perpetrated against Japanese Americans and Jews. The excerpt below is from an unpublished paper, written during World War II, which contained the crux of much of her thinking on racism in her sermons, speeches, and writings.

> Nor is there time to speak in any detail as to the effects of race prejudice in our own country. We are familiar with them. The Delaware Conference put it as succinctly as I have found it anywhere, "In our own country millions of people, especially American Negroes, are subjected to discrimination and unequal treatment in educational opportunities, in employment, wages and conditions of work, in access to professional and business opportunities, in housing, in transportation, in the administration of justice and even in the right to vote."
>
> Back of these fifty words lies an incalculable amount of human misery, frustration, the embarrassment of never knowing when one may be publicly rebuffed, the necessity of seeing one's children denied what is accorded to white children as their natural birthright. When a race riot breaks out in Los Angeles, Detroit, or Harlem, it is a spectacular event that makes the headlines. Back of every such outburst lies a multitude of unpublicized acts and attitudes of racial snobbery which are unchristian, undemocratic and in the truest sense, unAmerican.
>
> It is not surprising that as we fight a war to save democracy Negro Americans and Japanese Americans, segregated even in the very process of fighting for their country, should ask the pointed question, "What democracy?" As I heard it put recently by an impassioned Negro minister, "When our boys get to Europe or the Solomons are the bullets going to come marked 'For Whites Only'?" The surprising thing is not that there should be outcroppings of bitterness and even riots, but that there should be as few of them as there are. Were the tables turned, could the white people of this country show as much cooperation and restraint?
>
> The internment of 110,000 Japanese on the Pacific Coast, including more than 70,000 American citizens, will, I am sure, long remain a blot upon our democracy. It is a sobering fact that as war encircles the globe, Germany is the only country outside of the United States that has thought it necessary to intern any considerable number of its own citizens. I do not say that the treatment accorded to the Japanese in the relocation centers is comparable to the German concentration camp. Yet in the loss of economic security and professional opportunity, the uprooting of families and surrender of personal liberty that has been forced upon great numbers of our fellow citizens and loyal neighbors, there is something of which no American can be proud. One wonders whether, in the history books of the future, we shall try as hard to forget it as we now do the Mexican War.
>
> Anti-Semitism, though less conspicuously barbed in its racial discrimination, is always with us. Near my summer home in the Adirondacks is a sign which reads,

"Buena Vista, a Christian Club." The adjective "Christian" here is a euphemism which means simply, "No Jews need apply." It is somewhat paradoxical that the founder of the Christian religion, were he to return in the flesh today, would be kept out on this basis. In manifold subtler forms Christianity, not as a faith but as a culture, has become a mark of exclusiveness where it ought to be a leaven to increase the friendliness and creative mingling of men.[45]

6. *Sexism: "The church itself is the most impregnable stronghold of male dominance."* In 1924, Harkness published her first article in a religious journal, an essay directed against discrimination of women in professional and voluntary capacities in the church. And one of her last books, *Women in Church and Society*, written in 1971, addressed this same institutional evil. This first excerpt, from her remarks at the Oxford Conference in 1937, brought her into prominence as an advocate for the place of women in the church. She is taking a strong stand for the rights of her sex, while simultaneously seeking not to offend male leaders.

Women do much of the educational work of the local church and opportunities are increasing. Yet, it is a matter of grave concern that in many instances, the energy and intelligence of able women are being drained away from the Church to go into various secular enterprises, which may be very useful and important things to do, but which lie outside the Church. Again there are many reasons, and I shall speak of but one. In such secular enterprises and in professional life in general outside of the Church, women find an opportunity for *creative leadership*, for *expression of their talents on their own initiative*, and, in turn, a *recognition* which they do not ordinarily find in the Church. I am not now speaking of ordination, which is a tangled issue, but of the wider aspects of lay leadership.

This report affirms what we have heard many times in this Conference—*that the Church is a supra-national, supra-racial, supra-class fellowship.* May I remind you, without censoriousness, but with gratitude to you men for permitting us to be here, that the Church is also a supra-sex fellowship.

The second excerpt, from an article in *The Christian Century* of that year, further demonstrates Harkness's constant effort to take highly principled but practical stands on social issues.

Much of the detailed work of every church is done by women; yet women occupy a very minor place on governing boards, whether local or denominational. The trained woman who wishes to teach religion in a college—even the church college—finds the odds against her because there are plenty of men to be had. It is not now difficult for women to secure excellent preparation for educational or administrative work in the church, and in this training there is little sex discrimination. Yet it is difficult anywhere for women to secure placement, and harder still to win professional recognition on the basis of quality of service rendered.

It is a paradoxical fact that the Christian gospel has done more than any other agency for the emancipation of women; yet the church itself is the most impregnable stronghold of male dominance. It is this fact more than any other which makes women of intelligence and ability restive, and skeptical of the church as the most effective channel for their effort.

What is to be done under these circumstances? To speak to the last point first, there is no value in railing against the situation, which is so deep-rooted in social and ecclesiastical tradition that it will change but slowly. On the other hand, nothing is to be gained either for women or the church by acquiescing in it. Perhaps the first necessity is for the men of the church to become aware that the situation exists! The second is to realize that what women, like those of other underprivileged groups, desire is not charity but opportunity. I am not decrying chivalry, but paternalism often parades unrecognized under the cloak of chivalry. The third thing we women must do is to keep on doing the best work we can because it is worth doing—without expecting much recognition or reward. The women of the future may reap the results.[46]

7. Militarism: "A pacifist, I think, forevermore." Harkness committed herself to pacifism after World War I when she observed the devastation of Europe firsthand and affirmed that the guilt for the war lay upon the Americans and other allies, as well as the axis powers. In an excerpt from a letter to Edgar Brightman in the fall of 1921, she professes her feelings immediately after her participation in the "American Seminar" to Europe, led by Sherwood Eddy. She describes a gathering in Berlin on Sunday, August 3, of "thousands of people [estimated at 200,000] banked in for acres in front of the Reichstag . . . to commemorate the tenth anniversary of the beginning of the war."

> I liked the German people we met very much, and came away with a great deal better understanding of and sympathy for the German viewpoint than I have ever had before. . . . The economic conditions in Germany are improving, though they are still bad enough. . . . But it is tragic to find so much war bitterness and mutual misunderstanding, with the feeling in both countries that though war had done no good, there is no way out except more wars. My trip to Rheims and the battlefields, with what I saw in Germany of the effects of the hunger blockade and the "war-peace," have made me *a pacifist, I think, forevermore.* I came away with more sympathy, on the whole, for Germany than for France, for while there are still plenty of evidences of militarism in Germany I do not think many Americans realize what Germany has suffered from the hunger blockade, the injustice of the treaty, and the accusation of sole guilt—to say nothing of the Ruhr. [emphasis mine]

Throughout her life, Harkness maintained her pacifist stance. In her "Spiritual Pilgrimage," published in *The Christian Century* on the eve of World War II in 1939, she capsuled the essence of why some people, in the name of the church, needed to hold such an uncompromising position.

Perhaps I should explain why I have become a more convinced pacifist in a day when many better Christians than I have felt impelled to surrender their pacifism. The reasons are both pragmatic and theological. War destroys every value for which Christianity stands, and to oppose war by more war is only to deepen the morass into which humanity has fallen. I have talked with lovable, high-minded Japanese Christians who see nothing of aggression in what their country is doing. "Japan is fighting for two reasons only—to establish friendly relations with China and to preserve the peace of the Orient." When a military system does this to the minds of sane people it is time to repudiate forever the illusion that by fighting we shall have peace.

But deeper than this is the realism which has come with the shattering of whatever illusions our liberalism had. I believe that life is inevitably a sphere of conflict and that our choices are not often to be made between good and evil, but between alternative evils. I believe that in all of life's dark areas the triumph which shines through tragedy comes not with the sword which our Lord rejected, but with the cross toward which he walked. I believe that only in the union of justice with suffering love is any human force redemptive and permanently curative, for only in such union is force more than human.[47]

8. "Wanted—Prophets!" Calling Laity and Clergy to Their Prophetic Ministry. Laity and clergy alike were held accountable to their prophetic ministry by Georgia Harkness. This impassioned statement, which draws upon her evangelical liberal stance, was written in 1937. The world had never needed prophetic utterance as at that particular moment, she contended. However, it is the timelessness and application of her message to the end of the twentieth century that strikes Christians reading her words today.

If ever the world needed prophetic utterance it is today. This is not the *worst* period in the world's history, but it is by all odds the most complex. Though the world is probably even now growing better, one wonders whether the stream of progress has not got more than ordinarily impeded in an eddy. Economic strife, class cleavage, racial hatred and suspicion, militarism, religious indifference, moral laxity, muddled thinking—these are only a few of the issues which must give us pause if we think the world is moving placidly along toward the Kingdom of God.

When Amos came down the hills of Tekoa to disturb the serenity of the religious festival at Bethel, he came with no meek conventional message. He came to tell the self-satisfied company there assembled that they were too well pleased with themselves—that they could not hope to win the favor of Jehovah by going through the motions of religion while oppression, injustice and debauchery were rife in the land. The present time reveals many parallels. We have religious formalism and spiritual apathy, the economic oppression and wasteful extravagance, the hatred, suspicion and greed which confronted the eighth century prophets. There has been progress—

but after twenty-seven centuries we have not made such a vast amount of progress. If the church is to save the world or save itself, it must produce prophets to proclaim once more that justice must roll down as waters and righteousness as a mighty stream.

THREE INGREDIENTS ESSENTIAL

It takes three major ingredients to make a prophet. It takes religious insight, intellectual alertness, and social vision. A prophet speaks forth boldly what he sees—of things as they are and things as they ought to be. One can have no prophetic message unless he sees with the eye of religious devotion, intellectual clarity and social sympathy. And since vision becomes effective only in passion, to be a prophet means to have a passion for God, for straight thinking, and for humanity.

Is the church producing such prophets? In a measure, yes—perhaps. If the question were put to any group acquainted with the situation I doubt whether it would call forth a very unanimous or enthusiastic "yes." It is a significant fact that college students are turning their backs upon the church in large numbers because of its failure to speak a prophetic message. The judgment of youth is often immature, but its idealism is sound; and a church that spends its time in theological wrangles and doctrinal disputes while giant evils go unchallenged, the church had better look within before inveighing against the student for defaulting.

What are the churches doing in this crisis? Various things—some of them very commendable things. Most of our churches are trying in one way or another to develop the religious experience of individuals. The method varies from Holy Roller meetings to the most dignified of ritualistic service; but the aim of every church—at least of every church that has not fallen into such a torpor as to forget it has an aim—is the endeavor to cultivate spiritual values. And this is well. Without the aim we should have no church. Properly interpreted, it is probably the primary function of the church. Adequately achieved, it would carry us a long way toward the solution of the world's problems. It is a task which demands prophetic leadership—but it is not the only task.

MAKING PEOPLE THINK

Here and there a church is trying to make its people think. But only here and there. In general—let us face the ugly fact—the major part of the minister's activity goes to keeping the pews reasonably full, keeping the organizations going, keeping the finances up, and keeping everybody in good humor. Neither by pulpit nor pew is it expected that the minister will stir up the cortical areas of his hearers. Such is the inertia of human nature that the occupants of the pews prefer generally not to be made to think. And the minister, being made of the same human nature, prefers also not to be made to think. Meanwhile both minister and people follow the paths made familiar and congenial by long-accustomed habit—and think that they are thinking!

Still more rarely do we find a church where pastor and people have social vision. Social vision is the capacity to see with sympathy and intelligence the needs of another, and to see it through the other person's eyes. It means the ability, without callousness or sentimentality, to enter the experience of underpaid workers and over-rich possessors of unearned wealth. It means identifying one's self vicariously with the plight of share-croppers, ostracized negroes, prostitutes, underfed children, unemployed men—all those to whom is denied fulness of life. Social vision means not merely a vague feeling of benevolence and good will; it means an earnest effort by education and legislation to create a better world. It means the willingness to throw oneself into the struggle for an unpopular cause for conscience's sake, without restraint of prejudice or fear of entrenched opinion.

And this is where the rub comes. There are plenty of people who would like to see the world improved if the improvement could be brought about without too much inconvenience! But there are not many who are willing to act when action involves being thought queer. Candidates for the ministry used sometimes to be asked whether they were willing to be damned for the glory of God. Happily, theology has passed this stage. But unhappily many of us, both of clergy and laity, have not yet reached the stage where we are willing to face social disapproval for the glory of God or the relief of man's estate.

If the church is to have a prophetic function, Christian leaders must be willing to challenge comfortable, traditional modes of thought, and do it in terms not glossed over with vague generalities. Such challenge is imperative in the areas of economics, of militaristic nationalism and of race, and because in these areas we are now least Christian, it is in these most dangerous to be prophetic. It is safe to talk of social justice in general, but not to be a socialist; to read Isaiah's vision of a warless world and preach an eloquent sermon from it, but not to be a pacifist; to quote, "God hath made of one blood all nations of the earth," but not to invite a Negro to one's home or to one's pulpit. So one chooses the safer course, and tells himself he must not undermine his influence by rashness. Caution is the mother of pseudo-prophetism.

Prophetic courage, to be sure, should not be made an excuse for blundering obstinacy. Lyman Abbott had a wise adage, "Let courage teach you when to speak, and tact teach you how." But neither must expediency be made an excuse for retreat. There is need of a resurgence of the spirit of William Lloyd Garrison who said: "I am in earnest. I will not equivocate. I will not excuse. I will not retreat a single inch—and I will be heard."

If the church has not produced many prophets in our day, it is largely because congregations have not wanted them. Pulpit and pew must share the blame. "Passing the buck" is a practice at least as old as the story of the garden of Eden, and one which is antithetical to prophetism. What eventuates from it is lack of vision on both sides of the chancel rail. And where there is no vision, the people perish.[48]

Thelma Stevens

CHAPTER 11

THELMA STEVENS, CRUSADER FOR RACIAL JUSTICE

ALICE G. KNOTTS

Thelma Stevens, 1902–1990, Executive Secretary of the Department of Christian Social Relations and Local Church Activities, set out in 1940 with the support of the Woman's Division of The Methodist Church and a budget of $15,000 to lead Methodist women along paths intended to create a new social order. Her experiences and deep Christian faith led her to embark on her crusade to eliminate racism and work for a social order without racial barriers.

Born on May 11, 1902, on a farm near French Camp in Montgomery County, Mississippi, Thelma was the youngest of nine children of Larkin Stevens and Ida Palmer Stevens. Initially a talkative child, at age six she became quiet and reflective after her mother's death from pneumonia. Unable to speak with the rest of her family about her tremendous grief, a few months after her mother's death she decided to leave home. She walked past the garden and through the pasture where her family kept cows, horses, and mules. She came to a stream she would need to wade across to get away, but she became entangled in thorns and some embedded themselves in her left hand. She sat down to cry, wishing to escape her sadness. Suddenly Benjamin, an older brother, scooped her up in his arms and gently carried her home.

The thorn in Stevens' hand became for her a parable of life. Years later when she was grown, a thorn, long ago forgotten, festered and came out of her hand. As an adult, Stevens saw that racial bigotry was a festering thorn in the hand of church and society.

Soon after her mother died, Thelma went to live with her married older sister, Ethel, who provided a strong role model. In addition to rearing three children of her own and teaching school full-time, Ethel herself filled her husband's Methodist pulpit for two years while he suffered from illness. Stevens joined and was an active member of the local congregation of The Methodist Episcopal Church, South.

In Mississippi, school was held only a few months out of each year, but when she was old enough, Stevens attended regularly. She played with both African American and white children from nearby farms. Stevens noticed that the African American children were not allowed to attend her school, had no school of their own, and consequently had no opportunity to learn to read or obtain an education.

As a teenager, she found herself at odds with the teachings of the church primarily because devout white people practiced segregation and demonstrated little substantive concern for their poverty-stricken, uneducated African American neighbors. Stevens quietly observed the inequities she saw. Neither the church nor friends or neighbors were ready to acknowledge or talk about racial injustice.

After completing high school at age sixteen, Stevens taught at a one-room high school in Crystal Springs. Here occurred "the most devastating experience of my life."[1] One morning in 1921, members of the young women's basketball team that she coached arrived early for school and took Stevens for a bus ride to a secluded spot in the woods where a crowd, an African American teenager hanging from a tree, and the sound of gunfire told her that a lynching was in progress. Sickened by the event, she ordered her students onto the bus and the bus driver to leave immediately. The experience profoundly changed Stevens' life, for she vowed that "if the Lord would ever let me live long enough I would spend the rest of my life working for basic fairness and justice and safety for black people."[2] This commitment soon expanded to become a pledge to end racial barriers everywhere, between all races. At age eighty-one she reflected, "I've done the best I could in every instance that I've had access to, and I suppose it will be the priority of my life as long as I live."[3]

Stevens graduated from State Teachers' College at Hattiesburg (now the University of Southern Mississippi), but not before she had oriented her classmates, other prospective school teachers, through banned contacts with African American teachers, to the blighted condition of public education for African American students in Mississippi. As a college graduate and teacher of pedagogy at a junior college in Perkinson, Mississippi, she launched an experimental teaching project between herself, ten white college students, and local African American school teachers, to provide supplementary instruction in teaching methods to teachers with a fifth-grade education.

While Stevens attended State Teachers' College, a recruiter for the Methodist deaconess program spent a week on campus and tried to enlist her. (See document 1.) She would have none of it. From her perspective the church was too bigoted to be a place where she could work. Although the recruiter welcomed Stevens' opinions about religion, she knew that the local church did not live the kind of faith she held. She took the teaching position at Perkinson. Yet within five years, Stevens made a vocational turnaround and a different commitment to the church.

One day the mail brought an application form and offer of financial aid for graduate study at Scarritt College in Nashville. In retrospect, the mysterious arrival of that letter seemed to be an act of God, for as much as the hypocrisy of the church repelled Stevens, the opportunity for graduate education appealed to her. Her sister Ethel encouraged her, saying that nothing in the world would make her happier than to know that Thelma was working in the church.[4] In 1926 Thelma Stevens entered Scarritt College for Christian Workers in Nashville, Tennessee, completing a master's degree in 1928 and a thesis entitled "The Pharisees and Jesus." (See document 2.)

Stevens' vocational commitment changed as she discovered some Christians who were open to new ideas and whose social vision she shared. At Scarritt, Stevens entered an academic climate influenced by the social gospel and by forward-thinking southerners whose social consciousness led them to rub against the nap of the southern social fabric. Stevens found people with a concern and passion for helping to root out racism. She met professors who shared her theological understanding that people should be treated with justice regardless of race. Mabel Howell, Stevens' Professor of World Mission and Sociology, nurtured Stevens' understanding of Christian mission as action and engagement with issues of peace and justice in a global setting.

One of her great discoveries at Scarritt was a kindred spirit and mentor in her Professor of Sociology and Director of Field Work, Louise Young.[5] Young came to Scarritt from Paine College, where she had been the only white faculty member. At Scarritt, Young taught a course "The Negro in America." The two women formed a lifelong friendship.

From her New Testament studies, Stevens learned that Jesus handled criticism from religious leaders by finding a deeper authority coming directly from God. God's guidance and authority were confirmed by Jesus' own inner understanding of righteousness. She took this as her model for facing criticism from racists within the church.

Stevens spent two years working with members of Nashville's African American community at the Bethlehem Center under the supervision of Estelle Haskin, Director of the Center and a leader of Methodist women's work in race relations.[6] Stevens later wrote, "Miss Haskin was one of the great pioneers of women's history in Methodism. Her priority was *racial* justice."[7] Stevens decided that when she left Scarritt she would accept a job where she could work with African American people.

Gradually Stevens began to consider the possibility of working for The Methodist Episcopal Church, South, as a deaconess. Over the years since the lynching, she had reaffirmed her commitment to spend her life working to end the tension and injustice between races. She had decided to remain single so that she would not be limited by husband or family in pursuit of her professional aims. Now she applied to be a deaconess and was refused! Her doctor would not recommend her to the Deaconess Bureau because she had a bad ulcer and he didn't expect her to live more than three years.[8] Subsequently, friends who had expected her death within months celebrated the success of her major surgery.

One of her teachers helped Stevens find a job at Hampton Institute, a vocational and liberal arts studies institute for African American students, located in Virginia. Stevens was packing to move when, through assistance from Louise Young, she received the offer of work she preferred, a position as director of the Methodist women's sponsored Bethlehem Center in Augusta, Georgia.

From 1928 to 1940, Stevens served as Director of the Bethlehem Center. Here, with her friend and coworker, Dorothy Weber (Carter), Stevens managed a bustling community center, oversaw the construction of a new building, purchased a forty-acre campsite, and organized some of the earliest interracial camping programs in the nation.[9] During the Depression years, the Bethlehem Center helped people hold their lives together when normal social structures were in chaos and people were hungry and unemployed. Six hundred children attended the Vacation Bible School. Stevens used community organizing skills to involve members of the community in the leadership and development of programs designed to serve the neighborhood. She particularly enjoyed meeting with a group of African American pastors, teaching them Bible study skills, examining with them the sermon text for the following week, and hearing their sermons.

Stevens' location within an African American community in the South and her tie as an employee of the Woman's Missionary Council of The Methodist Episcopal Church, South, brought her into contact with other white southern Methodist women who were working to improve race relations. In 1928 Stevens met Dorothy Tilly, from Atlanta, whose monumental leadership in race relations with the Woman's Missionary Council, the Southern Regional Council, and the Fellowship of the Concerned spanned more than three decades.[10]

In 1930, it was Stevens who first took Tilly to eat with a group of African American churchwomen in the dining room at Paine College.[11] Stevens and Tilly were teaching at a summer school session for women of The Colored Methodist Episcopal Church. After a morning session, as they headed out for lunch, Stevens suggested that they eat in the dining room on campus. Tilly said, "Why, Thelma, I never ate with Negro people in my life!" Stevens responded, "Well, you don't mind, do you?" and Tilly replied, "Well, no, I don't mind. I just never have done it." With that, Stevens guided Dorothy Tilly along a new step in race relations.

Through the Woman's Committee of the Commission on Interracial Cooperation and its white director, Jessie Daniel Ames, a core group of southern African American women worked with white churchwomen, guiding them as they worked to change racial attitudes and public policies across the South.[12] In this ecumenical setting, white Methodist women from the Woman's Missionary Council of The Methodist Episcopal Church, South, worked closely with well-known leading African American public figures including Charlotte Hawkins Brown, Jennie Moton, Janie Porter Barrett, Mattie E. Coleman, Juliette Derricotte, Nannie Burroughs, and Mary McLeod Bethune, who were the heads of educational or social service institutions. Close ties between these prominent women with a strong commitment to racial justice made possible advances in race relations even under the cloak of segregation.

In 1930, noted southern Methodist leaders such as Louise Young, Estelle Haskin, and Dorothy Tilly helped Jessie Daniel Ames found the Association of Southern Women for the Prevention of Lynching (ASWPL). Stevens joined them in working to obtain the signatures of sheriffs, judges, and voters on an anti-lynching pledge.

In 1938, when Stevens was tapped by the Woman's Missionary Council to succeed Bertha Newell as head of the Bureau of Christian Social Relations, she was chosen for her strong commitment to racial justice, her knowledge of African American perspectives, and her bonds across racial lines to people with similar commitments. During her two years in Nashville as a staff member of the Woman's Missionary Council, Stevens became familiar with the broad scope of contemporary Christian social relations work addressing economic, social, and racial problems.

Stevens was selected to provide strong, capable leadership during a time when women from northern and southern Methodist missionary societies were preparing for merger of The Methodist Episcopal Church, Methodist Episcopal Church, South, and Methodist Protestant Church. At that time, the northern church women did not have missionary programs addressing problems of racial justice, but they supported institutional forms of mission to African American women and children.

Discussion of the proposed 1939 merger of northern and southern branches of Methodism accentuated the formation of attitudes among Methodist women that formally differed from the position of The Methodist Episcopal Church, South, on the issue of segregation.[13] Stevens, a vocal opponent of plans for merger that included racial segregation, refused the offer of a job with the Woman's Division of Christian Service in The Methodist Church. She felt that she could not work in good conscience in a denomination with a racially segregated governing structure. Stevens believed that she could do more good for race relations in a situation where she would not have to compromise her principles. But friends prevailed. Leaders of Methodist women persuaded Stevens to change her mind and work from inside The Methodist Church to eradicate racial barriers. Stevens lived to see the fruit of her work.

In 1940, at age thirty-eight, Thelma Stevens moved to New York and assumed her duties as full-time Executive Secretary of the Department of Christian Social Relations and Local Church Activities of the Woman's Division of Christian Service of The Board of Missions of The Methodist Church. Equal in title to the powerful heads of the Department of Foreign Missions and the Department of Home Missions, Stevens struggled to define new frontiers for Christian mission in areas of human relations. Many Methodist women, accustomed to institutional definitions of missions, could not see the value of the new department. They deemed it a competitor, siphoning precious missionary money away from schools and hospitals that provided needed services to women and children. (See document 3.)

Working closely with Louise Oldshue, the Chair of the Department of Christian Social Relations and Local Church Activities (CSR/LCA), and with the chairpersons of seven committees of the department, Stevens brought a global perspective, a passion for justice, and an acceptance of persons of all races to the Woman's Division.[14] By 1942, Stevens had hired the first non-Caucasian support staff member of the Woman's Division, Charlotte French. The Woman's Division also called on the federal government to release confined Japanese Americans, agreed to hold its meetings where hotels and restaurants would serve African American as well as white members of the Division, and was pressing the Board of Missions and the General Conference of The Methodist Church to do the same.

Taking as her mandate for Christian social action the teachings of Jesus and the Social Creed of The Methodist Church, Stevens led the Department of Christian Social Relations and Local Church Activities and the Woman's Division toward a new definition of Christian mission. The task of Jesus' disciples, she believed, was to build a new global social order based on the teachings of Jesus. Every Christian had a responsibility to shape public opinion and public policy, to oppose injustice in all forms and disguises, and to include people of all races and persuasions in the discussions essential to maintaining democracy and developing spiritual life in religious communities. One of the most influential projects of Methodist women in national life was their involvement with the President's Committee on Civil Rights in 1947. Thelma Stevens played an important role in helping Methodist women implement the goals of the report in their local communities. (See document 4.)

For more than forty years Stevens served as an interpreter of Christian life and action, particularly to churchwomen. She read widely from noted Christian authors and kept abreast of new developments in Christian thought. By continually leading workshops and seminars she participated in the dialogue which shaped new thinking about critical issues. In the same manner, Stevens stayed current on the subject of race by cultivating friendships, attending meetings, and reading books and magazines written by people of color. Frequently a public speaker at gatherings of Methodist women, Stevens expounded the meaning of verses of scripture to help her audiences understand new developments in the light of their faith traditions.

Stevens provided the initial idea or the chief initiative and leadership for numerous programs of the Wesleyan Service Guild and the Woman's Society of Christian Service. With help from Susie Jones and the Committee on Racial Practices, she represented the Woman's Division in contracting with Pauli Murray to write *States' Laws on Race and Color,* the first book ever to compile the nation's segregation laws. Murray was a graduate of Howard Law School and an aspiring civil rights attorney, already seasoned when her 1938 application for admission to the University of North Carolina was rejected solely on racial grounds.[15] Published in 1950, *States' Laws on Race and Color* guided attorneys as they filed suits in civil rights cases and helped Methodist women understand the complexities involved in integrating Methodist-owned hospitals, schools, and homes.

Stevens helped write much of the 1952 Charter on Racial Policies of the Woman's Division and promoted its adoption by Methodist women in conference and local societies. Once the charter was adopted, Stevens used it as a frame of reference to hold up ideals and goals for action. She encouraged Methodist women to work with local committees in every community to desegregate public schools, and in some places where this was done school desegregation quietly proceeded in the 1950s and 1960s.

Under Stevens' leadership, the Department of Christian Social Relations and Local Church Activities urged and trained Methodist women to write letters to government officials to press for the formation of a Fair Employment Practices Commission, to provide equal hiring opportunities for minorities in the military, in war industries, and in post–World War II employment. Methodist women participated in the campaign against lynching, and called for the end to the poll tax and racial discrimination in voter registration requirements. The Woman's Division supported extending social security legislation to include domestic and agricultural workers and lobbied for the formation of a Civil Rights Commission and for the creation of the Department of Housing and Urban Affairs. All of these actions broadened civil rights for minorities.

In providing leadership for a broad range of issues, Stevens remained in close contact with other organizations. She read *The Crisis,* a publication of the NAACP, and belonged to the Methodist Federation for Social Action, the Association of Southern Women for the Prevention of Lynching, the Southern Regional Council, the Fellowship of the Concerned, and United Church Women.

Stevens drafted much of the legislation coming from the Department of CSR/LCA and the Woman's Division that went to each quadrennial session of the General Conference of The Methodist Church. In 1944 the Woman's Division became the first official agency within The Methodist Church to call for the General Conference to publicly oppose racial segregation. Starting in 1944 and every four years following, the Woman's Division petitioned the General Conference to merge its racially segregated jurisdictions. In 1944, at the urging of the Woman's Division, the church formed the Commission to Consider the Relations of All Races in The Methodist Church. That commission wrote a powerful statement on The Methodist Church and race, which was adopted by the 1948 General Conference. The statement created a theological base from which Methodist women and others could work to end the segregated jurisdictional system, a process that took more than twenty years. In 1952, when The Methodist Church formed a Commission on World Peace and a Board of Temperance, the Woman's Division supported the formation of a Board of Economic and Social Relations so that the fuller spectrum of social issues could be addressed in an organized way by the church. Stevens then initiated cooperative programs, a series of nine regional Interracial Leadership Conferences co-sponsored with the new board and held in the years between 1955 and 1958. Concerns that surfaced in these conferences led her to envision a church-wide Conference on Human Rights, which was held in 1959 at Southern Methodist University and co-sponsored by ten boards and agencies of The Methodist Church. A statement issued by the Conference on Human Rights called on The Methodist Church to end its racially segregated jurisdictional system. In 1964, the General Conference concurred with this position, agreeing to a plan for merger with the Evangelical United Brethren Church that made no mention of race.

Between 1956 and 1966, the Department of Christian Social Relations sponsored visits and tours of the United States by four World Understanding teams. The Methodist women from other nations selected to participate on these teams included Africans, South Americans, and Central and East Asians from nations where Methodist women had supported mission programs. Educated, persons of color, Methodist, and leaders within their own countries, these women had many interests in common with those of the American women who came to hear their presentations. Thousands of Methodist women, attracted by the novelty of meeting women from exotic lands, had their first experiences of staying in integrated housing accommodations. Talking and eating with people of other races at World Understanding Workshops, they came away with changed attitudes about race relations.

In 1960, when sit-ins began and spread across the South, Stevens negotiated with committees and individuals in the Woman's Division to interpret the actions of youthful civil rights leaders in terms of individual and corporate responsibility to work for Christian principles of love and justice. Through mission study texts studied by local units of Methodist women, the groundwork had already been laid among Methodist women for a Christian understanding of the principles of nonviolence. Led by the Department of Christian Social Relations, the Woman's Division encouraged Methodist women to support the rights of students to use nonviolent forms of civil rights protests against segregation, to write to the owners of department store chains urging them to desegregate their services, and to raise bail for students who were jailed. Stevens, who had rallied support from Methodist women for passage of the 1964 Civil Rights Bill and the 1965 Voting Rights Act, persisted in urging Methodist women to work for local implementation of these federal laws. She still affirmed the 1940s motto of the Department of Christian Social Relations, "All action is local." For Stevens, racial justice and the elimination of racial barriers had come to include civil rights, human rights as established in the 1947 Universal Declaration of Human Rights, inclusion of persons of all colors, and deliberate efforts to provide equal opportunities for all persons.

Stevens was instrumental in building strong ties between Methodist women and the United Nations, starting with the Woman's Division's appointment in 1960 of Margaret Bender as official observer to the U.N. In 1962, in cooperation with the Board of Christian Social Concerns of The Methodist Church, the Woman's Division sponsored construction of the United Nations Center located directly across the plaza from the U.N. There groups from many churches could hold seminars and conferences, and churches could monitor and support international solutions to problems that often stemmed from racial and ethnic strife.

In 1968, when The United Methodist Church was born, Stevens retired from the Women's Division. Her retirement gave her new channels to work against another powerful and sinister "ism" that was wreaking damage in human relationships. She addressed sexism using skills she had mastered in her work against racism. She organized, spoke, wrote, lobbied, and called both church and society to account for attitudes and policies that perpetuated injustice. Stevens advised and contributed funds to a group of women who founded the Ecumenical Women's Institute in Chicago, gave countless volunteer hours to Church Women United, and helped with the formation of what became the United Methodist General Commission on the Status and Role of Women. She continued to exhort church leaders to work for justice for gay men and lesbians and serve as mentor to younger women as they moved into leadership positions. She spent her later retirement years at McKendree Towers in Hermitage, Tennessee, and Brooks-Howell Home in Asheville, North Carolina, dying at Brooks-Howell on December 18, 1990, at age eighty-eight.

When Stevens spoke on public occasions during her mature years, she described her vision of justice and peace using biblical language. She told the Eastern Pennsylvania Chapter of the Methodist Federation for Social Action at their annual conference gathering in 1982:

We need to remember again what one of the great Prophets of Justice, Isaiah, said many centuries ago—(42:9) "Behold, the former things have come to pass and new things I now declare; Before they spring forth I tell you of them." When this great Prophet of Justice sent this warning down through time, he also included the call for *justice and peace* found in the message that Jesus himself read when he preached his first sermon in the synagogue of Nazareth, his own home town. This event, as recorded in the Gospels, happened soon after his 40 days in the wilderness taking stock of his own priorities for his mission to the world. These priorities are timeless and provide the guidelines for all who come after him in every age and circumstance.

Listen again to the Prophet Isaiah (61:1-4, 8-11):

"The spirit of the Lord is upon me because the Lord has anointed me to bring good tidings to the afflicted; he has sent me to bind up the broken hearted, and to proclaim liberty to the captives, and the opening of prisons to those who are bound.

"For I the Lord love justice. I hate robbery or wrong; I will faithfully give them recompense and I will make an everlasting covenant with them.

"For as the earth brings forth its shoots and as a garden causes what is sown in it to spring up, so the Lord God will cause righteousness and praise to spring forth before all the nations."

This message from Isaiah—set forth by Jesus Christ himself—challenges us to its fulfillment, and brings hope to all who seek to heal a troubled world today— where justice and peace *can* prevail in the new century which calls us![16]

Always Stevens kept before herself and others words of the prophet Isaiah and the example of Jesus. She believed that the church, as an inheritor of the prophetic tradition of the Hebrew scriptures and the gospel message, should be a clear leader in the movement for racial justice, not simply adjust its policies to meet changing social standards.

Stevens, too, carried on the prophetic task. Challenging Christians to move forward, she paraphrased Jesus' central teachings:

You pick up where I leave off and carry on—seeking justice and liberation for the oppressed of every kind, doing the things that make for peace, and sharing my message and mission with the whole world—thereby building the foundations that make all of God's creation one people! You have many roots, many colors, many cultures, many religions. You are women and men—fully equal and fully responsible—in God's created Universe.—Never count the cost—but remember that God, the Creator, sent me to die that you might live and serve—healing the hurts of people—bringing peace with justice to all humankind.[17]

DOCUMENTS

1. *Excerpts from an Interview with Thelma Stevens.* Stevens struggled with the question of what to do with her life and how to relate her faith convictions to the church. Just a few months before graduating from State Teachers' College in Hattiesburg, Mississippi, she considered the possibility of working for the Woman's Missionary Society of The Methodist Episcopal Church, South. She was acquainted with the segregation, racism, and hypocrisy of the church, but did not find support there, in the local church, for her belief that God's love for all people should be translated in terms of acceptance and inclusion of all races without segregation.

And when I graduated, well, just a few months before I graduated, a recruiting woman personnel recruiter for [Methodist] mission programs came to the campus and stayed a week. She and I got to be good friends. We played tennis together. We did all sorts of things and she said, "Thelma, I think you ought to volunteer for work in the Woman's Missionary Society and be a deaconess and do the jobs, some of the jobs that need to be done." She said, "I think you could do a good job of it."

I said, "Not on your life. I'm not going to work for the church. Have no desire to work for the church and I have no intention of doing it."

And she said, "Why?"

I said, "Because the church doesn't believe in anything I believe in and I'm not going to work for the church."[18]

A few years later, Stevens was ready to graduate from Scarritt College for Christian Workers. Her studies, teachers, and experiences had changed her mind, and she was ready to become a deaconess. She failed to pass her physical exam because the doctor predicted that, because of ulcers, she would not live more than three years. About five years later, while serving as director of the Bethlehem Center in Augusta, Georgia, she grew to appreciate that turn of events.

Several of my friends, the black women in the community around there, would come to my office one at a time or two at a time. Just every once in a while they'd come in and sit down at my desk and they'd say, "Oh, Miss Stevens, we are glad you're not a deaconess." And I would say, "Why? Why are you glad I'm not a deaconess?" And they said, "Well, because if you were a deaconess, somebody would send you here whether you wanted to come or not, and because you're not a deaconess, you came because you wanted to and we like to have people that work with us black people, to work with us because they want—they're one of us—want to come and don't have somebody make them come."[19]

2. *Excerpts from Stevens' Master's Thesis, "The Pharisees and Jesus."* In her master's thesis, Thelma Stevens wrestled with the question of how to understand the ethical teachings of Christian faith. In this sample of her early writing (at age twenty-six), she explored the relationship of Jesus to the Pharisees, who were conservators of Jewish religious traditions. Stevens argued against legalism and an ethic of purity, claiming that Jesus overcame such boundaries by using a higher moral and spiritual sphere. Stevens asserted that Jesus rejected dualistic notions of spiritual and material realms and accepted all of life as permeable with the spirit of God. Spiritual laws are evident in the higher moral sphere. Human traditions may miss the mark.

> When questioned by the "legalistic" Pharisees, Jesus said that there was no such thing as religious impurity in the material sense. That can come only in the moral and spiritual sphere. Sin in the heart is the only possible way of defilement. . . . Jesus attacked [the Pharisees'] Traditions and accused them of giving up what God had commanded and holding only to what men had handed down. (Mark 7:8) Their zeal for righteousness did not rest on a true interest in the Law but in their own human Traditions.[20]

Part of Stevens' ability to take a position on racial issues that was critical of segregation and the racial views of the church and culture around her hinged on her understanding of the ethical position Jesus took in his interpretation and use of scripture. The key ethical question for Jesus' critics was, "By what authority do you do these things?" Jesus' answer, according to Stevens, was that he acted according to conscience. His guide was his sense of the presence and spirit of God, found not in scholastic arguments over chapter and verse, but in actions where God's love is known.

> The authority of Jesus is not that of any letter. . . . Jesus repudiated all claim to external authority and in return external authority through Tradition and Jewish hierarchy condemned him. That infallible outward authority on which the Scribes and Pharisees founded their religion did not exist for Jesus. He was endowed with the authority of holiness and love, the authority of the spirit not of legalism. . . .
>
> It was Jesus' purpose to create in his disciples a moral consciousness identical with his own. He laid down principles, applying them by way of example to a few particular cases, Sabbath, food fasting, etc. He authoritatively abrogated nothing. His principles came from the depths of human consciousness and when once proclaimed, conscience, must recognize it as its own and not some supernatural power. Jesus' revelation was not superim-

posed upon the conscience like that of Moses. "It is conscience itself raised to a higher power of clear sight and energy." Nothing external can spoil a man morally but it is that which is inward. This is the verdict of conscience upon that form of religion which it has superseded.[21]

3. The Gospel Message, the Role of the Church, and the Commitments of Methodist Women. In 1940, following the merger which created The Methodist Church, six women's missionary organizations from three uniting denominations became the Woman's Division of the Board of Missions. Thelma Stevens, head of the new Department of Christian Social Relations and Local Church Activities, outlined the task of the new department in relation to the gospel message, the role of the church, and the commitments of Methodist women. Here we see Stevens' vision of the ministries of Christian laywomen in church and society. She describes women as leaders, as disciples of Jesus, and as agents of social change. Spiritual interests overlap social concerns because they are inseparable.

From its very inception the fundamentals of Methodism have been concerned with the application of the Social Gospel in human relationships. Interpretations and emphases have varied with conditions and groups. During the past quarter of a century there has been an increasing interest and a more active participation in a program of Christian social action by church people in general. Women have taken the lead in many of these issues, and Methodist women have centralized their efforts to build Christian ideals for the individual and his society, believing such a goal to be basic for the permanent growth of Christian Missions throughout the world.

Such an organized movement among Methodist women has been channeled through various avenues, such as the World Citizenship Committee, the Committee on Christian Citizenship, The Ladies' Aid Association, the Bureau of Christian Social Relations, and other channels. As a result of such a movement pioneer groups have initiated studies and activities in an ever-widening area of social action, including many phases of human relations.

Recognizing the crying need for such widespread education and activity, the United Methodist Church provided for a major department in the Woman's Division of Christian Service, through which such lines of work might be promoted. This department of Christian Social Relations and Local Church Activities has been interpreted as follows: "It shall seek to make real and effective the teachings of Jesus as applied to individual, class, racial, and national relationships. It shall endeavor to enlist the participation of church women in such questions as have an important bearing on public welfare. It shall seek to inspire in the women of the local church a greater devotion to its spiritual interests; to co-operate with its educational agencies, and to develop Christian fellowship and a concern for the financial responsibilities of the church."

Such an interpretation would mean increased emphasis on study and Christian action in the realm of vital social questions of the day, as well as a more careful study of local church needs. The latter may be interpreted in terms of church projects, service, and activities, as well as an enlarged program of community activity. Many of the activities promoted by Ladies' Aid groups and Local Work Committees may well come within such a category. Such activities need to be properly evaluated in the light of the purpose of the department, looking always toward the broadening of the church's interest in building a Christian World Community. Groups of women with united effort in more than 45,000 Methodist Churches, can make a large imprint toward the building of the kingdom of God.

After a description of the organizational structure of the department, its officers, and staff, seven committees are listed. Note the variety of social concerns and Christian tasks in which Methodist women felt called to take action. Stevens invokes the teaching of Jesus that God calls people to use their talents.

Local Church and Community Co-operation—Mrs. J. Fulton of the Western Jurisdiction is chairman. This committee within the Division will attempt to recommend ways for co-ordinating projects and activities in the local church that come within the scope of the society. It shall seek to develop wider avenues of Christian fellowship and service; suggest ways for recruiting and training volunteer workers for work with community agencies, and seek to evaluate methods and motives for church and community activities. Much of the activity included in the programs of those agencies or committees responsible for local work in the church will probably come within the scope of this committee.

International Relations and World Peace—Mrs. E. R. Bartlett, Greencastle, Indiana, chairman. This committee shall recommend studies, activities, and social action that make for a peace-seeking world-minded citizenship.

Economic Relations—Mrs. Wm. H. Veenboor, Grand Rapids, Michigan, chairman. The function of this committee is basic in relation to all other committees. It shall gather and study facts regarding economic and industrial conditions at home and on mission fields and suggest studies and methods for working toward a Christian economic order.

Minority Groups and Interracial Co-operation—Mrs. David Jones, Greensboro, North Carolina, and Mrs. Paul Arrington, Waynesboro, Mississippi, are co-chairmen of this committee. This committee shall "study minority groups in the nation and seek to discover ways and means for the promotion of more Christian attitudes and relationships within the community life. It shall conduct studies, experiments, and demonstrations in Interracial Co-operation that tend to build a co-operative world community."

Christian Citizenship—Mrs. W. H. Ballengee, Edinburg, Virginia, chairman. This committee has a wide responsibility in the realm of legislation, the use of the ballot, working for better movies, a saner and more profitable use of the radio, improving facilities for public education, working for a reduction in delinquency and crime, and other activities.

Alcohol and Other Narcotics—Mrs. C. M. Randall, Seymour, Texas, chairman. This committee will seek to promote a wider and more practical educational program in this area; to encourage total abstinence and public sentiment against the use of alcohol at social functions, to promote enforcement and control of laws controlling traffic in alcohol and narcotic drugs, and co-operate with other agencies within the church seeking similar ends.

The Christian Family—Mrs. C. C. Weaver, Charlotte, North Carolina, chairman. This new committee will seek to promote an educational program that will build a stable family life and a Christian home. It shall co-operate with the Board of Education in promoting such a program.

The jurisdictions and conferences will choose from these areas the lines of work that seem most pertinent to their needs. The work will be promoted through jurisdictional and conference committees, and every effort made to integrate the interest and activity into the entire church program. Social action will be more effective when it grows out of a church-wide conscience and local church projects are the responsibility of the entire church membership.

Let the goal of this great new department be to make its program "worldwide in its concern and church-wide in its appeal," remembering that the continued success of our missionary program at home and abroad is determined by the kind of Christian philosophy we practice as individuals in our daily relationships. "It is God the Creator whom we, who know how to create, must serve if we are to be workers together with any God. Our Christ is not only a lamb, but the Son of Man, who has power to cast out devils, as we have! Our religion is not only a hymn to charity, but also the stern parable of the talents."[22]

4. A Response to To Secure These Rights, *the Report of the President's Committee on Civil Rights, 1947.* Dorothy Tilly, a Methodist from Georgia who devoted her life to improving race relations and who worked closely with Thelma Stevens for more than a quarter century, was appointed by President Harry S Truman to the President's Committee on Civil Rights (PCCR). She actively engaged churchwomen, especially Methodist women, in moving the nation toward eliminating racial barriers to making civil rights equally available to all. Stevens and other Methodist women provided documentation and testimony before the President's Committee on Civil Rights. When the report of the committee was published, both women distributed it widely, and used it to educate people about civil rights and to work actively for an end to discrimination. In March 1948, Thelma Stevens recommended the following actions in her monthly column in *The Methodist Woman.*

What Can We Do?

(1) Secure a copy or copies of the President's committee's report, *To Secure These Rights,* and encourage members of your Woman's Society and your Guild to read same. Ask your pastor and key *laymen* and *youth* of the church to read it. Initiate a series of forums and discussions on the report, using the best available resource people of your community. At least one or two specific group activities for bettering human relations and achieving *civil liberties for all* may grow out of such a study. The following are suggestive:

    1. What *Civil Rights Laws* are on your state's statute books? Are they enforced? Deal with specifics in your own community—are hotels, restaurants, and recreation facilities open to all? Can you start a movement for law enforcement in keeping with "our American heritage"?

    2. What discriminations are practiced in your state and community that violate the Fourteenth Amendment, which says that "no state shall make or enforce any law which shall abridge the privileges or immunities of citizens of the United States"? How does the term "separate but equal" relate to this issue in your state? One group of Christian women was so concerned over this issue that they made a study of the schools over widespread areas, taking pictures of facilities available to Negro children and to white children. They gathered ample evidence to prove that schools were "separate" but *not* "equal." Other comparative studies were made of public transportation facilities, and public services such as sewage disposal, paved streets, lights, etc. When we know the facts we usually act!

. . . . .

(3) "We urge that Woman's Society and Wesleyan Service Guild members be watchful and help to prevent the passage of local or state legislation which would infringe upon the civil rights of any group or individual . . ." (From the "Program of Action for 1948" of the Woman's Division)

(4) (a) You and other individuals who so desire may communicate with President Harry S. Truman at the White House, Washington, D.C., to: (1) Congratulate the President and the members of the committee for the excellent report. (2) Ask the President to exercise his power to make the following changes in accordance with the report: (a) To set up a Civil Rights section of the F.B.I. (b) Establish a permanent commission on civil rights in the Executive Office. (c) End discrimination and segregation in the armed forces together with a ban on any kind of discrimination against armed forces personnel by transportation facility, hotel, restaurant, and theater. (d) Ask for full hearings for federal employees whose loyalty has been challenged with a clear and public announcement of "loyalty" standards; the hearings to include specific charges and an opportunity to rebut.

(b) Express your Christian conviction to congressmen and senators concerning action on the following: (1) Drastic increase in fines and prison for police brutality under the Federal Criminal Code. (2) Enactment of a Federal Anti-Lynching Law carrying stiff penalty and giving the Federal Bureau of Investigation jurisdiction over all lynching cases. (3) Enactment of a Federal Anti-Poll Tax Law which would permit all qualified persons to participate in voting. (4) Enactment of a permanent Federal Fair Employment Practice Act to prohibit all forms of discrimination in private employment. (5) For the District of Columbia—Enactment of laws prohibiting discrimination and segregation in public schools, hospitals, housing projects, and recreation facilities. (6) Enactment of a law prohibiting discrimination or segregation based on race, color, creed, or national origin in interstate transportation.[23]

Alice Yun Chai

CHAPTER 12

THE STRUGGLE OF ASIAN AND ASIAN AMERICAN WOMEN TOWARD A TOTAL LIBERATION

A Korean Methodist Woman's Vocational Journey

ALICE YUN CHAI

ASIAN FEMINIST THEOLOGY OF SYNTHESIS AND A COMMON STRUGGLE FOR TOTAL LIBERATION

There is an emerging Third World and feminist theological scholarship, which postulates that theological analysis needs to be rooted in the experience and struggle of people in their historical, socio-economic circumstances.[1]

Presented here is a contextual theology derived from Asian foremothers' lived experiences, consciousness, and female cultural traditions, as well as from today's Asian women's struggles, which has been devised by groups of Asian women engaging in theology in their respective communities. This emerging Asian feminist theology is both collective and ecumenical in the sense that it is based on inter-faith dialogue among Asian and Asian American women during the last decade. Through contextualization, Asian women embrace historical female cultures with all their oppression and contradictions. This theology is also transformational in its contextualization, since it is based on the intersection of Asian female cultural heritage and the struggle for liberation, a process developed by the privileged class of educated Asian women. The process consists of listening, repenting, and changing their relationship with disadvantaged women in their respective societies to express solidarity with them in their struggle for survival and for a total liberation from all oppression.[2]

Historically, the religious environment of many Asian societies has been characterized by multiple indigenous belief systems and rituals and the introduction and indigenization of external religious heritages such as Christianity. Confucianism has co-existed with indigenous beliefs and religions such as Shamanism, Taoism, Buddhism, and other popular and formal religions in Korea and other East Asian societies. The dynamic interaction between these different traditions has been explored from Asian feminist theologians' point of view in recent years.[3] For example, in Korea, there were the folk ritual practices of Shamanism, which were performed predominantly by female shamans.

The introduction of organized religions, such as Confucianism, Buddhism, Shintoism, and Christianity into Asian societies such as Korea has brought mixed blessings to women. There was a double-edged character to Korean women's relationship to the church. Although the church provided principles and environments for resistance to the oppressive structures of the dominant society, it also helped to sustain both the hegemonic domination and the patriarchal relationships within the church and society. For example, the nineteenth-century missionary movement can be attributed to evangelical revivalism as well as to the West's military and political expansionism. Western missionaries demonstrated white supremacy and ethnocentrism in their belief that their race and their own culture and religion were inherently superior.[4]

The Christian missionary movement accompanied by Western cultural imperialism began to socialize Korean women in such a way that the women devalued their own cultural and female heritage, including female-centered Shamanism, which was considered "primitive" and "superstitious" by the missionaries. In addition, the emergence of Korean Christian women, who were educated and of the middle class, helped to create a new social stratification among women that was based on Western education, female professions, and Christianity.[5]

However, the introduction of Christianity to areas of male-dominated Confucianism had some liberating effects on women. Asian Christian women were inspired by the gospel message, which spoke of Jesus as a compassionate being who recognized their worth as human beings.[6] A ninety-one-year-old Korean woman who came to Hawaii as a sixteen-year-old picture bride in 1917 stated her reason for coming to Hawaii as follows: "My cousin in Hawaii told me that there were some good Korean Christian men in Hawaii who treated their wives better than non-Christian men in Korea. My mother was glad to let me go to Hawaii since she was very saddened [that] her two older daughters had been severely mistreated by their in-laws to the extent that one of them had committed suicide by drowning."

Christian churches attracted women because they allowed them to step outside familial roles of domestic work and seclusion to explore new possibilities, by attending schools and churches alongside their brothers and other men. Many Asian women who joined the Christian church were poor and lower-class widows, or daughters of upper-class women seeking education and the meaning of life.

A Korean American daughter of a picture bride proudly related how her mother had tried to overcome female seclusion in Korea as follows: "When my mother was attending Ewha Woman's University, she learned about freedom, but women could not even go outside by themselves. She and her friend used to wear boys' school uniforms to engage in underground political work for independence. She was caught by the Japanese police and was imprisoned for one year. She wanted to come to Hawaii to continue her education and political activities." In similar fashion, my mother and other Ewha Woman's University graduates formed a group of single women as adopted sisters in the 1920s, taking an oath to work for women, staying single the rest of their lives, and engraving tattoos on one anothers' arms. In time, all the women broke their oaths and married. My mother, at age twenty-eight, was the last to wed.[7]

Church women could learn to read, sing songs, enjoy the fellowship, and exercise some form of religious leadership in their local religious communities. Many of the Christian church activities specifically addressed women's issues, and allowed women to come together to talk about their problems and find ways and means to tackle them. A Korean Christian educator and writer, Pauline Kim, tells in her autobiography that Korean Christian schoolmates nurtured Platonic love relationships by exchanging letters, poems, clothes, and other gifts. She thinks that they learned this woman-to-woman love from American women missionary teachers.[8]

Western women missionaries with professional training provided female education and improved women's situation. The first girls' schools and women's shelters were founded by women missionaries in many Asian countries. Many women and girls started going to school, defying the norm that women's place should be in the home. Single women missionaries also inspired Asian women to receive education and training, and dedicate themselves to careers while forsaking marriage. Thus, women missionaries' work in the early Asian Christian churches provided Asian women an alternative to the dominant patriarchal culture and social relationships. For example, a ninety-two-year-old Korean woman who came to Hawaii as a nineteen-year-old picture bride in 1922 said that she had decided to come to Hawaii after meeting her single, American missionary woman teacher in a church Sunday school and realizing that American women did not have to get married but could have educational training and professions of their choice. Another ninety-two-year-old former Korean picture bride said that her ability to speak in public as a leader of women's groups in Hawaii was due to the work experience in door-to-door evangelism she had had since the age of eight with her grandmother in Korea.

In Korea, American women missionaries founded the first girls' school, Ewha Hak-dang, in 1886 in order to teach the Korean alphabet and English to enable the students to read the Bible, one of the requirements for conversion to Christianity.[9] In fact, educating Korean women by opening schools was a strategy of American missionaries, who found it impossible, otherwise, to convert Korean women because of the strict supervision of girls by their family elders. Consequently, the goal of converting Korean women to Christianity made them sufficiently literate and educated to become economically independent professionals such as "Bible women" and teachers.[10] "Bible women" or female evangelists, who were usually widows or single women, were employed to translate for the missionaries and to do evangelical work among women.

Christian churches also provided opportunities for Asian women to engage in organized activities and to build leadership skills in the public sphere. The Christian community, serving as an institutional base for sisterhood and fellowship, also provided the setting for organized actions against oppressive structures in society, including Confucian patriarchal traditions such as arranged marriage, concubinage, and funeral ceremonies and mourning customs. The Christian women participated in anti-traditional marriage customs, literacy campaigns, organized health-care programs, and women's associations.

Rosa Kuai Choi Cupfender, the daughter of a Korean Christian pioneer woman, Helen Choi, tells in her mother's biography that her mother entered Ewha Hak-dang in 1895. She met her prospective husband while teaching at her alma mater in 1906 at age nineteen, which culminated in 1912 in the first love marriage and marriage ceremony in Korea, in which the bride wore a Western bridal gown. Cupfender was the founder and the first president of the Korean Chapter of the Woman's Christian Temperance Union, in 1930.[11]

The turn of the century saw the rising aspirations of Asian people for national independence and self-determination. Koreans had striven for national independence ever since their country was colonized by Japan in 1910. Korean Christian immigrant women in Hawaii were in the forefront of the struggle between 1910 and 1945 to gain Korean national liberation from the Japanese colonization.[12]

During the last two decades, Asian women theologians' serious research into the hitherto unexplored women's historical, cultural, and religious resources has opened their eyes to the treasures therein. They have come to a new appraisal of women's tradition in Asia as they begin to raise questions from a feminist perspective. Since Christianity often came to Asia together with the expansion of Western military aggression, women are attempting to find new ways of engaging in theology that will liberate them and sustain their faith by indigenizing Christianity to Asian culture.[13]

The spiritual inheritance from Asian foremothers has raised a serious question for them: What is the connection between the lives of their foremothers and Christianity? To identify themselves as Asian, female, and Christian simultaneously is an enormously challenging task for them, because Asian identity is defined by participation in their cultural matrix and human relationships, while Christianity is often perceived to be bound up with Western philosophy, liturgy, and cultural symbols. In light of this, Asian women theologians have started looking at alternative texts such as local and native resources, folk literature, women's narratives, and popular religious texts to construct their theology. They have started to explore the possibility of engaging in Asian feminist theology in myths, poems, songs, stories, dances, rituals, and even lullabies by paying attention to alternative resources based on women's experiences.[14]

Among the new approaches being taken is that of Chinese feminist theologian Kwok Pui-lan. She has named as "dialogical imagination" the process of bringing the Asian people's story and the biblical story together by dialogue, which to the Chinese means mutuality, active listening, and solidarity with what others have to say.[15] Korean feminist theologians for their part have been reexamining the songs and dances in Shamanism, a folk religious tradition in which women often played significant symbolic and ritualistic roles. Indian women have been looking at their invaluable treasures of folk literature and the long tradition of goddess worship to uncover their significance for today.

The feminist transformation of culture and theology must be one of the most significant norms in selecting and appropriating alternative resources among Asian women theologians. Asian foremothers' religious experience and their quest for liberation point to the necessity of expanding their Christian identity and devising a more inclusive theology.[16]

Korean spiritual foremothers combined and synthesized all the spiritual resources available to them and established their own unique, familiar religious universe in their hearts. Since women were excluded from the public sphere of determining the meaning of religion, they were free to create a religion on their own by devising, in private, a spiritual whole that enabled them to survive and liberated them in the midst of their struggle for full humanity. A Korean feminist theologian, Chung Hyun Kyung, calls this "survival-liberation-centered syncretism."[17] It is their commitment to feminism that leads them to the multiple Asian female religious heritage their foremothers practiced.[18] What it means to them to be a Christian in view of our foremothers' religious syncretism is that they must use all of their foremothers' experiences to create a perspective on religion that is liberating for Asian women, a perspective that will enable them to claim their life-giving power to free all people.

The particular history that Asian women and other women's communities can identify with is that God is actively alive among people who seek to become full human beings. God is found in the life experiences of poor people, the majority of whom are women and children, and God is empowering them not only to survive amid wretched conditions but also to overcome those conditions.[19]

The unity of the church must be understood as an invitation to work together in a historical movement, not necessarily as religious doctrines and beliefs. Today, as Asian women pursue their own theology, they envision a more inclusive and multi-colored unity.[20] Current Asian socio-economic conditions affect women and, more often than not, perpetuate their exploitation, multiply their oppression, and intensify their suffering as women. We are alarmed by the increasing poverty and oppression engulfing many Asian societies today, resulting in the extreme degradation of women. It is the women who suffer most, caught in the interplay of foreign domination, state repression, militarization, and racial strife. Therefore, if Christianity is to be truly relevant to the Asian setting, there is a need for the societal and feminist theological transformation.

Korean women are adversely affected by the national division created in the aftermath of World War II. They live under a government preoccupied with national security and militarism, while at the same time remaining under the control of the Confucianism that supports male superiority in all aspects of society. Most young rural women have been driven out of their villages by family debts, dispossession of land, and devastation caused by the export-oriented economy and open-trade policy of the government. They go to the cities and are exploited by the low wages, long working hours, and poor working conditions of multinational corporations. Out of economic desperation, many poor Korean and Filipino women enter into prostitution to financially support their families. Widespread prostitution in Asia is the result of Asian governments' goal of obtaining foreign currencies and the negative stereotype of Asian women as passive servants, and in one of its forms includes the economic and sexual exploitation of Asian women on American military bases in Okinawa, Korea, and the Philippines and sex tourism.[21] Poverty, militarism, and sexual discrimination are at the root of prostitution and the violation of human rights for women.[22]

In the midst of political, economic, and cultural turmoil, strong grass-roots movements have emerged in many Asian societies. Church women in Asia contribute great force and militancy to these movements since some aspects of oppression of women cut across class, caste, creed, race, profession, and age.[23]

Asian women engaging in theology from the Asian field have come to see that structural inequalities require a collective movement for change, beginning at the grass-roots level. They have further discovered that women's oppression is linked with other oppression, particularly the oppression of rural and working class people.[24]

There is an emerging Asian feminist theology which envisions salvation as the liberation of women from all oppression; this is achieved when women become whole human beings, freed from all that dehumanizes them, including sexual exploitation, injustice, and poverty. Typical features of the Asian women's movement are organized actions against patriarchy and for political, national, and social liberation as embodied in various struggles for justice.

Exemplary are the leading groups in the Korean women's movement, who have been strongly connected with the general human rights and democratization movement. These women's groups have actively supported survival rights of factory workers and the rural and urban poor and working women. During the 1987 democratization movement in Korea, women's groups came together to form a coalition network. In the 1980s, church women of Korea became greatly concerned with the unification and democratization movements: They organized joint activities with students, laborers, farmers, and the urban poor, rallying around issues such as survival rights, peace, and ecology.[25] They saw the necessity of organized power in order to bring about changes at home, in the church, and in political life. Women carried the double and triple burdens of pushing for liberation in both the women's movement and the larger democratization movement.

Korean church women's groups have been working on issues relating to middle-class homemakers, factory and rural working women, women in squatter situations, and families of political prisoners. They have also been working with victims of police sex torture and domestic violence. More recently, Korean Christian women have been engaged in a massive effort to uncover and reclaim the forgotten history of approximately 200,000 Korean women called "comfort women" (or *Chongshindae,* a more inclusive term which includes those recruited for the mining and defense industries). Comfort women were drafted by the Japanese Imperial Military government between 1931 and 1945 for involuntary prostitution for Japanese military personnel in Japan, Manchuria, mainland China, the Pacific Islands, and southeast Asia during the Pacific war. Korean Church Women United, in coalition with feminist groups in Korea, Japan, and the United States, has been working to expose the experiences of these women to the world. The issue of comfort women forces us to look at women's sexual oppression in its totality, that is, in historical, political, economic, and social ways, by relating it to the structures of colonial, military state, race, and class oppression.[26]

In Korea, national unification cannot be achieved without restoring social justice and peace, realizable only by economic survival and liberating the oppressed and subordinated grass-roots people *(minjung).* The *minjung* are those who are "politically oppressed, economically exploited, socially marginalized, and culturally despised and ignored. They include a variety of overlapping categories of those who have shared in the deep, unresolved suffering, or *han,* of the Koreans."[27] The three socio-historic-cultural situations which are sources of gender specific women's *han* to be uncovered are: (1) religio-cultural gender ideology; (2) Japanese colonialism; and (3) neocolonialism, national division, and military dictatorship.[28] National unification will become a reality only when all the forces of oppression and exploitation are overcome and a genuine reconciliation is made among people from all walks of life and between the sexes in mutual respect for self-determination.

At the 1988 Women's Forum of the International Christian Consultation on Justice and Peace in Korea, women representatives from all over the world came to the consensus that the national division of Korea has reinforced the combined oppressive effects of the patriarchal structure and imperialistic militarism. They also agreed that the capitalistic economic system has deprived women of human rights and repressed democratization efforts.[29]

In a move toward change, the church women in South and North Korea have declared 1995, fifty years after the end of World War II, as "the Year of Jubilee" by taking a leading part in this community building as protectors and life-givers of the people, giving force to the "life movement."[30]

Feminism can be defined in today's Asian Christian women's circumstances as a movement against any and all forms of oppression, encompassing oppression in the household, the church, the state, and extending to global arenas of exploitation and domination. It purports to eliminate domination in all forms by transforming society as a whole, and this is to be accomplished by creating multiple fronts of struggle and by simultaneously being both autonomous and in solidarity with all other agents of change.

ASIAN AMERICAN SPIRITUALITY AND THE INTERSECTION OF GENDER, RACE, AND CLASS

Throughout the 1970s and 1980s, women of color and Third World women have insisted that a feminist analysis should uncover the complex interconnectedness of sexism, racism, neocolonialism, and class exploitation in women's lives.[31] I will describe and analyze how this interplay of sexism, racism, and classism has affected Asian American women.

The early Asian immigrant picture brides' strong religious faith, memories of their mothers' and grandmothers' resilience, and creation of women's culture and institutions provided them with dignity, strength, courage, and an enduring spirit to struggle to survive under severe economic hardship and domestic difficulties.[32] This apparent contradiction between the reality of women's multiple oppression and women's affirmation of their experiences can be understood by their creative female spirituality, which is based on their passion for life-giving activities and ingenious survival strategies for their families and themselves. It was achieved by using all the available, alternative, and newly created resources within their ethnic and women's communities. These ethnic and women's communities in turn also provided the wherewithal for their daily political strategies and for organized actions against oppressive structures such as the patriarchal family, capitalist economy, racism, imperialism, and colonialism.

In recent decades, since the passage of the 1965 liberal United States immigration laws allowing the unification of families and eliminating discrimination against Asians, and the 1975 and 1980 Southeast Refugee Acts, there has been a continuing influx of immigrants and refugees to the United States from Asian countries, especially from Korea, the Philippines, and Vietnam. Moreover, the combined effects of Asian immigrant women outnumbering men, the important roles women have played in political transformations taking place in many of the Asian countries in the 1980s, and the visibility of women's issues achieved by the women's movement have made the church aware of the urgent need to recognize Asian immigrant women as an important constituency group.

Despite the fact that the majority of recent women and men immigrants from Asia are college-educated, of urban middle-class backgrounds, and of childbearing age, they cannot find jobs in the United States that are commensurate with their education, training, and experience. The men resort to taking low-paying, unskilled or semi-skilled jobs. Because of occupational segregation based on gender, race, ethnicity, and national origin, immigrant women are too often locked into poorly paid, labor-intensive light manufacturing or service jobs in the garment, electronic, cannery, beauty, jewelry, food, hotel, tourist, or entertainment industries. The majority of them work long hours under adverse working conditions.[33] Many of these women who are not engaged in such outside employment work as unpaid workers in family businesses, which require even longer working hours during the weekdays, as well as on Saturdays. In their households, these women do almost all of the housework and also assume the childcare. On top of all this, the kitchen work in their churches on Sundays is frequently also their lot. Their demanding responsibilities at home, at workplaces, and churches, their belief in Confucianism and the American ideal of social mobility, confinement of their social and working lives within their ethnic communities, and their identification with their husbands as co-owners of family businesses generally prevent them from building a strong working-class consciousness to commit themselves to organizational activities such as unionization.

Consequently, the working mothers' health deteriorates under multiple burdens and the stress encountered as a result of their husbands' resistance to sharing home and childcare responsibilities. If they invite their mothers or mothers-in-law from Korea to come over and help them with housework and childcare, these relatives become additional emotional, financial, and physical burdens. The so-called success stories of Korean immigrant entrepreneurs and "super-kids" have been made possible only by the great sacrifices of these "Korean immigrant super-women." At the same time, the increase in runaway teenage children, wife battering, and divorce among Korean immigrant families, as reported recently in the Korean language newspapers, is partly related to the unequal gender and ethnic division of labor in the family and the workplace that is experienced by Korean immigrant women. In addition, many Korean women who are married to United States citizens are caught in abusive marriages for fear of deportation under the 1986 Immigration Marriage Fraud Amendment.

MY RELIGIOUS HERITAGE AND STRUGGLE
FOR TOTAL LIBERATION

Despite my third-generation Methodist family and predominantly Methodist educational background, I was reared in a multi-religious environment and hence felt little conflict with the different religious practices and belief systems to which I was exposed. Since my father was the male heir of his patrilineal lineage, he was responsible for conducting ancestral memorial services for his foremothers and forefathers of four ascending generations. My mother, female relatives on my father's side, and household helpers prepared food to serve to participating relatives. The elderly male relatives from the oldest generation on my father's side led the Christian memorial worship services. After the services, women relatives shared stories about the wisdom and strengths of their foremothers while the men talked about intellectual, political, and military achievements of their forefathers.

On Sundays, family members of both my mother's and my father's side attended Chung-dong First Methodist Church, the oldest Methodist church in Seoul. My parents were one of the few married Korean couples who sat together in the church; the majority of the married couples sat separately. One of the complaints I had about the church was that, even though my grandmother and other female relatives were more spiritual and hardworking members of the church, mostly my father and other male relatives with social status and wealth became church elders and officials. My great aunt, who devoted eighty-some years of her life to the church as a "Bible woman" (a lay woman evangelist), was finally allowed to give a prayer at the dedication ceremony of the new church building when she was nearly ninety years old.

While I was attending elementary and high school during the Japanese colonial occupation, I had to salute the Japanese flag every morning and once a week visit a Shinto shrine located on Mount Nam-san by climbing several hundred steps. This helped to build my leg muscles and I enjoyed the early morning fresh air! When school classes went on excursions, we visited Buddhist temples located on the tops of the mountains outside Seoul, ate delicious vegetarian meals, and watched some Korean women drinking, singing, dancing, and enjoying themselves in the temple court-yards. While visiting the countryside or non-Christian households in our neighborhood, we sometimes observed shamanistic rituals of dancing and dramatized narration conducted by female shamans dressed in multi-colored robes.

Since 1975, I have been teaching cross-cultural courses on women in the Women's Studies Program of the University of Hawaii and doing research on Asian immigrant women. The groups of women with whom I have built social networks consist of a handful of feminist women colleagues in Asia, Hawaii, and on the mainland United States whom I met at feminist and women's studies conferences. Most of these friends are women of color and Third World feminists engaged in grass-roots activism, feminist teaching, and feminist research. They constitute a very important support group for me.

Through my research work and political action regarding Asian immigrant women whose lives have been affected by the complex interplay of sexism, racism, and classism, I have come to believe in a broader definition of feminism that includes societal and personal transformation based on the elimination of all inequalities. In the early 1970s, women of color used to argue among ourselves or with working-class and lesbian women about ranking the relative importance of various oppression experienced by each group. Gradually, we came to an agreement that no category of oppression that women of color or any other multiply oppressed women face can be regarded as more or less important than another. The combined effects of multiple oppression—against gender, race, class, sexual orientation, and so forth—affect the lives of women differently and should be considered in totality.

In exploring and analyzing our experiences of oppression of gender, race, and class, I have come to realize that the diversity and complexity of women's life experiences are firmly grounded in the domination process, and that all systems of inequality are interconnected. It is not so much the differing viewpoints among women, but our refusal to admit to the privileges and power created and perpetuated in our society based on those differences, which is the chief cause of division among women.

Therefore, it is not only necessary to recognize the fact that there are differences among women, but even more crucial for us to accept that there are inequalities of power and resources, and conflicting interests among women based on the hierarchical system of class, race, nationality, religion, region, ethnicity, language, sexual orientation, age, generation, and different physical ability. I have painfully come to realize that we have to understand how history, culture, politics, religion, and economic realities coalesce in women's experiences in Asian and Asian American historical, cultural, and social situations.

In the process of exploring and analyzing our differences, Third World women and women of color in the First World have contributed greatly to broadening and redefining feminism as a movement against any and all forms of oppression, encompassing struggles in the household, the church, and state and global arenas. Exploitation and domination against women must be overcome.

As a result of my commitment to feminist scholarship, I have devised a theory of Asian American women's studies based on reclaiming Asian women's history and articulating their current realities through research on early and recent Asian immigrant women in Hawaii. This has led me to find my cultural and spiritual roots, which have been and continue to be essential in the process of my becoming a whole person. I have struggled to integrate my politics into a feminist world and into an Asian female world through my research work, as well as in my day-to-day political activism for the liberation of women from their gender, racial, economic, and cultural oppression.

Prior to my research experiences with Asian immigrant women, I felt very separated and alone in all the struggles and communities in which I participated. However, the discovery of our Asian spiritual foremothers through feminist historical research not only enabled me to integrate my experiences in the complex world of politics, but also transformed my fragmented self into a whole human being. My views have become clearer regarding the past history, present reality, and future relationship of Asian women to the family, the church, and society. Between 1981 and 1990, I worked as the Asian coordinator of the Coordinating Council, and have served as a co-founder of the Women of Color Caucus and the Asian and Asian-American Task Force of the National Women's Studies Association. I am a founding member of the International Women of Color Feminist Organization, which was founded in May 1991 in Chicago.

My urgent task as an Asian American feminist church woman has been to raise consciousness and to influence the church in challenging various contradictions as the church performs a complex series of functions which historically have upheld the interconnected hierarchies of domination and exploitation. As the only Asian female member of the California-Pacific Annual Conference Commission on the Status and Role of Women (1980–1988), I have constantly challenged white male supremacy, sexism, racism, classism, homophobia, ageism, and physical ableism in the church. In order to meet the urgent need of immigrant women's experience of racism and sexism by discriminatory immigration laws and vulnerability to domestic violence, I have since 1988 coordinated outreach and educational programs and the Bilingual Domestic and Legal Hotline for Korean immigrant women and Korean women married to United States military personnel. This has been made possible through a grant from the California-Pacific Annual Conference Commission on Church and Society in coalition with the Hawaii Women Lawyers' Domestic and Legal Hotline volunteers, the Interfaith Network Against Domestic Violence of the Hawaii Council of Churches, and the Advocates for Immigrant Women Committee of Hawaii. About two-thirds of the calls received in 1989–1990 have been cases involving both wife battering and the 1986 Amendment.

At the Hawaii district and my local Korean United Methodist church in Hawaii, I have devised a long-term planning strategy for the empowerment of all persons and groups regardless of gender, race, ethnicity, class, language ability, age, marital status, physical ability, and sexual orientation.

This long-term strategy, submitted to my Korean ethnic local church's Long-Range Planning Committee, has as some of its objectives: (1) to include a representative number of women at all levels of the church hierarchy, including the hiring of a fully ordained bilingual woman minister; (2) to recover and document women's contributions in our church archives and history publications; (3) to encourage critical thinking and questioning of sexist, racist, and classist interpretations of the Bible, church doctrines, and publications; (4) to implement educational and consciousness-raising programs, and encourage strong commitment to and active participation in social action for societal and global justice issues; (5) to encourage the sharing among men and women of physical service work, such as childcare and kitchen work, and leadership roles in children's and youth programs; and (6) to use inclusive language and content in relation to gender, class, race, ethnicity, culture, sexual orientation, age, different physical ability in the worship services, and in educational materials.

According to fifteen life-history interviews with recently immigrated Korean Methodist women leaders in Hawaii, which I have conducted in recent months, the most important obstacle to achieving these goals of having an inclusive church is the internalized oppression of women themselves. One-half of these women had Buddhist and shamanistic family backgrounds but had converted to Christianity, and the remaining women were born into Christian families. Most of those born into Christian families had devout female relatives such as grandmothers, mothers, or aunts as their spiritual mothers. Many of these spiritual mothers had been the first members in their families to become Christians, often against the wishes of their male relatives. Half of those interviewed had intense conversion experiences, including speaking in tongues, hot fire-like body temperature, heavy flowing of tears, and healing of physical illnesses during prayer meetings, youth community activities, and revival meetings.

To them, Christian faith predominantly means personal salvation, eternal life, and God's blessings and miraculous events in relation to personal and familial well-being and life crisis situations such as marital conflicts, serious illnesses, and adaptation to immigrant life. The most painful experiences they had were related to problems in marriage such as conflict with in-laws and husbands' extramarital affairs.

For the overwhelming majority, the Christian faith and service to God are the most important aspects of their daily life, evidenced by their intensive and extensive participation in church religious and volunteer service activities such as singing in the choir, Sunday and Wednesday evening services, early morning and Friday evening prayer meetings, revival meetings, Bible classes, study class (sok-hwe) attendance and leadership, and membership in the United Methodist Women. Since they spend most of their free time at the church or with church members, most of their friends are members of the church they belong to. Two-thirds of them desired to study theology and become professional women evangelists and wanted their children to inherit their Christian faith and dedicate their lives to God.

In regard to gender hierarchy and division of labor in the church, three-fourths of the women felt uncomfortable with having women elders and clergy women, especially married clergy women with young children. The women were either willing to or resigned to doing domestic chores in the church, including activities such as cooking, washing, and cleaning, or other "feminine" tasks, and were willing to assume subordinate roles either because they felt that these were God-given duties or because they believed that it was impossible to change men. During a recent United Methodist Women's meeting, they coordinated a churchwide food bazaar in a church, which raised $12,000 net profit for the church building fund. The majority of these women felt more comfortable and more enjoyed working with women in the church kitchen or in one another's homes as leaders of the United Methodist Women than in participating in male-dominated committees as token women, whose opinions they felt were often not taken seriously.

At the national level of The United Methodist Church, as the only Asian American female member of the General Commission on Archives and History of The United Methodist Church since 1988 to serve as the Chair of the Committee on Ethnic History and as a member of the Committee on Women's History, I have been advocating the feminist transformation of ethnic history and the integration of experiences of women of color into women's history.

At the general conference of the National Association of the Korean American United Methodist Church, which was held in March 1990 in Boston, I was elected vice-president of the organization. I have pledged myself to building a community of feminist women in the Korean American United Methodist Church toward making the Korean American churches in the United States more inclusive by raising their consciousness of sexism within the Korean American churches. I have worked with younger generation clergywomen and men and interracially married laywomen and immigrant women to organize their own autonomous networks and groups, which will empower them in order to transform the existing older-generation male and the clergy-dominant Korean American United Methodist Church hierarchy.

Upon receiving the Annual Barrier Breaker Award from the California-Pacific Annual Conference Commission on the Status and Role of Women in June 1989, I once again felt an intimate communion with Asian spiritual foremothers and feminists all over the world. They have baptized me with the fire of their life-giving spirituality and passionate politics so that I can continue to do my part to bring liberation and justice to the lives of all the oppressed in the world. They have given me the resources and strength to be constantly aware of the interconnectedness of the hierarchy of domination and oppression. They have inspired me to work toward building a better and more humane society by creating coalition politics with feminist, gay rights, labor rights, human rights, national sovereignty, and peace groups, which try to empower women, the indigenous, people of color, gay men and lesbians, the working class, the poor, the differently abled, the elderly, and other oppressed people of the world.

Rosalie Bentzinger

Carole Cartwright

May Chun

Jean Dickinson

Lois Hanna

Ruth Palmer

Barbara Scott

Ethelou Talbert

CHAPTER 13

ONE SPIRIT—MANY STORIES

*Contemporary Laywomen Share
Their Vocational Visions*

MARY ELIZABETH MULLINO MOORE

I entered this study of laywomen in The United Methodist Church with enthusiasm and biases, all of which I want to share in the early moments of this chapter. My enthusiasm has only grown during the time of preparation, but my biases have been stretched, bent, and reshaped as I have interviewed laywomen in many different settings of ministry. To be fair with you as readers, I will share my preliminary biases as we begin, as well as some of the surprises and contradictions that came to me in the course of the study.

I began with the assumption that laywomen in the United Methodist tradition would represent a wide range of commitments and vocational directions. Further, I expected to find that women often feel pulled in different directions, and that their vocational commitments often change dramatically over time. I assumed that many laywomen feel torn at times in their lives between a lay vocation and being ordained. I expected most laywomen to describe their vocation in relation to what they do for and with the church. And I assumed that women would often identify some difficult periods in regard to discerning their gifts, affirming their vocation, and experiencing the affirmation of others.[1]

The research consisted of interviews and biographical reviews of eight women representing various vocational directions, geographical regions, racial and ethnic groups, and ages. The sample was not a random or representative sample selected using statistical procedures. However, the sample was diverse, representing a broad span of The United Methodist Church. The purpose here is not so much to represent all United Methodist laywomen through statistical selection and analysis; that is a worthy project, but a much longer one for another kind of book. For this book of historical narratives, the purpose is to tell the stories of a few women who represent the tradition as they have experienced and acted within it.[2]

As for the expectations that formed the backdrop of this study, some were radically reformed in the course of the interviews. Certainly, I found that a wide range of commitments and vocational directions was represented, but the anticipated pulls in different directions were not evident in these single interviews. Two of the women interviewed spoke of their vocations as evolving, and three others spoke of their many interests and gifts coming together in what they now do in their vocation. The picture is one of women weaving their lives and gathering up their many experiences and unexpected surprises along the way like threads for weaving.[3] Only occasionally does one glimpse a picture of a woman traveling a road with forks, where decisions to take one route or another are sometimes needed. Even for those women who had dramatic moments of conversion or decisions to make, the life journey has been one of living into the decisions or building upon them, rather than rehearsing or repeating them. For this reason, the vocational commitments do not change dramatically over time; more accurately, the commitments accumulate and are reshaped by the women in emerging life circumstances.

Even the choice between lay and ordained vocations did not seem to be traumatic for these women. Many felt a strong tug at one point in their lives toward ordination, and many think they might have chosen ordination had they been born a few years later. These women were all active in the church, and often began telling their vocational sagas with stories of church involvement. On the other hand, they saw the whole of their lives as their vocation, and many discussed in great detail their roles with family, friends, and community agencies.

Most striking was the celebrative nature of these interviews. The women spoke of real struggles, but they spoke too of the inner strength that carried them through trying times. Again and again they emphasized their sense of God's presence; experiences of deep inner strength; gratitude for others who had given them guidance, support, and friendship; and personal satisfaction in the living of their vocation.

Meeting the stories of these women is encountering the Spirit that inspires them. Their stories are many, but common threads weave the many into a whole. You will discern commonality and uniqueness in these eight remarkable women as we begin now to weave their stories together.

IN THE BEGINNING

Virtually all the women began to tell their faith journeys at the point they named as the beginning, but those beginnings were different. May Chun introduced her faith journey with the most clear sense of a moment of beginning.

My faith journey started when I was 12 years old. My origins were in what I would consider a typical island Asian family. We were Buddhist in background, but neither my parents nor grandparents were practicing Buddhists. We laughed because we gathered for Buddhist holidays, but just to share food, like potlucks. Because of the family's being nonpracticing Buddhists, I think when I learned about Jesus Christ in Vacation Church School and Christian Endeavor, it was more easily accepted that I chose to go the Christian route. On the day I was supposed to be baptised and join the church, my Soloman's "Head of Christ" fell and the glass broke. My mother took the event as an omen that *might* be a bad sign. She asked me to wait, even though I was already dressed in my Easter finery and ready to go. I waited for a year, and then I was baptised and joined the church.

In reflecting on her beginnings as a twelve-year-old, May added a spontaneous comment at the end of her interview:

I do not know what my life would be if I hadn't begun this faith journey. Sometimes I wonder if it means even more to me because I wasn't born into it, but I came into this faith journey later in my life. I am glad I *had* the choice; I have no feeling of having lost something by missing those twelve years. It has made all the difference in my life to be on this faith journey. It has made me who I am.

In contrast to May's story is that of Jean Dickinson, who began by saying:

I guess that my faith journey was always very much a part of my life because I was raised in a home where faith was very much "the home." I was raised in the church and spiritual activities, and I never knew any different. My family put me into the faith community, and they modelled faith and Christianity. This was the basis or foundation for me, making me open to other experiences that came along to strengthen the foundations, such as experiences with young people, camps, and the environment of Christian fellowship all my life.

Another story of beginning is similar. Ethelou Talbert tells of her family, and most especially of her grandmother:

My faith journey started almost at birth because my mother was a teacher and church organist and my father was a mortician, quite a combination there. My grandmother lived with us. I'm one of four girls and we were taught by my grandmother at a very early age; she would devote Saturday mornings to conduct catechism for us. That's where we learned the books of the Bible and how to pray, and we sang together. After that time we were free to do whatever kids were doing. Because of my mother also, being a church organist, we would sing constantly, almost daily. So I learned to sing at a very early age, and as far back as I can remember I was part of a church choir. I came up in the Methodist church which was a Methodist Episcopal Church then, and most of my life has been in the church. I credit my life journey in the church to my grandmother primarily.

Rosalie Bentzinger also credits her family as the "primary moulder" of her faith. Rosalie thinks of her parents together because of the pervasive harmony in their relationship. When her father died, her brother said that their parents had "the marriage of the century." Certainly for both of them, the church was first in their lives.

Rosalie describes the beginnings of her faith journey with abundant reference to these family influences:

> I had parents to whom the church was of first import in their lives, and they made certain that their children were a part of the church from before we could even remember. We lived about two blocks from the Methodist church and our mother was the person who was responsible for youth ministries, children's ministries, choir, and almost everything else you could think of because she wanted good things to happen in that church, and I'm sure also, she had in mind that it was important for her family's growth. My father was Sunday School superintendent part of the time and always sang in the choir, always very much a part of everything that happened at the church. We sat always in the third row from the front on the left side of the sanctuary; it was near a door so if children did not behave themselves, they could be taken out rather quickly. My mother, who had been a public school teacher, had all kinds of creative ideas of what to do, things that were of interest to children, to youth. We always knew that we would be in church on Sunday morning and Sunday evening, and youth groups in between. Choir practice was sometimes held in our living room. I sat in with the choir at practice long before I became a member of the choir.

The significance of Rosalie's family involvement is a thread throughout her interview. She recalls that her parents were oriented to supporting the church and the pastor, so they did not allow critical talk of the pastor in their home, even when they did not fully approve of what the pastor was doing. She also recalls that they stood always for what they believed, and as a child, she knew better than to say, "Everyone is doing this." Their reply would always be, "I know, but *we* don't do this."

Reflecting on her church-oriented family, Rosalie says:

> When I hear now of youth rebelling against their parents, I find it foreign to my own experience, and the experience of my brother and sister as well. Somehow, our parents helped us to believe that the church was so important and that it must be first in our lives. I have wondered what kind of magic my parents had that made us feel this was wise. I think that we had so many opportunities for leadership roles in the church that we learned and grew a lot in that regard. We also had so much fun with our friends in the church and with our friends in other churches. We were, in a sense, a very isolated community as compared to today. Even though there were four denominations in that town, we always did many things together. I was surprised to learn in my later years that the ecumenical movement had not yet arrived.

Not all of the stories in this chapter find their beginnings in such faith-oriented and church-related families. Two of the women did not grow up in strongly church-related families, but in both cases, they grew up going to Sunday school in nearby churches. Lois Hanna tells with a smile how she used to go to the Methodist or Presbyterian church until her teenage years, when, moving to Lake Elsinore, the Methodist church attracted her because "that's where all the teenagers went and we learned to dance in the basement of the Methodist church with the minister turning the gramophone for us." She adds, "Then my senior year of high school we moved to Ontario and I went part of the time to the Ontario Methodist Church and part of the time to the Upland, depending on who my boyfriend was at the present time." After a time in a Baptist and United Brethren Church, she and her family settled after World War II into an Evangelical United Brethren Church, which continues now, many years later, to be her church home.

Another story is told by Carole Cartwright, who begins by saying, "I grew up in a home that was Baptist, and I spent many Sundays at church, unwillingly I might add." She continues:

> My sister and I did start out with a good Baptist upbringing, meaning Sunday School through church through healing services. As a result of that, I was baptized into the Baptist church, and that was really an experience for me. I chose to be baptized because in the Baptist church, you come when you are called. It's not automatic. When I was 9 or 10, I felt the need to go up at the service and say, "I'm ready." I had total immersion, which was wonderful. It felt like I was really going to be in the Lord and with the Lord. I felt really exhilarated. The church, however, was not prepared to help me maintain that exhilaration. At least that's my feeling. There was no organized Bible study; I was given the Bible, and it was up to me. I wasn't old enough to do it without nurturing. Eventually, the good feeling left. I still felt I had a good relationship with God, but that too sort of faded away.

For another interviewee, childhood experiences may have been less prominent in her faith journey than later events. Barbara Scott explains that she "grew up in the church," but she focuses the early story of her faith journey on her conversion experience at a junior high camp, and on her experience of trying to "process things" during her college and young adult years.

Ruth Palmer grew up in an interdenominational church, so her early experiences of church were less homogeneous than some, and she continued to sort out her religious identity in the years beyond college. Ruth grew up on a Texas farm, regularly attending the Sunday school in her interdenominational church. Her parents were Baptist, and the Baptist pastor came occasionally to her small church; she herself was baptized as a Baptist. In the small town church, however, the Methodist pastor came once a month, and in the years following college, Ruth found herself more at home in the Methodist church in Houston, which she visited with her roommate and later joined.

The stories of these laywomen and the beginning of their journeys introduce their lives. Their stories give a glimpse into the larger body of United Methodist laywomen, reflecting a variety of childhood experiences, diverse denominational backgrounds, and the various ways parents have embodied, encouraged, or remained neutral on matters of faith.

THE GIFT OF MENTORS

One striking feature of these stories is that all of the women interviewed expressed gratitude to mentors. In some cases the mentors were members of the family, or the family itself. In others, the mentors were pastors, older women in the church, friends, teachers, colleagues, famous persons; or they were communities such as a Christian girls' club, an all black elementary school, a congregation, a Sunday school class, or the United Methodist Women (and antecedent bodies). The roles of mentors were as diverse as the persons and communities. Some were longtime guides, companions, or friends; some were inspirational figures from afar; some were colleagues whose styles of collaborative work inspired and enhanced the work of others; and some were people who planted a vocational idea or called a person into a particular role at a particular time.

Some stories have already been told of mentors within family and childhood communities, but the power of this mentoring is often stressed by the women interviewed. Carole Cartwright, a very successful producer and manager in television programming, is now an independent video producer and consultant. She recalls the powerful mentoring that took place in her family and all-black elementary school:

> My parents, when I was growing up, were a strong influence on me in terms of where I was going to go. I always knew from the very beginning that I was part of a minority group. Being black, "colored" at that time according to my father (because where he came from, if you were colored you represented the best of Black Society), my father said you're always going to have to work harder, you're going to have to be better, you're going to have to have education. He and my mother were very influential in terms of the knowledge that you have to succeed and you really have to get your education.

Those messages were reinforced for Carole in school:

> I attended an all-black elementary school where there were at least two or three teachers who continued to foster that thought—that you are bright and it is your duty to go on. I credit them with giving me the self-confidence to feel that I could do it. That was the last time in my life, those eight years in elementary school, that I was ever in an all-black school or community. When I went to high school, I was forced out into the world. From that point on, I've been a minority in a majority. . . . That early beginning and confi-

dence that both my parents and teachers gave me have helped me not to worry about whether people are accepting me or not accepting me because of race. That background has given me some strength.

Carole later tells of the time in high school when she was counseled not to go to college but to consider a trade. She attributes her determination to go to college anyway to her parents and elementary school teachers. She says, "Had I not had that reinforcement at a younger age—that you are worth something, you can do anything you want, don't let anybody tell you you can't—I would have easily given up."

The enduring trait for Carole is determination; she still cannot wallow in problems: "Once I recognize a problem, I have to do something about it." She recognizes that many successes along the way have reinforced her determination, but the quality was born in her childhood. Even now, Carole is grateful for being black so that her sensitivities are increased: "For me, being black has been a great thing. I've been able to be aware of some problems in the world that others might not recognize, and that means that I've been able to do something about those problems. That includes problems such as AIDS today."

The church itself did not play a strong role in forming Carole's character in her early years; she credits her parents and teachers with that role. The church did teach her about God and Jesus, and she now appreciates that United Methodism offers "a learning process for our young people." Carole always longed for a church that would nourish her high moments such as her experience of baptism.

For Carole, however, mentors have also included colleagues; childhood influences have been joined by the influence of colleagues in adulthood, especially the unselfish volunteers she saw at work all over Chicago, like those at Operation ABLE (Ability Based on Long Experience), and some of the inspiring people more than fifty years of age who have been helped by ABLE to return to work or pursue other goals. Through her work, Carole has been inspired to do documentaries such as one on Alzheimer's disease, which she says "is one of the things I'm most proud of."

In addition to her community colleagues, Carole now describes her congregation as her family; the congregation as a whole is mentor. Carole's young adult daughter first planted the idea that the family needed "a church home." When they visited The United Methodist Church, all of them "felt that this is where we belong." The veteran, fatherly pastor had much to do with the appeal, as did the congregation, which was "welcoming but not overwhelming" and which did not communicate "a list of do's and don't's." What became especially important to Carole was learning of all the significant work the denomination was doing in the world, being in a congregation where she and her family felt people's caring, and engaging with others in strong Bible study. One moving time in their own family life was when Carole's husband suffered a severe heart attack. Carole says, "It was during that time that through the people in the church, I came to realize the value of prayer. When he was in the hospital and we were in church, he felt it and I felt it—this warm feeling that people care and God cares."

Carole tells of frustrations in some earlier church experiences during times when her work in television involved her in communicating stories of battered women, abused children, and men who had lost their jobs. She had to deal in her personal and spiritual life with these matters, and she found it difficult to go "to church where they were going to have a tea in three months and were wondering how they were going to decorate the room." Because of such frustrations, she dropped out. Carole experiences her present church and the denomination as more concerned with those pressing needs in the world, and this is why she has become so active. She has seen the church's involvement through the United Methodist Women, and she has found support within the connectional system "to make a difference in other than your own neighborhood." Carole's own appreciation for the mentoring and inspiration of the church has led her into many leadership roles; she is District Chair of the Council on Ministries, District Director of the Status and Role of Women, Lay Leader of her local church, and a lay speaker.

Jean Dickinson's mentors have often been individuals and groups in the church, especially her family and friends, who were centered in the church. Her experience was much like that of Ruth Palmer, Rosalie Bentzinger, and Ethelou Talbert because the family became a focal center of spiritual life and a connection to the church. Like those of some of the other women, not all of the church experiences were positive. Both Jean and Rosalie had uneasy reactions to the revivals that were part of their early church life, but in both cases, people within the church helped them to deal with their sense of guilt. Jean remembered one particular revival when she "couldn't work up any tears." She learned in time that tears and dramatic turnings were not necessary to faith. What Jean recalls positively about her journey, then, are not dramatic moments, but a "very quiet religious experience."

Jean's mentors were people who were present with her over time. She remembers a Sunday school teacher whose "presence and witness" were important to her, especially the teacher's "patience with us as teenagers." She recalls her dad's mentoring with her, and even now, she appreciates the encouragement he gave her to think: "He wanted me not just to speak, but to think things through. One time, during the Rosenberg trial, I said that the Rosenbergs ought to be executed. Dad asked me how I thought I had the right to be the judge about that. He was always challenging me like that to think and to try to be fair. This has carried through into my own family and work." Jean also names some pastors who have been particularly important in her life, one an admirable person whom she knew slightly but who witnessed his faith, one a close friend who pushes her to think, and another a colleague and good model of collegiality.

Further, Jean names some communities that have been formative for her, including the people in Appalachia with whom she did volunteer work during college, the Methodist Youth Caravan group and leaders with whom she worked on a World Peace Team the summer after college, the Stephen Ministry group in her present church, and the children with whom she taught for many years. Of the children, she says, "The children shared so many experiences that were learning and spiritual experiences for me. Children are basically honest and fresh; they taught me lessons of life and of love. They weren't trying to teach me, but they did."

Most of the women interviewed named many such individuals and communities within the church who had been important shapers and supporters of them in their spirituality and vocation. Four of the women accentuated the importance of the church community in sustaining them today. Ruth Palmer describes her Sunday school class as "a centering point" for her and her husband, and Lois Hanna comments, "When you've been in a church forty some years, you have a lot of support." Rosalie Bentzinger recalls how important it was for her to grow up in a church that really cared for children and "always considered the children part of the church." Now, she is aware that being in church on Sunday is still very important to her spirituality. On the other hand, Ethelou Talbert recognizes that, though she would enjoy being in her church now and singing in the choir, she needs to be "flexible as far as churches are concerned because I travel with Melvin quite a bit." She finds that churches expect the bishop's spouse to be there, and she has learned that she has the gift of flexibility and can play that role of traveling with her husband.

Another form of mentoring is the lifelong spiritual guidance of a spiritual father or mother. May Chun's story of her godmother is such a story. May chose her own godmother because this woman, the Director of Christian Education at her church, had first introduced her to Jesus Christ in Vacation Church School. May explains that she became active in the church, spending much time with this woman and the church youth and the Christian girls' club that the woman sponsored. Still today, the club meets occasionally, and they recently celebrated their mentor's eightieth birthday. May's spiritual journey is sprinkled with stories of her godmother, as is her view of the church's vocation with children. She tells of a recent conversation with a church leader who was looking for Vacation Church School teachers "because people are counting on it to babysit their children." May recalls her response: "I said I couldn't agree because Vacation Church School is much more than babysitting or recreation. All of these things served in a progression for me to keep my interest and help me be a disciple. We sometimes downplay what a person will understand and what will be important to start them off."

One of the striking features of most of the interviews is the role of mentors, often pastors, in calling the women into some particular service. Barbara Scott appreciates one pastor's role at a time when she was struggling with vocational questions; he gave her opportunities to serve in many different ways in the church. Ruth Palmer, Carole Cartwright, and Rosalie Bentzinger describe vocational turning points primarily as moments when someone came to them and asked them to consider a new role. Ruth was persuaded by the Executive Director of Wesley Community Center in Houston to leave her accounting business and become the new Executive Director, thus combining her longtime missional concerns with her business expertise. Carole was persuaded by her district superintendent to begin witnessing, which led her into lay speaking and later into district leadership under the persuasion of the same superintendent. Rosalie describes most of her vocational changes as initiated by an invitation from another person, usually a pastor, to participate in some new kind of ministry. She usually insisted that she was not prepared and was encouraged to join the team and prepare as she went along. So she did!

Another form of mentoring was quite common among the women interviewed—mentoring offered through the United Methodist Women. Lois Hanna began her young adulthood in The Evangelical United Brethren Church, and she was active in the Women's Society of World Service. In fact, she was so active that she used up her tenure and was not able to take Conference leadership roles in the United Methodist Women after the merger in 1968. She did carry on with active leadership in her local unit and district.

Lois's stories of the Women's Society and United Methodist Women are similar to several. As a young person, Lois appreciated her peers and the older women in the Women's Society, often pastors' wives, who were important role models and friends. She smiles as she tells about their car trips to meetings and the frequent journeys with visiting missionaries. These women reassured her:

> They always just took it for granted that I could lead. So even though sometimes I got up shaking in my boots, I'd think, "Now it's up to me to do this." These people are depending on me. I guess it showed me that life in the church could be so fulfilling and so much fun. In those days we didn't stay in hotels or motels; we slept on cots in the church. Lola Schafer, the D.S.'s wife, and I always bunked together and we became very good friends. Dot Grumbein has been a faithful friend all these years, and we still continue to be friends. We just know that we can depend on each other.

For Lois, the United Methodist Women made another important contribution to her vocational life. She credits the women, and also the educational ministry of her church, with preparing her for the work she has done later in her life. Not only did she take responsibilities in both arenas, but she took advantage of the special trainings, such as mission studies and laboratory schools. This prepared her for the eighteen years she taught preschool in her city, and for the many years of board leadership in church service agencies, such as the David and Margaret Home and Frazee Community Center. Lois points out that she did not have a college education, but "my education was all through the church."

Like Lois, Ruth Palmer and Carole Cartwright see the United Methodist Women as an important mentoring community for them. Ruth, like Lois, applauds the role of the older women as "mentors and role models," and both Ruth and Carole credit the women with educating them about the mission of the church in relation to needs in the world. For both, the United Methodist Women has also opened doors for them to respond to those needs.

We cannot leave the subject of mentors without noting the significance of adult family relationships for these women. Carole Cartwright, Ethelou Talbert, and Jean Dickinson describe at length the importance of their husbands to their spiritual journeys. For Ethelou, married to a bishop, and Jean, married to a pastor and seminary president, their vocations have been linked with their husbands'. Their husbands have been spiritual companions, and their vocations have been collegial with those of their spouses.

For Jean, the death of her husband was a religious crisis because of the closeness they had enjoyed. She says, "I didn't lose my faith, but I struggled with questions. Even though I knew answers, I needed to struggle. Even when I yelled out to God, I knew my faith was still there because I wouldn't yell to someone who isn't there." This religious experience influenced Jean's vocation; she spends much time now with persons facing crises. In her own crisis, she was bothered by persons who quickly told her that "your faith will get you through." She knew that and believed it, but she felt that "people sometimes negated my right to be hurt." She watches her own language very carefully now as she journeys with people through loss and grief.

MAKING A DECISION—TAKING A STAND

Another striking feature of the spiritual journeys of these laywomen is the influence of certain decisions on their lives and the daring to take an ethical stand that several of them exercised in their young adult lives. Two of the women, May Chun and Barbara Scott, refer particularly to decisions made as youth to give their lives to God. For May, this decision led her into Christianity, and for Barbara, the decision was "to commit my life to Christ." Both women refer back to those early decisions as reference points in shaping their vocations. For May, the decision has led her into a lifetime of "growing in discipleship," and she has given herself fully to being a disciple in her work as a librarian, in her church involvements (from local to general church levels), and in her family. For Barbara, the decision has led her to return to an earlier dream to enter representative ministry. In becoming a diaconal minister, she feels she has fulfilled an earlier call that has been reshaped into a service-oriented ministry in her church and community.

Some decisions are more painful. Both Barbara Scott and Carole Cartwright made decisions to divorce, and both wrestled hard in making the decision and in dealing with lingering doubts. Carole says, "A few years later, I realized it was a good decision, but at that point, I wondered if it was good enough." Both women acknowledge now that the turning point has been formative for them in positive ways.

Some decisions are to take bold ethical stands. Rosalie Bentzinger made such a stand in her first year out of college when she was teaching home economics in a high school. When members of the basketball team were doing failing work, she gave them failing grades. The coach came to her and asked her to change the grades so that the boys could still play basketball. This coach was also superintendent of the schools and her boss. Rosalie recalls,

> About the third or fourth time he came and I said I wouldn't change the grades, he said that *he* would change them. I went to him and said I couldn't teach there under those conditions, and therefore, I was submitting my resignation. Since I was under contract, I said I would stay until he could find someone, but I wanted him to find someone right away. Fortunately, there was another teacher involved who was the principal of the school and had been a teacher in the junior high earlier. . . . He had changed the grades when they asked him to, but thought better of it later. He resigned also. It was a big issue. One of the things that was disappointing to me was that persons who were in the church in that town and also on the School Board were not supportive of what I was saying by my resignation. We had a long discussion about it. I wept buckets of tears. . . . They asked me to reconsider. I said I would not. I left there.

In time the State Athletic Association heard rumors, which led to an investigation, and the school basketball team had to forfeit the county title.

Some of the decisions are made in partnership. May Chun is wrestling with decisions now about how to respond to the needs of homeless people in Hawaii. She realizes that a personal response to open her home in some way is hard to contemplate, because "you aren't the only one living in a home." All of the women interviewed recall moments of decision making when they were working together with their spouse, sister, parents, or children. Jean Dickinson recalls an ethical decision that she and her husband made together about how to respond to the racial controversy in Mississippi where her husband was serving a local church. She said that she did not want her children growing up in an unhealthful situation, and she and her husband felt they had to take a stand against segregation.

Together they decided that he would sign a statement of protest, "Born of Connection," with several other church leaders; this finally led them to leave the state and find their vocation elsewhere.

Some decisions lead to new insight regarding vocational action. One such decision was made by Carole Cartwright when she was working for a television station in Chicago. She says,

> I went into my station manager and told him that we needed to do something about the hunger problem in Chicago. The station manager, who lived in a wealthy suburb of Chicago, said, "What do you mean? There's no hunger in my neighborhood." I was shocked that he was so narrow that he could only think in terms of his own personal experience. What I did was to gather statistics and other kinds of information so I could convince him there was a major hunger problem in Chicago. When it was all over, we put together this brochure. It's one of the things I'm most proud of. The purpose of the brochure is to convince people that there is a hunger problem. Before people will act, they have to be convinced there is a problem.

In this case, Carole had already sensed that she wanted to do something about the hunger problem, but her specific actions were guided by her interchange with the station manager.

Finally, some decisions are made as a response to life circumstances. Ethelou Talbert has experienced many changes in life, being married to an itinerant elder who has been a local church pastor, district superintendent, General Secretary of the General Board of Discipleship, and now, bishop. Ethelou's first big move, however, was made at her own initiative. When I asked what led her to move from New Orleans to California in her young adulthood, her response was, "I guess God did." Ethelou has a strong sense of God's hand at work, and she acknowledges that she is gifted with flexibility. One of the changes in Ethelou's life was particularly traumatic, however. When she lost her singing voice, she had to decide how to respond to the situation. She tells her story:

> I've been out of my life's work now for ten years or so because my life calling was singing. Going up to Washington state where we were from 1980 until 1988, I lost my voice completely. I could not sing at all. That was traumatic for me, but I said, "If God wants me to sing, he gave me this voice, it will come." And since we've been down here, it's been coming back.

VOCATIONAL JOURNEY

The most clear common thread in the journeys of these eight women is that they all see their *vocation as a response to God's call.* Ruth Palmer says of her vocation in Wesley Community Center: "I think I was divinely led; this was not something I sought and worked for." May Chun says that she has "always felt the need to be prayerful about decisions." She explains that this has been her approach to everything in her life, including changes in jobs. She always prayed about decisions to send an application for a new position, and she prayed again if she sent the application: "All right, Lord, I have sent this in; bless it and guide me along the way."

Carole Cartwright expresses the understanding of many of the women that God's lead is not seen only by looking retrospectively into the past; it is active in her life now and will continue to lead her into the future. Carole says, "I still don't know what God has in store for me ultimately. I'm trying to let Him/Her direct where I go. When opportunities come, I try to listen to the inner voice and do it or not, based on what I feel my journey should be. Where that will end, I don't know."

The women interviewed also carry a *common thread of commitment, or what some of the women call stewardship.* Rosalie Bentzinger understands her vocation in terms of her "sense of stewardship of all of life." She explains "that we really are called to make the world a better place and we take our clues for that from the life of Jesus Christ."

Ruth Palmer also describes her vocation in terms of commitment and stewardship:

> My gift, I guess, is my commitment to the church and my belief that all people have the right to a good education for their children, a good quality of life (abundant life), food for their family, and opportunities to develop skills in order to work and to develop their God-given talents. I am trying to bring the resources of the church together with the needs of the community. I am also bringing other resources in the community into partnership with the church because public funds are available to meet the needs that are our priorities.

Ruth describes this work as a way of being "good stewards of the dreams of the women back in 1904" who founded the Wesley Center that she now directs.

The sense of commitment is not vague for these women, and some express very strong determination. Carole Cartwright describes her determination as "the feeling that I should be able to accomplish anything I want to"—the quality that has enabled her to persist when people have tried to discourage her. Rosalie Bentzinger describes herself as determined "not to give up on things that I feel are very important." Rosalie says that she does not give up hope; that does not mean being "rigid and uncompromising," but recognizing that "there are certain points on which you do not compromise."

Another mark of the vocational understandings among these women is their *sense of participation with others in the ministry of the church.* May Chun understands her ministry as one of partnership with others in the community, and she believes that her calling is often mediated through the community. May says, "Some of us didn't feel called to ministry in the ordained sense, but called to ministry because of our gifts—a ministry in partnership with the ordained ministers. If I am elected, chosen, or appointed to do something and I can do it, then I see that as my calling."

The sense of participation with others leads Barbara Scott and others to see themselves as calling and equipping others for ministry. Barbara says, "I chose diaconal ministry rather than ordained ministry because I see mine as a servant role. I see myself helping persons see who they are and what their gifts are. I see the interview process with new members as seeing what their gifts are. If they have gifts as teachers, then I invite them to teach. I am kind of like a personnel director."

For some of the women, participation in worship is another important role. Barbara Scott and Jean Dickinson regularly lead in worship and in pastoral prayers; both find that meaningful to themselves and to others in the congregation. Barbara finds that her role in educational ministry enhances the seasonal experiences and special liturgies that she can create with others, as for Good Friday. Jean recently had the experience of conducting a funeral service for someone who was special to her. The act of committing the person's body and soul was very powerful for her. She "felt really empowered" as she participated in this sacred act. Long before she served on a church staff, Jean had her first experience of serving communion. She found the feeling of serving communion to be different from receiving communion. She says, "I wish everyone could have that experience of serving, and many lay people never do."

The women interviewed have *an acute awareness of the problems in the world.* They particularly identify the problems of injustice related to race, economics, gender, and international politics. Some of the problem areas that arouse particular concern are child abuse, lack of education, homelessness, hunger, economic and racial exploitation, and prejudice. Barbara Scott links injustice with the urgency of peace-making, having been influenced particularly by Martin Luther King, Jr., and Dietrich Bonhoeffer. Lois Hanna is particularly concerned about "what's happened to the morals of our country." She sees families disintegrating, and she is concerned about what has happened to commitment. She says, "We have just let the standards of morality go down and down and down and down." Among all these women, the problems of the world are seen as interconnected; they identify interlocking problems requiring multiple responses.

Some of the women see themselves responding to the problems of the world in direct ways. May Chun is involved with approving grants for disaster relief through the General Board of Global Ministries and the United Methodist Committee on Relief (UMCOR). At the same time, she is seeking ways to respond to the persons who are hungry and homeless in her native Hawaii. She says, "The work of the General Board of Global Ministries has certainly opened my eyes. You don't serve on a board without becoming aware and wanting to respond, and not just *through* the Board."

Ruth Palmer also finds herself offering direct services to enhance the life opportunities of persons who come to Wesley Community Center. She also tries to address the gap between the rich and the poor and to eliminate prejudice across economic, racial, and ethnic boundaries. Ruth does this in part by involving affluent churches with Wesley Center and by encouraging work teams to spend time working there.

Rosalie Bentzinger responds to global needs through her efforts "to expand the vision of our diaconal ministry" so that persons will be empowered to move into new areas of ministry, such as ministries with persons facing AIDS, addictions, militarism, and poor health care. She also serves as an advocate for diaconal ministers as they seek to live out their vocations.

Jean Dickinson finds herself raising issues of gender and justice within the church, and she "speaks and acts with people in the church" on many issues. She recognizes that she is "not a political activist," that she has "a more indirect way of responding." Likewise, Ethelou Talbert has participated in some volunteer programs for homeless and hungry people, and she wishes she could do more. Her primary response, however, is providing a supportive environment for others: "I see that I enable Melvin to go out and fulfill some of these obligations. He's involved in so many things, and I make home a pleasant place for him to come back to. . . . And I've always wanted to be in a setting where I'm with young people. I'm now with Merritt College and there I work with students. . . . So I feel that I provide a support system for other people."

The women interviewed see their *vocations as shaped in large part by their gifts, given by God and nurtured by the people around them.* Ethelou expresses gratitude for her ability to sing. She says that she is sometimes surprised when old friends tell her how much her singing has meant to them. She adds, "I did know that I had something; I was given a gift that was far beyond my control. Sometimes I would hit certain notes and climb the octaves and think, 'I did that?' It was really amazing and it's not something you have through voice training; I think it was just a gift from God." Ethelou also sees herself as having a gift for following, which has been valuable in her life.

Leadership is a gift many of the women have discovered in themselves, sometimes recognizing it only slowly. Both Lois Hanna and May Chun took their first leadership roles reluctantly, comparing themselves with their talented predecessors. For both of them, friends and mentors spoke to their hesitation and encouraged them to use gifts of leadership that they did not even know they had.

All of the women describe how they have come to discern their gifts in relating to others and to their life situations. Other people have called them to do new things and encouraged them to value their talents. May

Chun's godmother was one of those encouragers, and for May, Lois, and Ruth, mentors were often their seniors in United Methodist Women. Jean Dickinson saw her gift for perceiving and analyzing life situations only when the principal of her school called her attention to it.

Life situations have also been important revealers of persons' gifts. Carole Cartwright has found that her natural gifts in listening and communication combine with her experiences of racism to shape her vocation in combating racism and building understanding. She says, "I think I'm an approachable person and that's a gift. Because of that, I've been able to meet and change people who are very bigoted."

May Chun has also found her life situations shaping her vocation. She tells her family story: "When our grandchild was stricken with illness four years ago, I was always meeting persons who had some crisis and who shared and helped me through. It happens over and over and over again. God doesn't leave us—doesn't let us suffer without that constant sense of presence and support." Now, May's vocation includes preparing dinner and spending five evenings a week with her grandchild; she and her husband do this together.

In a more humorous vein, May allowed her life situation to shape her vocation when she retired and joined the women who work at crafts in her church every week. She recalls, "I found out quickly that I am not an arts and crafts person. I finally gave up the crafts, especially after the things I had made didn't sell at the bazaar." She adds, "I think God gives us special gifts and we use whatever gifts we have."

Despite the accent on action and using their gifts, the women often describe their *vocations as embodied in the quality of their lives.* Jean Dickinson was particularly explicit about this, saying: "My calling is to be a person of integrity and honesty and fairness. My calling has more to do with the quality of my life. I could be a parent or a teacher or a volunteer, but my calling in whatever I do is to witness—to be the best I can be in who I am and in whatever I am doing at the time."

Lifting a similar theme is Carole Cartwright, who says, "My whole life is my vocation." She describes her family relationships and her involvements in the church. She also describes her approach to her career: "I've moved out of the corporate world into my own business, and one of the criteria I set up for myself was that I would not take on any project that I personally did not believe in."

Striking among the women interviewed is the degree to which they *recognize their multiple roles in work and family as part of their vocation.* Many began by describing their vocation in terms of what they do in and with the church, but they eventually included what they do in all of their lives. May Chun, Ethelou Talbert, and Jean Dickinson have seen their vocations intertwined with those of their husbands, often doing some things together, such as the care May and her husband give to their grandchild, or the church visitations that Ethelou and her husband make together.

The women with children describe the importance of parenting in their vocational lives. They speak with joy of their children and with seriousness of their roles as parents. Some of the women also talk about caring for parents, a role that was very important to Rosalie Bentzinger for several years, and some have played strong roles with sisters and brothers. Ethelou Talbert says, "I'm the eldest of the four of us and my relationship with my sisters and with their children is very special in that they've always looked up to me. I was the one who would discipline all the kids, but today, now that many of them are grown and have children, I still have the utmost respect from each one of them. They call me to help them make decisions."

These common threads weave through the vocational lives of the eight women. One last thread may be named—the common understanding of *vocation as evolving and being filled with surprises along the way*. This theme brings the weaving metaphor full circle; it is a reminder that the metaphor of weaving was suggested in the first place by the women's descriptions of themselves. The women seem to be weaving their lives—finding new threads as they live their lives and weaving those threads into an ever-changing fabric.

Characteristic of the weaving is a spirit of humility expressed by many of the women. Lois Hanna says, "I don't think I do anything very spectacular—just kind of live each day as it comes and do what has to be done wherever I'm led." For Lois, as for others, however, the humility is not self-deprecating, but more of a joyful appreciation for life. She says that her calling "is just doing things I like to do."

All of the women seem to experience much joy in the living of their vocations. Ruth Palmer says, "I feel very fortunate because if anyone had told me to seek the work I am doing now, I wouldn't have. It just kind of evolved." Carole Cartwright expresses joy not only in looking back over her vocation, but also in looking forward to what lies ahead. She says,

> The only thing I feel now is an excitement because I don't think I've reached where I'm supposed to be yet. I'm still moving on that journey and I keep coming to crossroads, but I'm still waiting for the revelation of what it is I'm ultimately supposed to contribute. Along the way, I hope I'm doing something. . . . I'm still on the way to where I'm supposed to be spiritually, and I am enjoying the trip.

DOCUMENTS

1. Interviews and Interviewees. The interviews in this chapter are too few to draw large generalizations about United Methodist laywomen, but they are too many to share full details of each person interviewed. Here I share some brief biographical data about each woman to give a glimpse into the marvels of their lives. I also include the interview questions for the sake of encouraging readers to continue exploring the stories of laywomen they know or wish to know.

The women were selected to represent diversity of geography, ethnic and cultural background, forms of service, locus of church involvement (local, district, conference, general), and age. These women have all made their mark, as have thousands of women I did not interview. The purpose here was not to speak for all women, however, and though I was stirred by my own desire to interview many more, the gift of these eight is itself priceless.

Of the eight women, two are employed by local churches, two are employed by denominational boards or agencies, and four have been employed outside the church while remaining active in the church. Six have been full-time homemakers and professional volunteers during some period of their lives. The women represent the states of Hawaii (1), California (3), Texas (1), Tennessee (1), Ohio (1), and Florida (1). The racial and ethnic groups represented are Chinese American (1), African American (2), and European American (5).[4] The women's ages vary from 45 to 80.

Rosalie Bentzinger is Associate General Secretary of the Board of Higher Education and Ministry, Division of Diaconal Ministry. Formerly she served local churches as Director of Christian Education, and she was on the Iowa Conference Council on Ministries staff. She has been President of the National Christian Educators Fellowship and of the Iowa Chapter. She was also a delegate to General and Jurisdictional Conferences and Vice Chair of the General Conference Committee on Discipleship.

Carole Cartwright administers Cartwright and Company, a video production and consultation company. She is former Director of Programming and Program Operations for KNBC-TV in Burbank, California, and former Manager of Community Programs for WMAQ-TV in Chicago, Illinois. In her local church she is Lay Leader, and she shares her faith story with other churches as a lay speaker. Carole is also Chair of the District Council on Ministries, District Director of the Commission on the Status and Role of Women, and Vice-Chair of the Conference Commission on the Status and Role of Women.

May Chun has been a teacher, librarian, and administrator. She is the former Assistant Superintendent of Education and State Librarian for Hawaii. She was also President of the United Methodist Women in the former Pacific and Southwest Annual Conference, and she was named Conference Lay Woman of the Year in 1984. She has served six years on the General Board of Global Ministries and as a frequent delegate to General and Jurisdictional Conferences.

Jean Dickinson was for many years a teacher of children in kindergarten and first grade. Jean provided support and hospitality for Methodist Theological School in Ohio when her late husband, Buford Dickinson, was

President. Now Jean serves the Worthington United Methodist Church (Ohio) in Adult and Membership Ministries, and she is a member of the World Methodist Council.

Lois Hanna is a retired teacher of preschool children. She is presently Lay Leader of her local church, District Lay Leader, Chair of the Board of Directors of David and Margaret Home, and member of the Pacific and Southwest Conference Board of Laity. She has held several offices on the Boards of Frazee Community Center, Church Women United, and the Pomona Valley Council of Churches. She has also served on the Conference Council on Ministries and was President of her district and local chapters of United Methodist Women.

Ruth Palmer is a diaconal minister serving as Executive Director of Wesley Community Center, a multiple-service center with six satellite centers in Houston, Texas. Ruth is former Chair of the Texas Conference Board of Diaconal Ministry and of the Wesley Community Center Board. She has held many leadership positions in her local church, including that of President of United Methodist Women, and was a third-time delegate to General and Jurisdictional Conferences in 1992. She is Past President of Houston Metropolitan Ministries Board, Coordinator of the Southwest Regional Hearing on Children in Poverty, Past Chair of the United Way Agency Executives Association, and a member of the Mayor's Human Services Advisory Commission.

Barbara Scott is Diaconal Minister of Program in the First United Methodist Church of Coral Gables, Florida. In Miami she serves on the Board of Directors for Habitat for Humanity, and she is also active in the Summertime Outreach in Liberty City. She is a former elementary school teacher.

Ethelou Talbert is a soloist, frequent choir member, and former teacher of music. At this time she is Technician in Learning Resources at Merritt College in the Learning Resource Center. Ethelou has moved often with her husband Bishop Melvin Talbert, so she has found many forms of service, including providing the support system for her husband and daughter. She is also former Information Representative for InfoServ, United Methodist Communications, and Director of Admissions and Recruitment at the School of Theology at Claremont.

The following questions were used in the interviews, with some more specific questions related to the unique sharing of each interviewee. The questions themselves were refined after the first three interviews into the form below, but all of the topics were covered in all of the interviews.

1) Tell me the story of your faith journey.
2) Who were significant people for you in your journey? Were some communities particularly significant to you?
3) What were the most critical decision points along the way for you (or times you had to struggle with decisions)?

4) How do you understand your calling (life's work)?

5) What do you think are your unique gifts?

6) What needs in the world trouble you most?

7) Do you see your life's work as a response in any way to those needs?

8) Describe your vocational life: What do you do and how do you do it?

9) Do you have anything else you would like to say about your spirituality or vocation?

2. *Writings of the Women.* The following selections are taken from inspirational writings by May Chun, Jean Dickinson, Lois Hanna, Ruth Palmer, and Ethelou Talbert. They represent only a small portion of the words written, spoken, and sung by the interviewees over their lifetimes of sharing.

OUT OF CONTROL

May Chun

On an already serendipitous car trip through the southern United States, we were privileged to enjoy the only U. S. showing of the treasures of Catherine the Great, Empress of Russia. Using a wheelchair powered and maneuvered by my daughter relieved a temporary walking problem for me.

Unexpectedly, the tour ended with discomforting nausea for me. Someone diagnosed it as a result of my being out of control because my movement through the exhibit was out of my hands, not self-directed or guided. That made sense to me, for being in control of self and circumstances is important for many of us. The thought of being out of control causes distress.

Reflecting on that experience, I became keenly aware of the many times I have been out of control in different ways. My life is not always grounded. I need guidance and direction.

It is God from whom I can receive the guidance I so often need. It is God on whom I can rely for direction. It is God whom I can trust for help.

I need to turn to God to see more clearly the way I should go, to serve as a disciple following Christ. I want to give God control, to fulfill the divine purpose in my life.[5]

WAIT FOR SURPRISES

Jean Dickinson

He was five years old. Tyrone was the youngest of five children, all with different last names, who lived with his single mother and another single mother with several children. A full house! He always arrived at school needing a bath, with unkempt clothes, and without a good breakfast. He had worn his shoes on the wrong feet long enough to mold them into some degree of comfort. A tough life for a little boy.

In the midst of our storytime one morning, he got up from his place among the children and snuggled close to me, obviously wanting to tell me something. I put my arm around him and asked him to wait until the end of my "not-to-be-interrupted" story. Given his chance, he leaned over and whispered, "Mrs. Dickinson, I love you." I had waited for a wonderful surprise.

As Tyrone's journey was not easy, we recall the difficult journey of Jesus through the forty days of Lent (springtime). Jesus experienced disappointment, ridicule, betrayal, pain and injustice. He prayed, he wept, he suffered and called out to God. The road to the cross was heavy.

I don't know how Tyrone's journey has unfolded. I do know that the journey of Jesus promises us a wonderful surprise on Easter morning. As we travel through Lent with our own crosses, we remember that Jesus gave his destiny to God. Can we wait for surprises? As we travel the road, can we wait patiently, in faith and hope for the Easter promises? I'm trying.[6]

YOU MAKE A DIFFERENCE

Lois Hanna

How do we go about carrying on God's creative activity? Most important, our love and relationship to Jesus Christ gives us the motivation and commitment to be used of God. The role of the laity as I see it is a threefold one:
1. Support your pastor—What do you expect of your pastor? . . . We need to be supportive of the pastor and family.
2. Support your church—How enthusiastic are you when you're telling someone about your church? . . . If you are the church, then you need to work with others to bring about changes that are acceptable to all.
3. Commitment and involvement—Each of us has something to contribute. Do you believe in the power of the Holy Spirit? If so, you will know that at least one of the gifts of the Spirit is yours. Everyone has a gift. Each gift is important in the total plan. If each of us uses our special gift, great things can happen. Maybe your gift is making coffee for the coffee hour, telephoning, visiting shut-ins, serving on a committee, baking cookies, teaching Sunday School, praying for the pastor, the church and the members, chairing the Ad Board, being President of UMW or UMM; maybe your gift is friendliness. . . .

Each one of us is important to the church, Christ's body, no matter who we are. Whether we are ordained ministers or those who greet visitors with a friendly smile, we are all needed to make the church complete so it can be what God intends it to be. Each of us is necessary or our Maker wouldn't have included us in Creation.[7]

LOOKING BACK . . . TO MOVE FORWARD

Ruth Palmer and Robert M. Reed

The last decade brought severe change to Houston. The economic slump resulted in lost jobs as well as lost homes and broken families.

During 1990 the world changed too with voices around the globe joining in a cry for freedom. The map of the world changed. Wesley Community Center continued the pace it began years ago. It reached out to those who were hurt most . . . to those whose lives were shaken . . . to those who wanted freedom from the imprisonment of poverty. We went to them—into their communities and into their homes—to help and encourage families.

Wesley, which has quietly served Houston's Near North Side for over 85 years, now provides assistance from six additional centers located throughout the Houston metropolitan area. We assisted over 35,000 people last year.

Families are being nurtured during their difficult times. We have learned that if we want to protect a child, we must help every member of the family in order to create security, stability and peace at home. . . .

With God's help and yours, Wesley will continue to be the hand that helps people win their struggle for freedom.[8]

TAKE TIME

Ethelou Talbert

I do not consider myself to have fully grasped it even now. But I do concentrate on this: I leave the past behind and with hands outstretched to whatever lies ahead I go straight for the goal—my reward the honor of my high calling by God in Christ Jesus. (Phil. 3:13-14, Phillips)

The past is over and done. What good is it to look back? It does not pay to look back unless you can profit from the experience of the past.

Recently I took time to look at myself. These are some of the questions I asked:

Who am I?

Where am I?

What am I doing for myself and the good of humankind?

Where do I hope to go?

Only you can answer these questions for you. Only I can answer these questions for me. The *now* is today. We must live it to its fullest. We must do what we really want and need to do. The possibilities of today are ours.

The future will break forth anew—the *New Age*. Will we be ready to face a new day? We must shape ourselves in the present to live in the future. We are the guides of the possibilities and potentialities of the future.

Stop, take an Inventory of your life. Are you heading in the direction you want to go? Are you who you want to be? Take time to look at yourself.[9]

Joyce Alford

Christine Bethke

Ellen Brubaker

*Sharon Brown
Christopher*

Judith Craig

Charlene Kammerer

Leontine Kelly

Susan Morrison

Kathy Sage

Nancy Grissom Self

Glenda Thomas

Patricia Toschak

CHAPTER 14

HONORING ONE ANOTHER
WITH OUR STORIES

Authority and Mutual Ministry Among
United Methodist Clergywomen in the
Last Decade of the Twentieth Century

BARBARA B. TROXELL

In the last third of the twentieth century, certain United Methodist clergywomen said yes to the call of the church to become district superintendents and bishops. The way was led by Evelyn Kandakai of Liberia in the
mid-sixties, followed in 1967 by Margaret Hendrichsen. After serving several rural churches, including a seven-point charge, the Reverend Hendrichsen was appointed superintendent of the Bangor (now Northern)
District of the Maine Annual Conference, the first woman superintendent
in The Methodist Church within the continental United States. Then, in
1980, after serving as superintendent of the Grand Traverse District of the
West Michigan Annual Conference, Marjorie Swank Matthews was elected
bishop, the first woman in any large Christian denomination so to serve.

Now in the summer of 1992, the number of bishops has grown to eight
and the number of women who have been or are superintendents exceeds
eighty. Of the five bishops one, Marjorie Matthews, has died, after serving
a four-year term and then moving into retirement. Leontine Kelly, the
only African American woman bishop, retired from the episcopacy in
1988, but is actively teaching and preaching in the San Francisco Bay area
and many other parts of the world. The active bishops and the large
majority of district superintendents are Caucasian, with three African
American, two Latino American, and one Native American woman serving
in this office; in addition there are five women ministering as superintendents in Central conferences in Africa and the Philippines. The bishops
are serving in the North Central, Northeastern, South Central, and Western jurisdictions. There are now women superintendents in every jurisdiction, though the first three were in the Northeastern, North Central, and
Western respectively.

What vocational vision has called us forth to such positions of authority
in the church? And once there, how have we nurtured our relationship

with God whom we have covenanted to love with all our heart and soul and strength and mind? What does it mean to "take authority" while encouraging mutual ministry of laity and clergy? How do we continue to deepen our special friendships, even as we move from one appointment to another where we are called to care for all sorts of persons and, in some cases, for an entire district or episcopal area of churches? How do our forms of spirituality, our ways of taking authority, and our friendships help or hinder us as women committed to justice and peace in God's world?

These are questions which addressed me time and again while I was a district superintendent in the late 1970s and early 1980s in northern California, and which continue to challenge my ministry. In 1990 I chose to ask these questions of twelve clergy sisters who are or were bishops, district superintendents, and general agency staff with a particular focus on the ministries of women.[1] Each of those interviewed has served or is now serving as pastor of a local church.

The responses shed insightful light on the lives and ministries of United Methodist clergywomen, who are "shaping the church"[2] as we move into the next millennium. Diverse ways of prayer and making connections, honest grappling with issues of authority and mutuality, and the healing power of trustworthy and supportive friendships undergird these women in positions of oversight within the church.

But in addition to insight into *their* ministries, these responses give voice to important concerns, possibilities, and challenges confronting the whole church. It is my hope that the whole people of God, lay and clergy, women and men, may be strengthened in our ministries of support and accountability through attention to these lively critical issues.

NURTURING OUR RELATIONSHIP WITH GOD

Foundational to empowering leadership is the affirmation of the source of our authority to lead. How do we nurture our fundamental relationship with the Source and Ground and Author of life? The bishops, superintendents, and former agency staff who were interviewed reflect many of the diverse ways of spiritual nurture of the more than 3,800 ordained women within The United Methodist Church.

For some, the traditional spiritual disciplines of regular prayer, meditation, Bible and other devotional reading, journaling, corporate worship, and relationship with a spiritual director are primary means of growth in faith. Solitude, silence, and slowing down, whether such rhythms are found at a retreat center, at a favorite lakeside home, at a spinning wheel, in reading the morning paper, or in daily quiet time, are reported by these women to be essential to their well-being.[3] In addition, those who knew Bishop Marjorie Matthews well, both in Michigan and in Wisconsin, tell of her "introspective listening, quiet reflection and internal dialogue with God about relationships with people and issues."[4] Many also spoke of walking outdoors, physical exercise, and the nourishment offered in bodies of water and other elements of the natural world.

One woman reflected on the value for her of four of Wesley's "means of grace": searching the Scriptures, prayer, Eucharist, and Christian conference. She connects these with feminist and world-embracing spiritual disciplines, as rich embodiments of the processes of word, meditation, celebration, and community.[5]

People are important resources for renewal: as gifted companions or as trusted cabinet members, who support and hold us accountable, and with whom we can play and pray, weep and laugh.[6] It is with such sisters and brothers—family members, friends, colleagues—that "Christian conference" occurs.

In addition, persons encountered in international, multicultural circumstances afford deep and broad spiritual nurture. One bishop, in her daily reading of the newspaper, finds herself vividly linked with those suffering and struggling to be faithful in other parts of the world. These women in leadership discover fresh depth in their faith and in their perspective on ministry through international travel, study, and mission. Spirituality, for each of these leaders within United Methodism, is strongly intertwined with and informed by social responsibility.

TAKING AUTHORITY AND ENCOURAGING MUTUALITY

When asked the question, "What does it mean to you to 'take authority' when we also want to encourage and model mutuality?" Leontine Kelly immediately responded:

> I don't see any dichotomy between authority and mutuality; if one is secure in God and in oneself, one seeks mutual ministry. Without losing authority, Jesus shared, and cared for people, and inspired people to take responsibility for caring themselves. "Get up and walk!" "You feed them!" In authoritative leadership we have an opportunity to model the joy that comes from mutuality.[7]

Bishop Kelly's response was echoed, in tones borne of their own unique experiences, by the other women interviewed. Their authority is rooted in the gospel authority given to *all* the people of God in their baptism. We live from the inner authority of God, who creates, redeems, sustains. Ordained ones, with a certain authority of office, are ever accountable to the community of faith, which has confirmed the call and selected them to be in positions of particular leadership.

One former superintendent notes that since authority is often linked with respect for the superintending office, it is essential to prepare well, to engage in adequate study, to model spiritual maturity and the continuing faith journey, and to show respect and appreciation for the life journeys of others.[8]

Furthermore, authority of office that is recognized by others as legitimate must be grounded, as one bishop states, "in respect for the autonomous authority and value of the other over whom you happen to be given authority."[9] One's authority within a supervisory position, whether as bishop, district superintendent, parish pastor, or active layperson, offers the possibility of providing space for prophetic and pastoral ministry to happen among all sorts of people. "To take authority means both encouraging folk who can provide the leadership in ministry we need and giving them the space to have that ministry happen."[10]

In reflecting on numerous regional training events of the Commission on the Status and Role of Women in which yellow stoles were distributed in remembrance of our baptism, former executive Nancy Grissom Self comments:

All of those stoles are a way of extending the invitation to take authority . . . to create what may, without your knowing it, be pivotal in somebody else's life. . . . You never know what God's interventions will be. . . . You feel like a midwife; you don't feel you've had anything to do with the birthing; you've only been there to help out.[11]

Another former agency executive, Kathy Sage, focuses the question toward a goal: "Take authority, for what and to do what?" She then replies: "To live free from the addictions of patriarchal culture and to be about creating a new culture that is consistent with feminist values." For Sage, significant exploration of co-dependency and addiction has helped her wrestle with the concept of authority. From her own experience as well as that of other clergywomen in their "wilderness wandering about questions of authority," she has discovered the importance of "cataloguing our compromises and addictions . . . [which become] cultural numbing agents." To do so, persons need to be in relationship with "other people who are willing to be accountable and to struggle and to support one another" in this process of acknowledgment and of truth telling.[12]

Being put on a pedestal by others is the experience of some of the women in positions of authority. One former superintendent (now parish pastor) struggles with the confusion that seems to arise when one manifests a collegial style of ministry, and then, apparently suddenly, one must take authority strongly over a given issue or personnel situation. She also speaks of the difficulty encountered when people project onto their pastor (or superintendent or bishop) the responsibility for the distinctive style or direction of a local church or district or conference. Projection in its multitude of forms requires heightened awareness and consciousness among all clergy.[13]

Superintendents serving in cabinets led by women bishops tell of their bishops modeling mutuality in cabinet meetings, inviting processes of consultation or discernment[14] at decision-making times, and being deeply pastoral with the clergy and laity of the conferences where they serve. At the same time, it is evident that each of the women interviewed, whether bishop or superintendent or agency executive, knows the meaning of clear decision making. Clarity and decisiveness are enhanced by the active listening and consulting practiced well by these women in authority.

Clergywomen in positions of prominent leadership understand that their authority of office gives them the power to aid other women and men to claim their own authority for ministry. Thus is mutuality served, as the gifts of all are evoked.

FRIENDSHIP AS THE FABRIC OF MUTUALITY

Our spiritual disciplines, our ways of taking authority, and our encouragement of mutual ministry are enhanced and encouraged by healthy friendships. To the question of how they continue to deepen their special friendships while they are in positions of authority often far from an earlier home base, many of the respondents began by describing the values of healthy friendships. They also spoke of the difficulties within some friendships once the power dynamics of role had changed.

My hypothesis that friendships are extremely important, intense, and life-sustaining for clergywomen was supported. But important nuances within this assumption were heard, which will require another time and place for focus alone on the subject of clergywomen's friendships.[15]

For each of the women interviewed, without exception, the nurturing of their friendships is a high priority. Supportive friends in their personal lives and in their professional ministries provide much of the human undergirding needed for them to move toward being the whole people these women desire to be.

One of the bishops defines friendship as "a relationship that has in it elements of intimacy, vulnerability, mutual risk, willingness to do more than the ordinary courtesies and kindnesses, trust, truth-telling, loving in spite of."[16] A superintendent speaks of the importance of "friendships that have stayed consistent and that are able to handle confidentiality and honesty."[17]

Another woman refers to friendship as part of her understanding of "home," which for her is now "no longer dependent upon geography [for I have] come to a strong sense of being home in God which transcends all geographical limitations."[18] She continues to see her friends as "a global network of people and relationships [who] are there with words of support and encouragement . . ., an element of grace that comes as such a gift."

Distinctions were made between long-term friends, who know each others' stories from early days in ministry or even from college, and those who are friends of recent acquaintance. The friends who have long histories with us know and honor our stories, even as we know and honor theirs. They remind us of our roots and of who we are as human beings, children of God and part of the *laos,* the whole people of God. When because of office others put us on pedestals, or when because of insecurity we engage in heavily controlling behavior, these long-term friends stand with us and help us remember who we are. Again and again came the grateful affirmation: Because they know our stories, with love they hold us accountable to our humanity before God and with one another.

Personality differences (of extraversion or introversion, for example) have led some women to be more expansive and others more contained in their friendships. Some who travel widely encounter numerous "friends" throughout the nation and the world. For others, these are "colleagues and acquaintances," with the term "friends" being reserved for those with whom there is more mutuality, a two-way relationship. Whatever the understanding of the circle or circles of friendship, whether the clergy-woman is single or married, it is significant that regular phone calls, notes, letters, visits, opportunities to meet are deliberately sought as essential to nurturing these valued relationships.

In probing the question further concerning friendship issues among "United Methodist clergywomen in general across the United States," I heard comments about the pain of isolation and mistrust: "I don't think we realize enough our essential need for a safety net . . . I wish for more candor. . . . Everywhere I go across the country, [clergywomen] are hungry for, longing for, anguishing about not feeling connected. And yet, they don't trust each other enough to say, 'I'm just not good at that; please help me.'"[19] Some interviewees spoke eloquently of the importance of acknowledging the sin (or addiction) of perfectionism; and of needing the support of others who will walk with them through that process of truth telling. "Friendship helps you not to be a paragon."[20] Friends honor one another and hold one another accountable with their stories.

Several of the women recalled differences in attitudes, by some whom they considered friends, after they were elected or appointed to their position as bishop or superintendent. They tried to deal with such situations by honestly confronting their own discomfort while holding to the awareness of their roles and offices. Their respect for the confidentiality of the cabinet came into conflict for some in their relationships with other clergywomen and clergymen.

One superintendent speaks appreciatively of the support given her by the other clergywomen of the conference, even as she has learned the difficult balance necessitated by her position.

> There have been moments when I have felt there have been obstacles to nurturing friendship, partly because of the level and type of information I'm suddenly party to. . . . It's a continuing challenge to know how to shift the particular role that you are called to on any given day. Yet because it is important to me to be a friend, I do feel like it's possible . . . [though at times] it's really difficult.[21]

FRIENDSHIP: MODEL FOR PARISH MINISTRY?

There are differences of opinion on whether friendship can be a model for parish ministry. Many affirm that the parish should be a community of friends: trusting, supportive, accountable, celebrative, nonpossessive, nonmanipulative friends. Yet parishes are sometimes like dysfunctional families, with manipulation, possessiveness, competition, and jealousy present among the members. These and other factors lead some interviewees to find "hospitality" to be a fuller, more realistic, and more inclusive metaphor for relationships in local churches.

The question of whether a pastor can be in mutual friendships with parishioners brought a variety of responses. The pastor (or bishop or superintendent) is to be available to people, to listen well to them, to be vulnerable with them. Several women interviewed understand clergywomen as less apt to go with the traditional advice that the pastor should not form friendships with parishioners. Part of the forming of friendships occurs not only because most pastors are "people-oriented," but also because in the sharing of common values and interests friendships begin to grow. Yet as one superintendent says: "It is not the kind of friendship where you burden them with your own personal matters. I would see doing that much more with colleagues. There may be rare exceptions, but by and large, if you are going to be their pastor, then it is not a mutual friendship."[22]

A healthy model of friendship in a parish setting includes an invitation for all to grow, and for the pastor not to be using parishioners to bolster her or his own self-esteem or need to be needed.[23] And when a pastor leaves a parish (or a district or an episcopal area), "You have to find a way to send them (even your friends) towards the new pastor and to keep your friendship out of that parish life."[24]

How one remains faithful to a particular role in a given time in one's life history, while continuing to deepen friendship and encourage mutuality in ministry, is a continuing life challenge.

FORMS OF SPIRITUALITY, AUTHORITY, AND FRIENDSHIP IN RELATION TO SOCIAL RESPONSIBILITY

Our relationships with God, with friends, and with positions of authority radically inform our commitments to justice seeking and peace making. Which is to say, "at root" the clergywomen who are official leaders in The United Methodist Church understand social responsibility to be integral to their vocation. "My call is to live a life that becomes the Gospel and has everything to do with integrity. . . . My way of being in the world flows from one Source, God, who calls me toward the living of a vision of life as God intends it to be."[25] One bishop's words resonate with those of others who use phrases like "holistic," "balance," "opportunity to open doors and to make connections," "part of the fabric of our lives as Christians."

Several interviewees speak of involvement in particular community ministries in their various appointments.[26] Others relate opportunities afforded them to speak and lead in ways that promote peace making and justice seeking, through preaching, leading retreats, marching in protest or affirmation, and in the daily living out of their ministries of oversight. "When I'm at my best in the exercise of authority," says Bishop Craig, "I think that is a peace-waging way of being. . . . [It is] the opportunity to open doors and to make connections." Bishop Christopher speaks of "the vision of the Gospel way of life" being the "safeguard against taking of authority inappropriately in a way that is ultimately unjust."[27]

Susan Morrison poses a real dilemma: "How do I model that I am the bishop for everyone, and yet speak out on things that I care deeply about [in a way] that won't cut off the fact of being bishop for everyone?"[28] A continuing tension for all in leadership, this question poses one of the issues most prominent for clergywomen. There is a strong desire and inclination to hear and relate with all sorts and conditions of persons. Modeling the open inclusivity of the gospel is evident among these clergywomen in positions of authority; it was named in one way or another by almost every woman interviewed.

In addition, each leader has deep convictions borne of her understanding of the biblical witness, and informed by the tradition of the church, her own experience, and the discernment arising from these sources. How does one listen with open ears and heart to the plurality of voices, even to those with whose positions one disagrees, so that others know that they are heard and supported by their leaders in the exercise of *their* ministries? Such listening, such hearing into speech, is part of doing justice.

At the same time, calling others to accountability, which may be perceived as a disruption of the peace, also is the responsibility of persons in leadership. The tension continues and will not easily be resolved. Justice seeking, peace making, and social responsibility inevitably involve conflict.

Women clergy leaders within United Methodism are alert to this dynamic and wrestle with it in their ministries with vision and with courage.

CONCLUSION

Women clergy in United Methodism in the 1990s are part of a highly diverse community. No longer are we so small in number that we can make common cause with one another just because we are women. The nine hundred women (and some invited men) who participated in the fifth United Methodist Clergywomen's Consultation in August 1991 lived for five days with this reality. We are diverse racially, ethnically, internationally, politically, theologically, culturally, physically, spiritually. We celebrate and struggle with our differences.

The plurality of perspectives expressed at the Consultation reflects the pluralism of the entire denomination. When the stories were told publicly, some were missing; except for a brief prayer litany, the journeys of lesbian clergywomen, as well as of women who have suffered sexual abuse, were not lifted in corporate worship. Deep pain was expressed in smaller groupings; and many did not recognize signs of hope. The pain of isolation, division, and disagreement among United Methodist clergywomen is real and can no longer be denied or ignored.

How do ordained women leaders within the denomination address the divisions and the pain among us? Though this was not a direct question in the interviews, several interviewees reflected on this concern. Several urge clergywomen to remember how we came to be where we are, "out of our mutual exercise of power for and on behalf of each other."[29] Others remind us that we are in danger of being numbed by the expectations of a church and a society that continues to perpetrate and perpetuate patriarchy. In this perspective, we are called to speak truth to ourselves and to one another in love and respect.

Part of the truth that must be spoken concerns a fresh exploration of the meaning of servant ministry and self-giving, as well as self-affirmation and empowerment. Jealousy and resentment of those who are in leadership is being felt among clergywomen. An apparent inability to hear others' stories without feeling threatened in one's own is evident. As one of the interviewees stated a year after the interview: "Surely I can make compassionate connections with the herstories out of which lack of trust, confusion about servanthood, and edges of selfishness are arising, but . . . I often feel a lack of hard, clear, mutually self-less searching that will be necessary for us [if we are to become] agents of change in the church."[30] A former agency staff member and a bishop both speak in their interviews of the pain of clergywomen who either leave the active ministry or are seriously considering such a move, because they feel they cannot be heard or received in the church as they are. Their stories are not honored. Yet these are some of the women who are the most courageous and gifted and visionary.[31]

The women interviewed are concerned not to be co-opted themselves. They expresss a strong need to be held accountable to the vision of the gospel by family and friends and colleagues. They desire continuing grounding in their relationships with God, with friends, with family, with one another. Would we be bearers of the Good News it is essential that we "continue to honor each other with our stories" and to listen with discernment to the stories of all the people whose lives touch ours.

DOCUMENTS

HONORING ONE ANOTHER WITH OUR STORIES

The documents consist primarily of quotations from interviews with twelve clergywomen held in summer and fall 1990. Excerpts from two articles on the women bishops are also included. Documents are organized around the five questions asked in the interviews and the additional question about "other clergywomen" raised with some respondents.

INTERVIEW QUESTIONS

1. How do you nurture your relationship with God?
2. What does it mean to you to "take authority," when we also want to encourage and model mutuality?
3. How do you continue to deepen your special friendships, even as you have moved among various appointments and now are appointed a bishop (superintendent, general agency staff person) of the whole United Methodist Church and are assigned to a particular area which is not your home area?
4. Do you see friendship as a model for parish ministry? If so, how would you describe such a model? If not, why not?
5. How do your forms of spirituality, your friendships, your ways of taking authority help or hinder you as a woman committed to justice and peace in God's world?
6. What is your impression of the ways that United Methodist clergywomen, in general, reflect on issues of spiritual nurture, authority-mutuality, and friendship?

IDENTIFYING THE INTERVIEWEES

Joyce Alford is superintendent of the South East District of the Wisconsin Annual Conference. She has served as a parish pastor; prior to her entry into ordained ministry she was director of nursing and a professor of nursing.

Christine Bethke is pastor of First United Methodist Church, Oshkosh, Wisconsin. Her earlier appointments include being the director of pastoral care at a United Methodist retirement center.

Ellen Brubaker is pastor of Aldersgate United Methodist Church, Grand Rapids, Michigan. She was superintendent of the Grand Rapids District of the West Michigan Annual Conference. She has served several parish appointments.

Sharon Brown Christopher is bishop of the Minnesota Area of The United Methodist Church. She has served parishes in Wisconsin, was a district superintendent 1980–1986, and was assistant to the bishop in the Wisconsin Annual Conference.

Judith Craig is bishop of West Ohio and was episcopal leader of the Michigan Area 1984–1992, at the time of these interviews. Judith Craig has served in parishes, as pastor and as Christian educator, in Ohio and Connecticut. She was East Ohio Conference Council on Ministries director, 1980–1984.

Charlene Kammerer is superintendent of the Tallahassee District, Florida Annual Conference. She served several parishes prior to her appointment to the superintendency.

Leontine Kelly, bishop in the retired relationship, was episcopal leader of the San Francisco Area, 1984–1988. She has served parishes in Virginia and in San Francisco. She was executive of the Section on Evangelism, Board of Discipleship.

Susan Morrison is bishop of the Philadelphia Area. She has served as parish pastor, district superintendent, council director in the Baltimore Conference , and missionary in Brazil.

Kathy Sage is a writer and retreat leader, living in the Southwest. Formerly she was Director, Support Systems and Spiritual Formation of The Division of Ordained Ministry of the Board of Higher Education and Ministry of The United Methodist Church.

Nancy Grissom Self is pastor, University United Methodist Church, Redlands, California. For eighteen years she was a member of the Executive Secretariat of the General Commission on the Status and Role of Women of the United Methodist Church. Earlier she was a campus pastor.

Glenda Thomas is pastor, Almaden Hills United Methodist Church, San José, California. From 1984 to 1990 she was superintendent of the Delta District, California-Nevada Conference. She has held several parish appointments.

Patricia Toschak is pastor of Sunrise United Methodist Church in Mound View, Minnesota. From 1985 to 1991 she was superintendent of the Northwest District of the Minnesota Annual Conference. She has served several parish appointments.

A. NURTURING YOUR RELATIONSHIP WITH GOD

1. *"How UM Women Bishops Center Their Spiritual Lives."* In February 1990, *The Flyer,* newsletter of the General Commission on the Status and Role of Women in The United Methodist Church, invited four women bishops to share their individual approaches to spiritual renewal. Excerpts from this article follow:[32]

[Sharon Brown Christopher:] I have developed a rhythm for myself between being engaged in ministry and *doing,* and being apart for awhile and *being.* [I] spend time every morning in reflection. . . . I begin with scripture and other reading, then move into meditation and prayer, and then journaling. . . . About once a quarter I spend two days in retreat at a retreat center. . . . I have been involved in some form of spiritual direction with someone with whom I can talk about my own soul. . . . The rhythm is enhanced by an exercise program. . . .

Another thing that nourishes me is reading. . . . I continue this rhythm with the recognition that it is imperative that I do so not only for myself, but for the sake of the church and the world.

[Judith Craig:] My best corporate renewal time is cabinet devotions. . . . It's some of the best proclamation, invitation, prayer time I have anywhere. . . . Cabinets do work that causes them to recognize how very dependent we are on the energy that guides the blessing, the permission of God. . . . There's a bonding that's born of a desperate dependence on God that becomes very rich to all of us. . . . I have some intimate friends who nurture my spirit: Sometimes we sit and read scripture together, sometimes we pray together, and sometimes we just play together. . . .

My most intensive prayer time is when I'm driving . . . [in] the long hours in the car alone. . . . I find myself looking for the theological significance in almost anything I hear and do. . . . It is the grace of God I go looking for. . . . And it's abundant.

[Leontine Kelly:] I find the morning a deeply spiritual time for me . . . [keeping] the hours of 5 to 7 a.m. for this kind of centering.

. . . My quiet time in the morning is a beautiful time, a time of beginning and reflecting, a good prayer time. . . . I also try to do some formal study at that time. . . .

. . . I seek a body of water when I'm deeply troubled. Water provides a deep spiritual wealth for me.

. . . My spirituality comes from the beginning of a new day and the need to know that it's clear and challenging and redeeming and forgiving.

[Susan Morrison:] I do my spiritual resourcing throughout the day. One of the major ways is in solitude because I'm often alone. . . . I'm one who pays a fair amount of attention to what's happening in the world. . . . I also read the sports page. . . . It's part of my way of being playful and helps put other things in perspective. . . .

As I reflect on the question of spiritual renewal, I realize that people are one of my resources.

2. Humor and Play as Spiritual Nurture. In May 1990, Sharon Zimmerman Rader interviewed bishops Brown Christopher, Craig, and Morrison for *WellSprings: A Journal of United Methodist Clergywomen.* The chief emphases of the interview, published in the fall of 1990, were on the formative experiences of the bishops and their participation in "shaping the church." Excerpts related to the elements of humor and play follow:[33]

[Morrison:] There's a sense of celebrating the absurdity of life. There's nothing we do that needs to be taken so seriously that grace can't move. The Spirit moves. Silence, solitude and play: that is a strange mixture, but it's part of how I move.

[Brown Christopher:] I want to be nonchalant . . . about the penultimate matters with which I'm called to deal. To do this, I need to be alone every day. But community is also important. Play is important.

[Craig:] Humor keeps balance for me. . . . It helps with reality checks. In the middle of the worst moments in an annual conference, it is humor that draws me back to the center.

3. Wesley's Means of Grace Related to Christian-Feminist Spiritual Nurture. In correspondence a year after her interview, Kathy Sage outlines a parallel pattern of spiritual nurture:[34]

At a meeting focused on the Wesleyan "means of grace" as a model for nurturing spiritual growth, I realized that while the traditional disciplines have been helpful for me, I wanted to see if there was a similar pattern in terms of feminist spiritual disciplines. The pattern would be:

Means of Grace (Wesleyan)	*Spiritual Nurture (Christian Feminist)*
1. Searching the Scripture	1. Sharing our Stories
2. Eucharist	2. Celebrating our Life Stories
3. Prayer	3. Centering and Meditation
4. Christian Conference	4. Community

Searching the Scripture has been the way we have come to hear the Biblical stories and their meaning for us. It is important for me, also, to listen to the stories of women through poetry, fiction, women's music, and feminist theologians.

Eucharist connects me with the global church. I remember going to a Mass in Nepal and feeling an overwhelmingly positive sense of the universality of the Church. I didn't understand a word of the local language, the symbols incorporated indigenous art, and yet I was at home in the liturgy and connected through it to the people of Nicaragua, the monks of Gethsemane, and every other place I share the Eucharist. At the same time, I need to find ways to celebrate the passages and events of women's lives. I need to participate in and help shape feminist/womanist liturgy and celebrations . . . [which include] concerns of a global vision for women.

I would make less of a delineation between *prayer* as a traditional means of grace and what I need to nurture my spirituality. . . . Different forms of prayer have been important, such as meditation, centering, and use of a daily office. Feminist contributions . . . include the global perspective and the intentional inclusion of the holistic in wellness.

Less familiar is the Wesleyan understanding of *Christian Conference.* I need accountability and community in my spiritual journey. I've been part of a spiritual direction support group of men and women for eight years. We meet twice a year for three days at a time and are accountable to one another for our spiritual growth. When there is accountability and intentionality community can really flourish.

B. TAKING AUTHORITY WHILE MODELING MUTUALITY

4. Authority Rooted in the Gospel. Sharon Brown Christopher speaks for many of the interviewees when she states that authority begins in one's life in God, signed in baptism and confirmation, and continues to be explored in discernment:[35]

Taking authority begins with the authority of the Gospel, which is signed in baptism and confirmation. . . . Within the broad umbrella of the authority of the Gospel, the church sets apart some folks to assume different roles and relationships to authority. . . . The taking of authority must be done in the context of the Gospel way of life, and in the context of individual and communal discernment. That becomes the safeguard against taking authority inappropriately in ways that are ultimately unjust. . . . There are two parts to authority: one is based on obedience to God (obedience at root means "to listen"); listening becomes the key to the exercise of that authority, listening to the undercurrent themes as well as listening to the lone quiet voice that sometimes announces God's truth. In addition to obedience, to the listening to God in the midst of life, there must also be the willingness to act or to step out.

5. Respect for Others and for the Office. Several women understand authority to include respect for others and for the office to which they have been called. Excerpts from certain interviews follow:

[Judith Craig:] Authority is grounded in respect for the autonomous author-ity and value of the other over whom you happen to be given authority. Authority always begins out of mutual respect. It has to do with being willing to be vulnerable, and being secure enough to be vulnerable.[36]

[Patricia Toschak:] Working with weaving and fibers over the last three years, a new image has begun to emerge which has abiding strength to it: that is, of many vessels filled with energy, each one a unique gift to be shared, connected by an intertwining cord. In this intricate web, each must assume and exercise their responsibility for the task or role given them. I try to encourage mutuality by respecting each person's gifts and role, affirming their work and calling them to accountability.[37]

[Glenda Thomas:] Authority has something to do with respect for the way one conducts herself in the office [to which she's been appointed]; to do a sloppy job in such positions is the quickest way to undermine your own authority. Thus I try: to model study and solid preparation; to talk about faith; to reflect seriously on my own spiritual growth; and to show respect and appreciation for other people's spirituality and their lives. . . . Mutuality is real for we are all in this ministry together. . . . I saw everything I did, as a superintendent, as a way to improve others' ministries.[38]

6. *Authority Encouraging Mutuality.* Statements from several interviewees affirm that the authority of their offices or roles facilitated the mutual ministry of laity and clergy alike.

[Nancy Grissom Self:] Taking authority for the ministry given to you in your baptism . . . [means] to extend the invitation to take authority. It is a "come on in, the water's fine" kind of invitation. . . . Another way to take authority is to say to someone . . . you have my permission to do what you are doing, even though it may not be the party-line. To take authority to create, with-out your knowing it, what may be pivotal in somebody else's life. . . . We've hardly ever done one of those regional training events [sponsored by the Commission on the Status and Role of Women] that somebody hasn't come to a new self-understanding of her relationship to God and the authority she has to move into something. That's breathtaking. You feel like a midwife. You don't feel like you've had anything to do with the birthing, you've only been there to help it out.[39]

[Susan Morrison:] For me to take authority means to provide space for prophetic and pastoral ministry to happen. That means both encouraging folk who can provide the kind of leadership we need in ministry, enabling them to be in the places where that can happen, and giving them the space in which that leadership can happen. It also means protecting space for them.[40]

[Charlene Kammerer:] It is important both to be in authority through your role and yet be able to listen to people with compassion and care. To attend to people in meetings, to follow through and be available to people over a period of time are expressions of mutuality within Christian authority. It means to stand with someone, both male and female, in their own ministries.[41]

[Joyce Alford, Christine Bethke:] Bishop Marjorie Matthews constantly sought opportunities to integrate mutuality and authority in her work with local congregations. She had the ability to draw people into open and honest relationships.[42]

7. *Reflections by Others on Authority and Mutuality in the Ministry of Women Bishops.* At the suggestion of one of the bishops interviewed, I talked with several women district superintendents who had served in cabinets with women bishops. Excerpts from their responses follow:

[Sharon Brown Christopher:] I saw Marjorie Matthews demonstrate mutuality in authority. I remember her coming to the first cabinet meeting in Wisconsin, and in a very quiet yet sure way laying out for us how she understood herself in relationship to the episcopacy and to us, from a biblical context. She was announcing before us her willingness to assume the authority that the church had given her to be the episcopal leader in the church and especially in Wisconsin. At the same time, as we worked together I sensed a highly consultative process. She was eager to hear from all in the decision-making processes.[43]

[Ellen Brubaker:] For Judy Craig, the role of bishop seems to be very important; yet it is difficult for her because the system has made it a position without adequate accountability. She does listen very well, and she is wonderfully creative. . . . She has asked her cabinet to hold her accountable.[44]

[Glenda Thomas:] Leontine Kelly was clear from the beginning that because she was bishop, she had to be clear. She could make hard decisions and would stand firm on them; when such decisions affected your life in a different way she stood behind you. In terms of mutuality, she was very pastoral with her cabinet. She cared about all of me, not just my professional side. Furthermore, she was willing to hear pros and cons, even though the decision to be taken would be hers. Very occasionally her strong pastoral heart would give her trouble with sticking to carefully considered administrative decisions.[45]

[Patricia Toschak:] Sharon Brown Christopher takes authority with great gentleness—what I would define as "controlled strength." She is clear in herself about the discipline out of which she must work both scripturally and in terms of polity. She seeks to understand as fully as possible the person or persons she is working with, so that she is sensitive to their perspectives and their hope. She then helps them to clarify and to understand where their position conflicts or meshes with the big picture. . . . She is not afraid to take her time in discernment. She models mutuality in a great variety of ways.[46]

C. IMPORTANCE OF FRIENDSHIP PERSONALLY AND AS A MODEL FOR MINISTRY

8. Definitions of Healthy Friendships. Two of the bishops began with definitions of healthy friendships, in response to the questions on friendship:

[Judith Craig:] Friendship is a relationship that has in it elements of intimacy, vulnerability, mutual risk, willingness to do more than the ordinary courtesies and kindnesses—trust, truth-telling, loving in spite of.[47]

[Sharon Brown Christopher:] "Home" is key term for me as I think about friendship. . . . I've really come to a strong sense of being home in God, which transcends all geographical limitations and means that anywhere I go geographically home is available to me. I have a real sense of home in the church, and know that I can go anywhere and the church is there. . . . I have a strong sense of home in my marriage, which is an anchor point and centering point for me. I have a sense of home in my friendships. . . . My friends are a global network of people and relationships not bound by geographical location. They are there with words of support and encouragement, elements of grace.[48]

9. Friends Supporting Us and Holding Us Accountable. The two former agency executives saw their friendships enhanced through their work connections. They, with others, describe their friends as both supportive and holding them accountable.

[Kathy Sage:] Rather than be a hindrance to friendship, work in the church facilitated the contacts with persons who became significant friends or colleagues. Most of my friends are in one way or another spiritual friends, *compañeros*. . . . The travel [of the job] got me to friends. Friends have come out of working together on projects that were important.[49]

[Nancy Grissom Self:] One of the things about a general agency position is that I can connect up with people when I travel. . . . I also try to make my house a place where people will come for nurture. . . . Also, friendship helps you not to be a paragon.[50]

10. Difficulties in Friendship While in Positions of Authority. Charlene Kammerer's description of the difficulties is echoed by several others in their interviews.

[Kammerer:] There have been times when I have known obstacles to nurturing friendship because of the level and type of information I am party to. . . . It's a continuing challenge to know how to shift the particular role that I am called to on any given day. It is not always possible to be in the role of friend. I have had some painful experiences around this issue.[51]

11. Friendship as a Model for Parish Ministry? There were differences of opinion around this question. Two views are reflected here, in four excerpts from interviews.

[Judith Craig:] A healthy model of friendship in a parish would have to do with relationships where the pastor is able to be playmate and proclaimer, able to weep with and scold, and allow others to weep with and scold in return. . . . To the degree that stays a fairly clean two-way street without becoming maudlin or self-centered or a manipulative kind of self-revelation, I think that can be healthy. . . . I don't think you have to play the old role that you can't be friends with your parishioners. I think you have to learn how you draw the line when you leave, and you have to find a way to send them toward the new pastor and keep your friendship out of that parish life.[52]

[Leontine Kelly:] Yes, I think friendship can be a model for ministry. . . . I think pastors should be prepared to love people and to receive love from people. It's got to be mutual. It can't work if it isn't. There will be people you are closer to, of course. Jesus called all twelve of his disciples "friends." Yet he had the close ones in that small circle, Peter and James and John.[53]

[Charlene Kammerer:] I am not sure if friendship would be a model. . . . I am more in tune with the image or metaphor of hospitality. My hospitality images are very rich. I see hospitality as broader and more inclusive.[54]

[Glenda Thomas:] I do see it as a model as long as you have alongside friendship the fact that you are always the pastor. What that has meant in my experience is being very available to people for whatever they want to share. At the same time it is not the kind of friendship where you burden [parishioners] with all of your personal problems. . . . By and large, if you are going to be their pastor, then it is not a completely mutual friendship.[55]

D. RELATION OF SPIRITUALITY, AUTHORITY-MUTUALITY, AND FRIENDSHIP WITH SOCIAL RESPONSIBILITY

12. Enhancing Integrity in One's Calling. Sharon Brown Christopher names integrity and embodiment as that which is enhanced through nurtured spirituality, a sense of authority in relation to mutual ministry, and the accountability of healthy friendships.

Remember the baptismal vow that parents make for their children that says: "do you promise to live before your child a life that becomes the Gospel?" I feel my call is to live a life that becomes the Gospel. It has to do with integrity and embodying the congruity between my words and my actions and my relationships. Somehow my way of being in the world flows from one Source, God, [who calls me] towards the living of the vision of life as God intends it to be.[56]

13. Socially Responsible Authority. Judith Craig speaks for many of the interviewees when she sees "making connections" as central to social responsibility, to justice and peace making.

If you use the concept of *shalom,* and the wellbeing of the other as the drive . . . and authority is exercised out of that, I understand my authority as opportunity to make connections for you, so that you can be the-best-you-can-be. I understand appointment-making as opening doors for congregations and pastors to meet each other to become what they can be, and *not* sending somebody just to do their job somewhere. When people say to me, "What do you like most about being bishop?" I think the thing I like and enjoy most is the opportunity to open doors and to make connections.[57]

14. Dilemmas of Inclusion and Conviction. Susan Morrison asks a crucial question:

If I am the bishop for everyone and seek to be present to that fact, how do I speak out on things that I care deeply about in a way that won't cut off the fact of being the bishop for everyone? What is the best way to address issues and take a stand where I am heard and have credibility, and yet be supportive? How do I speak out on things I care about and do it in a way in which I am the bishop for all and yet can enable the space for the things I care about to happen?[58]

E. HARD ISSUES CONFRONTING CLERGYWOMEN

15. Loneliness and Pain in Diversity. Susan Morrison and others speak about women leaving the ordained ministry:

[Morrison:] One concern that I have is that I am seeing good women leaving ministry. They are the women I had planned on being here to help vision a future in the church. [They seem to be leaving because] boundaries are too tight. That has to do with imagery of God, with worship, with music, with lifestyle, a series of things. . . . Some newer clergywomen don't seem to see these as important issues. I am seeing much more competition [among women], yet there is an inability to name it and to dialogue about it. I once dreamed we could model something different, and I'm beginning to wonder whether that is true.[59]

16. Numbness, Co-optation. One bishop speaks for many in terms of the need for continual truth telling and mutual accountability.

[Judith Craig:] I hope the sisters will not ricochet at defensive postures in the next decade vis-à-vis each other or vis-à-vis clergy*men*. I think we're in for a rough decade, frankly. The backlash is on and my plea is that they take their authority in good stride and remember how they came to be where they are out of their kind of mutual exercise of power for each other and on behalf of each other. I hope they will hold people like me accountable to that vision and will keep telling the truth to me and to each other.[60]

CONTRIBUTORS

Diane H. Lobody is Associate Professor of Church History at the Methodist
Theological School in Ohio and is an ordained United Methodist minister. Her doctoral dissertation, "Lost in the Ocean of Love: The Mystical Writings of Catherine Livingston Garrettson," was awarded a 1990
Bross Prize and has been submitted for publication. She is currently
immersed in a study of the interplay of gender, spirituality, and social
activism in the American Methodist tradition, a research project
funded by the Indiana University Center on Philanthropy and the Lilly
Endowment, Inc.

Ila Alexander Fisher is an ordained United Methodist minister and pastor of
Wellington Park United Methodist Church in Chicago. She holds a
B.A. from DePauw University, an M.A. from Goddard, and an M.Div.
from Garrett-Evangelical Theological Seminary.

Nancy A. Hardesty is an independent scholar, writer, and editor from South
Carolina. She is the author of numerous books, including, most
recently, the third edition of *All We're Meant To Be: Biblical Feminism for
Today* (Wm. B. Eerdmans Publishing Co., 1992). She is Visiting Assistant Professor of Religion at Clemson University, Clemson, South Carolina.

Adrienne Israel is an associate professor of history at Guilford College in
Greensboro, North Carolina. She has received support for research on
the life of Amanda Berry Smith from Guilford College faculty research
funds and in 1990–91 was a Scholar-in-Residence at the Schomburg
Center for Research in Black History and Culture in New York. Israel
received her Ph.D. from Johns Hopkins University and B.A. and M.A.

from Howard University. She has a full-length biography of Smith in progress.

Carolyn De Swarte Gifford is the editor of a selected edition of the journals of Frances E. Willard, to be published in 1994 by the University of Illinois Press. She serves on the editorial board of *Telling Women's Lives: A Chicago History* (an encyclopedia of Chicago women), and was associate editor of *Past and Promise: The Lives of New Jersey Women* (Scarecrow Press, 1990). She was the Women's History Project Coordinator, General Commission on Archives and History of The United Methodist Church, from 1983 to 1986.

Joanne Carlson Brown is Professor of Church History and Ecumenics at Saint Andrew's Theological College, a United Church of Canada seminary in Saskatoon, Saskatchewan. She is an ordained elder in the Pacific Northwest Conference of The United Methodist Church. Her fields of interest are nineteenth-century Methodism, women's history, and historical theology.

Kenneth E. Rowe is Professor of Church History and Methodist Librarian at Drew University. He is closely associated with the United Methodist Archives and History Center at Drew. Rowe has edited *The Methodist Union Catalogue* (Scarecrow, 1976), *Rethinking Methodist History* (Abingdon Press, 1985), and *United Methodist Studies Basic Bibliographies,* 3rd ed. (Abingdon Press, 1992), contributed to *United Methodism in America, a Compact History* (Abingdon Press, 1992), and he is coauthor with Russell Richey and Jean Miller Schmidt of *Methodist Experience in America* (forthcoming from Abingdon Press).

Emilie M. Townes is Assistant Professor of Christian Social Ethics at Saint Paul School of Theology in Kansas City, Missouri. She is an American Baptist clergywoman and concentrates her work in womanist ethics and spirituality. She is the author of *Womanist Justice, Womanist Hope* (Scholars, 1993), and the editor of *A Troubling in My Soul: Womanist Perspectives on Evil and Suffering* (Orbis Books, 1993).

Dana Hardwick earned her B.S. in Sociology from the University of Wisconsin in Milwaukee in 1967. She spent the next twenty years as a computer programmer-analyst in Washington, D.C., Chapel Hill, North Carolina, and Lexington, Kentucky. In 1986 she began to explore correctional chaplaincy and entered Lexington Theological Seminary in 1987, receiving her M.Div. in 1990. Ordained to the priesthood in 1990, she now serves Trinity Episcopal Church in Covington, Kentucky, as Associate Rector.

Kyung-Lim Shin-Lee received an M.Div. from Garrett-Evangelical Theological Seminary in 1988. She is now in the D.Min. program at Wesley Theological Seminary, where she is also Dean of Community Life. Lee is an ordained elder in the Baltimore-Washington Conference of The United Methodist Church.

Rosemary Skinner Keller is Dean and Vice-President of Academic Affairs and Professor of Religion and American Culture at Garrett-Evangelical Theological Seminary and a member of the Graduate Council of the Joint Northwestern University/Garrett-Evangelical Ph.D. program. She is a Diaconal Minister and a member of the Board of Directors of the General Commission on Christian Unity and Interreligious Concerns of The United Methodist Church. Her publications include *Georgia Harkness: For Such a Time as This* (Abingdon Press, 1992), and the three-volume *Women and Religion in America* with Rosemary Radford Ruether (HarperCollins, 1981, 1983, 1986).

Alice G. Knotts is an independent scholar living in Denver, Colorado, and is a facilitator with the National Corrective Training Institute. As a ministerial member of the Oregon-Idaho Conference, former Co-President of the Methodist Federation for Social Action, and fifth-generation United Methodist pastor, she is especially interested in United Methodist history and its meaning for Christian vocation and social witness today. Her dissertation, 1991 winner of the Jesse Lee Prize in United Methodist History, is entitled "Bound by the Spirit, Found on the Journey: The Methodist Women's Campaign for Southern Civil Rights, 1940–1968."

Alice Yun Chai was born in Seoul, Korea, attended Ewha Woman's University, received a bachelor's degree from Seoul National University and Ohio Wesleyan University, and Master's and Ph.D. degrees in Anthropology from Ohio State University. She taught anthropology at Ewha Woman's University, Seoul National University, and in the Women's Studies Program of the University of Hawaii. Her research publications focus on Asian immigrant women, Asian American, and Korean women.

Mary Elizabeth Mullino Moore is Professor of Theology and Christian Education at the School of Theology at Claremont, California, and a diaconal minister in The United Methodist Church. She is the author of *Education for Continuity and Change, Teaching from the Heart,* and several essays on theology and education. With Rosemary Keller and Gerald Moede, she coauthored *Called to Serve: The United Methodist Diaconate* (Board of Higher Education, The United Methodist Church, 1987).

Barbara B. Troxell is Assistant Professor of Practical Theology and Director of Field Education and Spiritual Formation at Garrett-Evangelical Theological Seminary, Evanston, Illinois. A ministerial member of the California-Nevada Annual Conference, she has served as pastor, student YWCA director, district superintendent, and dean of students at Pacific School of Religion. Earlier she was a pastor in New York and a university YWCA director-associate chaplain in Ohio. She leads retreats and workshops on issues of spirituality, authority, and women in ministry.

NOTES

CHAPTER 1

1. Catherine Livingston Garrettson in Diane H. Lobody, "Lost in the Ocean of Love: The Mystical Writings of Catherine Livingston Garrettson," Ph.D. dissertation, Drew University, 1990, p. 307. The Catherine Garrettson manuscript collection, which contains about two thousand pages of diaries, correspondence, and miscellaneous writings, is held in the Archives of The United Methodist Church at Drew University in Madison, New Jersey. Her first six diaries and a dream journal have been edited and may be found in the work cited at the beginning of this note; all other documents are still in manuscript only. In this essay, I have gently modernized Catherine's somewhat idiosyncratic and perplexing spelling and grammar, lest reading her materials become obtrusively difficult. Some of the delightful flavor of her writing is thereby lost, and readers are encouraged to take a look at the edition of her diaries, which adheres strictly to her form, or better yet treat yourselves to an archival adventure and lovingly read the originals themselves at Drew.
2. One of the continuing problems in writing women's history is the struggle of deciding which name to use when referring to women in our own narratives. Some scholars hold fast to the traditional use of the subject's last name; we do not, after all, customarily refer to Lincoln as Abraham in a historical study. Other scholars argue that no woman's last name is really her own—it is either her father's name or her husband's, and matters become confused if she marries and changes her surname. Further, they suggest that the use of a surname sounds artificial and that the intimate use of a woman's given name is more appropriate to feminist principles. For this essay, I refer to Catherine Livingston Garrettson as Catherine, primarily because there are too many other Livingstons and Garrettsons cluttering up the text. *Everybody* in this article is called by her or his first name. Were I writing about Catherine's network of evangelical women, half of whom were also named Catherine, I would be operating under rather different circumstances and would use quite a different system.
3. Catherine Livingston Garrettson (hereafter CLG), "Autobiography," pp. 2-3.
4. CLG to Mercy Otis Warren, August 18, 1781.
5. CLG, "Autobiography," p. 4.
6. Ibid.
7. CLG to Margaret Livingston, July 5, 1787.
8. CLG in Lobody, "Lost in the Ocean," p. 304.
9. For a masterful and succinct analysis of the alternative value system offered by early Methodism to white women and other marginalized persons, see Donald G. Mathews, "Evangelical America—The Methodist Ideology," in *Rethinking Methodist History: A Bicen-*

tennial Historical Consultation, ed. Russell E. Richey and Kenneth E. Rowe (Nashville: Kingswood Books, 1985), pp. 91-99.

10. An elegant description of the practical spiritual disciplines of early Methodists (albeit British Methodists, but the practices were readily translated to the American setting) may be found in Richard Heitzenrater, *Mirror and Memory: Reflections on Early Methodism* (Nashville: Abingdon Press, 1989), pp. 78-105.

11. This taxonomy of Christian mystical experience is unfolded in detail in Evelyn Underhill's classic *Mysticism* (New York: E. P. Dutton, 1961 repr. ed.).

12. CLG in Lobody, "Lost in the Ocean," p. 304.

13. See Doris Andrews, "Popular Religion and the Revolution in the Middle Atlantic Ports: The Rise of the Methodists 1778–1800," Ph.D. dissertation, University of Pennsylvania, 1986, pp. 196-200. Andrews also includes an insightful section on Catherine.

14. CLG to Catherine Rutsen, March 17, 1791.

15. Clare Brandt, *An American Aristocracy: The Livingstons* (New York: Doubleday, 1986), p. 146.

16. Pathbreaking studies of the impact of the Revolution upon women include Linda Kerber, *Women of the Republic: Intellect and Ideology in Revolutionary America* (Chapel Hill: University of North Carolina Press, 1980) and Mary Beth Norton, *Liberty's Daughters: The Revolutionary Experience of American Women, 1750–1850* (Boston: Little, Brown, & Co., 1980).

17. For a perceptive and lively treatment of the interplay of republican ideology and American Protestantism, see Nathan O. Hatch, *The Democratization of American Christianity* (New Haven: Yale University Press, 1989).

C H A P T E R   2

1. Abel Stevens, *The Women of Methodism* (New York: Carlton and Porter, 1866), p. 281.

2. Augustus Garrett to Jerry Clark, January 15, 1845. "Letterbook" of Augustus Garrett, 1843–1845. Archives of Northwestern University.

3. Ibid.

4. Craig Buettinger, "The Concept of Jacksonian Democracy, Chicago as a Text Case," Ph.D. Dissertation for Northwestern University, 1982, p. 19.

5. A. D. Field, *Worthies and Workers, Both Ministers and Laymen of the Rock Rivers Conference* (Cincinnati: Cranston and Curtis, 1896), pp. 313-14.

6. Chicago Bureau of Statistics and Municipal Library, *Chicago City Manual* (Chicago: Drovers Journal Publishing Company, 1911), p. 30.

7. Eliza Garrett to Mrs. Hamline, February 3, 1853. Garrett/Hamline file, Garrett-Evangelical Theological Seminary archives.

8. Alfred Theodore Andrea, *History of Chicago,* vol. 1 (Arne Press, 1875), p. 594.

9. Chicago Historical Society, File on Augustus Garrett, p. 6.

10. Field, *Worthies and Workers,* p. 128.

11. Ibid., p. 125.

12. A. D. Field, *Memorials of Methodism in the Bounds of the Rock River Conference* (Cincinnati: Cranston and Stowe, 1886), p. 423.

13. Field, *Worthies and Workers,* pp. 314, 315.

14. Chicago Historical Society, Augustus Garrett file, p. 2. The meaning of "the ancient Edward" cannot be determined.

15. Ibid., pp. 2, 3.

16. Buettinger, "The Concept of Jacksonian Democracy," pp. 45, 46.

17. Ibid., pp. 49-50.

18. A letter from Augustus Garrett to J. R. Malony, March 22, 1844, "Letterbook."

19. Letter from Augustus Garrett to John F. Seaman, January 5, 1845, "Letterbook."

20. Letter from Augustus Garrett to John F. Seaman, December 28, 1843.

21. *Chicago City Directory* (City of Chicago, 1844).

22. Stevens, *Women of Methodism,* p. 284.

23. Joseph Kirkland, *The Story of Chicago* (Chicago: Dibble Press, 1892), p. 225.

24. Lafayette Wallace Cast, *The Goodrich Family in America* (Chicago: Fergus Printing Company, 1889), p. 202.

25. Field, *Memorials of Methodism,* p. 406.
26. Almer M. Pennewell, *The Methodist Movement in Northern Illinois* (Sycamore, Ill.: Sycamore Tribune, 1942), p. 115.
27. Frederick A. Norwood, *Dawn to Midday at Garrett* (Evanston, Ill.: Garrett-Evangelical Theological Seminary, 1978), p. 11.
28. *Northwestern Christian Advocate,* vol. 2, no. 23, June 7, 1854, p. 90.
29. *Minutes of the Rock River Conference of the Methodist Episcopal Church* (Chicago: North West Christian Advocate, 1855), p. 3 (Appendix).
30. Frances E. Willard, *A Classic Town* (Chicago: Woman's Temperance Publishing Association, 1891), p. 404.
31. *Northwestern Christian Advocate,* January 6, 1855.
32. *Chicago Democrat,* January 5, 1855.
33. A letter from Grant Goodrich to D. P. Kidder on November 26, 1855.
34. *Weekly Chicago Democrat,* December 1, 1855, p. 1.
35. Kidder to Goodrich.
36. Information on Dr. Ebersole is based in part on conversations of Dr. Ebersole with Neal and Ila Fisher, August 1, 1990. Biographical dates were verified from a funeral biography.
37. *Women of Methodism,* pp. 285-86.
38. Charles Wesley Buoy, *Representative Women of Methodism* (New York: Hunt and Eaton, 1893), pp. 343-44.
39. *Northwestern Christian Advocate,* vol. 3, no. 48 (November 28, 1855), p. 191.

CHAPTER 3

1. Donald W. Dayton, *Discovering an Evangelical Heritage* (New York: Harper & Row, 1976), p. 96.
2. J. Krehbiel, in the introduction to Marshall W. Taylor, *The Life, Travels, Labours, and Helpers of Mrs. Amanda Smith* (Cincinnati: Cranston & Stowe, 1886), p. 10. Taylor's biography of Smith is based on a series of interviews he conducted with her.
3. Amanda Smith, *An Autobiography: The Story of the Lord's Dealings with Mrs. Amanda Smith, the Colored Evangelist* (Chicago: Meyer & Brother, Publishers, 1893; repr. ed., Noblesville, Ind.: Newby Book Room, 1972), p. vi. Page numbers for subsequent quotations will simply be placed in the text in parentheses. To date there has been no biography of Amanda Smith, but Adrienne Israel is working to remedy that situation. She expects to publish a biography of Smith in the near future.
4. *A.M.E. Review* 80 (January-March 1964): 6-7.
5. John H. Bracey, Jr., "Smith, Amanda Berry," *Notable American Women,* ed. Edward T. James (Cambridge, Mass.: Belknap Press of Harvard University Press, 1971), vol. 3, p. 304, gives her dates as January 23, 1837–February 24, 1915.
6. Although she does not mention Phoebe Palmer's Tuesday Meeting for the Promotion of Holiness prior to this event, she does mention it later and may have attended the meeting prior to her experience in John Inskip's church. The Inskips and the Palmers were close friends and colleagues. She notes on p. 81 that a friend of hers had told her that she "got the blessing through Mrs. Dr. Palmer" years previously in Canada, so she was certainly familiar with the Palmers' work.
7. The dates here are a bit confusing. On page 152 she says October 1870. This account begins on page 147 with the notation that "it was the third Sunday in November 1890" when she visited Fleet Street A.M.E. Church, but this is surely in error since this would have been about the time of her *return* from Africa.
8. C. Eric Lincoln and Lawrence H. Mamiya, *The Black Church in the African-American Experience* (Durham, N.C.: Duke University Press, 1990), pp. 276-80.
9. William L. Andrews, *Sisters of the Spirit: Three Black Women's Autobiographies of the Nineteenth Century* (Bloomington: Indiana University Press, 1986), p. 9.
10. Ibid. *Sisters of the Spirit* is a collection of the autobiographies of these three women.
11. Cheryl Townsend Gilkes, "'Some Mother's Son and Some Father's Daughter': Gender and Biblical Language in the Afro-Christian Worship Tradition," in *Shaping New Vision: Gender and Values in American Culture,* ed. Clarissa W. Atkinson, Constance H. Buchanan, and Margaret R. Miles (Ann Arbor: UMI Research Press, 1981), p. 78.

12. Ibid., p. 82. See also Lincoln and Mamiya, *Black Church in the African American Experience,* p. 274: "The pulpit has been viewed as 'men's space' and the pew as 'women's space.'"

13. Cheryl Townsend Gilkes, "'Together and in Harness': Women's Traditions in the Sanctified Church," *Signs* 10 (1985): 678-99. Gilkes uses "the Sanctified Church" to denote those denominations and congregations linked historically to the Holiness and Pentecostal movements of the late nineteenth and early twentieth centuries.

14. Gilkes, "Some Mother's Son and Some Father's Daughter," pp. 83-84.

15. Smith spells the name "Bordman," but she is obviously talking about William and Mary Boardman, well-known advocates of "the higher Christian life." On p. 196 she notes that Hannah Whitehall Smith was her friend.

16. *Autobiography,* p. 157, a "chance to preach" at Salem during a Thursday night prayer meeting. "We held meetings" she says on page 226 of a visit to Pitman church. The meetings were in a lecture hall, not the church sanctuary. In Scotland she speaks of herself as giving "the Gospel address" (p. 279). In Liberia she speaks of giving "a Bible reading" (p. 338).

17. Taylor, *Life, Travels, Labours, and Helpers,* pp. 26-27.

18. "Discovery," *Methodist History* 12 (April 1974): 61. Anna Oliver and Anna Howard Shaw were in 1880 the first two women to request full ordination from The Methodist Episcopal Church. They were denied ordination by the General Conference, and all preaching licenses to women were revoked. Shaw was immediately ordained by The Methodist Protestant Church.

19. She says there came upon the people "a spirit of revival," and prayer meetings were appointed for subsequent days. She notes that "on Wednesday and Thursday I gave some Bible readings."

20. Although the A.M.E. Zion did begin ordaining women in the 1890s, the A.M.E. Church did not grant women full ordination until 1948. See Lincoln and Mamiya, *Black Church in the African American Experience,* pp. 285-86. Smith's remarks echo those of Elizabeth, whose story is told in *Elizabeth, A Colored Minister of the Gospel Born in Slavery,* published in 1889 by Philadelphia Quakers. See Lincoln and Mamiya, *Black Church in the African American Experience,* p. 279. A comparison of that work and Smith's *Autobiography* might be fruitful.

21. See Gilkes, "Some Mother's Son and Some Father's Daughter," p. 88.

22. Eileen Southern, *Biographical Dictionary of Afro-American and African Musicians.* The Greenwood Encyclopedia of Black Music (Westport, Conn.: Greenwood Press, 1982), p. 342.

23. See Lincoln and Mamiya, *Black Church in the African American Experience,* p. 276, concerning women's roles in traditional African society.

24. Ibid., p. 281.

25. *The Union Signal* (February 5, 1891), p. 4. *The Union Signal* is the publication of the Woman's Christian Temperance Union. Smith had become a member of the Brooklyn WCTU in 1875.

26. *Christian Standard and Home Journal* (July 26, 1894), p. 7.

27. See Dorothy Salem, *To Better Our World: Black Women in Organized Reform, 1890–1920* (New York: Carlson Publishing, 1990).

28. *The Helper,* vol. 9, no. 10 (November 1907): 2. From the Moorland Spingarn Collection, Howard University, Washington, D.C.

CHAPTER 4

1. *Report of the International Council of Women, Assembled by the National Woman Suffrage Association* (March 25-April 1, 1888) (Washington, D.C.: Rufus Darby, printer, 1888), pp. 423-24.

2. Journal of Frances Willard, December 5, 1859 (hereafter referred to as Journal). The 49-volume journal kept by Frances Willard from 1855 to 1870, and 1893 and 1896 (along with three brief volumes from the 1880s), is deposited at the Frances E. Willard Memorial Library in the national headquarters of the Woman's Christian Temperance Union, Evanston, Illinois. The volumes have been microfilmed as an addendum (Series

5) to the *Temperance and Prohibition Papers* edited by Randall C. Jimerson, Francis X. Blouin, and Charles A. Isetts. A short typescript description of Series 5 prepared by Gary Kwiatek is available from the Bentley Historical Library. A complete transcription of the journal with accompanying short summaries of each volume, prepared by Carolyn De Swarte Gifford, has been placed at the Willard Library and is available for researchers. The portions of the journal included in this essay were transcribed from the original and not from the microfilm edition, so the citations do not contain information about the location of the entries on the microfilm.

3. Journal 16 (February-June 1861), p. 5 of front unnumbered pages.
4. Journal 24 (1867), p. 2.
5. Journal, July 22, 1860.
6. Frances E. Willard, *Glimpses of Fifty Years: The Autobiography of an American Woman* (Boston: Woman's Temperance Publication Association, 1889), p. 622.
7. Ibid.
8. Ibid., pp. 622-23.
9. Ibid., p. 623.
10. Journal, December 14, 1859.
11. Journal, May 5, 1861.
12. Quoted in Frederick A. Norwood, *From Dawn to Midday at Garrett* (Evanston, Ill.: Garrett-Evangelical Theological Seminary, 1978), p. 25.
13. Journal, February 23, 1862.
14. Journal, March 9, 10, 20, 1868.
15. Journal, February 6, 1869.
16. Journal, March 21, 1868; December 3, 1869.
17. Journal, December 3, 1869.
18. Journal 35 (March 1870), back page.
19. An earlier version of this essay was delivered as a public lecture of the Program on Women's Studies in Religion, Harvard Divinity School, February 1989.
20. Willard's speech, "The New Chivalry," appears in her autobiography, *Glimpses of Fifty Years,* pp. 576-89.
21. Ibid., p. 574.
22. Frances E. Willard, "The Woman's Cause Is Man's," in *The Arena* 5 (1892): 712-25.

CHAPTER 5

1. James Wm. McClendon, Jr., *Biography as Theology* (Nashville: Abingdon Press, 1974).
2. Frances Willard, *Woman and Temperance* (Chicago: Woman's Temperance Publishing Assn., 1883), p. 147.
3. Jennie Fowler Willing, *A Prince of the Realm* (Cincinnati: Cranston and Curts, 1895), p. 42.
4. Ibid., p. 103.
5. Willing, *Guide to Holiness* (November 1867), p. 138.
6. Willing, *Diamond Dust* (Cincinnati: Walden and Stowe, 1880), p. 159.
7. Ibid., p. 114.
8. Willing, *The Open Door* (September 1910): 17.
9. Willing, *The Only Way Out* (Boston: D. Lathrop and Co., 1886), p. 121.
10. Ann Douglas, *The Feminization of American Culture* (New York: Doubleday, 1977), p. 254.
11. Willing, *The Potential Woman* (Boston: McDonald, Gill, and Co., 1886), pp. 10-11.
12. Willing, *The Open Door* (March 1910): 7.
13. Willing, *The Ladies Repository,* June 1868, p. 444.
14. Willing, *The Open Door* (May/June 1909): 38.
15. Horace Bushnell, *The Moral Uses of Dark Things* (New York, 1868), p. 76.
16. Willing, *Woman's Home Missionary,* February 1883, p. 19.
17. Willing, "Methodist Women," *Heathen Woman's Friend,* May 1870, pp. 91-93.
18. Willing, *Guide to Holiness* (January 1896), pp. 22-23.
19. Ibid. (January 1898), pp. 21-23.
20. Ibid. (February 1898), pp. 54-55.
21. Willing, *God's Great Women* (Louisville: Pentecostal Publishing Co., n.d.), pp. 140-46.

CHAPTER 6

1. At the outset I wish to acknowledge the assistance of William T. Smith, layleader and historian of First United Methodist Church, Passaic, New Jersey, who provided much documentation and many research leads for this essay.
2. Her family lived on a farm across the Raritan River from New Brunswick in a municipality now known as Highland Park.
3. Her childhood nickname was "Oliver."
4. Not to be confused with Rutgers, the State University of New Jersey in New Brunswick, N.J., Rutgers Female Institute, later College, was founded in New York City in 1839 to provide higher education for young women in New York City. It flourished on Fifth Avenue between 41st and 42nd streets as an independent woman's college until 1894. In the middle of Anna's college course, the family moved from Brooklyn to Manhattan.
5. For instance, the 10th annual Woman's Rights Convention was held at the Cooper Institute in New York City in 1860. If Anna did not attend the public sessions featuring speeches by Lucy Stone and others, she surely read about them in the New York press.
6. Five recent studies tell the story of northern teachers of southern blacks: Ronald E. Butchart, *Northern Schools, Southern Blacks, and Reconstruction: Freedmen's Education 1862–1873* (Westport, Conn.: Greenwood Press, 1980); Jacqueline Jones, *Soldiers of Light and Love: Northern Teachers and Georgia Blacks, 1862–1875* (Chapel Hill, N.C.: University of North Carolina Press, 1980); Robert C. Morris, *Reading, 'Riting, and Reconstruction: The Education of Freedmen in the South, 1861–1870* (Chicago: University of Chicago Press, 1981); Joe M. Richardson, *Christian Reconstruction: The American Missionary Association and Southern Blacks, 1861–1890* (Athens, Ga.: University of Georgia Press, 1986); Allis Wolfe, *Women Who Dared: Northern Teachers of the Southern Freedmen 1862–1872* (unpublished doctoral dissertation, City University of New York, 1982). Richardson's 1986 study is best overall. He executes difficult expository moves successfully and presents a detailed accounting of the AMA with self-conscious balance.
7. The Storrs and Ayers schools were adjacent to the campus of Atlanta University, which had been founded three years earlier. At the end of 1869, the Ayers schoolhouse was sold to the Freedmen's Aid Society of The Methodist Episcopal Church as a site for Clark College. (American Missionary Association, *Twenty-Third Annual Report*, 1869, p. 46.)
8. Nancy F. Cott, *The Bonds of Womanhood: Woman's Sphere in New England 1780–1835* (New Haven: Yale University Press, 1977), pp. 140-41.
9. Richardson, *Christian Reconstruction*, p. 197.
10. Butchart, *Northern Schools, Southern Blacks*, p. 9.
11. Jones, *Soldiers of Light*, p. 11.
12. Stephen Angell, *Bishop Henry McNeal Turner and African American Religion in the South* (Knoxville, Tenn.: University of Tennessee Press, 1992), p. 212.
13. W. E. B. DuBois, *The Souls of Black Folk* (Chicago: McClurg, 1904), p. 31.
14. Anna Oliver to E. P. Smith, December 22, 1869, American Missionary Association Archives, Amistad Research Center, Tulane University, New Orleans. For the full text, see document 1.
15. Jones, *Soldiers of Light*, p. 105.
16. McMicken School of Design of the University of Cincinnati opened in January 1869. Thomas Satterwhite Noble (1835–1907) was the principal instructor in painting. Noble gained a national reputation when his paintings on slavery and Civil War themes were shown at the National Academy of Design in New York City in 1865–1866. Anna, who may have seen his work in New York, became one of his first students in Cincinnati. For the art scene in Cincinnati at the time, see Ripley Hitchcock, "The Western Art Movement," *Century Magazine*, vol. 32, n.s. 10 (August 1886), pp. 576-86.
17. Eight drawings and one oil painting, "Providential Spring at Andersonville Prison," drawn from life during her stay in Georgia, were chosen. *Fourth Annual Exhibition of the School of Design, Cincinnati University* (Cincinnati: Gazette Printing Co., 1873), p. 12.
18. For a modern critical history of the Ohio Crusade, see Joe Dannenbaum, *Drink and Disorder: Temperance Reform in Cincinnati from the Washingtonian Revival to the WCTU* (Urbana: University of Illinois Press, 1984), chap. 6.
19. "Rev. Anna Oliver's Story; How she was 'called' and the trouble she had in being 'cho-

sen,'" *New York World*, February 23, 1877, p. 2, col. 3. The sympathetic editor of *The Passaic Weekly Item* reprinted it in full on the front page of the March 24, 1877, issue of his paper on the eve of her departure from First Methodist Episcopal Church in that city.

20. Donald W. Dayton, *Discovering an Evangelical Heritage* (Peabody, Mass.: Hendrickson Publishers, 1988, 1976), pp. 41-43, 88-89.

21. "Rev. Anna Oliver's Story," p. 2, col. 3.

22. Anna was particularly disappointed when Princeton Theological Seminary would not accept her. Her great grandfather, the Reverend Samuel F. Snowden, was one of the founders of Princeton University and longtime pastor of the Presbyterian Church in Princeton.

23. Anna Oliver, "The Boston University True to Women," *Woman's Journal* (May 8, 1875), p. 152, cols. 1-2.

24. Ibid.

25. *Boston Globe*, June 8, 1876, p. 2, col. 4; see also *Boston Post*, June 8, 1876, p. 4, col. 2; *Boston Herald*, June 8, 1876, p. 4, cols. 3-4; and *Zion's Herald* (the Boston area's Methodist newspaper), June 15, 1876, p. 1, cols. 4-5.

26. M. Hawkins, "Women as Preachers of the Gospel," *The Methodist* (New York) 17/44 (October 28, 1876), p. 1.

27. Speakers included Mary Livermore, Maggie Newton Van Cott, Methodist Bishop Randolph S. Foster, Robert B. Snowden (Anna's brother and Episcopal priest), Henry White Warren, Methodist pastor in Brooklyn, and famous Brooklyn Congregationalist preacher, T. DeWitt Talmadge.

28. "Rev. Anna Oliver's Trials in the Passaic Pulpit," *Weekly Item*, Passaic, N.J., February 24, 1877, p. 3. A former slave and washerwoman, Amanda Smith began her ministry at a black church revival in Salem, New Jersey, in 1871. She became even more popular by preaching at white Holiness meetings in the years that followed. Her classic 1893 *Autobiography; the Story of the Lord's Dealings with Mrs. Amanda Smith, the Colored Evangelist*, has been reprinted by Oxford University Press (1988) with a helpful introduction by Jualynne E. Dodson. Long excerpts have been reprinted in William L. Andrews, *Sisters of the Spirit: Three Black Women's Autobiographies of the Nineteenth Century* (Bloomington, Ind.: Indiana University Press, 1986). Amanda Smith, like Anna Oliver, was licensed to preach by her denomination (African Methodist Episcopal Church) but never ordained. Like Oliver, Smith pressed a test case on the ordination of women before the General Conference of the African Methodist Episcopal General Conference and lost (1872). Like Oliver, Smith continued to preach. She acquired an international reputation as an evangelist, musician, and social reformer. See the essay on Amanda Smith by Nancy Hardesty and Adrienne Israel in this volume.

29. Centenary College, *Catalogue 1876-1877*. Centenary College was founded in 1869 by the Newark Conference of The Methodist Episcopal Church.

30. Oliver was elected first vice-president of the Passaic branch of the state WCTU (*Weekly Item*, November 25, 1876, p. 2, col. 5; p. 7, col. 1). She also gave temperance lectures in other New Jersey cities and towns, e.g., the *Weekly Item*, December 30, 1876, p. 2, col. 3, reports on her address at a temperance rally at Belleville, near Newark, N.J., December 23, 1876.

31. "Miss Anna Oliver's Discourse: 'The Needs of Passaic,'" *Weekly Item*, Passaic, N.J., March 24, 1877, p. 2.

32. In the second half of the nineteenth century, the water cure, or hydrotherapy, was popularized by women who were also involved in promoting dress reform, temperance, women's rights, and medical reform. The water cure consisted of numerous baths, exercise, simple food, and extended stays at a sanitarium. See Kathryn Kish Sklar, "All Hail to Pure Cold Water!" *American Heritage* 26/1 (1974), pp. 64-69, 100-101, and *Clara Barton and Dansville, Together with Supplementary Materials* (Dansville, N.Y.: privately printed, 1966).

33. Anna had been preaching in Brooklyn as early as the summers of 1875 and 1876.

34. The recently built church was in the latest Gothic style, of wood painted to look like stone, with high stained-glass windows, and it seated a thousand on the main floor and gallery extending around three sides of the building. Its original cost was $47,500, so at

$14,000 this was a bargain! (*Willoughby Ave. M.E. Church Annual,* 1881, p. 3). Miss Oliver paid $1,000 in cash and assumed a mortgage of $13,000.

35. "A Lady Pastor, A Surprise for the Wesley M. E. Church Members," *Brooklyn Daily Times,* March 25, 1879, p. 4, cols. 3-4.

36. The doctrinal statement in the Willoughby Ave. Church *Annual* is taken directly from Phoebe Palmer's 1871 summary, "What We Believe and Teach," published in her *Guide to Holiness* 59 (1871): 151-52, a journal to which Oliver probably subscribed. The summary was included in Richard Wheatley's *The Life and Letters of Mrs. Phoebe Palmer* (New York: W. C. Palmer, Jr., 1876), pp. 525-26. A more accessible source for the summary is *Phoebe Palmer: Selected Writings,* ed. Thomas C. Oden (New York: Paulist Press, 1988), pp. 305-6. The only theologically significant omission from the original five-paragraph statement that I can detect is the sentence "We have also long believed and taught, that all disciples of our Lord, under the present dispensation of power may, and *must* receive the *baptism of fire.*" For interpretations of Palmer in addition to the Oden volume in the Paulist Press Sources of American Spirituality series, see also Charles E. White, *The Beauty of Holiness: Phoebe Palmer as Theologian, Revivalist, Feminist, and Humanitarian* (Grand Rapids, Mich.: Francis Asbury Press, Zondervan, 1986) and Harold E. Raser, *Phoebe Palmer: Her Life and Thought* (Lewiston, Maine: Edwin Mellen Press, 1987).

37. "A Woman's Pulpit, Miss Anna Oliver's First Sermon in the Church She Has Bought, [and] a Talk About Finances," *New York Times,* April 7, 1879, p. 8, col. 4.

38. "The Rev. Anna Oliver's Difficulties," *New York Times,* July 13, 1879, p. 8, col. 6. See also "No Carpets but a Sermon, The Rev. Anna Oliver's Church, Despoiled of Its Furniture by a Rival Congregation, the Pastor Going on with Her Work, Yesterday's Services," *New York Times,* August 4, 1879, p. 8, col. 1.

39. For a more detailed story of the debate on the ordination of women at the 1880 conference, see my article "Ordination of Women, Round One: Anna Oliver and the Methodist General Conference of 1880," *Methodist History* 12 (April 1974): 60-72.

40. Willoughby Avenue Methodist Episcopal Church, Educational Committee. *1881 Methodist Annual* (Brooklyn, N.Y.: Eagle Job Print, 1881), p. 7. The *Annual* took special care to thank "our friends of the secular and religious press who have extensively reported our pastor's sermons, and have represented our general work with uniform fairness."

41. "Miss Oliver's Church Closed, the Reasons Which Led the Pastor to Give up Her Work Temporarily," *New York Times,* April 30, 1883, p. 8, col. 3. The full text of Oliver's public statement to her congregation and the community was published in the *Brooklyn Times* ("Anna Oliver Resigns the Pastorate of Willoughby Ave. M. E. Church," *Brooklyn Times,* March 12, 1883, p. 1). Oliver held the church property herself and in the end felt she could not ask persons to contribute the $13,000, which was due to complete the purchase. When attempts to sell the building to a Methodist Episcopal congregation failed, she sold it to a Reformed Presbyterian congregation and paid off the remaining mortgage.

42. "New York—Good News From Brooklyn," *The Union Signal,* January 21, 1886, pp. 11-12.

43. Unable to attend, Oliver sent a letter endorsing equal suffrage for women to the 1884 National Suffrage Convention in Washington (*History of Woman Suffrage,* ed. Susan B. Anthony and Ida Husted Harper [New York: Arno & The New York Times, 1969], vol. 4, p. 23). The dress reform movement, strong in the 1850s, disappeared during the Civil War but revived vigorously in the 1870s. See Robert E. Riegel, "Women's Clothes and Women's Rights," *American Quarterly* 15/3 (fall 1963): 390-401, and Frances E. Russell, "Dress Reform" in *The Encyclopedia of Social Reform,* ed. William D. Bliss (New York: Funk & Wagnalls Co., 1897), pp. 517-19.

44. The Methodist Episcopal Church had opened its first hospital in the nation in Brooklyn in 1881. Since James M. Buckley was prime mover in the enterprise, Oliver probably did not volunteer as a nurses' aid! See David C. Crummey, *Factors in the Rise of Methodist Hospitals and Homes,* unpublished doctoral dissertation, University of Chicago, 1963.

45. Elizabeth Cady Stanton, et al., *History of Woman Suffrage* (New York: Arno and the New York Times, 1969), vol. 4, pp. 206-7. Anna Oliver left $1,000 to the National Woman's Suffrage Association according to a footnote in the Stanton book, vol. 4, p. 207.

46. Copied from original in American Missionary Association Archives, Amistad Research Center at Tulane University, New Orleans, La.

CHAPTER 7

1. Dorothy Sterling, *Black Foremothers: Three Lives* (Old Westbury, N.Y.: Feminist Press, 1979), pp. 64-65. Revels was the first African American United States Senator. In 1874, Revels moved to Holly Springs to become a presiding elder in The African Methodist Episcopal Church. Also in 1874, Hill, who was a close Wells family friend and ex-slave, became Mississippi's secretary of state.
2. Ibid., p. 65. W. Augustus Low and Virgil A. Clift, eds., *Encyclopedia of Black America* (New York: McGraw Hill, 1981; repr., New York: Da Capo Press, 1981), p. 737. Rust College, at Holly Springs, Mississippi, was founded in 1866 by The Methodist Episcopal Church, North. Rust College is named for Richard Rust, a white antislavery advocate who was active in the Freedmen's Aid Society. Its early mission was to teach ex-slaves how to read and write. In later years it offered courses in agricultural and domestic sciences. Rust made it possible for many of its students to qualify for predominantly white colleges.
3. Ida B. Wells, Diary, February 8, 1885, Special Collections, Joseph Regenstein Library, University of Chicago.
4. Ibid., February 1, 1886.
5. Ibid., April 24, 1887.
6. Ibid., January 18, 1887.
7. Ibid., February 20, 1887.
8. Ibid., July 16, 1887.
9. Ibid., September 4, 1886.
10. Sterling, *Black Foremothers*, pp. 71-72.
11. Paula Giddings, *When and Where I Enter: The Impact of Black Women on Race and Sex in America* (New York: William Morrow and Company, 1984), p. 23.
12. Wells, Diary, December 4, 1886.
13. Ibid., April 11, 1887. The editor of the *Scimitar* was General Taylor.
14. Ibid., February 8, 1887.
15. Ibid., August 12, 1887. This convention was composed of writers, editors, and publishers of black papers and was held in Louisville, Kentucky. In her autobiography, Wells writes, "I went to Louisville to the first press convention I had ever attended and was tickled pink over the attention I received from those veterans of the press." Ida B. Wells, *Crusade for Justice: The Autobiography of Ida B. Wells*, ed. Alfreda Duster (Chicago: University of Chicago Press, 1970), p. 32. She also notes that she was the first woman representative at the convention.
16. I. Garland Penn, *The Afro-American Press, and Its Editors* (Springfield, Mass.: Willey and Co. Publishers, 1891), p. 408. At an 1889 press convention, Lucy W. Smith wrote of Wells' ability to reach both men and women in her articles. Smith credited Wells' touch with the political implications of the race question and her knowledge of household issues and concerns. Smith also considered Wells a role model for young writers.
17. Also lynched with Moss were Calvin McDowell and Henry Stewart. These three men were business partners in the People's Grocery Company.
18. Wells, *Crusade for Justice*, p. 70.
19. Moss's last words were, "Tell my people to go West—there is no justice for them here." Wells, *Crusade for Justice*, p. 51.
20. The Reverend Norman B. Wood, *The White Side of a Black Subject* (Chicago: American Publishing House, 1897), p. 381.
21. Arna Bontemps and Jack Conroy, *They Seek A City* (Garden City, N.Y.: Doubleday, Doran and Co., 1945), pp. 80-81.
22. Wells, "The Reign of Mob Law, Iola's Opinion of Doings in the Southern Field," *New York Age*, February 18, 1893. TMs, Special Collections, Joseph Regenstein Library, University of Chicago.
23. Wells, *Weekly Call* (Topeka, Kansas), April 22, 1893.
24. Wells, "Ida B. Wells Speaks," handwritten draft dated September 2. No year given, no paper cited. Special Collections, Joseph Regenstein Library, University of Chicago.

25. Wells, "Lynch Law in America," *The Arena,* January 1900.
26. Wells was among those who initially accepted the rape charge against black men. In *Crusade for Justice* she writes, "I had accepted the idea meant to be conveyed— that although lynching was irregular and contrary to law and order, unreasoning anger over the terrible crime of rape led to the lynching; that perhaps the brute deserved death anyhow and the mob was justified in taking his life," p. 64. Later in the same work, Wells comments on Frederick Douglass' initial acceptance as well: "He had been troubled by the increasing number of lynchings, and had begun to believe it true that there was increasing lasciviousness on the part of Negroes," p. 72.
27. Wells, "Lynch Law in All Its Phases," *Our Day,* vol. 11, no. 64 (May 1893): 338.
28. Sterling, *Black Foremothers,* pp. 82-83.
29. Wells, *A Red Record: Tabulated Statistics and Alleged Causes of Lynching in the United States, 1892–1893–1894* (Chicago: Donohue and Henneberry, Printers, Binders and Publishers, 1894; repr., *On Lynching: Southern Horrors, A Red Record, Mob Rule in New Orleans,* New York: Arno Press, 1969), p. 82.
30. Sterling, *Black Foremothers,* pp. 91-92.
31. Ibid., pp. 82-83. This bill gave the federal government control of the national elections in several states. The black vote had been systematically suppressed since 1875 in the southern states. Many believed, along with Wells, that the bill would have given blacks the protection of the federal government and assured blacks access to the ballot box.
32. Ibid., p. 83.
33. Wells, *Red Record,* p. 80, and *Cleveland Gazette,* November 24, 1894.
34. *Cleveland Gazette,* November 24, 1894.
35. Wells, *Red Record,* p. 89.
36. Ibid., pp. 89-90.
37. Ibid., p. 87.
38. The children's names in order of birth were Ferdinand, Charles, Herman, Ida, and Alfreda.
39. Wells-Barnett, handwritten letter to her daughters regretting her inability to be with them to help celebrate Halloween, October 30, 1920.
40. Wells-Barnett, *Crusade for Justice,* p. 251.
41. Ibid., p. 378.
42. Wells-Barnett, "The Negro's Case in Equity," *The Independent* 26 (April 1900): 1010.
43. Ibid.
44. Wells-Barnett, *Crusade for Justice,* p. 331.
45. Bontemps and Conroy, *They Seek A City,* p. 81.
46. Wells-Barnett, *Crusade for Justice,* p. 319.
47. Ibid., pp. 397-404.
48. Wells-Barnett, "How Enfranchisement Stops Lynchings," *Original Rights Magazine,* June 1910, p. 46.
49. Wells-Barnett, Diary, March 25, 1930.
50. Sterling, *Black Foremothers,* p. 116. No source given.
51. Wells-Barnett, *Crusade for Justice,* p. 83.
52. Wells-Barnett, "Lynch Law in America," in *The Arena,* January 1900, pp. 15-24.
53. Wells-Barnett, "The Negro's Case in Equity" in *The Independent* 52 (April 26, 1900): 1010-11.
54. Wells-Barnett, *Crusade for Justice,* pp. 355-58.
55. Ibid., pp. 401-3.

CHAPTER 8

1. Katharine Bushnell, *The Badge of Guilt and Shame* (Oakland, Calif.: by the author, n.d.), p. 7.
2. Katharine C. Bushnell, *God's Word to Women: One Hundred Bible Studies on Woman's Place in the Divine Economy,* 4th ed. (Piedmont, Calif.: by the author, 1930), par. 619.
3. Katharine C. Bushnell, *Dr. Katharine C. Bushnell: A Brief Sketch of her Life Work* (Hertford, England: Rose & Sons, 1932), pp. 3-4.

4. "Our Third and Fourth Round-The-World Missionaries in the Orient," *The Union Signal* 20 (August 23, 1894), p. 4 (WCTU microfilm ed., roll 9, frame 569).
5. Bushnell, *A Brief Sketch*, p. 4.
6. Ibid., p. 20.
7. *The Union Signal* (Chicago) (March 4, 1886).
8. Frances Willard, "Our White Ribbon Anchorage," *The Union Signal* 18 (October 20, 1892), p. 9 (WCTU microfilm ed., roll 8, frame 282).
9. Bushnell, *God's Word*, Lessons 77-79, par. 616-44; Bushnell, *A Brief Sketch*, p. 20.
10. Bushnell, *A Brief Sketch*, p. 20.
11. Ibid.
12. *The Union Signal* 15 (January 10, 1889), p. 1 (WCTU microfilm ed., roll 5, frame 314).
13. "Where Satan Rules," *Milwaukee Journal*, February 7, 1887, as reprinted in Bushnell's report to the WCTU National Convention, October 18, 1888.
14. Katharine Bushnell, "Work in Northern Wisconsin: Dr. Bushnell's Investigation," *W.C.T.U. State Work* (Madison, Wisconsin) 1 (November 1888): 1-7.
15. *The Union Signal* 15 (January 10, 1889), p. 1 (WCTU microfilm ed., roll 5, frame 314).
16. Bushnell, "Work in Northern Wisconsin," 5.
17. Bushnell, *A Brief Sketch*, p. 6.
18. *The Union Signal* 14 (November 8, 1888), p. 4 (WCTU microfilm ed., roll 5, frame 234).
19. Bushnell, "Work in Northern Wisconsin," 3.
20. Ibid., 7.
21. Bushnell, "The Facts in the Case," *The Union Signal* 15 (7 March 1889): 5 (WCTU microfilm ed., roll 5, frame 382).
22. "Truth About the Fielding Case," *W.C.T.U. State Work* 4 (June 1889): 5 (photocopy).
23. Bushnell, *A Brief Sketch*, p. 7.
24. *Oakland Tribune* (California), February 10, 1946, obituary; Bushnell, *A Brief Sketch*, p. 7.
25. Bushnell, *A Brief Sketch*, p. 7.
26. "Sustain Dr. Kate Bushnell," *W.C.T.U. State Work* 4 (March 1889): 4 (no author); *The Union Signal* 15 (April 11, 1889), p. 5; (February 21, 1889), p. 8; (June 6, 1889), p. 11; (January 31, 1889); etc. (all from WCTU microfilm ed., roll 5).
27. Bushnell, *A Brief Sketch*, p. 7.
28. Ibid., p. 8.
29. Ibid.
30. Glen Petrie, *A Singular Iniquity: The Campaigns of Josephine Butler* (New York: Viking Press, 1971), p. 267.
31. *The Union Signal* 16 (December 25, 1890), p. 16 (WCTU microfilm ed., roll 6, frame 563); Frances Willard, "Dr. Kate Bushnell, A Sketch," *The Union Signal* 16 (November 20, 1890), p. 4.
32. *The Union Signal* 16 (December 25, 1890), p. 11 (WCTU microfilm ed., roll 9, frame 560).
33. Elizabeth Andrew and Katharine Bushnell, *Queen's Daughters in India* (London: Morgan and Scott, 1899), pp. 18-22.
34. Ibid., p. 25.
35. Elizabeth Wheeler Andrew, "A Winter's Purity Campaign in India," *The Union Signal* 19 (May 11, 1893), p. 2 (WCTU microfilm ed., roll 8, frame 578).
36. Andrew and Bushnell, *Queen's Daughters*, pp. 31-32.
37. Ibid., pp. 45-53.
38. Bushnell, *A Brief Sketch*, p. 13.
39. Enid Hester Chataway Moberly Bell, *Josephine Butler: Flame of Fire* (London: Constable and Co., Ltd., 1962), p. 231.
40. Andrew and Bushnell, *Queen's Daughters*, pp. 95-96. Katharine Bushnell, "An Appeal to Purity Workers," *The Union Signal* 20 (March 29, 1894), p. 5 (WCTU microfilm ed., roll 9, frame 405).
41. Bushnell, *A Brief Sketch*, p. 18.
42. Ibid., p. 19.
43. Elizabeth Andrew and Katharine Bushnell, *Heathen Slaves and Christian Rulers* (Oakland, Calif.: Messiah's Advocate, 1907), p. 63.
44. Ibid., p. 126.

45. Ibid., pp. 137-39.
46. *The Union Signal* 20 (July 5, 1894), p. 1 (WCTU microfilm ed., roll 9, frame 529).
47. Bushnell, *A Brief Sketch,* p. 22.
48. Ibid., p. 23.
49. Ibid., pp. 24-25.
50. Katharine Bushnell, M.D., "What's Going On: A Report of Investigations by Katharine C. Bushnell, Regarding Certain Social and Legal Abuses in California That Have Been in Part Aggravated and in Part Created by the Federal Social Hygiene Programme" (Oakland, Calif.: by the author, 1919).
51. Ibid., p. 2.
52. Ibid., p. 4.
53. Ibid., p. 12.
54. From the full title of *God's Word to Women.*
55. Willard, "Bushnell, A Sketch," p. 4.
56. Bushnell, *A Brief Sketch,* p. 20.
57. Bushnell, *Badge of Guilt and Shame,* p. 7.
58. Katharine Bushnell, *The Reverend Doctor and His Doctor Daughter* (Oakland, Calif.: by the author, 1927), pp. 54-55.
59. *The Union Signal* (February 21, 1889), p. 8.
60. Bushnell, *God's Word to Women,* par. 466.
61. Ibid., par. 412.
62. Dowd, Sharyn, "1 Corinthians 14:34-35 as a Corinthian Slogan: The Old Roots of a 'New' Interpretation," an unpublished paper read at the Southeastern Regional Meeting of the Society of Biblical Literature, March 16, 1990.
63. Katharine Bushnell, *Covet to Prophesy* (Oakland, Calif.: by the author, n.d.), pp. 3-5.
64. *The Union Signal* (September 12, 1889), p. 7.

CHAPTER 9

1. Christian Literature Society, *The Korea Mission Field,* vol. 6, no. 1 (January 1910), p. 15.
2. Methodist Episcopal Church, *Women's Foreign Missionary Society, Annual Report,* 1885, p. 48.
3. William F. Warren, ed., *The Heathen Woman's Friend,* vol. 17, no. 10 (April 1886), p. 249.
4. *Women's Foreign Missionary Society, Annual Report* (1896), p. 81.
5. Ewha Women's University, *The History of Eighty Years of Ewha* (Seoul: Ewha Woman's University Press, 1965), p. 66.
6. Horace N. Allen, ed., *The Korean Repository,* vol. 4, no. 8 (1897), p. 295.
7. *Heathen Woman's Friend,* vol. 25, no. 1 (July 1893), p. 16.
8. *The Korea Mission Field,* vol. 6, no. 1 (January 1910), p. 13.
9. *Heathen Woman's Friend,* vol. 26, no. 4 (October 1894), p. 102.
10. *Woman's Missionary Friend,* vol. 41, no. 5 (May 1909), p. 167.
11. Lulu Frey, "Mrs. M. Scranton," Sadie B. Harbargh, ed., *The Korea Methodist* vol. 1, no. 5 (1905), pp. 49-50.
12. *Women's Foreign Missionary Society, Annual Report* (1899–1900), p. 84.
13. Mary Scranton, "Woman's Work in Korea," *The Korean Repository,* vol. 3, no. 1, pp. 2-3.
14. *Women's Foreign Missionary Society, Annual Report* (1886), pp. 47-48.
15. *The Korean Repository,* vol. 5, no. 12 (1898), p. 479.
16. *The Korean Repository,* vol. 4, no. 8 (1897), p. 297.
17. *The Korea Mission Field,* vol. 11, no. 10 (October 1915), p. 294.
18. Ibid., p. 295.
19. *The History of Eighty Years of Ewha,* p. 610.
20. Jeannette Walter, *Aunt Jean* (Colorado: Johnson Publishing Co., n. d.), p. 77.
21. *The Korea Mission Field,* vol. 18, no. 12 (December 1922), pp. 267-68.
22. Mary Isham, *Valorous Ventures* (Boston; WFMS Publication Office, 1936), p. 277.
23. Elizabeth M. Lee, *In Memoriam Alice Rebecca Appenzeller,* unpublished article (April 23, 1950), p. 5.
24. Alice R. Appenzeller, "To Innocents Returning Home," *The Korea Mission Field,* vol. 18, no. 1 (January 1922), p. 17.

25. Ibid.
26. Alice R. Appenzeller, "How Can We Help the Young People in Their Social Life?" *The Korea Mission Field*, vol. 22, no. 1 (January 1926), p. 11.
27. Ibid.
28. Ibid.
29. Ibid., p. 12.
30. Ibid.
31. *Women's Foreign Missionary Society, Annual Report* (1932), p. 36.
32. *Women's Foreign Missionary Society, Annual Report* (1927), p. 55.
33. *The Korea Mission Field*, vol. 8, no. 1 (January 1912), p. 9.
34. Helen Kim, *Grace Sufficient* (Nashville: The Upper Room and Other Devotional Literature, 1964), p. 93.
35. *Women's Foreign Missionary Society, Annual Report* (1932), pp. 40-41.
36. Helen Kim, *Grace Sufficient*, p. 120.
37. Lulu E. Frey, "The Need for Higher Education for Korean Women," *The Korea Mission Field*, vol. 6, no. 7 (July 1910), pp. 179-81.
38. "Some Remarks on Woman's Work," *The Korea Mission Field*, vol. 11, no. 10 (October 1915), pp. 294-96.
39. Moneta Troxel, "As Workmen Unashamed," *The Korea Mission Field*, vol. 29, no. 1 (January 1933), p. 14.
40. Jeannette Walter, "The Preparation of the Worker, or Why I Became a Missionary," *The Korea Mission Field*, vol. 10, no. 1 (January 1914), p. 9.

CHAPTER 10

1. Georgia Harkness, "One in Christ Jesus," *Journal of the First General Conference of the Methodist Church* (Nashville: Methodist Publishing House, 1940), pp. 777, 778.
2. Helen Johnson, "Georgia Harkness: She Made Theology Understandable," *United Methodists Today* (October 1974), p. 55.
3. Rosemary Skinner Keller, *Georgia Harkness: For Such a Time as This* (Nashville: Abingdon Press, 1992), is the first biography of Harkness.
4. Georgia Harkness, "Days of My Years," unpublished autobiographical sketch written for the Pacific Coast Theological Group (1950s), Harkness Collection, Garrett-Evangelical Theological Seminary, pp. 2, 3.
5. Such titles as *Understanding the Christian Faith* (Nashville/New York: Abingdon-Cokesbury Press, 1947), *Prayer and the Common Life* (Nashville/New York: Abingdon-Cokesbury Press, 1948), and *Religious Living* (New York: Association Press, 1953) attest to this commitment.
6. Georgia Harkness, *Grace Abounding* (Nashville/New York: Abingdon Press, 1963), p. 34.
7. Donald Dayton, *Discovering an Evangelical Heritage* (New York: Harper & Row, 1976). Chapter 2 provides a good revisionistic introduction to Finney.
8. Harkness, "Days of My Years," p. 9.
9. Ibid.
10. Ibid., p. 13.
11. Ibid.
12. Ibid., pp. 14, 15, 16.
13. Ibid., p. 18.
14. Ibid.
15. Georgia Harkness, *Religious Living* (New York: Hazen Foundation, 1940), pp. 1, 35; Georgia Harkness, *The Recovery of Ideals* (New York: Scribner's, 1937), pp. viii, 13, 49, 62.
16. *Recovery of Ideals*, pp. 46, 190.
17. Harkness, "Days of My Years," pp. 20, 21.
18. Ibid., pp. 24, 25.
19. Ibid., p. 26.
20. Ibid., p. 23.
21. Georgia Harkness, *The Dark Night of the Soul* (Nashville/New York: Abingdon-Cokesbury Press, 1945).
22. Harkness, "Days of My Years," pp. 25, 26.

23. Harkness, *Dark Night of the Soul*, p. 10.
24. Harkness, "The Racial Issue and the Church," unpublished paper in the Harkness Collection, G-ETS, p. 2.
25. Georgia Harkness, *Christian Ethics* (Nashville/New York: Abingdon Press, 1957) and "The Racial Issue and the Church" contain her fullest discussion of the biblical and theological bases for racial inclusivity and equality.
26. *Daily Christian Advocate: The Northeastern Jurisdictional Conference of The Methodist Church* (June 13 and 16, 1956), pp. 43, 44, 68. See also letter from G. Bromley Oxnam to Georgia Harkness (July 3, 1956), Harkness Collection, G-ETS.
27. *Journal of the Last Session of the General Conference of the Evangelical United Brethren Church, Last Session of The Methodist Church, and The United Conference of The United Methodist Church, and the General Conference of The United Methodist Church*, vol. 1 (Nashville: United Methodist Publishing House, 1968), pp. 524-31 and 536, 537.
28. Georgia Harkness, "Letter to the Editor: Methodist-E.U.B. Union," *The Christian Century* (April 1967), p. 501.
29. Georgia Harkness, "Young Women Leaders in the New Methodist Church," *World Outlook* (January 1939), p. 30.
30. *Journal of the 1948 General Conference of The Methodist Church*, pp. 397, 398, 429, 430.
31. Tabulation of the questionnaire is given in "Women in the Ministry: A Report to the Church by Georgia Harkness" (1951–1952), Harkness Collection, G-ETS.
32. *Daily Christian Advocate: Proceedings of the 1956 General Conference of The Methodist Church* (May 7, 1956), p. 534.
33. Ibid.
34. Ibid.
35. "The Christian Conscience and Weapons of Mass Destruction," Report of a Commission appointed by the Federal Council of the Churches of Christ in America, p. 3.
36. Ibid.
37. Ibid., p. 4.
38. Ibid., pp. 7-8.
39. Interview: Rosemary Keller with John C. Bennett, Pilgrim Place, Claremont, California, September 7, 1990.
40. Harkness, "Days of My Years," p. 28.
41. Ibid., pp. 9, 10, 14.
42. Ibid., pp. 23, 24; Georgia Harkness, "If I Make My Bed in Hell," *The Christian Century*, January 14, 1942, pp. 45-48; Harkness, *Dark Night of the Soul*, pp. 10-12.
43. Georgia Harkness, "A Spiritual Pilgrimage," Ninth Article in the Series "How My Mind Has Changed in This Decade." Copyright © 1939 Christian Century Foundation. Reprinted by permission from the March 15, 1939, issue of *The Christian Century*, p. 349.
44. Georgia Harkness, *World Call*, November 1942, Cover. Quoted from *The Glory of God*. Copyright renewal © 1974 by Georgia Harkness. Reprinted by permission of Abingdon Press.
45. Harkness, "The Racial Issue and the Church," pp. 10, 12.
46. "Remarks of Dr. Georgia Harkness at the Oxford Conference," Summer 1937, Harkness Collection, G-ETS; "Women and the Church." Copyright © 1937 Christian Century Foundation. Reprinted by permission from the June 2, 1937, issue of *The Christian Century*, p. 708.
47. Georgia Harkness to Edgar Brightman (September 21, 1921), Brightman Collection, Mugar Library, Boston University; "A Spiritual Pilgrimage," *The Christian Century* (March 15, 1939), p. 350.
48. "Wanted—Prophets!" *The Presbyterian Tribune*, October 14, 1937, pp. 9, 10.

CHAPTER 11

1. Thelma Stevens, "Thelma Stevens' 'Thorns That Fester': An Oral (Auto)biography and Interview," Alice G. Knotts, ed. (New York: Women's Division, General Board of Global Ministries, The United Methodist Church, December 5-7, 1983), p. 278.
2. Ibid., pp. 280-81.
3. Ibid., p. 281.
4. Ibid., pp. 18-20.

5. Thelma Stevens to Alice G. Knotts, letter, February 2, 1984, p. 3.
6. Ibid., p. 3.
7. Ibid.
8. Thelma Stevens, "Thorns That Fester," p. 20.
9. Ibid., pp. 40-41.
10. Thelma Stevens to Alice G. Knotts, letter, February 29, 1984, p. 4.
11. Thelma Stevens, "Thorns That Fester," p. 290.
12. Alice G. Knotts, "Southern Methodist Women and Interracial Relations in the 1930s," *Methodist History* 27 (July 1989): 230-40.
13. Alice G. Knotts, "The Debates Over Race and Women's Ordination in the 1939 Methodist Merger," *Methodist History* 29 (October 1990): 37-43.
14. Alice G. Knotts, "Bound by the Spirit, Found on the Journey: The Methodist Women's Campaign for Southern Civil Rights, 1940–1968," Ph.D. Dissertation, The Iliff School of Theology and the University of Denver, 1989, pp. 92-105.
15. Pauli Murray, *Song in a Weary Throat, An American Pilgrimage* (New York: Harper & Row, Publishers, 1987), p. 115. Murray, who early recognized the links between racism and sexism, later was ordained a priest in the Episcopal Church.
16. Thelma Stevens, "Former Things Have Come to Pass and New Things I Now Declare," a speech presented to the Methodist Federation for Social Action, Eastern Pennsylvania Conference, Reading, Pa., June 9, 1982, pp. 3-5.
17. Thelma Stevens, "Empowering Women for the Decades of Methodism's Third Century," manuscript of a speech to United Methodist Women, January 22, 1983.
18. Thelma Stevens, "Thorns That Fester," p. 13.
19. Ibid., p. 21.
20. Thelma Stevens, "The Pharisees and Jesus," M.A. Thesis, June 1928, Scarritt College for Christian Workers, p. 22.
21. Ibid., pp. 60-62.
22. Thelma Stevens, "Committees and Chairmen," *The Methodist Woman* (Woman's Division of Christian Service, Board of Missions, The Methodist Church) 1 (October 1940): 24-25.
23. Thelma Stevens, "Our American Heritage," *The Methodist Woman* (March 1948): 22-23.

CHAPTER 12

1. Lois M. Wilson, "Turning the World Upside Down," *In God's Image* (Spring 1991), p. 8.
2. "Introduction," in Susan Brooks Thistlethwaite and Mary Potter Engle, eds., *Lift Every Voice: Constructing Christian Theologies from the Underside* (San Francisco, Calif.: Harper & Row, Publishers, 1990), pp. 1-17; Ai Young Kim, "Reflections and Future Vision of Korean Feminist Theology in the 1980s," in *A Decade of Korean Feminist Theology* (Seoul: Korean Association of Women Theologians, 1990), pp. 4-40; Wilson, "Turning the World," p. 8; Chung Hyun Kyung, *Struggle to Be the Sun Again: Introducing Asian Women's Theology* (Maryknoll, N.Y.: Orbis Books, 1991); Rita Nakashima Brock, *Journeys by Heart: A Christology of Erotic Power* (N.Y.: Crossroad, 1988).
3. Kwok Pui-Lan, "The Emergence of Asian Feminist Consciousness of Culture and Theology," in Virginia Fabella and Sun Ai Lee Park, eds., *We Dare to Dream* (Hong Kong: Asian Women's Resource Center for Culture and Theology, 1989), p. 97.
4. Ibid., pp. 92-94.
5. Ibid.
6. Kwok Pui-lan, "Mothers and Daughters, Writers and Fighters," in Letty M. Russell, et al., *Inheriting Our Mothers' Gardens* (Philadelphia: Westminster Press, 1988), pp. 26-27.
7. An interview with the ninety-year-old mother of the author, Margaret Cho Yun, who graduated from Ewha Hak-dang in 1926.
8. Pauline Kim, *Ninety Years of My life with Jesus* (Seoul: Voice Publishing Co., 1989), pp. 92-93.
9. Young-Chung Kim, *Women of Korea: A History from Ancient Times to 1945* (Seoul: Ewha Woman's University Press, 1976), p. 218.
10. Ok Kyung Min, "An Ewha Alumni Who Seeks Truth, Goodness, and Beauty with Reverence of God, Interview with Margaret Cho Yun," *Ewha Alumni* 47 (May 1991): 6-8, Seoul, Korea; Kwok, "The Emergence," pp. 92-94.

11. Rosa Choi Cupfender, *Helen Choi, A True Christian* (Seoul: Naratmal Publishing Co., 1991).
12. Alice Chai, "Korean Women in Hawaii: 1903–1945," in Hilah Thomas and Rosemary Keller, eds., *Women in New Worlds* (Nashville: Abingdon, 1981), pp. 328-44, 425-27.
13. Kwok, "Mothers and Daughters," pp. 24-26.
14. Korean Association of Women Theologians, "Feminist Theological Lighting on Goddess Image Imposed in Korean Folk Beliefs," *In God's Image* (September 1990): 48-52; Kwok, "The Emergence," p. 98.
15. Kwok Pui-lan, "Discovering the Bible in the Non-Biblical World," in Thistlethwaite and Engel, eds., *Lift Every Voice,* pp. 270-82.
16. Kwok, "The Emergence," pp. 98-99.
17. Chung, Hyun Kyung, "Following Naked Dancing and Long Dreaming," in Letty M. Russell, et al., eds., *Inheriting Our Mothers' Gardens* (Philadelphia: Westminster Press, 1988), pp. 66-67.
18. Kwok, "Mothers and Daughters," p. 31.
19. Chung, "Following Naked," p. 69.
20. Kwok, "Mothers and Daughters," pp. 31-33.
21. Elizabeth Dominiquez, "Biblical Concept of Human Sexuality; Challenge to Tourism," in Fabella and Sun Ai Lee, eds., *We Dare to Dream,* pp. 88-91.
22. Ibid., pp. 90-91.
23. Fabella and Sun Ai Lee, "Final Statement: Asian Church Women Speak," in Fabella and Sun Ai Lee, eds., *We Dare to Dream,* pp. 148-49.
24. Letty M. Russell, "Introduction: Crossing Bridges of No Return," in Wha Soon Cho, *Let the Weak Be Strong: A Woman's Struggle for Justice* (Bloomington, Ind.: Meyer Stone Books, 1988), p. 1.
25. Park Young Sook, "Justice, Peace, and the Integrity of Creation—Justice and Peace—Life Movement and Korean Women," *In God's Image* (Spring 1991): 41-49.
26. Park Soon Keu, Lee Hyo Jae, and Yun Chung Ok, eds., *Jung-shin-dae Munjae Cheryojip I— The Collected Data on the Jungshindae Issue, Volume 1* (Seoul: Korean Council for the Women Drafted Under the Japanese Rule, 1991); *Songso reul Tonghaeso bon Jung-shin-dae Yosongui Konan: Yosong Shinhakchok Haesok—Biblical Look at the Suffering of Jung-shin-dae Women: A Feminist Theological Analysis* (Seoul: Korean Association of Women Theologians, 1991).
27. *Korean Feminist Theology and Korean National Reunification* (Seoul: Korean Association of Women Theologians, 1989); Sun Ai Lee, "Peace, Unification and Women: II. A Theological Reflection," in Fabella and Sun Ai Lee, eds., *We Dare to Dream,* pp. 72-82.
28. Chung Hyun Kyung, "Han-puri: Doing Theology from Korean Women's Perspective," in Virginia Fabella and Sun Ai Lee Park, eds., *We Dare To Dream* (Hong Kong: Asian Women's Resource Center for Culture and Theology, 1989), pp. 135-36.
29. "Statement of the Women's Forum of the International Christian Consultation on Justice and Peace in Korea," *Women's Forum Report: A Proceedings of International Consultation on Justice and Peace in Korea* (Seoul, Korea: National Council of Churches in Korea, 1988), pp. 105-6.
30. Letty M. Russell, "Introduction: Crossing Bridges of No Return," in Cho Wha Soon, *Let the Weak Be Strong: A Woman's Struggle for Justice* (Bloomington, Ind.: Meyer Stone Books, 1988), p. 2.
31. Naomi Southard and Rita Nakashima Brock, "The Other Half of the Basket: Asian American Women and the Search for a Theological Home," *Journal of Feminist Studies in Religion* 3 (Fall 1987): 135-50; Naomi Southard, "An Asian-American Woman Reflects on Racism, Classism, and Sexism," in Virginia Ramey Mollenkott, ed., *Women of Faith in Dialogue* (New York: Crossroads, 1987), pp. 51-60.
32. Alice Yun Chai, "Women's History in the Public: 'Picture Brides' of Hawaii," *Women's Studies Quarterly* 1:2 (Spring-Summer 1988): 51-62.
33. Alice Yun Chai, "Adaptive Strategies of Recent Korean Immigrant Women in Hawaii," in *Beyond the Domestic/Public Dichotomy: Contemporary Perspectives on Women's Public Lives,* ed. Janet Sharistanian (New York: Greenwood Press, 1987), p. 76.

CHAPTER 13

1. These assumptions were not formed as hypotheses, but were identified at the outset of the study in order to be honest about some of my expectations as a researcher, and in order to take these into account in interpreting the findings of the interviews.
2. A description of the interviewees and a list of the interview questions is included with the documents at the end of the chapter. The method of research was to interview each woman, recording the full text of the interview. Analysis of the interviews included: listing the women's experiences, ideas, and issues; grouping these into thematic patterns; identifying the frequently occurring patterns and those that diverged from the norms; and compiling the patterns into narrative form so that each pattern was represented in the chapter by some of the representative data.
3. Such an image is reminiscent of the dominant metaphor of improvisation in: Mary Catherine Bateson, *Composing a Life* (New York: Atlantic Monthly Press, 1989).
4. The cancellation of three interviews because of the women's heavy schedules, and my own surgery soon after, meant that the ethnic diversity is less than what was originally intended. This is unfortunate, and it will be an important challenge for future research.
5. May Chun, "Out of Control," *The Upper Room: Special 1992 General Conference Issue* (Nashville: Upper Room, May 14, 1992).
6. *The Messenger,* Worthington United Methodist Church, vol. 7, no. 6 (March 6, 1990).
7. Devotional presented in Riverside District Conference, 1990.
8. *1990 Annual Report: Wesley Community Center,* pp. 2-3.
9. Janice Grana, compiler, *Images: Women in Transition* (Nashville: Upper Room, 1979), p. 16.

CHAPTER 14

1. Women interviewed were: Sharon Brown Christopher, Judith Craig, Leontine Kelly, Susan Morrison (bishops); Joyce Alford, Ellen Brubaker, Charlene Kammerer, Glenda Thomas, Patricia Toschak (superintendents or former superintendents); Christine Bethke (parish pastor who knew Bishop Marjorie Matthews well, as did Alford, Brubaker, Christopher); Kathy Sage, Nancy Grissom Self (former agency executives whose position descriptions included direct work with U.M. clergywomen). With one exception, the persons interviewed are Caucasian women; all interviewed were born and live in the United States. Thus this is a limited sample. In other studies, it will be important to include clergywomen from Central conferences and African American, Asian American, Hispanic, and Native American clergywomen.
2. The image of "women shaping the church" is found in many sources but most aptly for this chapter in *WellSprings: A Journal of United Methodist Clergywomen,* vol. 3, no. 2 (Fall 1990), especially "Women Shaping the Church: An Interview with Bishops Craig, Morrison, and Brown Christopher," by Sharon Zimmerman Rader.
3. For enlightening reflections on this theme by the four living women bishops, see "How UM Women Bishops Center Their Spiritual Lives," *The Flyer* (The General Commission on the Status and Role of Women in The United Methodist Church), vol. 10, no. 4 (February 1990), pp. 9-10.
4. From a personal interview with Ellen Brubaker, July 1990.
5. See document 3, which gives Kathy Sage's description of these four reinterpreted means of grace.
6. Susan Morrison speaks of play, "a sense of celebrating the absurdity of life," as being centering for her; and Judith Craig says, "Humor keeps balance for me," in "Women Shaping the Church," pp. 13-14. Joyce Alford and Christine Bethke (interview, July 1990) tell of Marjorie Matthews seeing people she enjoyed as one of the best ways of nurturing her relationship with God.
7. Leontine Kelly, in interview, June 1990.
8. Glenda Thomas, former superintendent of Delta District, California-Nevada Conference, in an interview, November 1990.

9. Judith Craig, in a personal interview, July 1990.
10. Susan Morrison, in telephone interview, July 1990.
11. In personal interview, July 1990. For eighteen years, Nancy Grissom Self was part of the Executive Secretariat of the General Commission on the Status and Role of Women in The United Methodist Church.
12. From 1980 to 1990, Kathy Sage was Director, Support Systems and Spiritual Formation of The Division of Ordained Ministry of The Board of Higher Education and Ministry of The United Methodist Church. Her comments were made in a telephone interview, August 1990, and updated in later correspondence with the author.
13. Reported by Ellen Brubaker in personal interview, August 1990.
14. For Sharon Brown Christopher (interview, October 1990), discernment is an essential element of authority. Patricia Toschak, then superintendent of Northwest District, Minnesota Conference (in interview, November 1990), underscores Bishop Christopher's emphasis on discernment.
15. Mary E. Hunt, in her recent book, *Fierce Tenderness: A Feminist Theology of Friendship* (New York: Crossroads, 1991), has made an important contribution through her model of the four elements she suggests are present in women's friendships: love, power, embodiment, and spirituality. She also notes that attention, generativity, community, and justice-seeking are strong dimensions of women's friendships. (See especially chaps. 6 and 7.) Her excellent work, focusing on friendships between women, has aided my thinking. In inquiring about clergywomen and their friendships, however, I have been open to their friendship patterns with one another, with other women, with men, and with children.
16. Craig, personal interview, July 1990.
17. Toschak, in telephone interview, November 1990.
18. Christopher, October 1990; other quotations in this paragraph are from that interview.
19. Nancy Grissom Self, in interview, July 1990.
20. Ibid.
21. Charlene Kammerer, Superintendent of the Tallahassee District, Florida Annual Conference.
22. Thomas, in telephone interview, November 1990.
23. Kathy Sage speaks of the parish for some clergy as a "stash."
24. Craig, interview.
25. Christopher, interview.
26. Charlene Kammerer (in telephone interview, August 1990) says: "It's been important for me . . . to find in every place I've lived a particular expression of justice ministry that I want to make a commitment to; some of the time the congregations or settings I've served in have been part of that with me and sometimes not." Kathy Sage (in telephone interview, August 1990) speaks of the connections between living with peasant families in Nicaragua during a study leave, awareness of addiction to caffeine, and our global addiction to war. Leontine Kelly, as resident bishop of the San Francisco Area 1984–88, was a presence of justice and peace in numerous ways, including actions of civil disobedience at a nuclear weapons laboratory on Good Friday. She spoke (in the telephone interview, June 1990) of being supported by some friends and colleagues, who themselves might not march but who respected her and prayed for her.
27. Christopher, interview.
28. Morrison, interview.
29. Craig, interview.
30. Name withheld by request.
31. Morrison, interview.
32. Excerpts from *The Flyer,* pp. 9-10.
33. Excerpts from Sharon Zimmerman Rader (interviewer), "Women Shaping the Church."
34. Excerpted from Kathy Sage, September 1991 correspondence with author, updating and clarifying transcription of interview, August 1990.
35. Excerpts from interview with Sharon Brown Christopher, October 1990.
36. Craig, interview.
37. Toschak, interview.
38. Thomas, interview.

39. Self, interview.
40. Morrison, interview.
41. Kammerer, interview.
42. Joyce Alford and Christine Bethke, speaking of Marjorie Matthews while she was bishop of the Wisconsin Area, interview, July 1990.
43. Sharon Brown Christopher, who served on cabinet in Wisconsin, when Marjorie Matthews was bishop, interview, 1990.
44. Ellen Brubaker, former Grand Rapids District Superintendent, who served on cabinet with Judith Craig as bishop, interview.
45. Glenda Thomas served on the cabinet of the California-Nevada Conference with Leontine Kelly as bishop; interview.
46. Patricia Toschak served on the Minnesota Conference Cabinet with Sharon Brown Christopher as bishop; interview.
47. Craig, interview.
48. Christopher, interview.
49. Sage, interview.
50. Self, interview.
51. Kammerer, interview.
52. Craig, interview.
53. Kelly, interview.
54. Kammerer, interview.
55. Thomas, interview.
56. Christopher, interview.
57. Craig, interview.
58. Morrison, interview.
59. Ibid.
60. Craig, interview.

INDEX